DOUBLE DUTY IN THE CIVIL WAR

DOUBLE DUTY IN THE CIVIL WAR

THE LETTERS OF SAILOR AND SOLDIER EDWARD W. BACON

EDITED BY GEORGE S. BURKHARDT

SOUTHERN ILLINOIS UNIVERSITY PRESS / CARBONDALE

12 11 10 09   4 3 2 1

Library of Congress Cataloging-in-Publication Data
Bacon, Edward W. (Edward Woolsey), 1843–1887.
  Double duty in the Civil War : the letters of sailor and soldier Edward W. Bacon / edited
by George S. Burkhardt.
    p. cm.
Includes bibliographical references and index.
ISBN-13: 978-0-8093-2910-6 (cloth : alk. paper)
ISBN-10: 0-8093-2910-7 (cloth : alk. paper)
1. Bacon, Edward W. (Edward Woolsey), 1843–1887—Correspondence. 2. United States—
History—Civil War, 1861–1865—Naval operations. 3. United States. Army. Connecticut
Infantry Regiment, 29th (1864–1865) 4. United States—History—Civil War, 1861–1865—
Personal narratives. 5. Connecticut—History—Civil War, 1861–1865—Personal narratives.
6. Sailors—United States—Correspondence. 7. Soldiers—United States—Corrrespondence.
I. Burkhardt, George S., 1927– II. Title.
E601.B15 2009
973.7'5—dc22   2008040696

Printed on recycled paper. ♻
The paper used in this publication meets the minimum requirements of American National
Standard for Information Sciences—Permanence of Paper for Printed Library Materials,
ANSI Z39.48-1992. ∞

In memoriam—
my mother, Antoinette (Tony) Frances (née O'Brien)
and
my father, George (Chub) Stedman Burkhardt

CONTENTS

ILLUSTRATIONS

ACKNOWLEDGMENTS

AS USUAL, PEOPLE FROM ALL OVER THE UNITED STATES AND some from abroad helped, encouraged, corrected, and advised during this endeavor. Always it is refreshing and grand that total strangers will expend time and effort to assist in clarifying a Connecticut Yankee's Civil War letters and diary.

First I must thank Thomas Knoles, curator of manuscripts, and Susan M. Anderson, assistant curator, American Antiquarian Society, Worcester, Massachusetts. They made available the complete Edward W. Bacon Papers, including photographs and Bacon's hand-drawn map, from their collections. Without their cooperation, this work would not exist.

Almost from the beginning, Sylvia Frank Rodrigue, Southern Illinois University Press executive editor, displayed a positive interest, offering encouragement and advice. Though always most professional and capable, she guides authors and editors with a warm sense of humor. Barb B. Martin, design and production manager at the same press, cheerfully provided valuable guidance on photograph, map, and art problems. I am very grateful to both for their unstinting aid.

Curators, librarians, archivists, and their assistants readily searched for and furnished documents, photographs, and information. Repeatedly, the patient James W. Campbell and Amy L. Trout, curators at the New Haven Museum and Historical Society, fielded requests for odd or obscure facts about nineteenth-century New Haven. The staff at the Connecticut Historical Society in Hartford also received many queries, and Barbara Austen, Jill Padelford, and Sharon V. Steinberg cheerfully responded. I thank them all.

Yale University library staffers also handled many letters and e-mails asking for this and that from their collections and from the Bacon Family Papers, held in their libraries. Graciously helpful were Diane Kaplan, Cynthia Ostroff, and Laura Tatum.

John T. Magill, curator and head of research services at the Historic New Orleans Collection, answered many questions about that city during the early Civil War years, questions ranging from the types of streetcar lines in the city to the location of various buildings. He invariably provided the answers.

T. Juliette Arai and Brenda B. Kepley, Old Military and Civil Records at the National Archives, went out of their way to search the records on an obscure matter. Olga Tsapina and Lita Garcia researched manuscripts on another equally obscure subject at the Henry E. Huntington Library, San Marino, California.

Michael J. Crawford, head of the Early History Branch, U.S. Naval Historical Center, surely tired of the many queries about Civil War ships, ratings, personnel, customs, and practices but kindly replied to all requests. His colleague, Robert A. Hanshew, photographic curator, was most generous in providing many ship images for selection.

Much appreciated was the research undertaken by Megan G. Sheils and Sara Schoo of the Department of State's Ralph J. Bunche Library in Washington, D.C. They confirmed the service of a nineteenth-century American consul, a matter that had defied my best efforts.

Petitions for copies of manuscripts or photographs uniformly received quick attention from obliging people such as Cynthia Luckie, Alabama Department of Archives and History; Charles Greifenstein, American Philosophical Society; M'Lissa Kesterman, Cincinnati Historical Society; Diane Shelton and Lynne Hollingsworth, Kentucky Historical Society; and Dennis Northcott, Missouri Historical Society.

Charlene Bonnette and Judy Smith, Louisiana State Library, assisted with a needed photograph, while Raynelda Calderon, the New York City Public Library's manuscripts and archives division, arranged to send a sailor's lengthy Civil War journal.

University library professionals often exerted themselves to satisfy pleas for documents. Among them were Dwayne Cox and John Varner at Auburn University; Elizabeth B. Dunn at Duke; Peter X. Accardo at Harvard; Sue Presnell, Indiana University; Janet Bloom at the Clements Library, University of Michigan; Graham Duncan, University of South Carolina; and Courtney Chartier, University of Texas, Austin.

Many individuals also contributed to the completion of this work. Bob Huddleston of Northglenn, Colorado, supplied the answer to a nagging question about button arrangements on Civil War army uniforms. Hugh Davis, Ph.D., author of *Leonard Bacon*, generously replied to questions about the Bacon family.

Professor Laurence Horn, Yale University, and his fellow members of the American Dialect Society, amazingly had the answers to puzzling nineteenth-century idioms and deciphered an example of Bacon's sometimes baffling hand script. Dave Neville, publisher of *Military Images* magazine, courteously assisted with the Medical Cadet program. Ethan Bishop, a contributor to the www.findagrave.com site, showed the way to finding a photograph.

Lawrence T. Jones III, coauthor of *Civil War and Revolution on the Rio Grande Frontier*, most kindly allowed use of a period photograph from his extensive and private collection.

Some anonymous workers also deserve mention. First are those at the Library of Congress, the National Archives, and other agencies who have placed high-resolution photographs on their sites, available for downloading by the public. Though a commercial site, still credit must go to Ancestry.com. Their collection of census pages, Civil War soldier records, and obituary notices enables researchers to identify people with no claim to fame. Then Cornell University has digitalized and placed on the World Wide Web the Civil War's *Official Records* for both the armies and the navies. And thank heavens for the Internet and the Web—life and work are now a thousand times easier for those of us who engage in historical research.

Essential to this account is the work of George Skoch, master mapmaker. It is he who produced the clear maps and diagrams showing Bacon's activities, battles, and travels, as well as the tracks of the USS *Iroquois* and the CSS *Sumter* as they played cat and mouse on the high seas.

For support and encouragement here at home, I must thank my wife, Qiao Hua, who never grumbles at my lengthy vanishing acts while huddled in my study; my daughter, Cynthia Dewey, who exuberantly urges me on; and brother-in-law Hendrik de Kanter, who is always interested in my progress.

Lastly, here is the usual disclaimer: if I have overlooked anyone, it was inadvertent and by no means indicates a lack of gratitude.

DOUBLE DUTY IN THE CIVIL WAR

INTRODUCTION

BY THE HUNDREDS OF THOUSANDS, NORTHERN MEN ANSWERED the call to arms during the Civil War, moved by patriotism, a sense of duty, idealism, peer pressure, or—sometimes—just a longing for adventure or a desire for the hefty bounties paid to some volunteers. Most were young men, with twenty-five as the mean age for more than a million Federal soldiers. However, the largest age classes were those just eighteen, followed by the nineteen-year-olds.[1]

As a youth of eighteen in 1861, Edward Woolsey Bacon was not unusual in leaving his home in quiet New Haven, Connecticut, to serve his country. Few, however, of any age or position experienced such a panoramic exposure to the conflict as Bacon. In the navy, he chased Confederate commerce raiders around the Caribbean and down to South America, endured boring blockade duty, and took part in riverine warfare on the Mississippi. As an infantry officer, he perspired near Charleston, South Carolina, fought and shivered in the trenches on the Petersburg-Richmond front in Virginia, and chafed at occupation duty in "wretched" Texas.

He emerged unscathed after shore batteries targeted his ship, when a Confederate ironclad shot up his Mississippi squadron, and when mortar and artillery shells, snipers, and ordinary enemy riflemen sent missiles his way in Virginia. With a candor and honesty not often found in Civil War letters, he confessed his fear during battle in letters to friends (though not to family).

More agreeably, during his naval service he strolled the streets of colorful foreign ports, attended fetes with English officers and their ladies, met diplomats, and chatted with famous admirals and captains.

Hundreds of men served in both the army and the navy during the war, though most had first joined the army as ordinary soldiers. Some volunteered for naval service, thinking they would have an easier time of it aboard ship, enjoying three good meals a day and a comfortable bed every night; many more found themselves involuntarily transferred to sea service when the navy ran short of sailors. Again, Bacon was twice over an exception: he entered the navy first and he was a captain's clerk, associating with officers and sometimes acting as one.[2]

The Rev. Leonard Bacon, his father, was a prominent New England clergyman and an abolitionist, albeit a moderate voice in that movement. In a compilation of his writings about slavery published in 1846, the elder Bacon asserted
that if Southern slavery was "not wrong, nothing is wrong." Abraham Lincoln
famously repeated those words in 1864. Yet both Bacon and Lincoln placed the
nation's unity first and foremost. For them and most Northerners, preservation
of the Union was the primary goal, contrary to the wishes of fervent abolitionists or the Radical Republicans in the Congress.[3]

Undoubtedly, the father's thinking and stance on slavery and the war
influenced the sons. Yet throughout the war, Edward W. Bacon never suggested he fought to free the slaves. He spoke of duty to the country, though
he sometimes wavered on that score when he wearied of it all. Older brothers
Theodore and Francis (Frank) answered Lincoln's first call for troops, marching off with the 1st and 2nd Connecticut Volunteer Infantry regiments, both
three-month units. Young Edward enviously watched them go. He had some
military training at a private academy and drilled some Yale men when the
war started. Probably his father and family curbed his initial impulses to
somehow accompany his brothers, fearing that his health would suffer if he
became a soldier. They thought sea service far more suitable and beneficial,
apparently believing that would assure him plenty of fresh, healthy ocean air,
dry quarters, and regular meals.[4]

Reality differed sharply from those expectations. True enough, plenty of
fresh air circulated on deck at sea, but below, the ventilation was poor and the
air was musty and damp, filled with many unpleasant odors. Sleeping on deck
might be healthier, except when it snowed or rained or the wind blew spray
everywhere. As for the food, generally the daily diet was more regular and better
than a soldier's fare. Still, scurvy often afflicted naval personnel because they
lacked enough fresh vegetables or fruit to ward off that often deadly illness.
While Bacon fared better as a captain's clerk, meals aboard ship frequently were
monotonous and uninviting.[5]

On the USS *Vanderbilt*, a large side-wheel steamer that scoured the Atlantic
for Confederate raiders, a marine listed the menu on July 4, 1863: bread poultice
and coffee for breakfast, bean soup and pork at midday, hardtack and coffee
for dinner (or supper). On the Western rivers aboard a small gunboat, the bill
of fare differed little. Steward John Swift, aboard the USS *Silver Cloud*, wrote
that "breakfast is coffee (watery) & hardtack, dinner pork and beans one day,
salt beef next day while supper is coffee & hard tack." Worse yet, Swift said, was
that their cook dished out fried cockroaches and pork mixed together.[6]

More life-threatening were the frequent shipboard accidents and the diseases that spread more rapidly within a vessel's confined quarters. Contagious
diseases ranged from annoying colds to lethal tuberculosis and smallpox.

Then mosquito-borne viral illness, such as dengue, malaria, and yellow fever, disabled crews on blockade duty close to shore or assigned to Southern river squadrons. Typhus and typhoid fever, both bacterial diseases, also sickened sailors. Sometimes shipmates would not realize that a man was sick or had expired. However, Bacon knew it when he contracted dengue or "break-bone fever," as it was called then. Though not usually fatal, it is a painful, debilitating ailment and even today no vaccine exists for it.[7]

Early in his naval service another infirmity affected Bacon. He complained of sensitive eyes, variously described as "weak" or "sore," worsened by exposure to bright sunlight. This suggests that a modern physical examination would have resulted in his rejection or acceptance only for limited service.[8]

Yet despite his defective vision, Bacon began a second war career as an infantry officer. Again, his father and upbringing surely influenced him: he chose to lead black troops. Though the senior Bacon was an abolitionist, he also favored colonization for African-Americans, an aim opposed by many free blacks. This was at a time when a strong prejudice against blacks gripped Connecticut and the North.[9]

In early 1864, when Edward W. Bacon joined the 29th Connecticut Volunteer Infantry (Colored), most white Federals still resented, distrusted, and scorned black soldiers. From high commander to low private, Yankees openly voiced disdain and disgust that blacks had joined their ranks and gained at least a semblance of equality. Major General William T. Sherman, famous for his march to the sea, wanted "a white man's war," refused to have black troops with his armies, and flatly said he did not trust them. More extreme, an Illinois infantry private wrote home that if he had to fight next to a black soldier, he would "shute the negro first and then the Rebles." Further, officers of white regiments made known their contempt for black troops and those who led them, regarding both as inferior and third-rate.[10]

Bacon apparently escaped such snubs and insults, because the officers of white troops with whom he associated almost exclusively served in Connecticut regiments. So, given his family's standing, the young officer heard few slurs about his association with black troops. In the close-knit Connecticut community, many also knew that his two older brothers had volunteered for the first three-month units, then joined the 7th Connecticut Volunteer Infantry, a three-year regiment.[11]

The brothers came from a large family, even for those days. Leonard Bacon, the patriarch, sired nine sons and five daughters, so their connections and relations with others were widespread. As a prominent and respected church leader, he wrote and lectured extensively, besides guiding his congregation in New Haven. Always, however, he teetered on the edge of financial failure, even to losing the family home. Yet poor as they were, the father still managed to provide an education for his children. Edward W. Bacon, for instance, attended a private academy and then Yale before leaving for the navy.[12]

Throughout his service in the army and navy from age eighteen to twenty-two, Bacon depended on his father for counsel and guidance. Such deference to a father's views and direction, even to young maturity, was commonplace and accepted in American society at that time. While it might seem odd today for a battle-tested soldier to ask his father for a ruling about his future, it was not so then. After Lincoln issued his Emancipation Proclamation, for instance, a Federal soldier's father advised him to abandon the "abolishun" war as soon as possible and the youth did just that by quickly deserting. But even Bacon demonstrated that filial deference was not absolute—he did join the army, though his father and family preferred that he make some other choice.[13]

Whatever he did, though, his family encouraged and assisted him. Much emotional and practical support during the war years came from two sisters. Katherine, or Kate, as Bacon always addressed her in his letters, was younger by about six years. Born in 1848, she was only twelve or thirteen when Bacon first sailed away in late 1861 on the USS *Iroquois*. Always she was his faithful correspondent and responded to his many requests for clothing, supplies, and information. Katherine was his lifeline to home and all that was familiar and yet so distant. Rebecca, born in 1826, was much older than Edward, born in 1843. She was the family's mainstay when both mother and stepmother became invalids. Rebecca kept the home together, concerned herself about the three brothers away at war, and apparently trembled only when financial pressures mounted on their father. She also wrote Bacon and helped to satisfy his many requests for clothing and sundries.[14]

For a young man who grew up in such a tight-knit household, ruled by a father who was a dedicated opponent of slavery and an unbending abolitionist, his dearth of expression on these matter is somewhat puzzling. In his letters and diary, Edward W. Bacon never utters the word "abolition" or rants about slavery. On only one occasion were his sentiments evident. In New Orleans he rejoices when he has the opportunity to physically remove the shackles from a young male slave. He was pleased to report that he would have the handcuffs and neck ring with padlock as souvenirs, as an example of "Secession jewels."[15]

At best, Bacon is patronizing toward his black troops; at worst he denigrates them as men and soldiers. Summing it up, Bacon once wrote, "I have no doubt that negro troops can be made equal to any. There is no doubt that now they are inferior. As a rule their discipline is good but there the goodness ends." That was scarcely an uncommon view. Edwin A. Thorpe, a fellow captain in the 29th Connecticut, described his mostly free black soldiers as "tractable and brave." More critical was a Massachusetts officer who declared that "Negroes are not the most active persons in the world" and that they were "the hardest people to reason with."[16]

Leonard Bacon's family

Lucy Johnson	Leonard Bacon	Catherine E. Terry
1800–1844	1802–1881	1813–1882

Rebecca Taylor Bacon
1826–1876

Benjamin Wisner Bacon
1827–1848

Leonard Woolsey Bacon
1830–1907

Francis Bacon
1831–1912

Theodore Bacon
1834–1900

George Blagden Bacon
1836–1876

James Hillhouse Bacon
1838–1840

Lucy Bacon
1841–1854

Edward Woolsey Bacon
1843–1887

Katherine Wadsworth Bacon
1848–1915

Thomas Rutherford Bacon
1850–1913

Alfred Terry Bacon
1852–1901

Ellen Brinley Bacon
1856–?

Alice Mabel Bacon
1858–1918

Though condescending and imbued with a sense of white superiority, Bacon still concerned himself with the welfare of his men, praised their achievements, and exerted himself to secure recognition for individual acts of bravery. In one instance, Bacon sought "favorable notice" for a soldier who "had assisted materially in silencing one of the many guns opened upon us" and who, as a result, would lose a leg, if not his life. Like the good officer he became, Bacon also watched out for his men in more mundane matters. He went to great pains to recover money from shifty characters who had taken advantage of an unsophisticated soldier, he admonished another soldier to relieve a mother's worries by writing home, and agitated for a healthier diet when scurvy began killing the men.[17]

A hasty consideration of Bacon's attitudes and the treatment of his men might suggest inconsistency, even contradictory or paradoxical behavior on his part. Such was not the case. Bacon regarded his black soldiers as dependents, his immature charges. He told his father that he had acquired facial wrinkles because of the "the constant care of my large family." Biased or arrogant as that might seem, his conduct was far superior to that of virulently racist white officers who physically and verbally abused black soldiers. Bitter and frustrated, a 43rd USCT infantryman wrote, "There are men in this regiment who were born free . . . and will not stand being punched with swords and driven around like a dog."[18]

Bacon and many other Yankees had probably never encountered many African- Americans before the war. In Bacon's Connecticut, the total population in 1860 was 460,000, of whom only 8,600 were blacks. That relatively small group was not dispersed throughout the population but lived in enclaves or in isolation. What white New Englanders thought they knew about blacks mostly came to them secondhand. In New Haven, where Bacon grew up, much anti-abolition sentiment and anti-Negro rancor existed. His father, for instance, viewed blacks, free or slave, as degraded and one of the foremost "pollutions" in American society.[19]

Bacon's initial experience with numbers of African-American came when he joined the navy. Before the war, the navy, unlike the army, had enlisted free black men as sailors. When the navy rapidly expanded and, at the same time, could not find enough white men to man the ever-increasing number of warships, the navy enrolled more native and foreign free blacks and then began accepting contrabands, former slaves, by the thousands. Because of incomplete or missing records, figures vary for their numbers. Michael J. Bennett, the author of a recent study, wrote, "Historians have been unable to agree on the exact number of African-American sailors" in the Civil War Federal navy. Probably at least 18,000 blacks were among the 118,000 men who served for varying enlistment periods. They comprised about 15 percent of the navy's strength, though an official estimate in 1902 placed the figure at 25 percent.[20]

While those aboard each ship ranged from just a few to almost the entire complement of some gunboats, they certainly helped man the two warships on which Bacon served. These were the *Iroquois* and the much larger USS *Hartford* with its crew of 310. Not once, however, in letters and diary does Bacon mention that African-Americans fought for their country on Federal warships.[21]

That changed when he joined the 29th Connecticut Infantry (Colored) and later shifted to the 117th U.S. Colored Infantry. He shared the popular belief that the free Northern blacks made better soldiers than former Southern slaves. Otherwise his letters lacked comments about race, black equality, or polemics about slavery. That reticence was in sharp contrast to the outspoken and frank rhetoric of many other young men serving in the armed forces at that time. They often expressed strong opinions about black soldiers and sailors and seldom hesitated to voice those views. But perhaps Bacon had heard enough of that when he grew up in an abolitionist household and felt that there was no need to declare himself when his correspondents already knew how he felt. Moreover, by electing to join the unpopular black regiments, Bacon had made his position clear.[22]

THE BACKGROUND

Since the Civil War, a steady stream of memoirs, regimental histories, diaries, and letter collections have rolled off the presses. Of these almost countless volumes, most have concerned the armies. Comparatively few primary works, those written by men who were there, have described naval life and operations. Probably the best-known works came from higher-ranking officers, though some subordinate sailors and marines have provided excellent accounts. Just a few exist by captains' clerks, Bacon's position.[23]

This want of primary sailor narratives is easily explained. The opposing armies, with more than three million men serving at one time or another, had many times the number of prospective writers as the two navies. At its peak, the Confederate navy mustered just 5,200 officers and men, while the Union navy had its top strength of 58,000 officers and men at war's end, though a total of 118,000 men served for varying terms during the conflict.[24]

Historians have focused on land campaigns, resulting in far fewer studies of the navies. Yet Yankee sailors contributed mightily to the Union's final victory and Confederate raiders drove American-flagged ships from the high seas, with that effect lingering to this day. Playing a much more vital role than its much smaller Southern counterpart, the Federal navy transported troops, mounted a blockade that seriously hampered the Confederate war effort, chased Southern raiders, and engaged in amphibious assaults with the army. Its warships forced the fall of New Orleans, and gunboats played a major role on the Western rivers.[25]

Scholars still debate the Confederate navy's importance during the struggle while generally agreeing on the significant contribution made by the North's navy. Admiral Bern Anderson, in his 1962 study *By Sea and by River: The Naval History of the Civil War,* concluded that the Confederate navy's effort was "little more than annoyance to the Union" but "[t]he Union Navy . . . tipped the balance in favor of its cause." In 2006, Spencer C. Tucker, in his *Blue & Gray Navies: The Civil War Afloat,* decided that the Confederate sailors made a "credible showing" and "[t]here is no question that the U.S. Navy played a crucial role in the Union victory."[26]

In the 1990s and the first few years of the twenty-first century, several excellent works appeared about shipboard life in the Federal service. These welcome additions to Civil War literature, particularly to knowledge about the naval experience, have drawn extensively on primary documents—the letters and diaries of ordinary sailors and lower-ranking officers. Among them are Dennis J. Ringle's *Life in Mr. Lincoln's Navy*, Steven J. Ramold's *Slaves, Sailors, Citizens*, and Michael J. Bennett's *Union Jacks: Yankee Sailors in the Civil War*.

Bacon's letters and diaries also help expand another area of limited knowledge—that is, life in the black regiments. Approximately two hundred thousand black soldiers served the Union cause during the war, but many were illiterate and only a handful rendered accounts. Notable among them are Joseph T. Wilson's *The Black Phalanx*, a comprehensive work by a man who served in two black regiments; James H. Gooding's *On the Altar of Freedom* (edited by Virginia M. Adams), a black soldier's dispatches from the 54th Massachusetts to the New Bedford *Mercury*; and editor Donald Yacovone's *A Voice of Thunder*, the reporting of a man who also served in the 54th Massachusetts Volunteer Infantry (Colored). Edwin S. Redkey's *A Grand Army of Black Men* is a valuable compilation of wartime letters from black soldiers and sailors to several African-American periodicals. R. J. M. Blackett edited *Thomas Morris Chester, Black Civil War Correspondent*, another informative collection.

Several white officers compiled black regimental histories in the postwar era, though these varied considerably in quality. Some contain only very brief sketches of the unit's service, lengthier biographies of officers, and a bare roster of enlisted men. Examples of valuable primary works are Luis F. Emilio's *A Brave Black Regiment*, an oft-cited history of the 54th Massachusetts Infantry (Colored), Joseph M. Califf's story of the 7th U.S. Colored Infantry, and Edwin M. Main's narrative about the 3rd U.S. Colored Cavalry, one of only seven black cavalry regiments.

Considering the relative scarcity of eyewitness testimony to naval affairs and about black soldiers, Bacon's letters are doubly valuable. Further, his letters allow the reader to know the youth and the young man and to evaluate him as a human being.

METHODOLOGY

Usually Bacon wrote in a clear, even hand, though some letters show signs of haste or weariness. Occasionally, he and his sister Rebecca used a form of the then outdated slanted "*f*" look-alike for an interior or ending "s," and sometimes he was careless in forming the florid capital letters of the day. Now and then, a word defies transcription because it is illegible or, less frequently, because of ink faintness or a paper fold or blemish. In those instances, the word or words are noted as illegible. When uncertain whether a word has been correctly read, I enclosed the questioned word in brackets and followed it with a question mark, or placed a bracketed question mark after it, as so [?]. His father's letters proved very difficult to transcribe, because he joined most words in a sentence.

Bacon's grammar, punctuation, and vocabulary testify to his good education. For the most part, spelling failed him only with names. He was prone to phonetic or common spellings of proper names, which could and did cause some trouble. Misspelled names have been corrected, usually without making a fuss about it. On this subject, Bacon normally referred to friends and colleagues by their last names but used first names for relatives.

His observations were fairly accurate, except when he gave credence to rumors, many of which swirled through the armies and ships during the war. Most of the rumors he bandied about represented wishful thinking, hope for change for the better.

Problems mostly arose with the identities of people fleetingly mentioned. Despite strenuous effort, it proved impossible to identify all and so some remain unknown.

Another problem exists with portions of his diary. An unknown typist transcribed diary pages, probably in the middle of the twentieth century. But some of the originals are no longer extant, so there is no way to determine the fidelity of the typed copies. However, a comparison of typed diary pages with surviving originals reveals only minor errors.

PART ONE ⟶ THE SAILOR, 1861–62

(1) HIGH SEAS HUNT

EDWARD WOOLSEY BACON TURNED EIGHTEEN AS OTHER YOUNG men volunteered for service when the Civil War began in 1861. "My duty urges me to it," wrote a South Carolina youth on April 14, 1861, and a German immigrant declared it was his "holy duty" to soldier for the Union. An Illinois infantry officer expanded on that theme, telling his wife, "I thought God & my Country was calling upon me, & I tried . . . to walk in the path of duty."

While duty called North and South, their sharply opposing motives defined the war. Northerners fought to preserve the Union; Southerners sought to defend their semifeudal slave society and to win independence. Speaking for most Yankees, two brothers who joined the navy early on said the "holy cause" was to save "that *blessed* and *glorious* Union" and to crush the "wicked and threatening rebellion." But for Confederates, it was not rebellion but only a right and necessary withdrawal from a tyrannical Union, a perfectly legal secession. They fought to defend their rights and to win liberty and independence.[1]

North and South, people fervently believed in their clashing goals. Captain Elias Davis, 8th Alabama Infantry, said his "cause is just," and Sergeant Wash Vosburgh, 115th New York Infantry, wrote that "we are doing what is right." Most also felt the Deity backed their righteous aims, as long as they did not offend Him in some way. In a cogent expression of the Southern view, Private J. T. Kern, 45th Mississippi Infantry, told his mother, "God surely will not suffer such inhuman monsters to torture us much longer, but will dash them to pieces in his wrath." Montgomery C. Meigs, the Union army's quartermaster general, decided, "God does not intend to give us peace until we expiate our crime . . . until the last shackle is stricken from the wrist of the black man."[2]

However, relatively few Northern men volunteered to fight and perhaps die to free the slaves. For Bacon, a sense of duty, preservation of the Union, and family obligation motivated him. Leonard Bacon, the patriarch, though a moderate abolitionist, strongly supported the fight "to preserve the government, the Union, and the Constitution," as his biographer puts it. Two of Bacon's older brothers promptly went off to war, one as a regiment's assistant surgeon, the other as an infantry captain, and this apparently made Edward all the more eager to join the struggle.[3]

Doubtless a sense of urgency also sharpened Bacon's desire to take part. When the conflict began, most Americans envisioned a brief and civilized contest staged to the sound of stirring martial music. Marching under bright flags, the gathering hosts would clash and soon settle the quarrel. A New Hampshire volunteer explained that they "thought a war with the South would be a nice thing—a mere play, an army of 100 000 could go through them like a dose of Salts." Some people might get hurt in the process, but few gave that much thought. Many youths, anxious for adventure, glory, and excitement, worried that the war might end before they reached the Virginia battlegrounds. Victory would be swift, sure, and sweet. That was the popular view on both sides.[4]

That wildly misplaced optimism influenced high and low. On April 15, 1861, Lincoln initially called for only seventy-five thousand volunteers for just three months' service to suppress the Southern insurgency, as he termed it. They would reinforce a widely scattered and small Regular Army of just sixteen thousand officers and men. Bacon's brother Frank, who had studied medicine at Yale, quickly left for Virginia with the 2nd Connecticut Volunteer Infantry, one of those three-month regiments.[5]

Short service regiment or not, Bacon's father thought Edward too frail for army field service, and his dutiful son took heed. Instead, the father suggested service afloat, surely assuming that the naval service meant healthy sea air, good food, comfortable quarters, association with Christian gentlemen and social equals, minimal danger, and a well-ordered existence. This would prove beneficial and, at the same time, satisfy the need to serve.

Soon young Bacon would learn that while the ocean air was invigorating, its moisture permeated every corner of ships, making the interior always damp. Meals were regular, but that was about the only virtue of monotonous, malnutritious shipboard dining.[6]

Whether officer or lowest rating, all found warship living quarters extremely cramped. Robley D. Evans, later a rear admiral, recalled that the tight confines caused much stress and many fights among crewmen after long, tedious days at sea. They had little room to stow personal possessions or clothing, sometimes of shoddy issue. Old navy ranking officers might be upright Christian gentlemen, but the war's exigencies required an influx of volunteer officers and men of varying character and background. As Bacon soon would discover, he was not the equal of captains and admirals and the lower ranks were a mixed lot, many given to profanity, drink, skulduggery, brawling, whoring, laziness, and every other kind of misconduct.[7]

Given the self-contained day-and-night operation of a warship, discipline was necessarily strict and captains were kings, as Evans explained. Many were petty tyrants and reigned as autocrats with a stern, harsh hand. Infractions, such as "carelessness," "being dirty at muster," and "insolence," merited instant confinement for days in shackles or double irons and a bread-and-water diet. As reported by a black sailor, the more serious offense of striking an officer fetched one culprit a sentence of six years in prison.[8]

Still, the popular notion that sailors faced a minimal risk of death in battle had some validity and appeal for recruits. It was true enough that by any statistical measure fewer sailors than soldiers were killed in action. Of the recorded 118,000 men who served in the navy during the war, just a few more than 2,100 died in battle. But—and it is a big but—when gunfire or mines sank a ship or an enemy shell exploded its steam boilers, a very high percentage of the crew often lost their lives. Further, a bewildering variety of accidents, many horrific in nature and peculiar to the sea service, killed sailors. Falls from high masts or into holds left sailors lifeless, men slipped overboard and drowned, cannon burst upon firing and shredded crews, and thick hawsers snapped and whipped into deck hands. In one odd accident, an officer "bled profusely" when a cutlass slipped from its scabbard above his bunk and slashed his head.[9]

Infectious diseases posed another grim threat in a ship's close confines, as Bacon also learned. Deaths from tuberculosis and other respiratory ailments were not uncommon, smallpox struck, and fleets on the lower Mississippi sometimes were almost incapacitated by fevers. Shipboard sanitary conditions were primitive and were not improved by swarms of germ-carrying vermin. Symmes E. Browne, an ensign on the river gunboat USS *Tyler*, complained that "the boat is actually alive with roaches and rats, mosquitoes and flies, gnats and bugs, of every description. . . . I never saw a place like it. The boat is awful dirty. . . ." On the high seas, one sailor swore that when a flying fish landed on deck, rats would instantly pounce and devour it before he could move. That might have been a sea story but many sailors said rats and cockroaches abounded on their ships.[10]

Ignorant of these unpleasant realities, Bacon's father somehow learned about the unusual and anomalous position of captain's clerk in the navy. Nothing comparable exists today. Then, a ship's captain selected his clerk, who served at that officer's pleasure. Though paid by the government and listed on a ship's muster rolls, the clerk could forfeit his job if the captain lost his command. A contemporary description of the clerk's job stipulated that he must have a "fair hand" in writing and would receive five hundred dollars yearly or about forty-two dollars a month, the same as a midshipman. At the time, a seaman's pay was fourteen dollars a month, while an ensign, the lowest-ranking commissioned officer in the navy, received one hundred dollars monthly. Like the position itself, the pay was betwixt and between enlisted and commissioned salary scales. Primarily, the clerk's duties were to act as the captain's personal secretary and stenographer, but he also might serve as an aide, messenger boy, extra officer, companion, or emissary. Each captain defined his clerk's status and duties aboard ship, so a clerk's standing and tasks could vary considerably from captain to captain, ship to ship.[11]

If there was one thing certain about the position, it was that many fathers sought that supposedly safe and comfortable but honorable berth for their sons. Bacon's father, an influential man with many friends in high places, began to work on his son's behalf. He turned to Captain Andrew H. Foote, a New Haven native with almost forty years service and a high-ranking officer in the still small but rapidly expanding navy. On June 10, 1861, Foote wrote from the Brooklyn Navy Yard and promised to help if he could, but offered little encouragement. By the end of the month, however, Foote had positive news, and soon young Bacon was struggling to find his sea legs as a captain's clerk on the USS *Iroquois*.[12]

%

**[Diary] U.S. Steam Sloop of War *Iroquois*,
At Sea, off Nantucket Shoals, July 17, 1861**

On Sunday, July 14th we left our dock at the Navy Yard, Brooklyn, and under the direction of the Pilot, steamed down the East River, thru New York Bay and the Narrows into the Atlantic Ocean. Just as we passed Sandy Hook our Ship began to roll, for it was a windy morning and the *Iroquois* is apt to roll in a very even sea. Like all who commence an ocean life, I was, of course, made sea sick, but rather gloried in that I did not yield until one, at least, had led the way.

For two or three days I have been very small in my own estimation, but my officers have "made a great deal of me." Capt. Palmer, especially, has been very kind in having me to dine with him and in giving me his best Cider, Wines and Brandy.[13]

The cruise of the *Iroquois* thus far has been anything but an eventful one; beyond speaking [to] several vessels we have nothing to enliven us. I have spent all my well hours in the Cabin reading to the Captain or writing up the Ship's Log. I am therefore very well situated except that my mess mates are very bad fellows. Only one of them, Cromwell, is a decent fellow.[14]

New Haven, Sept. 6, 1861

Dear Edward,

We are pleased to get your frequent letters from Hampton Roads. Two came yesterday & one to day. Your position seems to be, almost every way, as good as you could reasonably ask for. I trust you are not only performing your duties to the satisfaction of Capt. Palmer, but are also acquiring physical health & business habits which will prepare you for usefulness in coming years.[15]

Theodore has been raising a company, of which he is to be captain, for the 7th Regiment (Alfred Terry's). His lieutenants are [William] Charnley and

[Chauncey H.] Keeler. The company is nearly full, & will probably be accepted by the state tomorrow. Part of the men are already in camp (on Oyster Point just below Mr. Hallock's). Others who are enlisted are coming in, & new recruits are obtained every day. Frank is Surgeon of the same regiment, with two assistants; and Adrian Terry will probably be quartermaster. Two regiments, the 6th & 7th, are required to rendezvous here & will march in a week or two. The 8th & 9th (the 9th being Irish "Forward the North!") are required to rendezvous at Hartford & will be ready almost as soon as these at New Haven.[16]

We are beginning to get our house ready for winter. [proper name illegible] has been working today putting in new registers [?] preparatory to a new furnace, the old one having been condemned as not worth repairing. I shall be somewhat troubled to pay some of the bills for your outfit, particularly the large one at Knevals's. Can you not send an order on the Navy Agent at New York for a portion of your monthly pay? There is a printed form of such orders by which men in the Navy assign a portion of their pay for the support of their families. If you will send me such an order, I will see that whatever may accrue after paying the bills is deposited in a Savings Bank or otherwise invested at interest to accumulate till you need it.[17]

In haste, your aff. Father, Leonard Bacon

Let it be your encouragement, under trials or danger, that if you are serving your country in the spirit of self-sacrifice, you are serving God. Look for strength as your day, & grace according to your need.

%

After his initial landlubber's seasickness, Bacon experienced a fruitless hunt for a Confederate privateer and boring blockade duty.

No matter how many Federal ships guarded Southern ports, some blockade runners always managed to slip through the cordon. Even after more than three years of effort, Rear Adm. Samuel P. Lee, commanding the North Atlantic Blockading Squadron, declared that the blockade was still "very weak." One ship's officer wrote home that the blockade runners "come upon us & flit by like a phantom." Sailors, including Bacon, found the duty very disagreeable and, as one said, a man "might as well be in prison."[18]

Though the Federal navy had only forty-two ships in commission when the war began, they still surpassed the South's nonexistent fleet. Further, the Confederacy lacked the means, machinery, or materials to construct large steam-powered warships. They seized or bought what vessels they could use as fighting ships but could never hope to match the ever-enlarging Yankee force. So they concentrated on defending vital points on inland waterways, sought to break the blockade with ironclad ships, and moved to disrupt the Yankee shipping trade.[19]

In this last design the South succeeded, at least in part. By the initial use of privateers and then with Confederate States Navy commerce raiders, they drove the American flag from the high seas. That decline in the American merchant marine has persisted to this day, excepting for the artificial and temporary stimulus experienced during the two world wars. After the Civil War, other factors—such as a 1797 law forbidding the repatriation of a ship once expatriated or transferred to another flag; foreign advances in iron or steel ship building; wage, safety, and working condition requirements for seamen on American ships—all have acted to continue that decline. But it was the Confederate cruisers that caused the once thriving American merchant marine to founder.[20]

When those raiders began to prey on merchant vessels, insurance rates skyrocketed for cargo and ship. In competition with foreign carriers, American ship owners could not raise their shipping rates to compensate for the drastic increases in insurance or the war risk and, in any event, foreign and domestic customers were loath to lose their goods to a raider. Consequently, American hulls began to sail under foreign flags. At first, many transfers were in name only, but that ploy soon failed. Then Northern owners shifted title legally and often permanently to neutral owners.

Lincoln set the tone for the Northern reaction when he defined the Confederate marauders as pirates and declared the crews subject to hanging. High officials, the U.S. Navy, the public, and the Northern press followed suit. That position proved untenable, especially when Confederate president Jefferson Davis vowed to hang Yankee captives in retaliation.[21]

While a number of privateers initially sailed with letters of marque, the necessary governmental authorization, the wind went out of their sails when it proved very difficult to get their prizes into Southern ports and when they risked prison or death if captured by Federal warships. Before privateers retired, Bacon's *Iroquois* vainly hunted for one of them, the *Jeff Davis*. Confederates enjoyed much greater success with their navy's raiders. That success was and is not measured solely by the number of ships captured or sunk. Just as important was the disruption to trade and the diversion of precious resources to protect shipping and to search for the Southern predators.[22]

The best of these raiders, the *Alabama, Florida, Georgia,* and *Shenandoah,* came from British shipyards. By subterfuge and with the British government's indulgence, Confederate agents contracted for the construction of those and several other warships. Charles Francis Adams, Lincoln's minister to Great Britain, protested the shipbuilding but to no avail. Alone the *Alabama* destroyed or captured sixty-nine ships in her two-year career under Commander Raphael Semmes, CSN.[23]

Semmes, a former U.S. Navy officer who had fought in the Mexican War, began his marauding in a much less impressive vessel, the *Sumter.* Originally

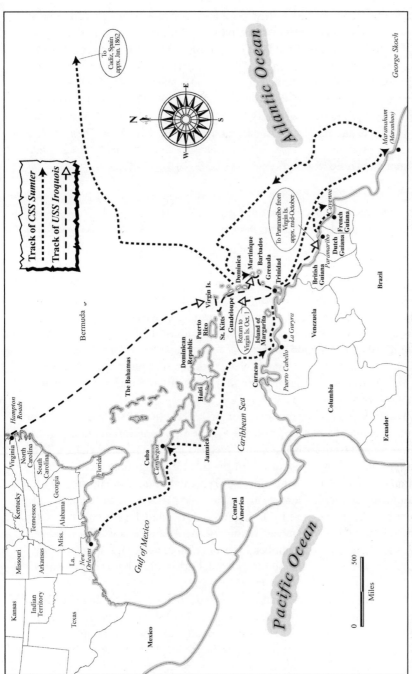

Tracks of the *Sumter* and the *Iroquois*. When the Confederate sea raider CSS *Sumter* escaped from New Orleans and began to capture Yankee merchant ships, Bacon's USS *Iroquois* soon joined the hunt for the "pirate." Their tracks converged at the French island of Martinique in late November 1861. There the raider tricked and eluded the *Iroquois* but almost foundered while crossing the Atlantic Ocean. George Skoch.

built for the Havana–New Orleans run and named *Habana*, she was a bark-rigged, single-propeller steamer of almost five hundred tons with a top speed of about ten knots and limited steaming range. The Confederate government bought her and ordered Semmes to New Orleans to oversee her transformation into a warship with four broadside guns and one eight-inch shell pivot gun. Alteration work proceeded slowly, but on June 30, 1861, she evaded the blockade and put to sea with a crew of ninety-two men, including twenty marines. On the third day out, she captured and burned her first Yankee vessel. Then the CSS *Sumter* was well on her way, sparking a relentless hunt for her by the *Iroquois* and many other Federal warships.[24]

%%

[Diary] U.S.S. *Iroquois,* Harbor of Port of Spain, Trinidad, October 1st, 1861

The cruise after the *Jeff Davis* proved fruitless; having been at sea, cruising between Nantucket South Shoals and the Capes of Delaware, we returned to New York on the 24th of July. Our boilers needing some repairs, we remained at the Navy Yard for some ten days, while I took leave of absence and went home.[25]

I found the family at North Haven in summer quarters. Staying at home for a few days I returned to New York on Aug. 29th, stopping over a train to call at Stamford on my friend Skiddy.[26]

On the first of August we left New York for Hampton Roads, which we reached on the 6th. We coaled here and then set sail for Savannah, Geo., which port we were ordered to blockade.

In due time we arrived off the mouth of the Savannah River and cast anchor about nine miles from shore, near the Frigate *St. Lawrence*, but out of sight of land. Here we lay under banked fires, ready to make immediate chase for any thing hostile, rolling constantly with the tide for a month, the only object to remind us of *terra firma* being the top of Tybee light-house and the tops of very distant trees behind it. During this whole dreary time not a sail hove in sight except the *Harriet Lane* which brought us a little mail, for me only one letter from Skiddy, which was indeed a windfall. As August was spent, so was our coal, and on the 1st of September I was once more at Hampton Roads. Com. Stringham was away in the *Minnesota* and, Capt. Palmer being our officer, we were performing the duties of Flag Ship for our whole stay.[27]

On the 4th we received orders detaching us from the Blockading Squadron, under Com. Stringham, and detailing us for special service in pursuit of the pirate steamer *Sumpter* [*Sumter*]. Accordingly, on the 6th we left Hampton Roads, and on the 13th were at anchor in the harbor of St. Thomas, West Indies.[28]

At St. Thomas we spent several days very pleasantly. I there attended the Jews' Synagogue, and saw the beautiful women of the island, and the English church and heard the first sermon for two months or more. Time slipped away fast with the luxuries from the North in the way of ices and fresh meats; with cool pleasant moon light evenings in the Public Gardens and the music from the Band of the Garrison in the old fort, which would try to defend the place.

On Wednesday, the day we left St. T., steamed around St. Croix, and the next morning sighted and passed Saba and St. Eastalia [Eustatius] and cast anchor at St. Kitts—stopping only to get the news, we went on, passed Nevis–Mt. Serrat [Montserrat] and next day, which was Friday, anchored at St. Pitre, Guadeloupe. Remaining one day, seeing the town, of wood, all built since 1843—when an earthquake threw down all the buildings here.

Saturday night we passed Dominica and Sunday morning stopped at Port Royal, Martinique. Lt. [David B.] Harmony was sent on shore to confer with the Governor as to the news, the Consul living not here but at Port Prince, some seven miles hence, we therefore sailed away, the sound of church bells following us, this being the first time for months since our ears had been gladdened thus. Touching at Port Prince, we saw the Consul and then made way for St. Lucia, which we passed in the night and next morning made Barbados, a long and comparatively low island, evidently under high and successful cultivation.[29]

Mr. Edward Trowbridge, the U.S. Consul, came on board and was welcomed by me as an old friend; I felt at once at home.

Going ashore the next day, Mr. T. R. Trowbridge Jr. an old neighbor and playmate of mine, was very polite and in a new buggy, just out from New Haven. I was taken by him all over several fine estates and to the Trowbridge residence, where I dined in the pleasantest manner. Through all my visit at Barbados, and we stayed until Thursday, I never wanted for kindness or attention.[30]

From Barbados, we steered for the Grenadines, and passing them all, cast anchor at the last, Grenada, in the harbor of St. Georges. Here we coaled and the next day, Saturday, were off for Trinidad, the Port au Spain [Port of Spain].

U.S.S. *Iroquois*, Off Paramaribo,
Surinam[e] River, October 17th 1861

Dear George,[31]

You are doubtless posted as to my cruise in these waters, and know partly from your own experience, how pleasant it has been and how fortunate I am in being in the fastest vessel in the Navy, so as to be used in chasing pirates, rather than blockading in the winter some port on our Southern coast. My only objection to the change is the entire absence of all news from home, my latest date since Aug. 6 being a short note from Father, received just as we were leaving Hampton Roads on Sept. 6th.

We are now, Sunday, 20, just going to sail in a great hurry, having received some news from the *Sumpter*, which I do not know.

We probably go to Maranhan, on the Brazil Coast, just below the Amazon River. Very likely before we return we will run further South, to Rio, where we have a Naval Store House.

Though this place is uninteresting, except as that which Capt. Semmes (pronounced Sims) threatened to batter down if not supplied with coal, I am having a very pleasant time indeed, going to all sorts of places which never hoped to see and learning a great deal of practical geography, even at the expense of several brilliant actions and lots of letters north.[32]

I wish you would continue to write to Hampton Roads [so] that I may have successive dates awaiting me there.

Very truly, Your aff. Brother, Edw. W. Bacon

I will write again by the first opportunity, this goes in some ship to Boston and will be received by you some time during next December, I presume.

Very truly—EWB

The *Sumpter* is drifting along the coast 100 miles to the eastward. We take her to morrow or next day.

Oct. 24: "Veni, vidi, vici," we expected to be able to say to day, but the fates have decreed otherwise; we know that the pirate is near us, was where I said, but as it proved, we were not to meet her. We are out of coal, but are now filling up—on Saturday we leave Paramaribo, either for Trinidad or for the little islands in the neighborhood of Curacao. We have now only a month's provisions in the ship, and, unless we find ourselves close on the *Sumpter*, we return to Hampton Roads.[33]

I am quite well. Edw.

[Diary] Paramaribo, Suriname River, Dutch Guiana, Wednesday, Oct. 23rd, 1861

On Sunday morning we reached Port au Spain, Trinidad. We found no trace of the *Sumpter*. Coaling, painting ship, etc., detained us until Tuesday of the next week. We found Trinidad a very delightful place; our time passed very quickly with horseback rides into the splendid tropical country, with visits to and from the English Sloop of War *Cadmus*, whose officers had met those of the *Iroquois* in the Mediterranean in the years of 1859 and 1860, and with cool, refreshing visits to the Ice Establishment, an institution established by some Boston firm, who make by it immense sums of money.

On the Thursday evening of our stay we, the "Captain and Officers" were invited to a ball, given by Dr. Bury Irwin Dasent. It was a very brilliant and pleasant affair. The English Army and Navy officers and the deputation from the *Iroquois* made a pleasing diversity of dress, the ladies were some of them quite beautiful, but of a kind of faded beauty, they were languid and seemed careworn, though worn from want of care; they were shallow, without conversational ability, and without the usual characteristic of shallow girls, a faculty, usually much cultivated, for flirting. The gentlemen were heavy and, like their wives and daughters, without any powers of conversation, but with great power for drinking and eating. The officers of H.B.M.S. *Cadmus* showed themselves great gentlemen and atoned for their brethren of the Army, who, esteemed models of Military men, leaned lazily against the walls, in the windows and doorways with their hands in their pockets, or tippled so seriously at the refreshment tables as to make dancing rather an unsteady movement.[34]

In fact, my first insight into English society did not at all tend to lessen my preferences for American society.

Dr. Dasent's supper was a triumph in the culinary line not often seen, and was very thoroughly demolished by the company, who eat very much like animals, and doubtless retired to jeer the American indecent haste at meals, which really cannot compare with theirs.

On Monday night Capt. Palmer returned the compliment by having the Governor and a few other guests on board, with music and dancing and all the customary addenda. At both these parties I was forced to show myself, but more especially and more against my will on board the *Iroquois*.

On Tuesday we left Trinidad, full of pleasant memories of our week therein, and, after an unusual run of two days and one half, reached St. Thomas on Thursday evening, on our way home, or to the United States. We found here, much to our surprise, the U.S. Steamer *Powhatan*, Cmdr. Porter, on her way north from an unsuccessful cruise after the *Sumpter*, which had eluded her grasp as well as ours. On Friday the U.S. Str. *San Jacinto*, Capt. Wilkes, arrived from the coast of Africa, and the same evening there came in a brig which been spoken by the *Sumpter* in latitude 50, near Trinidad on the 5th. Capt. Wilkes, as senior officer, at once ordered the *Iroquois* back to the south in chase again and so, instead of going home ourselves, we were obliged to send letters saying that like an unlucky school-boy, we had been sent back to learn our lesson. On Saturday evening we left St. Thomas and, after a disagreeable passage, reached Paramaribo on Saturday afternoon following.[35]

Expecting to coal here, we hauled our fires and leisurely were waiting until Monday, when on Sunday a French war steamer came in bringing the report that the *Sumpter* was distant only 100 miles along the coast to the Ed [eastward]. We had sixty-five men ashore on liberty, nearly all of our officers were likewise ashore; at four o'clock we ran up the "Cornet" and sent a Corporal to find the men and at seven o'clock all, save one, were aboard, our ship in full sea trim and "all-hands-up-anchor" had been piped. Everyone worked to his utmost ability, the men at the Capstan bars whirled up the anchor with greatest jest, crying, "Now for the *Sumpter*"—"Here's for the *Sumpter*"—"Now then boys, heave away, don't lose the *Sumpter*."[36]

We steamed away and on Monday morning anchored off the mouth of the [Marino] river which forms the boundary between Dutch and French Guiana; up this river lay the brig from which the French Man of War got his news, and which had been boarded by the *Sumpter*. For complete information we dispatched Lieut. [David B.] Harmony in the 1st Cutter to board the brig and get the news. He returned on Wednesday, before daylight, reporting the *Sumpter* as steering Wd after boarding the brig—our game had escaped us once more. Out of coal, we are obliged to return to Paramaribo and fill up before we can chase again, but soon we will be underweigh [under way] once more tracking, and, we believe, finally taking this villain.

[Diary] Paramaribo, Oct. 26, [1861,] Saturday evening

We are still here, trying to coal, yet continually disappointed. There are prospects of our getting underweigh tomorrow morning, yet, should more coal be attainable, we may remain longer. Meantime the *Sumpter* is trying her best to escape us.

I have enjoyed myself quite a good deal, though prevented by weak eyes from going abroad into the bright sun.

Through Capt. Palmer I have made the acquaintance of the Misses Bixbes who were educated at Andover, Mass., and their sister, Mrs. Mentz, who are very pleasant and charming ladies.[37]

Yesterday I sent letters home by the barque *Alice Talton*, of and for Boston, though sailing under Dutch colors to escape the *Sumpter*. She expects to reach Boston in twenty-five days, and, though we may be at Hampton Roads before the expiration of that time, I was glad of the opportunity.

From this we go, I presume, to Trinidad, not finding the pirate there, proceed on to Curacao, and the little islands near there. We have but provisions for one month on board, and, should we not get upon the direct track of our prey in two weeks we, at the end of the time, will turn northward, either to Hampton Roads or to New York, and I think likely to New York.

[Diary] Port of Spain, Trinidad, October 30th, 1861

We left Paramaribo on Sunday morning, the 27th, got out of the river in the afternoon and sighted this island yesterday morning, Coasting around its southern and western sides, we cast anchor here last evening at 10:30. We find here American dates to Oct. 3rd, but no news of importance and no intelligence of the *Sumpter*. We, I am ashamed to say, lie here several days, when such is perfectly useless waste of time.

Iroquois, Trinidad, October 31st—1861

Dear Geo,

We still keep going after the *Sumpter* and she still escapes us. I wrote from Surinam[e] by a Boston barque, but on arriving here from Surinam on the 29th I found that a mail leaves here on the 6th, through in 16 days.

We are filling up very full with coal—our water tanks are also overflowing almost—and we are prepared for a long and effectual chase if we can sight any suspicious vessel.

Our next port, I presume, will be Curacao where the *S* once refitted and at or near which we expect she is now again refitting—not taking her or getting any late news of her there, we will go at once to Hampton Roads—or some Northern port to provision, as we have less than a month's supply on hand.[38]

I write under many difficulties, having two boils on my right eye.

Our dates are to Oct. 3rd. From all the Naval items which we see, I am very much of the opinion of every one else that on our arrival north, with or without the pirate, Capt. Palmer will be transferred, and very probably to shore duty—this would throw me out of employment for some time before I could get another place, and could bring me home before my three years are one third gone. As I have said before, I hope to gain so much strength in the sea that I may before long, if the war lasts, get an Adjutancy or some Army office where I can do something—the only objection which I have to the Naval Service is that I do not know how to do anything, and am therefore like a "cat in a strange garret."

In case I do not have such a run of good fortune as to have all these air-castles become real, I shall have at least strength enough to settle down to a good battle with books and get my education which I never yet have enough sight of. I find that Capt. Palmer still demands six or eight and some times ten hours of my time each day, so that study is impossible on ship-board as it would be in the Army. Active service is not by any means so near, for we have only been under fire once and then did not answer.[39]

Edw. W. Bacon

[Diary] St. Thomas, Nov. 28th, 1861

The doings of the last month have been more eventful than any previously recorded.

Leaving Port of Spain, we ran down the Coast of Venezuela to the Island of Margarita, a barren, uncultivated place, boasting of a fishing hamlet as its "Chief sea-port," called Pampatar, on its southern side. Here we were told that a few days before the *Sumter* passed the island, and that a few days after that she was off La Guaira on the mainland. We accordingly ran around the Island, thinking that she might be at another hamlet there, but she was not. Our next port was La Guaira where we saw the *Macedonian* and found that the miserable inhabitants of more miserable (were it possible) Pampatar had lied to us; the *Sumter* had not been off the Venezuelan Coast since her first appearance, two months before.[40]

I was much pleased with the coast all the way from the Dragon's Mouths to Porto Cabello, which was our next port; higher than any land I ever before had seen, it was at the same time very fertile and steep, presenting a beautiful and varied appearance.

In Porto Cabello I saw a sample of a South American Republic. The streets barricaded, the streets filled with miserable looking beggarly soldiers, than whom a town pauper in New England is better, the streets narrow and crowded with Spaniards, darkies, dogs, mules and the rascally, ill disciplined soldiers, the streets stinking and the people and animals likewise filthy. Such is a town in a South American "Republic." Happy Union of the North! A greater blessing than any "republicanism" is denied to you; the blessing of Christianity and its true freedom.[41]

From this specimen town we ran still farther west to the nice, cleanly Dutch Island of Curacao. Here the stupid Dutch Governor sent off to us word that we would only be allowed to remain in port 48 hours, a space of time to which the *Sumpter* was also restricted.

This insult to the Flag of the third power of the world was almost too much for his manly nature to bear, and Capt. Palmer turned away for St. Thomas, refusing to enter the Dutch port.

We reached St. Thomas on Monday the 11th of November, and proceeded to repair our machinery and to coal.

On Tuesday, however, at sundown a mail packet arrived from Martinique bringing news that the *Sumpter* was coaling at Fort Royal, Martinique, on the 8th. A brig had before arrived which on the 8th was boarded by the S. off Guadeloupe.

%%

In his next letter Bacon describes the encounter of the *Iroquois* and the *Sumter*. But to understand his account, the reader needs additional information, but not so much as to get ahead of the story.

Before leaving St. Thomas, Captain Palmer recruited a civilian pilot who agreed to assist if they came across the *Sumter* in a neutral port. This obliging pilot would signal the blockading *Iroquois* from shore when the raider left port and indicate her direction by signal lights. They executed this plan when the *Iroquois* did indeed find the raider in a neutral port.

Aside from that missing element, Bacon's narrative is clear and accurate.

%

[Diary] St. Thomas, December 9th [1861]

As soon as the Mail Packet confirmed the news of the *Sumpter's* whereabouts, we ceased coaling, got up steam and six hours after the Packet's arrival, we were out to sea bound for Martinique.

On Thursday, 13 November 1861, we made the northern point of Martinique and at three o'clock p.m., we were off the harbor of St. Pierre, which is the northernmost of the two ports which the Island affords, situated on an open roadstead, some fifteen miles wide at its mouth, opening toward the west.

As we doubled the point into the harbor we discovered a suspicious steamer apparently coaling at the wharves, which as we drew near displayed the Secession flag and was the *Sumpter*. We ran in under Danish Colors and, when quite near the *Sumpter*, hauled them down and ran up the American Ensign, amid the greatest consternation among the rebel crew, who crowded on their forecastle, and the rebel officers who left their drinks untasted at the bar and rushed aboard their ship.[42]

We did not anchor, but cruised around the harbor within half gunshot of the *Sumpter* all the night, occasionally running in so close that they supposed [us] about to board and the crowd of civilians on the shore grew more and more anxious and fearful.

The next day, but one, the Governor answered a communication from Capt. Palmer, requesting him to send the *Sumpter* away, and said that on account of the neutrality of the French government and the "generous disposition of the Emperor" he could not order the "vessel of the Southern States" away, but would invite us to anchor, when he would offer us the same civilities which the Southerners enjoyed.

We accordingly anchored where he directed, a mile or two from the *Sumpter*, and were at once visited by the Commander of the French War Steamer *Acheron*, then in port, who wished to impress upon us that we should, according to International Law, remain twenty-four hours after the departure of the *Sumpter*. We at once weighed anchor, with him on board, fearing lest the *Sumpter* should get away before us, and ran out three miles from land, outside of French dominion, where we remained keeping a close watch on the *Sumpter* day and night.[43]

Meantime, the French officials threw every obstacle in the way of our communicating with the shore, and strove to make our position in every way as unpleasant as possible.

After supper on the night of the 23d of November, I was sitting on the ladder of our starboard-gangway, looking toward the town, the lights of which I could just see, the moon not rising until near midnight. It was near eight o'clock and presumably the flash of the gun at the fort ashore, followed in half a minute by its report, reminded me, as on our blockade we burned no lights, of turning in. I sat, however, for six or eight minutes longer when I observed a bright but small light suddenly appear among the shipping, which grew larger and larger until I sprang from the ladder shouting with the gourd "Blue lights" and ran below, got on my side arms, returned on deck to find all at their quarters and our ship, almost ready for action, going to the Sd at a tremendous speed, for in that direction we were signalled the *Sumpter* had slipped.

We ran down the Island, standing in for the land, when we observed two lights of a vessel over a red one close in shore and immediately after them a very dim light close to the water moving very fast. These in a very few moments disappeared and we, fearful of getting too close in to the land, stood more off. South we still ran as far as Fort Royal light, when, seeing no signs of the *Sumpter*, and losing the scent in that direction, we turned to the northward and ran back to the harbor—we ran close in but could see nothing of the *Sumpter* there. Trusting to see some trace to the northward further, we ran up along the land, but saw nothing; smoke was then reported on our port bow, we ran off, but found the clouds had deceived us.

Then Capt. Palmer gave up all hopes and turning to me said, "Mr. Bacon, tell Mr. [John M. B.] Clitz to beat the retreat and secure the guns" and ordered Mr. [Frederick V.] McNair to "shape our course for St. Thomas." We reached this, in a run of twenty-four hours, on Monday morning very early. Here we found that the U.S.S. *Dacotah*, Capt. [James P.] McKinstry, had taken in tow the schooner *E. J. Talbot*, which we had dispatched to St. Thomas for coal and provisions, and had gone to our relief.[44]

After waiting for their return for four days, or more, we again put to sea, having news of the *Sumpter* to the Ed and cruised for four days in the Anagada Passage.[45]

On our return on Monday, a week from our former arrival, we found the *Dacotah* and the *Talbot* there.

I subjoin the report of the man who signalized us of the *Sumter*'s departure. He was engaged by us on leaving St. Thomas as a pilot, on reaching St. Pierre we discharged him, having the same time an engagement with him in regard to matters ashore. The arrangement was: "One blue light for Nd, two for the Sd."

※

Bacon's abridged copy of the pilot's report is replaced with the full version as found at *ORN* 1:216–17, H. A. Anandale, Dec. 3, 1861.

※

Captain Palmer
U.S.S. *Iroquois*
Sir,

On my arrival at St. Pierre, Martinique, I immediately took up my quarters on board the American topsail schooner, *Windward*, Steele, master, where I was cordially received as soon as I made known my mission. I engaged Mr. Rice, mate of the late schooner *Daniel Trowbridge*, who has lately been released from captivity on board the *Sumter*, Mr. Partnage, mate of the schooner *Windward* and Mr. Crocker, 2nd mate of the same, for the purpose of keeping watch on the position of the Str. *Sumter* and the *Iroquois*, which was duly made known to me at each relief of watch.

I obtained a powerful night-glass, as without it I found it impossible to keep watch on the *Sumter*, in consequence of the almost impenetrable darkness under the high land of Martinique. Watch was strictly kept up to the night of the 23d ultimo. At 8 o'clock p.m. on the 23d of November, the *Sumter* cast off her stern lines, slipped her port chain and steamed out, heading S.W. at about five knots an hour. When I perceived her two miles distant from her mooring and about two thirds of a mile from the southern point of the Bay of St. Pierre, I discharged one blue-light and thirty seconds after discharged a second light.

I immediately discovered the *Iroquois* standing in for the land, both vessels in sight, the *Sumter* inshore, where she could easily discern the position of the *Iroquois*. On the approach of the latter the *Sumter* ported her helm, stood back for the harbor, and stopped fifteen minutes under the stern of the French war steamer *Acheron*.

The *Iroquois* continued to the southward until hidden from sight by the southern point of the harbor. As soon as the *Sumter* perceived the *Iroquois* standing into Fort Royal Bay, she steamed up the land to the northward, about one-half cable length from shore. Thirty-five minutes after the departure of the *Iroquois* she came in sight again at full speed, standing into the harbor, as if to observe whether the *Sumter* had not returned to her moorings, and then continued to the northward.[46]

I should have signalized the return of the *Sumter*, but immediately after the second blue light was fired the captain's gig of the *Acheron*, with an officer of that vessel, was alongside the schooner, and I was not able to come off in consequence of all communication with the *Iroquois* being prohibited and a special armed force being placed immediately over the vessel in which I kept watch.

I am fully convinced that every facility was afforded the *Sumter* in her escape. She had an experienced pilot on board for the purpose of taking her through the reefs to the eastward of Martinique in case of pursuit by the *Iroquois*. I have been correctly informed that the *Sumter* took refuge under the northern point of the island and there lay for two hours and thirty minutes, when she discharged her pilot and proceeded to sea. One of the French war steamer's boats was in the vicinity of the spot where the *Sumter* took refuge. I, as all engaged in watching the *Sumter*, was fully convinced of the utter impossibility of her being discovered by the *Iroquois* in the offshore position which the authorities of Martinique compelled her to observe.

As soon as possible after the departure of both vessels I took passage on board the U.S.S. *Dacotah* for St. Thomas, and in compliance with Captain McKinstry's orders piloted that vessel to Basse Terre and Pointe à Pitre, Guadeloupe, from thence to St. Eustatius and St. Bartholomew, and then to St, Thomas, where I arrived and reported myself at the consulate of the United States of America.

I have the honor to be, sir, your
obedient servant, H. A. Anandale

※

Palmer had predicted the encounter with the *Sumter* would end badly. On November 18, five days before Semmes made his run for the open sea, Palmer presciently wrote,

> I feel more and more convinced that the Sumter will yet escape me, in spite of all our vigilance and zeal, even admitting that I can outsteam her, which is a question.
>
> To blockade such a bay as this, which is almost an open roadstead, 15 miles in width, the surrounding land very high and the water very bold, obliged, as we are by the neutrality laws, to blockade 3 miles' distance, it would require at least two more fast steamers, and a vessel of war of any description in port to notify us by signal of her departure, to give any reasonable hope of preventing her escape.

Palmer noted other critical disadvantages: Semmes could always see the *Iroquois* to seaward while he could not see the *Sumter* against the land's dark shadow; he could not depend upon his spies ashore because they feared the French officials and the wrath of the populace, both very sympathetic to the Southern cause; and French authorities aided the raider while hindering him.[47]

Semmes disputed the last, protesting that Martinique's governor failed to do enough to maintain the port's neutrality by preventing incursions by the enemy's small boats or "signals given to him" from shore. Also, he said Palmer had pushed the boundaries of international law by dropping anchor in the harbor and then immediately steaming back out to sea and he had placed a spy on shore. But at least Palmer had not attacked the *Sumter* in a neutral harbor, though the raider's crew had thought he might do just that and had sharpened their swords and buckled on pistols to repel boarders. However, despite Semmes' complaints, both the French and the English bent the rules to favor the Confederacy and its vessels during much of the war.[48]

Still, all hands agreed on the basic facts of the *Sumter*'s escape on the night of November 23, 1861. First she feinted southward, then after a pause, raced northward and was gone in the darkness and far reaches of the ocean. Palmer's early presentiment proved most accurate. With only the *Iroquois* confronting her, the odds strongly favored the raider. Short of attacking her while at anchor in a strong and important European power's port, Palmer had done everything possible within his means to capture or destroy the *Sumter*. His adversaries concurred. Semmes wrote that Palmer "did all that vigilance and skill could do" and his executive officer, John M. Kell, expressed sympathy for the Yankee captain.[49]

%

Iroquois, St. Thomas, Dec. 10 [1861]
Dear Kate,

The Norwegian Man of War which was to have left for New York on Sunday, the 8th, has not yet sailed, and we are making up another mail-bag.

We sail some time to day, not for Bermudas, for we have heard of the *Sumter* to the Ed, we therefore go in that direction, possibly stopping at Barbados before we return, but very likely having a good two weeks cruise without seeing land. The rainy season has set in with vigor; night before last, it blew almost a hurricane and rained as I never saw it at home, driving me from my hammock.[50]

We have no dates later than Nov. 16—but some body had seen a gentleman arrived from St. Domingo who says that he saw there a paper of the 27th which contained accounts of the advance from Charleston, that the troops of the Government were only fifteen miles from the city.

Though I trust it is so, I place very little reliance upon the story.[51]

We will be back here in about the 26th, expecting then to receive letters from home and orders from Washington.

P.S. The next[?] mail is due here on the 12th. So therefore postponed our departure, hoping to get news or orders even.

I, myself, do not expect either until by the next mail after.

I wish I had some more photographs of the family. I have only one of Father and that you sent me. Yours has only slightly discolored, Father's is perfect. That one of mine which I retained, seeking in vain for some one who cared for it, is all discolored. It makes my left eye look very jaundiced and my left foot induces the belief that I had just stepped into a bucket of white wash.

I have just noticed in a [illegible] Post that the Seventh Connecticut, Col. [Alfred H.] Terry, was the first to land at Beaufort. I should feel glad could I know that they were now the garrison of Fort Sumter.[52]

%

Though the *Iroquois* and other Federal warships continued to search the Caribbean, the elusive *Sumter* had vanished over the horizon, bound for safer European waters and more plentiful prey. But what the U.S. Navy could not do, the mighty Atlantic and the *Sumter's* own frailty almost wrought. John M. Kell, her executive officer, confirmed that "the voyage across the Atlantic was a severe test of her seaworthiness," one that the little ship nearly failed. When less than halfway across, the coal supply ran out and Semmes had to switch to the wind and sails for the rest of the voyage. Then on December 11, a furious gale struck, the first tempest of many that almost sank the creaking, leaky little craft. William P. Brooks, the 2nd assistant engineer, recalled it as a trying and hazardous time. He wrote, "The ship leaking very badly—the men without sufficient or proper clothing and the provisions bad and scant. . . . Prisoners as well as captors were obliged to take their turn at the hand pumps to keep the ship afloat."[53]

Finally they reached Cadiz, where Spanish authorities proved inhospitable and the *Sumter* sailed for Gibraltar. She took her last two prizes in international waters just off that British possession. There they could neither obtain coal nor make necessary repairs, and there Semmes abandoned the *Sumter.* Subsequently, she was sold to a British firm, turned into a blockade runner, and then, after the war, foundered during a gale in the North Sea.[54]

※

[Diary] At Sea, December 22nd, 1861

We remained two weeks in the harbor of St. Thomas, waiting for the arrival of the Northern mails, expecting to receive from Washington orders for home. On the 13th the mails came but we got no letters.

On the 15th, Sunday, we left St. Thomas on a cruise to the S. and Ed and this afternoon have been a week at sea, and since Wednesday, sailing under banked fires. Of course we have not seen, nor heard of the *Sumpter,* nor do I expect ever to see her again.

We are now on the Atlantic, about 700 miles from St. Thomas, and about 500 east of Barbados, I presume that in a day or two we will run in to Barbados, and then back through the Islands to St. Thomas, reaching that by the first of January, 1862, receiving there letters from our friends and orders home. Coaling up, we leave St. Thomas by the 7th and reach New York by the 18th. I then will be at home by the 20th and be able to say goodbye to a sea-life.

Capt. Palmer has asked for a Court of Inquiry on the *Sumpter* escape case and, much as I regret it, I fear they will relieve him of his command. This is conjecture; let time show how much of it comes to fact.[55]

[Diary] Bridgetown, Barbados, January 1st, 1862

After cruising fifteen days, under banked fires the most of the time, we arrived at Barbados on Tuesday the 31st day of December, 1861.

We have found dates to Dec. 11th and from the news are much inclined to fear a British War.[56]

I found New Haven papers and news down to Dec. 5th.

This afternoon H.M.S. *Cadmus* arrived from St. Thomas in two days, bringing news to the 19th ult.

She reports the U.S.S. *Quaker City* at St. Thomas, having on board for the *Iroquois* Commander John De Camp, who will relieve Comdr. Palmer, he returning to New York in the *Quaker City*, whether under arrest or not we do not know. We are to sail for St. Thomas on Friday or Saturday; there we will hear all.[57]

This causes me some exercise of judgment. Shall I, if offered by Capt. De Camp a Clerkship, accept it and remain in the *Iroquois*, or shall I return to the United States?

I have the whole two days trip to St. Thomas in which to dispose of the perplexing query. If I do decide right it will be well, for it is rarely that a young man is correct in his first independent decisions.

(2) RIVERINE WARFARE

RIGHTLY OR WRONGLY, BACON DECIDED TO RETURN TO THE north with Palmer, arriving at Hampton Roads in late January. From there he went to his home in New Haven.

Palmer, meanwhile, faced an inquiry into the *Sumter* affair. Semmes, Palmer's nemesis, correctly noted that "when my escape became known to his countrymen, he had all Yankeeland down on him." Palmer told Secretary of the Navy Gideon Welles that some people doubted his loyalty and that "some of my own officers had expressed dissatisfaction." He also forecast that newspapers would publish "some of these unjust accusations and base insinuations."

Indeed, the press soon published derogatory hearsay and calumnies in abundance, vilifying Palmer as the antihero of the saga. Apparently the news of the *Sumter's* flight first reached the *New York Times* on December 12, 1861, by private letters from St. Thomas. More letters followed, including one from Palmer when he wrote, "*Twenty Sumters might get out of that port with only one vessel to blockade it.*" But one of his officers, who wrote anonymously, declared, "The *crew* all say that we ran away from her, and I think so myself."[1]

Instead of a formal court of inquiry, however, Palmer appeared before a Navy Retiring Board in New York to examine his fitness for duty. That board also probed into how the *Sumter* slipped away from Martinique. One witness was Bacon, who testified in support of his captain. Board members found Palmer fit for duty; and on March 17, 1862, Welles wrote him, "The Department fully exonerated you from all blame."[2]

Meantime, Bacon enjoyed about two months of home leave. This gave him time to rest, tell his sea stories, and prepare for the next tour of duty.

With Palmer absolved and again assigned to command the *Iroquois*, Bacon's long leave ended. He and Palmer sailed to New Orleans to rejoin their ship. Along with hundreds of other deep water sailors, they then embarked upon a new kind of warfare on the Mississippi River. On comparatively shallow fresh waters, they would fight enemy land batteries, warships, and riflemen sniping at them from hidden positions on river banks. In addition, they had to contend with lethal diseases and fevers endemic to the lower Mississippi. In that time of primitive medicine, hygiene, and sanitation, debilitating illnesses often disabled many in a ship's crew.[3]

Control of the Mississippi was one aspect of General-in-Chief Winfield Scott's "Anaconda Plan" and of later strategic thinking: squeeze the Confederacy from all sides. Gaining sway over the vital north-south river would split the Confederacy into two unequal parts. Texas, parts of Louisiana, Arkansas, and Missouri would be isolated in the Trans-Mississippi. This would deny the eastern sections the troops, supplies, foodstuffs, horses, and revenue that came from across the river. Conversely, success would give Federal ships and troops free movement on the waterway, enabling the North to make gains in the West. This strategy required the capture of New Orleans, the South's largest city, and the reduction of fortified Vicksburg, the upstream bastion which enabled the South to hold the river.[4]

For the rest of his naval service, Bacon took part in the fight for the Mississippi. He missed the battle for New Orleans, when Flag Officer David G. Farragut's twenty-four wooden warships braved the guns of Forts Jackson and St. Philip, river obstructions, and many fire rafts, then routed or sank a small flotilla of thirteen Confederate warships, thus winning the day, the battle, and the city with light casualties. Farragut listed thirty-six killed and thirty-five wounded, while just one ship was lost, though others, including the *Iroquois*, suffered varying amounts of damage.[5]

That was the beginning of a complex, fifteen-month-long combined water and land campaign to clear the river. By April 1862, Federal naval and army forces to the north had won control of the Tennessee and Cumberland Rivers and by early June had cleared the Mississippi as far south as Vicksburg.[6]

First, Farragut and about five thousand soldiers moved northward from New Orleans toward Vicksburg. But the navy alone could not take that city-fortress, and the troops available fell far short of the number needed. Consequently, the effort to take Vicksburg became an arduous, frustrating, and lengthy campaign with many twists and turns, including a canal-digging venture to bypass the bastion's big guns. Grant assumed command in late October 1862, but Vicksburg did not fall until July 4, 1863, about eleven months after Bacon had left the navy.

Still, he saw much action in the campaign's first four months, more than enough to enable him to talk of "'smoke and shell' pretty loudly," as he put it.[7]

Bacon proved himself steadfast under fire, concealing his fears and dread from shipmates and revealing his apprehensions only to male friends. He also had other adventures, some of which he described with boyish enthusiasm. As his letters show, eventually these experiences exerted a sobering, maturing influence upon the young man. He became a veteran, knowledgeable about ships, men, the navy, and war.[8]

%

[Diary] Continental Hotel,
Philadelphia, April 3d, 1862

Since my last entry I have (on January 13th) resigned my Clerkship, have sailed (Jan. 14) for home, arriving Jan. 28 in America at Hampton Road and reaching home on the 30th. I have in the month of February attended the Naval Retiring Board as a witness in the case of Comdr. Palmer, in which case he was acquitted.

Upon Capt. Palmer's being ordered back again to the *Iroquois*, I received again the appointment of Captain's Clerk and orders to report in Philadelphia.

I have come here in obedience to these orders and am now awaiting the departure of the supply str. *Rhode Island* in which I take passage with my captain for the *Iroquois* now off the mouth of the Mississippi River and soon to go up to New Orleans.[9]

U.S.S. *Rhode Island*, Off Wilmington,
N. C., April 14, 1862

My Dear Kate,

We are having a very fine trip down the coast. The severe storm which we encountered in Hampton Roads seems to have exhausted the winds and we are almost without any roughness.

Since leaving the Roads we have seen or heard nothing of the *Merrimac* or of Yorktown, but off Beaufort, a beautiful little village, we came within range of Fort Macon and saw very distinctly the smoke of Burnside's guns trying the range.[10]

We learned that on Tuesday, to-morrow, the attack upon the fort was to open by both land and water.

It seemed to me a sure thing that Burnside takes the fort, isolated as it is.[11]

Early this morning we stopped, to supply the *Cambridge* off New Inlet, to the Wd of Cape Fear and since then we have been boarding vessels, quite a fleet of which have been around us. Unfortunately, none of them were liable to capture.[12]

We make Wilmington presently, supply the *Monticello, Mt. Vernon* and *Jamestown*, (the two first of which have rendered great service in the present war, especially the *Monticello* under Lt. Braine; and then are off for Port Royal and Tybee where I mail this and see, if possible, Frank and Theodore.[13]

It will be, probably, eighteen or twenty days before I reach South West Pass where we expect to meet the *Iroquois*.[14]

I expect a very pleasant time on the River, for I find we are to be in the Stream and not outside, under the influence of the disgusting ground swell which always exists at sea upon soundings. Capt. Palmer tells me that I am right in my belief that New Orleans is not yet taken and that it will not be taken for some weeks after we get there, Com. Porter's schooners to the contrary notwithstanding; and that they are not bound to S. W. Pass, that announcement being either a mistake or a ruse.[15]

My address I think I gave in my letter from Old Point, "U.S.S. *Iroquois*, Western Gulf Blockading Squadron." If you have occasion to send anything more than letters or papers, direct as above, "Care Naval Lyceum, Brooklyn, N. Y."

Your gingerbread has been a very capital thing. I am sorry to find the bottom of the box making its appearance, though I have enough to carry me to Key West at least, where we are to use two days in coaling ship. I shall call there upon Mrs. [illegible] whom we met in Litchfield and who was so urgent to have me when I saw her in New Haven.[16]

Remember me to all my friends and
Believe me with love to all,
Very truly your brother, Edward W. Bacon

P. S. Off Charleston, 18th April

The *Nashville* ran into Georgetown the other day, coaled, and ran out, while the blockading vessel was down at Port Royal for supplies, and the blockader's fire on Saturday last blew out of the water a schooner which refused to heave to. We have rumors from Pulaski, but shall know facts when we get there.[17]

EWB

⅍

This next letter to his father is a lengthy journal missive, a running day-by-day account of the situation in New Orleans.

⅍

U.S. Str. *Rhode Island*, Quarantine,
Mississippi River, April 30, 1862

Dear Father,

The great battle has been fought and New Orleans is ours, while I, the most unfortunate of warriors, have been wasting twenty five precious days between Philadelphia and my vessel.

Fort Jackson and Fort St. Philip surrendered on Saturday morning after a very hard fought battle and the great city of the South followed their example yesterday, except that the civilians did not fight.[18]

The stories as we get them are so wild and contradictory that I forbear to give them in detail, preferring to refer you to official dispatches, which are of course correct. The outline of the story seems to be that Porter bombarded for six days and nights, that on the sixth night the heavy chain across the river at the Fort was destroyed and that on the seventh morning, last Friday, our fleet ran the gauntlet of the fort and attacked above them the Secesh fleet of 13 vessels, including the Hollins [illegible word] *Manassas* after she had sunk the gunboat *Varuna*, whose wreck now lies on our starboard bow, but the frigate planted a shell just at the foot of her smokestack and utterly ruined the impregnable ram. The other rebel boats were run down and sunk in detail, not one of the 13 escaping. Our prisoners from them amount to 400.[19]

Monday night I arrived at Ship Island and on Thursday morning went ashore, where I saw the 13th C. V. [Connecticut Volunteer Infantry] and called on Mr. [Chaplain Charles C.] Salter and Capt. [Homer B.] Sprague; they were quite well, the whole Rgt.[20]

Thursday night brought us in South West Pass and this morning we began to ascend the river. The first objects that met our eyes were Porter's Mortar Schooners all stripped of their rigging and painted a yellow mud color, just like the waters of the river. Among these miserable looking craft was a dirty ragged steamer, her top mast housed, all her rigging to her shrouds sent down and her sides hung with chains, as I described in my Key West letter. Her cutwater and bowsprit were carried away; just forward of the smoke stack a shell had struck and carried away her bulwark, her sides were patched with bits of unpainted plank and her appearance was unseaworthy and wretched in the extreme. I learned that the pivot gun forward had been cleared of its men, 8 being killed and 10 or 12 wounded, and a Master's Mate [George W.] Cole had been killed. This was the heaviest loss in the fleet and I could hardly believe my eyes as I recognized in the still beautiful model before me the pride of our navy, the *Iroquois*.[21]

The beautiful ship had been in the very thickest of the fight and had acquitted herself gloriously, though with many scars.

We did not go aboard, for we have to report to the Flag Officer (who is at New Orleans, keeping in order the citizens, who are very insulting in their conduct) but steamed past our vessel and on upstream, passing quantities of empty shell boxes, bits of burned cotton, showing what work had been above. Every now and then we would pass the remains of a rebel gunboat, burned down to the water's edge, constantly saw exhausted fire rafts sent down from above but failed of their object, while too often we saw flocks of Buzzards settling over some poor tar which had floated down stream and been lost among the cane brakes.[22]

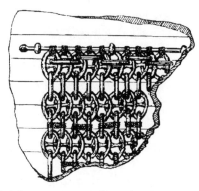

To deflect enemy projectiles, sailors draped chains on the sides of their ships, and Bacon wrote (April 30, 1862) that his *Iroquois* was so armored. From *Battles and Leaders*.

New Orleans, May 1, 1862

This is moving day and we have observed the New York custom by moving up.

We lay at anchor just above Quarantine all last night and early this morning were under weigh once more.

We passed George's old ship, the *Portsmouth*, of the same dirty color as the others and chain clad like them too.[23]

We saw more rebel gun boats, or rather, a few charred timbers to show where they burned and sunk, and passed close to the harmless mass of rusty iron which goes by the name *Manassas* and which seems to follow its namesake. My attention was of course especially attracted by the forts, Jackson and St. Philip, the former of some strength, the latter a mere earthwork strengthened by two water batteries but of small importance because of light guns. Fort Jackson seemed a good deal damaged by our attack, two guns or more were evidently dismounted and the brick walls much defaced; it must be confessed, however, that its walls looked much better than our forlorn gun boats. Fort Jackson seems very badly built, the casemates are sunk to the level of the river, and are said, during the present high water, to be inundated so that the shot from the casemate's guns would have to rustle through the grass of the river bank, and then skim the surface of the water before striking the mark for which it was destined. The barbet [barbette] guns were good in numbers but entirely exposed to the fire of the howitzers in the tops of the large vessels which cleared them of their gunners. I consider the resistance of these forts as manly and good for they are not very strong affairs, especially Fort St. Philip.[24]

Our run this morning has had fewer traces of war and the scenery has wonderfully improved. In all my West Indian cruise I never saw land so rich and seeming so well cultivated as that through which we sailed this morning, and our New England meadows are mere barrens as compared to it. The scenery, too, is very beautiful, for although there are no hills nor any rise of ground for the whole 170 miles, there are magnificent forests of every shade of green, sometimes close to the river bank and sometimes far, and broad plantations of thriving sugar cane of a bright green like that of our young cornfields, only covering many times as much space. And, lest even such a vast variety of foliage should tire us, at pleasant intervals we came upon large and hospitable plantation houses, surrounded by Magnolias and orange trees with dark and beautiful evergreens, while in contrast to the "big house," which we found always closed, were the strait clean rows of Negro quarters, always open and the occupants always cheering us on. It was a great change from yesterday; then everything was smoking and in ruins; now everything is thrifty, the negroes are working the fields and the teams are crawling along the flat roads as if never disturbed.[25]

As we drew near the city we discovered strong and well constructed earth-works on both sides the river which would have entirely prevented a landing of our troops and could have worried our fleet very much as it passed up the stream, but these, after a few moments sharp firing were altogether deserted, and New Orleans itself lay directly behind them. 50[,]000 troops are said to have manned these works and garrisoned the place, but, with the exception of a few prisoners, they prudently drew off into the country.[26]

We are anchored just above the Flag Ship, off the "Memphis Packet Land-ing," as a large white sign board tells us in plain black letters. Although not inclined to leave the war part of sea life, I cannot but think that the citizens have argued for truth in not tearing down the sign. In the rear of this quiet and empty landing is, a few streets back, a very handsome and New York like church tower of brown stone, just below it is the Custom House of the United States with our flag flying over it; then, a few steps below that is a larger Cathedral having three spires and a large wing on either side in a very aristocratic and French style of architecture, while the prevailing sentiments of the natives in this [illegible] of ours while "we're marching on," an expression in the name of "The Tehamitipee House," which repeats itself three times on the walls of a brick building of three stories, within rifle shot of our cabin window. I am afraid, however, that since those words were painted there, these flighty people have altered their doctrines, for everything with steam aboard, down to the very ferry-boats, had gone some days ago in a direction entirely opposite to this paradise of fillibusters.[27]

But I expect that I am wearying you rather too much. This is a great city; it rivals and perhaps excels the last great city that I saw, Philadelphia. The pecu-liar ingenuity of its inhabitants appalls me, Yankee as I am, for even on their ferryboats they economize by putting two boats together and but one paddle wheel between them, by which very simple and unique contrivance, I presume half the pressure of these hard, hard times and half the heavy, heavy taxes of this wretched [illegible] are obviated.

I hope soon to have a closer inspection of the big town of King Cotton, for Gen'l Butler, who this moment passed by my window, is landing his forces and will make it safe for a "Cursed Yankee" like me to run about these sacred streets unarmed.[28]

U.S.S. *Iroquois*, New Orleans, May 5th, 1862
I have been ashore for a whole day, (on the 2nd inst., just after Butler had landed his troops) and have pretty thoroughly explored the place. My companion was

a passenger who came aboard at Ship Island, a very clever fellow and a son of Prof. Longfellow.[29]

We went first to the St. Charles, which was quite dismal with a big card on the main entrance saying "House Closed." So chilly was our reception there that we went down to the Custom House where we found in front the remains of a great bonfire of gun carriages, which the Secesh tried to destroy when they saw them falling into our hands.[30]

Seeing enough there, we took a car and rode way out of town to the Marine Hospital, where we found ourselves outside of all pickets and in a lonely neighborhood, one of us in uniform, but armed only with a pocket-knife. We, therefore, on reflection, decided to turn back and took a stroll through the French quarter, buying on our way some very bitter oranges from a man who was delighted to see us and professed to come from Boston. On our way back to the Memphis landing I saw the sign "M. Greenwood," a very familiar name, over a fine, large store, but the premises, like most there in the city, were closed. Curious as to how he fared, I stepped into the next store, the door of which was open, to inquire; but the proprietor, a very [illegible] manly looking man, so soon as he saw me coming, turned square about and walked aft. Not at all daunted I followed him up and when alongside turned to him and asked him if he could please tell what had become of Mr. Greenwood, next door! He turned his back to me again and saying in a most insulting tone, "I have nothing in the world to do with you, Sir!" walked off. I answered, "Very well," and also went my way. Such was the conduct of very many to whom I spoke, while some few were glad to see us and talked as if they had just come out from under a featherbed.[31]

I remarked the dullness of the place. All the stores were closed and, though all the people were in the streets and very excited, their good clothes, which they were plainly sporting, looked exceedingly seedy; indeed I did not see half a dozen well dressed men the whole day. In the streets near the river even, where all the business and bustle of the city was, the grass was growing in thick tufts and on the levee opposite our present anchorage there is a fine large patch of wheat, some two feet high.

I was somewhat surprised, too, to see no darkies; they, I presume, were all carried up-country by their owners, for though "slave pens" in abundance were seen, they were all closed.[32]

In the afternoon a larger party of us were ashore again and visited the Custom House and Post Office, when we did the first job at pillaging in which I ever joined, save once in Virginia. I enclose some Confederate Postage Stamps and send you by this mail some choice newspapers, also a pamphlet which I took from the office containing the proceedings of the Episcopal Church of the Confederate States of America in Convention, Bp. [Bishop William] Meade presiding. I shall try to work in, too, a little of the remains of some $1,000,000 worth of cotton which these rascals burned so soon as the *Iroquois* (the front vessel) appeared before the place.[33]

When I went ashore I took $5.00 in hard gold which I got changed for shinplasters. The man who first gave me change said that my coin was the first he had seen since Sept. 12, 1861, and that he did not think there was another piece of money in the city, in which remark I fully agree, for there is nothing here but irredeemable paper. The eager grasp put upon my metal showed that the populace were glad to see the Yankees on one account at least. I expect that Butler is setting things to rights now, though.[34]

Saturday evening we came aboard the *Iroquois* with the usual ceremonies.

My poor ship is knocked almost to pieces. I could show you one of our guns with a great dent on it when a round shot struck it and bounded off to kill some of the next gun crew; fore and aft our bulwarks are torn to kindling-wood, while by way of defense our inner wood-work is daubed with a blue mud colored paint which looks gloomy and dirty enough. Our loss was 8 killed and 24 wounded; the heaviest in the fleet for our number of men. Our poor wretch of a Master's Mate died very bravely indeed; his right arm was carried clean away, save one little ribband of skin to which the hand still hung; the ball then entered the chest and tore everything out, it left nothing.

The poor fellow dropped to the deck and when his gun's crew ran to him, he cried out to them, "Don't stop for me, boys, I'm gone, go ahead and give it to 'em.!" Notwithstanding his terrible wounds, he lived 25 minutes and gave minute directions as to the dispositions of his things.[35]

The very heavy firing which we had on the way up from Fort Jackson had such an effect upon the remains that they were buried in the river. All our men were killed in the same way, torn to pieces. The head of a powder boy was blown away and never found. Our decks, and the steerage and Ward Room were soaked in blood.

When I get home I can give you "lots of yarns," but today I am very busy and write only by snatches.

Tomorrow morning we go up the river to Baton Rouge and perhaps will have some firing. When we return we are to go to Mobile, after the capture of which, in which we are promised a forward part, we may return home, for our boilers were condemned by a Board of Survey this morning and we made last night, lying here at anchor, only sixteen inches of water. I am afraid Forts Jackson and St. Philip have done us no good beyond our reputation. Everyone says the *Iroquois* did more than her duty. Old De Camp (drunk all the time, I suppose) fought her splendidly, sitting straddle of our after pivot gun smoking a cigar.[36]

By the way, I met ashore Capt. Jno. De Forest and a good many others in the 12th C.V.[37]

I am very well and in good spirits, anxious to meet the enemy up stream.

This place is fearfully filthy, every gutter overflowing with stagnant matter. Yellow fever must appear here in a very little time; thank goodness it's not our station.

> Very Aff. and with much love
> to all, Your obedient son,
> Edward W. Bacon

P. S. I get pay from April 1st, the time I left home. When you have read this will you send Tom with it to Dr. Whiting's, No. 20 Elm St., for my old chum Isham. It is the only letter I have been able to write and I would like him to see what I am doing. He will return it after taking some of the trophies. Capt. Palmer has made me signal and boat officer. I am not idle by a great deal.[38]

> **U.S.S. *Iroquois*, Baton Rouge,**
> **La., May 10th, 1862**

My Dear Kate,

My last letter, long and hastily written, I mailed at New Orleans.

On the morning of the 6th we weighed anchor and steamed up the river, which above the city continued as beautiful as below it.

Our day's trip was not specially exciting, there having passed up before us the *Brooklyn* and some gun-boats, bound for Vicksburg, could they reach it. We anchored for the night opposite the plantation of Ex. Gov. Roman and about fifteen miles below Donelsonville, once, in times long passed, the capital of the State. Having come to, a Lt. and myself were sent ashore upon a reconnaissance, which was quite entertaining. We were the first to have trodden the sacred soil at that particular spot.[39]

[Frederick V.] McNair, the Lt., seized upon a Frenchman while I nabbed the darkies. They told us that the last Sesesh left on Saturday, two days before; that quite a force of gunboats similar to those we sunk at the Forts had gone up a few days before us, and had rumors of our recent great defeat before Yorktown. The unanimous expression of the Contrabands was "By golly, Masr, dey *neber* tink you get past dem forts" and they remarked also "How different dese folks talks from five months 'go." They said all the folks about there were Sesesh and were not quite despairing, but were many of them quite hopeful in the prospect of their friend "Yellow Jack."[40]

I urged my nigs. to steal and bring off to us some Sesesh grub, which they did in the Mid-watch—when all was quiet.[41]

Next day we passed the inconsiderable place of Donaldsonville, and anchored at night off Baton Rouge, a very fine appearing place upon the first land ascending the valley which is not below the water level.

This Bluff is some 40 feet high and is surmounted by a very fine State House, the best ever State House building I ever yet saw, a large and well planned Deaf and Dumb Asylum, several churches and, higher up the river, not in sight as we approached, the U.S. Arsenal and Barracks, which occupy some 20 acres of land. Between these more prominent objects very neat and pretty cottage houses contrast with the thick trees and shrubbery, making the whole scene one of much beauty.[42]

This beautiful town, the Capital of this Confederate State, is now ours, of the *Iroquois*.

We were the first to communicate with the shore which we did on the evening of the 8th by a summons to surrender which was answered by a refusal to surrender to "any power upon earth," and the assurance that the place was "entirely without any means of defense," but that our occupation of it would wound the sensibilities of its peaceable and inoffensive inhabitants.

Accordingly, yesterday morning we landed a force of some 60 men and a howitzer and marched up to the Arsenal, having out a strong force of pickets to protect our advance. When we reached the Arsenal gate, I, being in advance of all, found it locked, but squeezing through was the first to tread Uncle Sam's property in his name. I at once spied a man dodging behind one of the biggest of the buildings and gave chase. In a few moments I had over taken him and compelled him to surrender at discretion, taking from him the key of the Comdts Office, of which he called himself the custodian, and leading him to the Chief of the Expedition, compelled him to disgorge his information, which was valuable.

I then received instructions (being Aide-de-camp) to overhaul the different buildings, so shouldering an immense bunch of keys, I began to act the "ruthless invader" to the utmost of my ability. My exertions were chiefly upon the Arsenal proper in which I found a lot of old files, some splendid clubs, some powder boxes and a quantity of oils and paints—everything else had been carefully removed.

The Laboratory was nearly perfect, and there were some shot and shell, but nothing of much consequence in the whole premises.

In the Commandant's Office I found a quantity of old papers—some loose gunpowder, some empty gin bottles and an iron bedstead, while over the chimneypiece was fixed the only prize I found, a very pretty pair of Antlers. I tore them down and have them now on board as a relic of my first active expedition, a very important one, and all the more so because bloodless.

After we had marched back again with our drums beating and colors flying above us and on the U.S. Property, we sent a letter of [to] Mayor [Benjamin F.] Bryan, assuring him that, if he suffered our flag to be molested, his town would pay the bitterest penalties. This correspondence you will probably see. The Mayor in his reply to our warning begs a good deal more than is proper for a man who will "surrender to no power on earth."[43]

Below Natchez, May 12th

We are now getting up to Natchez, which place we have orders to treat as we did Baton Rouge. We are to reach there by sundown, will coal ship and the gunboats in our train, and send them on to Vicksburg while we await the arrival of the Flag Officer. When any thing occurs worthy of mention or of interest I will add a postscript, unless I find a chance to send sooner.

Natchez, May 14th

We are as far up as we can go, for at Vicksburg, the next town to Natchez, the rebel batteries command the river for three miles and one half, and when we get there we can stop and think how much it will cost to go past. I have no doubt, however, that vessels which can pass a casemated fort, like Jackson, can run through four miles of batteries.[44]

We appeared before this place on the afternoon of the 12th, and sent on shore a summons to surrender, which the people at the landing refused to receive. We then, on her return to our side [of] the river (for, on account of the height of the Bluffs, we have to get across the river from the city to train our guns on it), seized the Ferryboat, and put aboard of her a heavy force of Seamen and Marines and two howitzers, and proceeded across the river. But as soon as we landed, a delegation met us, saying that they begged we would land no force but that they would make no resistance and apologized for all the performance of the morning—and the Mayor in his reply frankly surrendered his city, saying that "Formalities are vain in the presence of such realities." After which, too, when we sent ashore an Officer to communicate in regard to details, they were very kind to him indeed.[45]

I anticipate no further trouble here atall—that after six months are gone and the outrageous lies of these leaders are proved fully false, they will gladly return to their allegiance.

The Flag [officer] comes up to night and Capt. Palmer will try hard to get to Vicksburg, in which we all trust he will succeed. So that if you heard that Foote and Farragut have shaken hands at Memphis, you may be pretty sure that the *Iroquois* has added something to her laurels.[46]

I have not time to write more, for I have been working hard all day and am going ashore pretty soon to eat blackberries and rest myself.

Pray do not let my friends think I forget them but tell them I am well and ask after them.

With much love to all, Very truly and
aff. your brother, Edward W. Bacon

[Diary] USS *Iroquois*, Off Vicksburg, May 28, 1862

I rejoined my vessel on May 3d after a very long trip down the coast of 28 days.

New Orleans had been taken so that I had nothing to do but enjoy the fruits of victory. We had a trip up the river which I must describe at my next leisure, for it was one of much interest. We took the city of Baton Rouge without opposition, hoisting the Federal flag once more on the United States arsenal. Thence we went to Natchez which also surrendered to us. From Natchez we were ordered down to the mouth of Red River to protect some supposed Unionist there, and on our return were ordered to proceed up the river to Vicksburg which place we reached on the 23d of May and commenced the offensive Blockade which we are now engaged upon.

U.S.S. *Iroquois*, Passing Palmyra
(Jeff's plantation), June 14th, 1862

My dear Kate,

This is the third time I have passed the Jeff Davis Estate and it was our intention to stop & see whether Jeff had burned his cotton, Capt. Palmer, having promised to give Palmyra into my tender mercies, but the reception of the news that our Squadron of the Upper Mississippi on Tuesday made us hasten our speed.[47]

I wrote on Monday evening [June 9] a very hurried letter to Mother, telling how & why we had left Vicksburg & bombarded Grand Gulf. The *Itasca* left early on Tuesday morning, taking the *Katahdin*'s company with her down to Red River where she was sent to look for more batteries.[48]

In the afternoon, at the same hour as on Monday, when the sun shone well into the enemy, we got under weigh, steaming & slowly dropping down the river, giving a couple of broadsides as we passed & then turning to come up again, more slowly & with much heavier fire. After this, with capital aim, thrown our shells for some two hours, into the Battery & Shrapnel, Grape & canister in to the town, producing anything but a beneficial effect upon the wooden houses, we landed a force from the *Wissahickon*, *Sciota* &*Winona*, lighting the town in four places which soon became a very fine sight. Four huge pillars of flame, rising & growing more brilliant as the sun went down, supporting a great canopy of smoke over our heads, for the breeze had gone down, must have terrified the population for miles around.[49]

The enemy did not respond from his Battery, but kept up a constant firing of musketry on the Bluff & in the trees, the practice was not good, the balls falling near us, but taking no effect.

I presume there will be much capital made of the "Burning of Grand Gulf," but it will be from the whole cloth.[50]

Our transports & Store vessels were fired into long & Gen. Williams declined to punish the town. Subsequently, when Comdr. [John] De Camp made his appearance before the place, he expressly told the Authorities that any insult to any of the Federal vessels would be severely punished & that the work on the Battery must be stopped. Heedless of this warning, before dawn the next morning, the Battery opened on the sleeping crews of our gunboats, driving them off, though they also deserted their work. Passing the place yesterday, we found it still smoking.[51]

[The next two pages are unreadable because the ink from opposing and folded pages soaked through, blurring all except a word here and there. Only the postscript is legible, although parts may be missing.]

Yours truly & aff., Edward W. Bacon

Sunday June 15th

Our mail leaves to-night.

The heat to day is fearful—so much worse, not by the mercury but by the effect on us, than the West Indies as to make us long to have that climate once more.

The enemy are busy strengthening their defenses & the *Sciota* is under orders to prevent the mounting of a big gun which was brought down to a point.[52]

※

Encouraged by his success at New Orleans, Farragut apparently thought he could achieve the same result at Vicksburg. He was mistaken—the upriver city was a self-contained land fortress. Vicksburg and its defenses on high ground were one and the same; distant Forts Jackson and St. Philip protected New Orleans but left the city defenseless once they had been passed.

Nevertheless, Farragut "suddenly had the confidence to take Vicksburg," as historian Michael B. Ballard put it. On June 25 he ordered his fleet and the mortar boats up the river to anchor below the city. Sited on high bluffs and rolling hills, Vicksburg's guns commanded the river. On the twenty-sixth, the giant thirteen-inch mortars began hurling their high-arching 220-pound explosive missiles toward shore batteries and the city. Samuel H. Lockett, chief engineer at Vicksburg, asserted the blast from one mortar shell left a seventeen-foot-deep crater in hard clay but that "few soldiers and civilians were killed" and the bombardment caused little material damage. However, he conceded, "The howling and bursting shells had a very demoralizing effect on those not accustomed to them." That would include just about everyone in or near Vicksburg.[53]

On the next day, Farragut's ships joined the bombardment. Then, early on June 28, 1862, the Union fleet forged past the fortified city in the morning darkness, shore batteries and ships rapidly exchanging fire. David D. Porter, commanding the mortar boats, recalled, "The air seemed to be filled with projectiles." Brigadier General Martin L. Smith, Vicksburg's commander, quite agreed. In his official report, Smith said that "loud explosions shook the city to its foundations; shot and shell went hissing and tearing through the trees and walls, scattering fragments far and wide in their terrific flight; men, women, and children rushed into the streets, and, amid the crash of falling houses, commenced their hasty flight to the country for safety." Almost apologetically, Albert D. Bache, a captain's clerk on the USS *Hartford*, admitted, "The [Confederate] batteries are so situated that we cannot fire at them without destroying the town."[54]

For all the noisy fireworks, neither side sustained much damage. Farragut's sailors suffered some casualties, and Confederates' often plunging fire damaged some ships, but none were lost. Vicksburg was bruised but unbowed. It was clear that naval firepower alone could not compel the city's surrender. Porter wrote, "Ships . . . can not crawl up hills 300 feet high, and it is that part of Vicksburg which must be taken by the army." Farragut concurred, advising Major General Henry W. Halleck, the department commander, that they would need more troops to take Vicksburg. As Farragut ruefully told Secretary of the Navy Welles, "I passed up the river . . . but to no purpose."[55]

In this next letter Bacon first describes the fears he experienced in battle.

%

USS *Iroquois*, Above Vicksburg, June 30, 1862

My Dear Isham,

I wrote you just as we had ceased firing the 28th, a very short scrawl announcing that we had passed the Batteries of Vicksburg without the loss of a man, tho our rigging was a great deal cut and a shell exploded on our decks.[56]

I will try now to give you a little detail of the action, but all particulars are so disjointed as to make the task very difficult.

We had been looking for the Flag Officer to bring up the rear of the Mortars and Men of War for several days, when, on the 25th, we arrived. That night the Mortars went into position and the next p.m. opened fire upon the town and Batteries, without much effect for the practice was poor.

The bombardment continued at intervals until the evening of the 27th when word was passed to the different vessels to be ready next morning. At 2 a.m. the Flagship showed her two red lights and we all got underweigh, the *Iroquois* in the van, and proceeded up the river. We were much delayed by the slowness of the *Oneida* and other vessels in getting their position, so that it was about a quarter to four when we first got in range of the battery, marked on the little sketch which I enclose.[57]

Much to our surprise, the enemy were asleep, for the Mortars had let them rest that night, and [they] did not discover our movement.

We kept on a fair speed and, when more than half past the No. 1 Battery, they opened on us at 4 precisely, we answering with our pivots. Several more shots were fired by the Battery, which, like the first, missed us.

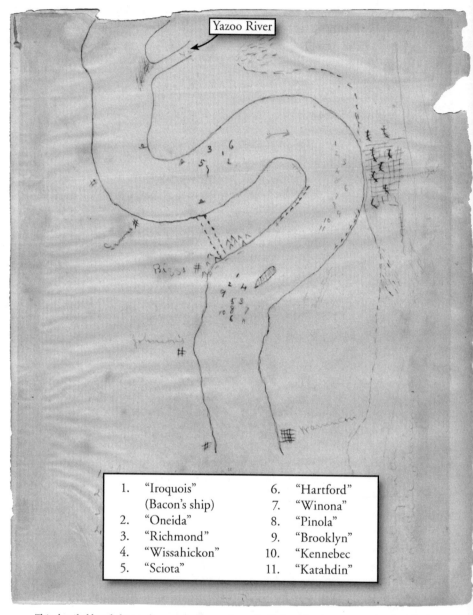

1.	"Iroquois" (Bacon's ship)	6.	"Hartford"
		7.	"Winona"
2.	"Oneida"	8.	"Pinola"
3.	"Richmond"	9.	"Brooklyn"
4.	"Wissahickon"	10.	"Kennebec
5.	"Sciota"	11.	"Katahdin"

This detailed hand-drawn diagram by Bacon shows the Federal fleet's upriver movement, early on June 28, 1862, in three successive stages through the gauntlet of fire from Vicksburg's batteries. His ship, the USS *Iroquois*, is number 1 and in the van as the ships steam upstream. He also shows (at bottom of the river's hairpin bend) the outline of the bypass canal digging effort.

The hospital Battery next received our attention, when suddenly on our bow there opened two new batteries of which we had not dreamed before. These were well served and the shot flew briskly all around us, cutting the rigging close above our heads. It was a shot from these Batteries to which I alluded in my last letter as passing just back of my head and in front of the captain as we stood near each other on the poop.[58]

We all the while had been steaming up against a powerful current but now Palmer ordered the engines merely to hold their own and we began to pour in our shell just as fast as we could load and fire our guns, which, with our well-disciplined crew, is very fast. Observing the vessels in the rear closing on us, we left the enemy here to the tender mercies of the guns of *Richmond*, throwing 1,000 pounds of shell at each broadside and proceeded to draw out the Batteries farther up. It is much the same story right thru, dull, like any reported battle to you, the reader, but as exciting as if the whole world were swimming around you to the participator. As soon as we fairly engaged one Battery, another seemed to open just a little on our bow, and then, a little higher up, another still, commanding that.[59]

But the worst guns of all and by far the best served, were the last which opened on us, a Battery of two or three rifled guns, marked no. 6 on my map. These guns did not open at their longest range, nor did any of them, but waited until they could rake us fore and aft as we steamed up the river. When they saw the time was come, they poured down upon us from a height of some 30 feet a succession of admirable shots, their shell bursting on every side and above us. I have now near me a piece of one of these tremendous projectiles.[60]

Not only did this Battery annoy us while below it but they turned their guns as we ran up and, when we were way past and imagined ourselves quite in safety, a number of raking shots from aft forward made us and the *Hartford* feel quite uneasy, for we were unable to answer them.[61]

I regard this as superior to all the other works, in elevation just sufficient, not like No. 1 on the top of a hill of some 200 feet, and protected by another commanding Battery above and a little to the left of it.

Now we were fairly through the gauntlet and I looked around to see what our loss might be. Our mainstays of wire rope some 1 ½ inches in diameter were cut and hung over the side, our mizzen rigging, under which I stood, was cut in several places, and a ricochet shot had struck the water close overboard by me, bounded over, cutting windsail halyards which were swinging loose some 6 feet above our heads, and entered the water the other side. I need not worry you with twenty other stories of similar character, but you will see what narrow escapes a battle brings.[62]

Looking back, I could see the *Oneida* just emerging from the smoke and the flash of her last guns, while just behind her came the *Richmond* with her magnificent broadsides.

The *Sciota* came through signaling for a medical officer, for her surgeon had been sent home, condemned by a Medical Survey as too ill for duty, and she had two killed and a number wounded. The *Wissahickon* continued on, her dashing commander De Camp feeling bound not to stop till he found something to bar his progress. He has gone, I believe, up the Yazoo.[63]

The *Brooklyn, Katahdin* and *Kennebec* did not come through for some reason not known to me. There is something suspicious in the fact that the *Kennebec*, tho wholly uninjured, failed to get through the forts below. It is as well to divide our forces, though the Flag Officer did not intend it. The *Hartford* reports that as she came through, the enemy were running from the lower Batteries, so that an adequate land force could have taken the place without material loss. Now, upon arrival of Grant, we must run the gauntlet again and perhaps with greater loss. Alas, Mismanagement![64]

We are expecting the arrival of some 20,000 troops from above in a few days, when the place will be taken and *Iroquois*, in obedience to positive verbal orders, will proceed direct to New York.[65]

Meanwhile, General Williams, with his 4,000 men, is digging a canal or "cut off," which I have dotted on my map. He sent down the river day before yesterday and now has at work 200 of Jeff Davis' negroes, whom he had brought up. This canal will soon be cut and then Vicksburg, ours or not, will be, in time, away from the business channel of the river, and Butler will receive all his stores and reinforcements via Memphis. In this way I hope to receive all my future letters before we leave for New Orleans and home; they should be directed, as before, with the addition of "via Cairo," not Memphis, as I wrote on the 28th.[66]

The *Tennessee* has arrived below and I was fortunate enough to receive a letter from home of June 3, later than anyone else, I think, but none from you. Now, old fellow, I have forborne to urge my case, knowing how intensely wrapped up you are in musty books, but really, you have not quite done the fair thing. It is three months since I left home, yet you have not found a moment to say that you are well and succeeding in your duties. Is it really so, old fel?[67]

You shut yourself up so no one else can see you (my sister speaks of all my friends almost, with the one melancholy exception), but you are such a book worm that the outside world, even the grave minister's family, know nothing of you. Indeed, I verily believe that my letters, so carefully penned, so many and so heavy, on which, too, I have always prepaid the postage, are all in one huge dusty pile in the New Haven Post Office, unhonored and unread, as well as unanswered. If it were not that I like to see and encourage laudable exertions to study in young men, I should have pricked you before about this—however, you are stubborn enough to escape any harm this reproof might do you.

I regret to learn that my friends have been injudicious enough to print some of my lucubrations in the local journals. I am more concerned in that my chances for the Presidency may be thereby endangered, believing with the Rev. Homer Wilbur, "A. M., etc, etc," in regard to the baneful effects of letters candidatial.[68]

July 1st, 1862, Tuesday

I remarked in my last the intense fatigue, the horrible prostration which I felt on coming out of Battle. I dread this in looking forward to our second conflict, almost as much as the falling shells. The tension of one's nerves and the work of the mind is dreadful. You have to force yourself to be cool. You see the flash of a gun and in a second hear the shriek of shell—yet in the intervening period my mind goes thro this—this shell may hit me. If I get below, if I fall down, run under cover, I may save my life (and my body starts to do so). But I can't permit this. My duty is here—on deck—ready, ready to jump forward in a minute—I must assist my captain—tell him when I see Batteries, where the following vessels are. I am sworn to do this duty. I can't save myself. Perhaps God will protect me. Every time I see that the guns in the hills flash, comes that irresistible impulse to run, to dissolve, which exhausts itself in a dodge of the head. . . .

Believe me very affectionately, your
sincere friend, Edward W. Bacon

Iroquois, Above Vicksburg, July 3rd, 1862

Dear Kate,

I wrote to Rebecca [sister] yesterday, but our mail facilities are growing so rapidly that I am inclined to keep you more fully posted as regards the *Iroquois* than before even, and indeed, as our position here becomes more and more the center of interest, and improves in interest to us day by day, my frequent advices may not be altogether without interest.

The Siege still continues, a pretty regular firing of Mortars being almost the only matter of interest in the whole day. Davis' Mortars opened yesterday p.m. close by us, throwing their shells across the point into the town. The enemy must have been a good deal startled at this new attack. Occasionally, too, we hear the shriek of the shell from the big rifles of the enemy, we are just too far off for them, but they try hard to hit us. I went ashore on the point yesterday at sundown and had them nearly over me quite often.[69]

The canal goes bravely on, it ought to be finished by the time the upper army gets here, but how soon that is I do not pretend to guess. I hope it may be soon.[70]

Further than this I know nothing. Capt. Palmer learned yesterday the death of his brother, Col. Palmer of the Topogs.[71]

We are going, of course, to celebrate to-morrow. I am going to let this lay by until a chance for a mail or more news occurs.

Aff. your brother, Edward W. Bacon

4th

We have nothing new—but papers to the 28th, which show our affairs on James Island.[72]

(3) TURNING POINT

WHILE THE NAVY HAD DEMONSTRATED ITS ABILITY TO PASS Vicksburg's guns, Farragut and his men could do no more than that. The North needed ground troops to capture the "Gibraltar of the West," and soldiers simply were not available in sufficient numbers. Ships and crews served no purpose anchored above the citadel city and many, including Farragut, wanted to escape to healthier climes and more rewarding duty.

Then a command shuffle occurred when Captain Thomas T. Craven quarreled with Farragut. Very shortly the junior officer went home, and Palmer assumed command of the flagship *Hartford*, Craven's ship. Palmer asked Bacon to accompany him, and that brought to a head the simmering uneasiness and ennui that apparently troubled Bacon. He felt himself caught in a dilemma.

Some of Bacon's quandary was self-created, but much was real. He wanted to serve—it was his patriotic duty—but maybe not there; he had proved himself under fire and perhaps that was enough; the *Hartford* was too big, too crowded, and his new shipmates would be riffraff, not the sort with whom he would gladly associate; yet Palmer had requested his presence and because he owed him much, it might not be right to turn him down, resign, and run for home. Yet if they stayed there on the river, in that fever-ridden oppressive heat, his health might fail, and then he would be of no use to anyone, let alone Uncle Sam or Palmer. He also worried that he grew old, soon leaving his teens, without an education to prepare him for suitable civilian employment, and he was not sure what to do about that dim prospect. Finally, he believed that the war rapidly drew to a successful conclusion for the North. Accordingly, his patriotic services really would not be needed much longer.

Why Bacon thought that victory neared is a puzzle. Confederates had repeatedly repulsed or defeated Federal forces on the main Eastern battlegrounds, and, aside from New Orleans, they still held strong positions in the West. Perhaps he indulged in wishful thinking or had only an incomplete grasp of the war's progress. From 1861 to the summer of 1863, Southern men and women expressed a justified optimism that they marched toward victory and independence. In June 1861, a 17th Mississippi infantryman was sure the "Abolitionists of the North" could never conquer the South, and in November 1862, Ada W. Bacot, a Confederate nurse, wrote that "the Yankees will never subjecate us." Northerners fretted that they were losing the struggle to preserve the Union. On July 4, 1862, a 9th Michigan Infantry soldier declared "many think . . . that we have got

whiped" and in January 1863, a surgeon with the 13th Iowa gloomily predicted
Confederates would win their bid for independence.[1]

Bacon wrote his father, expressing his concerns about staying in the navy.
He sought his father's guidance, probably hoping for some simple unraveling
of his mostly self-tied Gordian knots.

But by midsummer, Bacon learned that Lincoln had called for another three
hundred thousand volunteers to serve for three years. That news deflated his
earlier fancy that the war neared a happy conclusion. By the end of September
1862, he had reversed himself completely, sinking into despair and defeatism.
He was convinced that the Union's leaders, including Lincoln, had failed the
nation. In particular, the president had reduced civil liberties and had allowed
the nation to suffer many defeats. Exercising hindsight, Bacon thought Lincoln
should have called for a million volunteers and mobilized 150,000 black soldiers.
Given that brave and determined Southerners were bent on either independence
or death, pursuing the war was "foolish," because he felt that now the only goal
was the acquisition of territory.[2]

Nevertheless, duty still beckoned.

///

Above Vicksburg, July 5th, 1862

Dear Father,

My relations on board the *Iroquois* are about to be changed. Capt. [Thomas T.]
Craven, having quarreled in some way with the Flag Officer, has gone home,
and Fleet Capt. [Henry H.] Bell has taken the *Brooklyn*. This, of course, makes
a change upon Farragut's staff and he has appointed Commander Palmer Fleet
Captain. When the *Iroquois* goes home, I presume he will enter upon his duties,
but not before, I trust. But that will be soon, for Farragut told me this a.m. that
he intended to go below in a very few days. Captain Palmer has asked me to go
aboard the Flagship with him and I have the matter now under consideration.

My objections are chiefly the unpleasantness of the situation, the *Hartford*
being but a small ship for the Flag and very much crowded. Her steerage is not
a great deal larger than ours and yet the mess is 13 in number. Then, too, with
a Flag Officer, Fleet Capt. and the *Hartford's* Commander, the Cabin is pretty
well crowded and a Flag Officer's Secretary and two Captain's Clerks are not
likely to harmonize in every way. In addition to the crowded state of the vessel,
her discipline is very wretched and she is noted as the dirtiest ship in the fleet.
From all I can learn, there is not the greatest harmony among her officers.[3]

But all these considerations aside, if I finally see it my duty to go aboard in
this new capacity.

Perhaps I owe it to Capt. Palmer not to leave him, having come out with
him; yet in the strict terms of my engagement, he has no claim upon me, I being

clerk of the *Iroquois*, not Capt. Palmer's Clerk, and my transfer will involve my resignation and reappointment. Yet my chief reason has not been stated for accepting the appointment. My pay of $600 a year will cease with my resignation and I will be without employment, as I was a year ago and back at my studies at home, when, perhaps, I ought to be supporting myself and laying by some money for future use. This is my greatest reason.

On the other hand, comparing myself with what I was a year ago, I am at a stand-still, if I have not fallen back, in a knowledge of books, though I know a great deal better how to get along in the world. This is, perhaps, more valuable than one year of school, and I am rapidly reaching an age when, I suppose, study becomes harder, so, at least, they told me when I was a good deal younger. With my education so little advanced, with my teens getting behind me, ought I not to be preparing myself for those places in society which I ought, and which is my desire, to fill?[4]

This, indeed, was my feeling when I returned home six months ago and, further back, when I first left home. But, at first, I left for patriotism, knowing, too, that I could not study, and, when I came back, after so sad a defeat as that at Martinique, not having seen smoke, I could not stay without thinking myself and knowing others to be thinking that I was sick of war, afraid of battle and glad to make my escape. Now I have been in battle, have shown my willingness to fight for my country and have proved myself, I am told, not a coward. My health I deem better than ever before; the war, I am induced to hope, is beginning to draw to a successful close, and my services can do nothing to hasten that conclusion. The most I could do was by example and that has ceased to exert its influence.[5]

Then, too, the work here, when we shall have passed these Batteries again, will be so dull, the weather so hot, and a climate so wearing, that it seems (as a measure for the care of my health, often too feeble) necessary to leave the station. At the same time, I shall, in case the war continues, be willing to go again and stay as long as the War calls for me. But a dull War, as this will hereafter be, we hope, seems a waste of time and too great a sacrifice for me who have so much to do beside.[6]

The upshot will be, I presume, that I will tell Palmer that, unless he can procure another clerk, and if he is very anxious to have me stay and thinks he cannot get along without me, I will stay until something turns up. Otherwise, I will go home in the *Iroquois*.

I wish you would write me a few lines to correct my opinions and express your wishes as to what disposal you would have me make of myself. If you write via Cairo, I may receive your answer before Captain Palmer makes the contemplated change in his position.[7]

I am very affectionately, your
son, Edward W. Bacon

Iroquois, **Above Vicksburg, July 6, 1862**

Dear Kate,

We are to night in receipt of the cheering rumor that Richmond is captured with 50,000 prisoners—of course, that means taken and some 5,000 half starved secesh—like these poor fellows whom we take and who come off to us here. We learn from Halleck, too, that in a few weeks, as soon as he can get together his army, he will visit Vicksburg with men enough to take and occupy it, so that by Sept. 1st you may hear of the fall of this "last ditch."[8]

My affairs are a little disturbed just now. Capt. Craven has been sent home and Captain Bell has taken command of the *Brooklyn*. Capt. Palmer has been made Fleet Captain so that you won't hear of me much longer as Captain's Clerk of the *Iroquois*. I have not quite decided whether to go aboard the Flag Ship or not, but in the course of two or three weeks, when Palmer takes up his quarters there, you will know. I am sorry that the change has occurred, as I hoped to go home in the *Iroquois* and, if the war continued and I continued in it, to go out with him in a much larger, better ship.[9]

However, I hope the wretched fight will give way to peace pretty soon, so that neither Flag Ship nor any other ship will call me her Captain's Clerk.

You speak of transcribing one of my letters for Frank & Theodore; I wish you would do the same for me to one of theirs occasionally, for I would like to know how they are getting on. I have not yet learned what part they took in the Pulaski affair, how they liked it and what they did, but, if they and I too go home, we may meet and be able to talk over affairs together.[10]

I wrote to Theodore a day or two ago. My postage stamps are all gone and I was going to write to send me some, but conclude it isn't wise, for I may get some around here.

Our Bombardment continues not quite so lively as before, but still quite annoying to the Vicksburg people, I expect.[11]

Tomorrow or next day we are going up to the mouth of the Yazoo River to get some fresh grub, for we are really starving. The Steerage has eaten in the last Quarter 21 gallons of Beans! It is no wonder we have scurvy.[12]

Com. Farragut told me this morning that he intended to pass down the river in three or four days, but perhaps the news from Halleck will make him change his mind. This is as good a place as any.[13]

With love & remembrance to all my friends, I
am very truly your brother, Edward W. Bacon

Iroquois, **Above Vicksburg, July 11, 1862**

Dear Kate,

For the past few days we have been on a little vacation up the river, looking after fresh food and recreation for our men. We were for the most time anchored off a Dr. Buckner's, brother-in-law of P. M. G. Blair, and a very nice gentleman. I took tea at his house & spent a very pleasant evening. He is less secession than many, but is utterly resigned. We got plenty of chickens, sheep, and geese, corn, with eggs and milk but are without butter. I managed, too, to get a very few clothes washed, the first since I left Key West, 22nd last April.[14]

We are now again "Above Vicksburg"—anxiously waiting for something to turn up. If we only had 15,000 troops.

We received a mail yesterday & I got a letter from New Rochelle of the 8th June, but none from you, who are my only home correspondent. Today we have from up river Chicago papers of the 7th July, which tell us that "Vicksburg is taken, but no particulars."[15]

What do folks say of McClellan in New England now? I can not make out whether he is beaten or whether he is victorious; opinion in the fleet, where everyone admires & worships him, is that we are beaten before Richmond. Our advices from Arkansas do not look encouraging & truly our fix here is deplorable.[16]

We are all much amused by Hunter's letter to that wretch Wickliffe of Kentucky.[17]

We have no news. The water falls so steadily that the canal diggers can only just keep up with it, so, unless we have a rise of some feet, the ditch must wait until next year.[18]

No one knows when we go past. Farragut is child enough to tell every one & make all arrangements for passing at a certain time, but immediately will postpone the attack. I am content to remain here rather than at New Orleans, as long as need be, for this is much the healthier place, and we will reach New Orleans soon enough as it is.

The fever becomes every day more and more severe, yet I am mercifully spared; our list yesterday was 30 [?] of which I helped bury one, a seaman, opposite Dr. Buckner's. Other ships are almost as debilitated as we are. We can not muster a full gun's crew in any of our divisions.[19]

I have been thinking over my offer as Fleet Clerk and shall let the matter hinge on the accommodations they may be pleased to give me on the Flag Ship. My principal objection is the probable great sickness which must sweep us all who remain during the summer.

The Captain's Clerk of the *Richmond* is desirous of changing with me, for he wants to go home. The *Richmond* is the pleasantest ship to be aboard in the squadron, but I should stick to Comdr. Palmer.[20]

We are looking at the river banks very seriously tonight: They are some 20 or 25 feet higher now than when we first saw Vicksburg and the water is yet steadily falling. If we do not get that army soon, we will retire in disgrace from Vicksburg, defeated not by rebels alone, but by the river too. What can ail Halleck, if his army be really victorious?[21]

I hope to hear via Cairo [Illinois] in a day or two.

Very aff. with love to all, Edward W. Bacon

July 13—We have no news to send. This post to morrow by Cairo. I am looking for news from New Haven. Love to all, EWB

New Haven, 17 July 1862

My Dear Edward,

Yours of the 6th inst. was received yesterday. I could not reply till I had taken a little time for consideration.

Your question whether to accept Capt. Palmer's invitation to go with him from the *Iroquois* to the *Hartford* is one on which I should have had no doubt at all but for the explanations which accompany your statement of it. I should have advised that the transfer of your Captain to another ship & to another post of duty could make no difference in your relations to him. But after considering all the particulars which you mention, I am quite willing to leave the decision of the question to your own judgment.

Let me say, however, that the fact of your supporting yourself, & perhaps saving something out of your pay, ought not to have much weight. Whenever your way home is clear in other respects & you find that you can devote yourself to study in preparation for any employment which you may choose, do not hesitate for one moment on account of any question about means.

But some other things must be considered.

1. The war is not ended nor likely to be just yet. We are now creating a new army of 800,000 men, & if you were at home, you would hardly be contented with the idea of remaining here. Your present situation, even with the circumstances incidental to your proposed transfer, is better suited to your capabilities than any other which you would be likely to get—especially in the army.[22]

2. It seems not improbable that service in the Navy will be quite as important in the year to come as it has been for the last year. Unless my impressions are very erroneous, the great danger just now is the danger of some foreign interference—French more likely than any other.[23]

3. It seems to me that Capt. Palmer's *feelings*, as well as his technical *rights*, should be considered. Should you find that he is quite willing to part with you & will not regard your going away as any serious inconvenience to himself, such a circumstance would have no inconsiderable weight.

4. If you find your health failing, you had better take this opportunity of resigning & coming home. But if you have a fair prospect of health, the inconveniences & discomforts of the *Hartford* could be endured, at least for a while. You will need much forbearance, patience & discretion—as well as Christian steadfastness—in the new associations to which the change will introduce you,

& if you find it your duty to accept the change, I trust you will be on your guard
& that your strength to resist every temptation will be as your [illegible].

On the whole, let me say, ask God to counsel you & decide for yourself.

We are all in usual health. Frank came home on Saturday July 5, quite worn
down & somewhat ill. He is now at Washington, but will return to us & perhaps
obtain a somewhat longer leave of absence before he goes back to Port Royal. His
furlough expired on the 22d, but he is too ill as yet to resume his duties. Rebecca
is working hard in the Hospital & so is Emeline Brockway who has come down
for that purpose. Katy has just gone to visit her cousin Mrs. Phillips.[24]

Your friend George Shepherd, now serving at the Hospital, wants to be
Hospital Steward in the Navy. Com. Foote tells me that the appointment is in
the gift of the surgeon. If there is any chance for him in your fleet, he can have
ample certificates from the Surgeons at our Hospital.

With much love from your Mother & from all,

Your aff. Father, Leonard Bacon

Iroquois, **Above Vicksburg, July 13, 1862**

My Dear Skiddy,[25]

Though I have not heard from you, I am willing to ascribe the fact to the same
cause which detains all my other letters, irregularity in the mails. Firmly believing that this is in answer to a letter of about 15th June, now on its way to
me, I take your name from my list in its regular order, discovering that your
month is up and a little past.

You know from the papers all about our passing Vicksburg and can feel
satisfied, I trust, that "Bloodthirsty Bake," as they call me here, "has seen a
muss."[26]

I do not mean to worry you with a long story of how we thought we were
to attack, how we were disappointed, how we at last did go and how we came
safely through. For all this I may refer you to Isham, to whom I wrote when
the fight was still news. But I do mean to put forth a few claims respecting the
attack, which as regards the principal object was certainly not victorious—and
as regards the mere passage of the place, not altogether as successful as was
intended, for all the vessels not of the Mortar Fleet were ordered to pass, yet
some of them failed. But I want to compare our affair with the passage of the
Batteries of [Island] No. 10 by the *Carondelet* last winter. The *Carondelet* was
roofed and plated with iron; we were open and of wood. She ran down stream,
merely for the sake of passing and did not stop to fire a gun while we struggled
against a powerful current and, though exposed to the greatest havoc of their
plunging shot, we stopped in front of their most powerful Battery and fought it
until the pressure of the hinder vessels forced us on. Surely, with all allowance
for personal feeling, the latter was the more brilliant of the two affairs.[27]

※

Before Bacon could finish his letter, the war intervened. Early on July 15, the ironclad CSS *Arkansas* suddenly bore down on the Federal fleet, her guns blazing. Farragut had doubted that "she will ever come forth," and some had even questioned her existence. All doubts vanished as the ram, painted a dull brown, steamed straight at them.[28]

Confederates had moved the unfinished *Arkansas* downriver from Memphis when Union forces neared and towed her far up the Yazoo River for safety and completion. Lieutenant Isaac N. Brown, CSN, took command and, under adverse conditions, readied the 165-foot-long twin-screw ram for battle. Only partially covered with railroad iron and equipped with faulty, unreliable engines, the ironclad had a crew of two hundred, mounted ten guns, and listed a top speed of eight knots.[29]

As it chanced, on July 14 Federal commanders had decided to scout the Yazoo River to ascertain the ram's condition and location. Three army ships, commanded by naval officers, entered the tributary river early on the 15th. They were the ironclad *Carondelet* with fourteen guns, the wooden side-wheel *Tyler*, a former river steamer converted into a gunboat with seven cannons, and the side-wheel wooden ram *Queen of the West*.[30]

As they went up the Yazoo, down came the *Arkansas*. She battered the *Carondelet*, running her aground, then pursued the *Tyler* and the *Queen of the West* while they put on all steam to escape. Lieutenant William Gwin, the *Tyler's* captain, reported thirteen of his men killed, thirty-four wounded and ten missing. Master's Mate S. B. Coleman said that one shell from the *Arkansas* had exploded on the deck and "had horribly mutilated and instantly killed" one officer and five sailors, decapitating four of them. Upon reaching the Mississippi the two army ships avoided further damage and casualties by dodging into the Federal flotilla.[31]

Boldly the *Arkansas* steered straight for the Union fleet of thirty-three warships, surprising and stunning Farragut's sailors. Most ships had their fires banked, so they lacked the steam to move. Stationary, many could not fire on the enemy, because other Federal warships blocked their line of fire. One vessel, the army ram *Lancaster*, did have steam up and bravely tried to ram the intruder. But the *Arkansas* sent a shell through her boiler, spraying scalding steam over her decks and crew, forcing a dozen men to leap into the river. Sylvester Doss, a river pilot, afterward wrote, "I was on the Lancaster when she was Blowen up on the 15th day of July 1862 at 7 A. M. in fite with Arkansas Ram. . . . myself was Scolded very bad, my right Shoulder Broken, Left Ribbs Broken and my teeth Blowen out." Though severely injured, Doss survived, and so did the disabled *Lancaster*, saved when the tug *Champion* chugged out into the stream and towed her to shore.[32]

By then, Federal warships with clear fields of fire had begun to fire solid shot, shells, grape, and even rifle balls at the *Arkansas*. Edward M. Galligan, a sailor on the army's ironclad *Essex*, noted in his diary that "all the vessels laying there had a crack at her as she passed." Lieutenant Brown, the *Arkansas*' captain, reported that all his guns fired rapidly in every direction "without the fear of hitting a friend or missing an enemy." At the same time, Brown added, "The shock of missiles hitting our sides was literally continuous." One of those missiles, an eleven-inch solid shot, pierced his ship above a gun port, killing two gunners and the powder boy, and wounding three others. That same projectile, possibly from the *Iroquois*, then passed through the smokestack to kill eight and wound three men of another gun crew on the ram's other side.[33]

Though fearfully outgunned and outnumbered, not only by wooden vessels but also by Federal ironclads, and with its smokestack "shot to pieces" so that the inadequate draft prevented Brown from keeping up steam, still the *Arkansas* slowly pushed through the storm of metal hurled at her and reached safety beneath Vicksburg's batteries. Brown reported ten men killed and fifteen wounded during his turtle-paced passage through the mighty Union fleet. On that score alone, Brown had the best of it, for his adversaries suffered eighteen killed, fifty wounded, and ten missing.[34]

But casualty counts were not the defining criteria in the saga. Rather, it was that the audacious *Arkansas* had surprised and pushed through an entire Federal fleet to safety beneath Vicksburg's guns, and remained a potent threat to Federal arms, aims, and strategy. More than a minor vexation, greater than a niggling embarrassment, it was an acutely humiliating event for Farragut, his men and the Union. Indeed, Farragut confessed to "deep mortification," while Secretary of the Navy Welles called it a "serious mortification." Both made the Confederate ram's destruction the top priority, "at all hazards."[35]

%

Iroquois, Below Vicksburg, July 16, 1862

Dear Skid,

I left my scrawl the other day thinking to take it up when I should feel more inclined, but not guessing that I should have a very livelier subject matter than I began with. Here, however, it seems I was mistaken. I venture to say that never were any warriors as astounded as we were of Farragut's and they of Davis' fleets yesterday morning. At half past four an expedition had started up Yazoo River with the intention of capturing the splendid river boats secreted up its long and crooked channel and of explaining the myth with which we had so long busied our imagination of the rebel Ram *Arkansas*.

In order that there might be no lack of preparation, a detachment of volunteers had been placed aboard one of the Gun Boats. At half past six sharp,

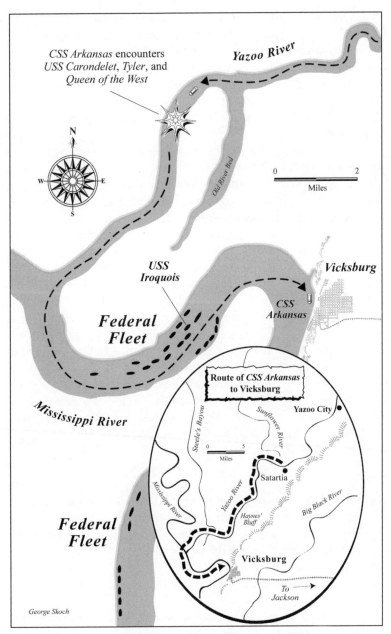

Romp of the CSS *Arkansas* through a large Federal fleet above Vicksburg, Mississippi. The CSS *Arkansas*, a jerry-built ironclad ram, surprised Federal warships on her first foray. She met three Federal warships on the Yazoo River, grounded one, put the other two to hasty flight, then shot her way through an entire Federal fleet anchored in the Mississippi River above Vicksburg on July 15, 1862. George Skoch.

cannonading was heard in the direction of Yazoo River but no notice was taken of it, except that the Flagship signalled us to get up steam, for we and several other vessels had several days before hauled our fires in order to save the scanty stock of coal we had. At 7½, however, the Gun Boat *Tyler* was observed backing round the point above us and followed by a stranger engaged with her in quite lively style.

We at once beat to quarters and I was turned out of a very comfortable snooze, much to my disgust, to go into a fight on an empty stomach. Down these two came and one after another we were engaged, but we lay so badly that many vessels could not fire on account of the danger to others.

The *Richmond* and *Hartford* gave the enemy a broadside apiece and, as she came on, we managed to bring in again ahead of *Oneida*, which was nearly covered by us, and again astern, when we gave her a solid 11 inch shot which ricochetted and then struck right amidships, between wind and water. It must have hurt her for we were only 800 yards distant. When the officers on the poop of the Flag saw the shot, they cheered right heartily, as did we also. The *Benton*, being exactly on our starboard beam, could not fire a shot, but dropped down, hoping to engage the Ram below in which she also failed. So this "*Merrimac*" passed by, giving us her guns at leisure, one shell from which is bedded in our port side. (I have a piece of it, since dug out.)[36]

Here was the end of the most cool and impudent attack on a fleet of some 18 vessels (not to speak of Ellet's Rams, one of which was blown up) that ever could be imagined by a little nondescript of only ten guns.[37]

The no longer mythical *Arkansas* passed victoriously under the guns of Vicksburg. Rather disgraceful, wasn't it? Of course, [there] was the greatest excitement: in an hour, everything that could carry a pot and a handful of shavings had "steam up" and plenty of it, but then the *Arkansas* was out of our reach.

July 17

A good deal disgusted at the cool impudence displayed in the morning and believing that we had so injured the Ram as to make her an easy prey, at 6:20 [P.M.] Farragut signalled to weigh and form the line of attack in two columns, as we had it coming up (the *Iroquois* in the van).

We therefore stood immediately for the upper Battery, which is a new one of some two guns, above the rifle Battery which I suspect as being the best served of the whole range.

The *Benton* and two other ironclads had preceded us about half a hour engaging lightly the upper Battery and under orders to draw the fire of both upper Batteries while we passed to the attack. It was now 7 o'clock as we passed the head of their line and had the mortification of seeing the iron boats get behind the fire over us, when they should have been well down in the stream. We were immediately under fire, but the enemy seemed to have been frightened last time and replied very poorly, their shot flying over us, as their guns were not enough depressed. Of course we at once answered with all our port Battery, giving them a dose of 5" shell and then shrapnel, [and] on we came. Our next shot was from the town which was crammed with musketeers and field pieces. We gave them grape and canister, which we could hear very distinctly rattle on the wooden houses. We received more annoyance from musket balls than anything else; they were thick as mosquitoes in this Western paradise.[38]

Here, in front of the town, we must have received a 6 pd. shot from a field piece which cut a hole in our bow between wind and water. We were now about half way through. Looking back we could see the smoke of those who followed making Vicksburg rather too hot a place for residence, while near the Court House a large fire was blazing which some of us had lighted. Directly overhead were passing the bombs from our mortars and, right in advance of us, the lower hill Battery opened its first gun, raking high over our heads. I now reported to the Captain that I thought I saw the Ram, her newly painted sides reflecting the flash of our guns, but she did not seem to fire and appeared dead. Just then, as I expected to hear the order "Starboard your helm" and to turn in to find and ram her, our propeller suddenly turned more slowly, stopped—and made some effort and then refused to move. Our worn out engines, never trustworthy, now had failed us in our greatest need and, instead of capturing the Ram, we drifted down stream subject to any attack she might wish to make, had she herself not been disabled.[39]

We were thus for twenty minutes under fire without the power to budge an inch except just as the current took us and a disagreeable twenty minutes they were. We found, however, that the dense darkness now closing in made the Batteries fire wildly and so we learned to disregard their shot.

When we were well out of range our journals were cooled enough to allow us to steam once more, so Capt. Palmer, though more wisely he would have remained below, stood back for the Batteries to seek [another] chance at the *Arkansas*. But when we were just getting under fire again, we were hailed by the *Brooklyn*, who told us the Flag was already below us and at anchor and so we dropped down again and received orders to anchor.[40]

We are again most fortunate in having none lost or injured; the other vessels all lost some. One of our "bummers"—cowardly fellow—on seeing the Ram in the morning, coolly blew up his schooner, because she happened to be aground, and retired to a safe place, in which he should be in future kept.[41]

We are now coaling, expecting an expedition every hour to destroy the Ram. The old Flag Officer [Farragut] seems to know that if he does not "skedaddle" her now, his reputation is gone as suddenly as it came. The Iron Fleet, though it ought to take her, seems very backward in anything of the kind.

Deserters reported aboard the *Hartford* the evening of the 14th that the *Arkansas* was on her way down but were told that "we had heard that before." Consequently, the next morning saw us without steam and at the mercy of our bold and brilliant enemy. She is commanded, I think (from the fact that he burned the *Van Dorn* up Yazoo), by Commander Pinckney [Pinkney], formerly of our Navy, but some say by Lt. I. N. Brown, formerly of the *Niag[a]ra*.[42]

I am and have been since the 13th suffering from the fever which is killing our Army at the rate of one a day and which makes us all miserable. If I do not get better soon, I shall become much disgusted, especially if we have any more fighting to do. Fighting comes hard when a man is living on quinine alone and has no appetite at that!

So, you see, Skid, war has its unpleasant times and when you have the break-bone fever is one of those times.[43]

Hoping to hear very soon from you and that you can make out this letter which I do not feel like making legible, I drop your letter until next month rolls around.

My regards to your Father and Mother and family. I should be very happy to be spending a pleasant evening in Stamford rather than on this horrid, muddy river, watching the lazy maneuvers of an ugly nondescript.

I shall very likely write you next from the Flagship, where I shall be Fleet Clerk, for it is pretty well understood that Palmer will be Fleet Captain.

You may direct as before "via Cairo."

Believe me ever your sincere
friend, Edward W. Bacon

℀

In his next letter Bacon assumed that his father will have read all about the *Arkansas* pushing through the fleet. Though the mails depended upon slow steamers, telegraph connections at key points could move the news very quickly to Eastern centers. Here Bacon described the effort to destroy the ram at her mooring under Vicksburg's guns.

℀

Iroquois, **Below Vicksburg, July 16, 1862**

Dear Father,

After a good deal of change in the programme, we got underweigh last night at 6:30 and proceeded down to the Batteries, the *Iroquois* leading as before, Davis' Iron Clads having already engaged lightly the upper Battery and all the remaining Mortars, above and below, busily bombarding the town. As we were within range of the first Battery, though we had not quite opened the point and a few moments later we were engaged with a new one or two-gun Battery above the splendid rifle Battery, formerly the first. The plan was to run the Batteries and capture the Ram or destroy her, so at once we put on all the steam we dared to carry on our worn out boilers and went ahead fast, firing our guns as rapidly as possible and subjected to a severe fire from the rifle Battery so beautifully handled. Our first discharges were five second shell, then shrapnel and, when we got well abreast the town, plenty of grape and canister, which we could hear patter against the wooden houses very distinctly. This passage differed from that of June 28th in the great numbers of sharp shooters along our whole course. Musket balls were flying about our decks in a very uncomfortable manner. We were now well down the river.

Davis was still above the upper Battery and the *Oneida* was following some little distance behind us. It was dark as any smuggler could wish and we were straining our eyes to distinguish our exact position and to discover, if possible, the Ram. I now saw her, the bright flashes of our guns and the light of a large fire in the upper part of the town reflecting on her freshly painted side. She seemed dead, emitting very little, if any smoke, and no sign of life was about her. I looked at the Captain as I reported her to him and saw him searching in the same direction. I was expecting to hear the word "Starboard your helm!" and to run in for her, when suddenly our propeller began to revolve less and less, stopped, turned again in a few last efforts and then remained motionless.[44]

Our journals were so heated the shaft could not turn, though a stream of water from a large hose played constantly upon them. What a horrible position! The current drifting us just as it became too dark to see and the Batteries probably only half passed. Moreover, we were losing our chance of capturing the Ram; some other vessel would be sure to take her. However, we hoped for the best and looked about us. We must be farther down than we supposed, for the shells from the Mortars are passing splendidly exactly over our heads. There, too, the lower Battery on the crown of the bluff is firing at us up the stream. We are therefore off the Hospital and must look out for the Ram and the lower Battery only.

The Ram did not seem to fire and the Battery was very poorly served. Thus we drifted down, perfectly helpless until almost out of range, when our journals were cool enough to allow the shaft to revolve once more.[45]

Once more, in mercy, we suffered no loss. We received in our port side forward a six-pounder rifled shell and grape flew above us as thick as the mosquitoes on this wretched river. We passed the *Brooklyn*; heard from her that the *Hartford* and *Richmond* were already below us and, dropping down, issued orders to anchor.[46]

Tho the enemy evidently had more guns than before, they did not serve them by any means as well. Their firing was wild and very irregular. The last part of the run, this may have been owing to the darkness, but there was plenty of light, except for the smoke, all the first third of the way. Their only improvement was the increase of sharp shooters, but even they must have been badly scared, for I hear of no one injured by their balls. As for the damage we did them, I do not think that very great, though probably greater than last time because they exposed more men.

I regret to say, I was much disappointed in the conduct of [Charles H.] Davis' Flotilla. Unless the *Benton* be excepted, not one of them was fairly exposed to the fire of the enemy and when we, open and vulnerable, passed them to receive the full weight of metal, they persisted in firing over our heads to our great annoyance, not to say danger.[47]

They confess they have not been used to as close quarters as the *Arkansas* gave them, but they never ought to allow open wooden vessels to bear the brunt for which they were specially constructed. There are some, however, who cannot get used to the screech of a shell. Last night, going forward, I pulled a miserable little powderboy out from under a lot of spars, stowed along side our smoke stack, who was actually terrified and there were a few others who were in a similar state, but very few, for all stood up to their work and did it like men.[48]

As an instance of the fear in which some are, the commander of one of the mortar vessels, which happened to be aground on our side of the river, like a coward blew her up when the *Arkansas*, disabled, made her appearance.[49]

Affly. Edward W. Bacon

※

Fixated on destroying the *Arkansas* at any cost, Farragut made another attempt on July 22, after the first effort a week earlier proved a failure.

Flag Officer Charles H. Davis, commanding the upper fleet, had opposed a second attack. He told Farragut that he did not think it wise to attack "without any regard to the consequences to ourselves." But Farragut, almost obsessive about the ram, was adamant. He replied, "I see no way now but to attack him . . . under the batteries, and take our chances." In this he had the eager support of Commander William D. Porter of the *Essex*, and Lieutenant Colonel Alfred W. Ellet, commanding the *Queen of the West*. Their ships would make the attack.[50]

"Got under way at sunrise," reported an *Essex* crewman, "and in company with the ram *Queen of the West* ran down river for Vicksburgh." Their battle plan was simple: steer straight for the *Arkansas* at her mooring and ram and sink her. Upper and lower Union fleets would be ready to assist if the Confederate ironclad ventured out into the stream. Accordingly, most Federals were only spectators as the drama unfolded. Bartholomew Diggins, a sailor aboard the USS *Hartford* recalled that "officers and men crowded the rigging and sails to witness the fight between the two ironclads."[51]

Bacon also watched the exciting scene, though soon the clash became shrouded in clouds of black powder smoke belching from the shore batteries and the ships' cannons. Both the *Essex* and *Queen* struck only glancing blows, and *Essex* ran aground on the riverbank. There the shore batteries pounded her during the ten long minutes it took to wrench free. Both Federal rams then withdrew.[52]

Farragut said that the time between the first shot and when the *Essex* escaped downstream was forty-nine minutes. In that time, the *Queen* was so "very much damaged" that she would have to go north for repairs, while the *Essex* sustained less damage but counted one man killed and three wounded in the fight. *Arkansas* had eight killed and six wounded during the encounter but remained afloat and defiant.[53]

※

Iroquois, Below Vicksburg, July 22nd, 1862

Dear Father,

My last date was July 17 under which I gave some account of the Raid of the Ram and of our second passage of the Batteries of Vicksburg. When I closed the letter we were coaling and anxiously wishing the destruction of the Ram.

So several days have passed until yesterday, when all arrangements were made for the lower squadron to come down at about five o'clock. The plan, however, was postponed until dawn this morning when the *Essex*, Iron-clad, attacked the Ram from above, the others of Davis' vessels being within supporting distance. One of Ellet's Rams was visible also from our decks. We were immediately under weigh, ready to go up should the enemy be driven under the lower Batteries, but he did not come down. The *Essex* came, though, and is now tied up on our port-beam. I have not yet learned what damage was done the Ram, though she looks much the same as ever.

Since the *Iroquois* failed in her motive power so seriously the other night, Farragut has concluded not to make her bear the brunt any more. Our place this morning was about the Center and therefore we were not in action. The *Oneida* fired her rifle several times. Farragut also received orders to go down the river and to order a survey upon the *Iroquois*. So Vicksburg will be left to Davis, who has fallen to below freezing point in estimation here. Yazoo River is a blur [blot?] on his Mississippi career.[54]

It was a very beautiful fight we witnessed this morning, though too short to accomplish anything. The two Rams were closed for a few moments as nearly as were the *Monitor* and the *Merrimac* and that under a very heavy fire from the Batteries. But we had no Worden in here, for Porter left the *Arkansas* and steamed down stream having been engaged not more than fifteen minutes and with but one man killed and two wounded. Evidently we have not a man among us with pluck or sense of duty sufficient for the present emergency. We may write down more defeat for our poor Union cause.[55]

Porter's story of the affair this morning is that he came upon the Ram as she was lying head down stream but, before he reached her, she had slewed around. He rammed her once but without effect and ran himself aground. He succeeded, he says, in putting three nine inch shot through her before he left her, but was finally carried down by the tremendous current which he *could not stem* (The *Arkansas* can stem it.). Ellet's Ram is said to have struck one blow but without effect. Our total loss is one killed and two wounded. The Ram has steam up this evening and is as well as ever. We do nothing more to her for our orders are for all hands to proceed down the River tomorrow. This move will be a great deliverance.[56]

Our soldiers, who have been of not the remotest use here, are dying by dozens. The 30th Mass. came up with 864 effective men. Now they muster 300 for camp duty and, for action, could not form a line of more than 200.[57]

Our sick list amounts today to 32 only. We cannot work our guns with one third the speed we used to. Officers and men are exhausted. Today at 10 a.m. our deck thermometer showed 95° under a wetted awning and a dampened deck. Below what must it be![58]

July 23d

Our latest is not encouraging. Two of our mail and hospital boats have been burned and their charred remains were found floating down the river. Flying artillery are doing much damage to our transports both above and below.[59]

Above New Orleans, July 27th

Dear Father,

We left Vicksburg on the 24th. We came down slowly, occasionally firing a gun into the woods to rouse out any stray "gorillas." But our retreat was undisputed. We anchored off Baton Rouge yesterday p.m. and I went ashore but was much disappointed in my first impression of the place. From the River it is very pretty but the houses are mostly poor and not in very good repair. We grabbed several Secesh in a boat off Red River and made them prisoners, as they refused to take the oath.[60]

You will see in the *Democrat* the Vicksburg account of that brilliant run of the *Arkansas*. People along the River bank ask us if she sunk more than ten of our vessels.[61]

New Orleans, July 28th, 1862

We are at anchorage and find the city much improved, much more like a city than when we were here before.

There are 1,500 troops in the city proper, however, and were it not for the guns of the fleet, there would be a violent outbreak tonight.[62]

Affly., your son, Edward W. Bacon

Iroquois, New Orleans, Aug. 1st, 1862

Dear Kate,

So that I can be always ready for something to turn up in the way of mail to New York, I commence now a little note with only one piece of information and that of no great consequence. We have been for some days in the hands of a Board of Survey which has examined us very carefully & decided that we can carry ten pounds of steam and therefore can remain out until our new boilers are ready for us at New York—some two months. This decision is very satisfactory to me, for it decides Capt. Palmer's going aboard the Flag Ship—now I presume he will not do so. We are to remain here for some days repairs and our destination is not yet divulged—though I suppose it will be Pensacola with the rest of the fleet.[63]

I spend most of my leisure time at the Barracks of the 13th C. I. [Connecticut Infantry], who are nicely quartered in the Custom House. This is the cleanest Regt. I have seen in our army—They appear on parade with white gloves & very bright muskets and plates—looking like a body of regulars, though their drill greatly lacks snap and precision.[64]

I wish very much I had a lieutenancy there. I dined the other day with Lt. Col. [Alexander] Warner, a very nice kind of man, and Capt. [Homer B.] Sprague & I take much comfort in comparing our notes upon the Contrabands. I was very sorry to find Chaplain [Charles C.] Salter gone home and for such unpleasant reasons; the Regt. were very much attached to him.[65]

Everybody is delighted with Butler, though he is yet too timid as regards the Contrabands. Without the knowledge of the Gen'l or anybody else, Capt. Sprague tells me he has enlisted in the new regiment forming here a number of white slaves, who are very fine fellows.[66]

Last night, as I was in the Custom House, a boy came in with his wrists handcuffed and quite a stout chain fastened around his neck by a good sized padlock. I had the pleasure of filing the chain so as to let loose his head and have the promise of the iron to add to my stock of examples of Secession jewels.[67]

We are looking anxiously for the arrival of a mail from New York, but are thus far disappointed. I observe that the 7th C. I. has gone to Richmond, for which I am sorry, for they were so nicely off before. I would like to know their new address.[68]

Monday Aug. 4th

A mail leaves us to-morrow, & I though I do not give you much news, I am going to venture this.

Reports reached us last night of Batteries between this & Baton Rouge & we were ordered to up at about midnight to investigate the matter. We had our Engines in pieces, however, & so got off. There is some doubt as to whether this ship will go to Pensacola with the others. The Flag talks of giving Palmer the command at Baton Rouge. Our fate will be decided probably today.

No mail has arrived from the North since July 9th and great anxiety is felt in regard to the safety of the *Creole*, which has the mails of three steamers and left New York on the 19th ult. A propeller is reported ashore some where in the Bahamas, probably the missing steamer.[69]

I am in much better health since we came down the river and since we had a chance to exercise properly ashore. But every one is very much debilitated. Those who have been in New Orleans & the lower river are much better than we from above are.

I meet pretty frequently Capt. Blynn [Blinn] of the Kent company—a very fine company & the Capt. a very good and very handsome officer. I believe the Capt. was George's special admiration in the military line.[70]

I wish you would write me quite a long letter when you receive this—for I shall lose all the letters sent "via Cairo," of which I have received not one. Thus this will be a blank of a month or two in my news from home.[71]

I hope to add our destination when we leave New Orleans, before I close this scrawl—but, let them send us where they may, our address will be the same as always before.

This city is quite free from Yellow Jack and as healthy, as the papers show, as New York.

I send much love to all,

> Believe me very aff. Your brother,
> Edward W. Bacon

Aug. 5th

It has been decided that we remain here for some time—probably four or five weeks before we go—though now the word is only two.

The *Creole* and the *Roanoke* have arrived this morning. I look for one or two letters, but then no more for two months yet.[72]

> Very Aff., Edward W. Bacon

We are busy caulking ship & the noise overhead is very painful.

There are widespread rumors of the advance of Breckinridge & 20,000 men on New Orleans & Butler seems to credit them. That is the cause of our remaining here. I have got no letters yet but the *Creole*'s mail is not yet sorted.[73]

New Orleans, Aug. 17, 1862

Dear Father,

Your answer to mine of July 5 last in regard to going to the Flagship as the Fleet Clerk is not received; but, what ever may have been the contents of your letter, the call for 300,000 more men made any thought of leaving the war to take care of itself and showing myself in the peaceful state of Connecticut worse than absurd.[74]

In some capacity somewhere I must be in the United States service, but how many places may turn past my hand which would be far better than a miserable Clerkship. Here I have nothing to do, nothing to interest me, no responsibility to make me really feel as if I cared about what happened. A few years of such a life, when I know I am qualified for a higher, would practically kill me. If I am capable of doing anything, I must get where I can do it. I hope some time to get your letter with those views for which I asked.

Aff. your son, Edward W. Bacon

USS Iroquois, New Orleans, August 21, 1862

My Dear Shepherd,[75]

Although somewhat out of season, for I have as yet received no acknowledgment of my last, dated June 8th, I am constrained to write you a few words of caution and advice.

My father, writing under date of July 27, 1862, which I received day before yesterday, mentions the fact that my friend Shepherd is anxious to obtain the situation of Hospital Steward in the Navy and infers that I would do a friendly office could I obtain such a place for you in this squadron.

Let me ask you if you know what the situation of Hospital Steward in the Navy is?

It is only [in] the last two years that he has been allowed to prefix *Mr.* to his name but has ever been held and is now almost at a par with the *shipped men.* He is allowed to wear the Navy button on his jacket but he must never venture aft the main-mast nor make any complaint or communication but "at the mast," like the common sailor. He swings his hammock in the most respectable part of the Berth Deck, where day and night for the three years for which he ships, his ears (if he be a person of any education or refinement) are tormented by that concentrated billingsgate which can be found only among the crew of a Man of War. When he takes his meals, it is in the same choice company and his food is of the coarsest "salt horse and hard tack," to which we of the steerage come once in a great while, after we have made soup of all of our old boat-legs.[76]

As for the amount of practice and experience you have, our surgeon tells me it is not worth the cruise. The diseases of a Man of War are mostly of one class—venereal—and a situation in an Army Hospital, where you see so much and such an endless variety of "*all* the ills that flesh is heir to" is ten times more valuable, as well as ten times more pleasant.[77]

I trust you see now that, should I try to secure for you the position of Hospital Steward in the Western Gulf Squadron, instead of doing you a service, I would be throwing around you a very disagreeable noose, an act for which, in truth, you could never thank me.

I am aware that Alf. Minor is aboard the *Sumpter* in the capacity in question but, unless his situation is most exceptional, he would gladly change off with some "Medical Cadet."[78]

Could you secure the position of Asst. Paymaster, drawing $1,800 a year, or were you far enough advanced to pass the examination of an Asst. Surgeon, entering the Ward Room—or could you take the lazy, nondescript berth of Captain's Clerk in the Steerage, I doubt not you would find the Naval Service pleasant and profitable. But beware of how you throw yourself among the shipped men of the forecastle: aboard a Man of War you can find a sample of every kind of life, from Fifth Avenue to Five Points, and the Forecastle is the Five Points.[79]

I am quite sorry to put such a wet towel over the bright water color you must have sketched of Medical Life in the Navy but I hope my advice, coming from "one who knows" the practical workings of a Man of War, may not be too late.

I suppose you have been quite busy with the wounded from Richmond, as everyone seems to be at home, but if the commencement of the war is to have such an effect, what at its close will be the duty of correspondents? Surely you must have a little spare time.[80]

We left New Orleans on Tuesday and today, Thursday, are in Pensacola Bay. Tomorrow or next day I move my quarters to the Flag Ship, of which Capt. Palmer is to take command. We are here to arrange and prepare for the attack upon Mobile or, rather, upon Forts Gaines and Morgan, which will give us a worse fight than we have yet seen, the passage of Forts Jackson and St. Philip not excepted.[81]

The victory there won, we may repose upon our Laurels for a time, for Galveston only will remain uncaptured in the dominion of Capt. Farragut.[82]

My letters may be addressed:
Captain's Clerk,
U.S. Flag Ship Hartford
Western Gulf Squadron
Pray let me know what is going on in New Haven.

My regards to your Father and Mother and family and believe me, Very truly, your friend and old school-mate, Edward W Bacon

In his next, Bacon referred to an incident on September 4, 1862, off Mobile and believed the family would know about it by the time they received this letter. Again a Confederate raider had embarrassed the U.S. Navy, "mortifying" Farragut and reminding Bacon of the *Sumter's* escape. Now, though he lacked all the facts, Bacon was critical.

In this latest discomfiture, the CSS *Florida*, the Confederacy's first British-built commerce raider, approached blockaders outside Mobile while flying a British warship's colors. That ruse worked long enough for the *Florida* to evade Commander George H. Preble's USS *Oneida* and another Federal warship and to reach safety in port.

With the exploits of CSS *Sumter* and the *Arkansas* still offending Northern sensibilities, Secretary of the Navy Welles dismissed Preble from the navy, though Lincoln restored him to duty in early 1863.[83]

%

Flag Ship *Hartford*, Pensacola, Sept. 6th, 1862

Dear Rebecca,

Things here are pretty much in *status quo* and I am as usual now very busy.

You will hear by this mail of the miserable mismanagement at Mobile, where the *Oneida* has made the *Iroquois* reputation glorious.

I am very sorry for poor Capt. Preble, who will & ought to be severely blamed, for as regards character etc, he is one of the very best officers I have met. But he is very slow & I suppose fearful of the awful responsibility of firing into a British Man of War.

Our yellow fever excitement is pretty much gone, though [the] people ashore won't let us get off our washed clothes yet. We will probably put up in the *Hartford* those plates of iron which the *Iroquois* was to use. They have been brought round here and the Admiral, for fear the enemy may get them again, wants us to use them thus.[84]

Farragut is a very clever old salt, without much [unreadable word] of reverence or much faculty for discipline or organization. He is very free in his expression of opinions. Says he don't see what McClellan has done to claim the honors of a great general; he don't see what he has waited so long for.[85]

Farragut does not wait. After the passage of the Forts, he pushed on to attack Vicksburg with a squadron of vessels utterly unseaworthy. The *Brooklyn* has now been discovered to have been terribly crushed by the [CSS] *Manassas*, a space of some 40 feet amidships being splintered and broken—this too under her coppers. The *Hartford* has through her main mast a shot hole, so that the least strain of sail would snap the mast.[86]

The *Mississippi* and *Susquehanna* are so that a gale of wind would destroy their motive power and you know what the *Iroquois* is. There is not one of those "splendid gunboats," with which the *Herald* is to flog England, but in time of peace would have to undergo three months repairs to fit her for an ordinary cruise, so serious have been the Battles of New Orleans and Vicksburg. Yet with such a Squadron as this, Farragut does not hesitate to attack Mobile nor does he wait the arrival of reinforcements and only had the most absolutely necessary repairs.[87]

I have often wished that our Admiral had been given command on James River below Fort Darling, which is not near so bad as Vicksburg, with a fleet of iron vessels.

I am pretty well and hope to grow better constantly. I think I am well now of all traces of Vicksburg fever. I did not send by the *Rhode Island* as fear she will not be allowed South next month.

I send by Mr. Blackman, Paymaster's Clerk of the *Connecticut*, for some little articles.[88]

I got no letters by the *Rhode Island* and since yours of July 26 have not a word from home. The *Connecticut*, too, brought me nothing, yet she left New York on 23rd August, almost a month later than my last date. However, there are probably some letters for me at New Orleans.

> Give my love to all at home and believe me,
> very truly and aff., Edward W. Bacon

Palmer is putting this ship into really splendid discipline and order. He has got from the *Potomac* an executive officer who is the best, most quiet & most thorough I have ever seen.[89]

※

Bacon's family worried about his health, and concern mounted after they received his letter of August 1 to Kate. He had visited the 13th Connecticut Infantry in New Orleans and declared, "I wish very much I had a lieutenancy there."

Leonard Bacon quickly wrote his son, warning him that his "want of physical strength" might result in a quick collapse were he to serve in the army. These were not idle fears: apparently Bacon was never robust and very likely carried tuberculosis bacteria. His mother died of consumption, as tuberculosis was then called, just a year after his birth. Given her active disease, his mother may well have transmitted it to him as an infant. An older brother, Benjamin, had succumbed to the then prevalent disease, and possibly it also killed James and Lucy, older siblings who died as children.[90]

Further, early in his naval career Bacon had complained of "weak eyes," and he again mentioned his "sore eyes" in a later letter to a 13th Connecticut officer. Modern ophthalmologists consulted about this condition said that eye sensitivity could well result from tuberculosis bacteria affecting his vision. Whether his family knew of his eye problems is unknown, but in any event they probably would not connect that impairment with consumption.[91]

However, the family worried needlessly about him transferring to the 13th. The regiment's colonel had resisted giving the vacant lieutenancy to an outsider and had instead promoted a soldier from the ranks.

Perhaps that was fortunate for Bacon. John T. Wheeler, appointed to the vacancy, and other 13th Connecticut men boarded a train carrying passengers and war materiel in early November. Somehow the train's ammunition cars exploded at a railroad crossing in Louisiana, and among the many killed were Wheeler and three other 13th Connecticut men.[92]

※

Dear Edward,

Your last letter is not now before me. I must have left it in New Haven, though I intended to bring it with me. So I may forget something which a reference to it would have brought to mind.

I wrote quite a long reply to your letter from near Vicksburg when you thought of resigning. But as I directed my letter by way of Cairo, it failed to reach you.[94]

As for your proposal now to leave the Navy and go into our Thirteenth Regiment, I would make no objection to it but for one reason. I fear the want of physical strength in your constitution. You are very serviceable where you now are. Perhaps you might be, for a little while, more serviceable as a lieutenant in the army. To a man of adequate constitution, the danger is about the same in one position or the other. But in your case there is this difference. The experience of a year has shown that you can endure the service on shipboard but it is to me quite probable, as it was when you first proposed to apply for a place in one of our three months' regiments, that you would soon break down & become unserviceable if you were in the army. If you were as "able-bodied" as Theodore, I would not object to your accepting such an offer as that made to you by Capt. Sprague.[95]

Having occasion to call upon Gen. [William H.] Russell day before yesterday, I presented to him your congratulations on his appointment. He enquired after you very kindly & desired me to say to you that his opinion agrees with mine on the question of your exchanging the navy for the army.

Ruddie is to begin next week at the C. C. I. by way of experiment, as you did six years ago. His lessons will be few & light at first, in hope that the exercise of the drill will give him health & strength for serious study.[96]

Theodore, at our latest intelligence from him (Aug. 31, I believe) was with Gen. Terry & Staff, performing quarantine in St. Helena Island. The *Delaware* steamer, in which the General performed his tour of inspection, took on board some passengers at Key West & therefore on her arrived at Hilton Head, though she had had no case of fever & though she had been almost long enough from that port to take away all suspicion of infestation, was required by Gen. Hunter to undergo fourteen days of waiting before landing anybody. Theodore is quite impatient of being shut up so long in a Department where there is so little to do & Gen. Terry, I believe, is no better satisfied than he is.[97]

Frank is now Medical Director in Gen. Casey's Division at Washington. As Gen. C. has command of all the new forces arriving so rapidly, Frank's duty is very laborious. It is very difficult for us to get any intelligence from him—he has so little time for anything but work.[98]

Your Mother has been here now for six or seven weeks. She has gained some relief from pain & some increase of strength by the change of air; but she suffers much every day. She expects to remain here till the middle or the end of October. The little boys, you know, have been here all summer. Katy has been here about four weeks. She & Ruddie will go home on Saturday to begin their attendance at School. Alfred will remain to wait on his mother. I brought Ellen & Alice with me when I began my vacation three weeks ago & when I went home last week, they went home with me. I am to have two Sundays more in my vacation. My going home for the last Sabbath was because three young ladies (one of whom is Fanny Bostwick & another Rebecca G. Bacon) were to be received to communion in the church. Mr. Bostwick probably has not long to live.[99]

Evening Since I began to write, yours from the *Iroquois* Aug. 23 & from the *Hartford* Aug. 29, has come to hand, having been forwarded from New Haven by Rebecca. I know not that I need to add anything to what I have said about exchanging your present place for a commission in one of our regiments. Your letter gives us some anxiety about your exposure to a new danger. May He who has shielded you in the day of battle defend you from the Pestilence that walketh in darkness. Let your mind be at peace, trusting in the love & wisdom of God. His will be done![100]

I reserve the remaining page for your Mother, who hopes that she may be able to write a few lines before the closing of the mail in the morning.

God be with you, my dear son, Leonard Bacon

Friday 12 Sept.

Your mother is afflicted this morning with one of her ill turns & cannot write. She sends her best love.

We are waiting today with great anxiety for the results of the battle which was fought yesterday—no doubt—before Cincinnati & with almost equal anxiety for news from Maryland. What a time is this! Is it possible that in God's wise good providence our country is to become the prey & the abode of barbarians? Our confidence in human leaders & values is failing, but God reigns forever & does all things well.[101]

L. B.

Flag Ship *Hartford*, Pensacola
Bay, Sept. 15, 1862

Dear Kate,

I am in receipt of a very welcome letter from you of July 30, the only news from home since Rebecca's note.

The Paymaster's Clerk of the *Connecticut* (a fellow by the name of Blackman, who has rather thrust himself upon me here with offers of his service) will probably call at our house before he leaves on his next trip with a letter of introduction from me to father.[102]

Will you please send down by him those pantaloons of blue cloth of which I have spoken, to be made at Mason & Rockwell's on the measure of those flannel ones I got when at home, but not quite so high in the hips. Please send me, too, a pair of those cloth Congress gaiters at Bristol & Hall's. Fenn knows my size, some where between 6½ and 7½.[103]

That new cap I brought out with me I lost overboard in the Mississippi and my old one, after five months constant use on top of the 7 mos. before, is no longer sea worthy. Please get me a new one at from $7½ to $9: the usual band and the simple gold embroidered wreath of one side oak & the other laurel leaves. The cap should be of this shape, , but the other, , will do on a pinch. My size is 6⅞. The oil silk cover should come gratis.

Since I have risen to the dignity [of] a State Room and no longer lash my bedding up every morning, I begin to feel the need of some covering for my bed. Are there not some young ladies in New Haven or vicinity who could send me out something thin and which will do to look at in the Cabin? My Bedstead is about the usual length and just wide enough for one pillow.[104]

I shall need, too, another box of paper collars, for this climate is very destructive of linen or paper either. I wear the turn down "Baryon" 13½ inches. The price should be $2.50. I have left about a third of a box, but, as you can get them at about half the Sutler's prices, I prefer sending for reinforcements by this early opportunity.[105]

Please send me the amount paid on each article that my books may know how I stand.

If you find the bill isn't getting too large, you may put in a pair of Oxford ties at B & H's.[106]

I have got a lot of *trophies* which I meant to send by this opportunity but I will not have time to pack them up.

I am in pretty good health, though the Gulf is not like New England.

We have no news, but are in a state of anxiety about Washington and Cincinnati. Our dates, received yesterday (17) are to the 3rd. We had a large mail down to Aug 30 but I got nothing.[107]

Give much love to all and believe me, very truly and aff. Your brother,

Edward W. Bacon

P.S. 18th—*Connecticut* leaves this p.m.

Flag Ship *Hartford*, Pensacola
Bay, Sept. 28, 1862

Dear George,[108]

Your letter of the 10th reached me a day or two ago and was very welcome, if even from the fact that it is so long a time since I last heard from you.

You set forth your very moderate and goodly conservative views. As I have had no one for a long time ask me to blow off for his edification, I cannot fail to improve this opportunity and make the most of this compliment.

In the first place, I do not doubt that God will overrule all things for the best, provided we make the best use of the means which he has seen fit to place before our hands.

Secondly, I do not doubt that we must render all service to our present Chiefs, just so long as their directions and acts are strictly just and entirely liberal.

Thirdly, I do not doubt that Lincoln will use all the means in his power quite as soon as he feels himself justified in doing so.

But I believe in the *first place* that God's ideas of what is best may differ from his.

I believe in the *second place* that the Chief's acts are not always strictly just nor entirely liberal.

I believe in the *third place* that the time for President Lincoln to use all means in his power has gone by, will not return, and that he has *not* felt himself justified in using them.

My first belief may be sufficiently established by reference to our frequent defeats and to the fact that for a whole sixteen months, the South has held its own.

The frequent imprisonments for unknown reasons and discharges without the investigations demanded; the censorship of the press and the persecution of those who object or are thought to object, not to our glorious Constitution nor to our plain and simple form of government, but to the mere instruments, those who are at present commissioned with the execution of the Government, all these acts seem to me as if some of our present Chiefs, however well-intentioned they may be, were not *strictly* just nor *entirely* liberal.[109]

Had President Lincoln commenced the war by calling for 800,000 or 1,000,000 men and arming of all intelligent and willing negroes (of whom there would not have been more than 150,000 at the utmost), and had Congress, at the same time, passed a most rigid Confiscation Act, we would have seen the war well nigh successfully ended by now. For then the South was unable to stand alone against such a shock: a strict blockade had deprived them of foreign supplies while what was native was untouched and the North, which was over-supplied with them, was able to turn all its immense resources against them. Now, however, the South is overcoming the blockade, manufactories of all necessary articles are springing up, immense quantities of army stores are now gathered in place of the Cotton Crop. The new government is working smoothly and admirably and the people are willingly accommodating themselves to circumstances. They are a determined, brave and self-denying people.[110]

I had great opportunities for seeing those of the interior just after sustaining their worst defeat and I am obliged to confess that the universal sentiment of all classes among them was that the war should end in their recognition or extermination. There are no Unionists in the South except the slaves. I am therefore convinced, too sorry to admit it, that further continuation of this war is foolish, that a people who for 16 months have held their own under such disadvantages, can hold their own for a longer time in future and that hereafter this will be a war for the mere accession of territory, which you and I used always to condemn.[111]

"The glory of Israel has departed." But I am not going to talk longer of such a mournful subject.[112]

You see that I am aboard the *Hartford*, tho not as Fleet Clerk, for at the death of Comdr. Wainwright the command devolved upon Capt. Palmer. I am sorry that your opinions of Captain Palmer differ so seriously from those of all who have seen him in action, but first impressions I know are stubborn. I have here a very pleasant mess and am better off than aboard the *Iroquois*, though in some little, prickly matters I am changed for the worse.[113]

You speak of entering the Navy. I do not want to be arrested for discouraging enlistments but I strongly advise you to stay where you are. There are several Clerkships vacant in this Squadron now: the *Susquehanna* (side-wheel, old frigate), Capt. [Robert B.] Hitchcock, who is certainly the most amiable Naval Officer I have ever met. This ship I very strongly recommend, not only as very comfortable but as disabled and likely to go home soon.[114]

The *Winona*, gunboat, leaking so badly her pumps can't free her, her Captain just recovering from an attack of *delirium tremens* and under the investigation of a Court of Inquiry, is without a Clerk.[115]

The *Iroquois*, Commander Edw. P. Nichols, whom I can very highly recommend, is now at New York for repairs and probably next cruise will be minus a Clerk, tho that is uncertain. This would be a nice vessel could you get no larger one, but I never again will cruise in one of her size. There may be some other vessels but I do not remember them.

But you had better stay home. True, I have never regretted entering the service but I much regret remaining more than fifteen months in it or after two or three fights, just enough to say "smoke and shell" pretty loudly.

You are generally thrown among such companions as you would not recognize on shore. A *good* Midshipmen's Mess is very pleasant though these days almost never found. I know of no other than mine in this squadron. Master's Mates are, almost without exception, the vilest characters.[116]

There are very few opportunities for doing good on board ship. You will always find that the discipline and work of the ship will interfere with everything.

A Captain's Clerk, too, is of no earthly use in action. I have probably passed six or eight orders in all the four actions in which I have been. The position is therefore the most trying on deck, for having nothing to do, you see each flash of the enemy's guns and wonder whether the ball from that gun will blow you to pieces. To remain perfectly cool and perfectly idle under heavy fire is the most trying of all the ordeals of war, everybody admits. Allow me then to advise you to stay at home where you are, serving your country as an upright citizen rather than to put yourself among unaccustomed temptations and uselessly to expose your life in the most unpleasant manner.[117]

I quite forgive your long silence if you will write me very often in the future, for I trust the chidings of your own conscience will be punishment enough. I hope you will not let my friends in Hartford forget me but assure them of my kind remembrances. Take lots of the same for yourself and believe me your coz. and true friend.

I am in no expectations of a fight for some months.

Affly., Edward W. Bacon

**Flag Ship *Hartford*, Pensacola
Bay, 29th Sept. 1862**

Dear Rebecca,

I received the other day your welcome letter of the 17th August, which gave me more news than I had heard in two months before, a fact which makes me hope you will find time to write again soon; and one from Kate dated at Colebrook, from which I see that I made a mistake when I wrote to her (I think it was) about some clothing, etc. As Kate is not at home, will somebody attend to giving the necessary orders, though I am sorry to put you to trouble with your very numerous Hospital duties.

I sent home in the *Iroquois* by Dr. Ireland $30.00 which I presume will be sufficient to defray expenses.[118]

I find my stock of Cotton socks of medium firmness getting lamentably short and though I have at times tried to darn them, yet I never found them after I had performed that operation quite as comfortable as new ones. Will you please send me out about a dozen pairs of the length of the thread I enclose?

I will try to send home some more $ by the next opportunity that offers, but so many leakages have been reported in the mail bags of the Transports that I do not trust them.[119]

We have no news later than the 17th and are very anxious about our Army of Virginia. We, however, learned this morning some facts in regard to Mobile. The place will be much more difficult to take than I had imagined.[120]

You know that only 9 feet of water can go to the City and that vessels of 15 & 16 ft. can get only about five miles inside Fort Morgan, within almost pistol shot of which the channel lies. This fort & immediate outworks mount a few over 100 guns; inside the fort is the place for the 16 ft. vessels to maneuver.[121]

[Here Bacon drew a small unintelligible sketch, not included, apparently showing Mobile Bay channels, Fort Morgan, and other unidentified objects.]

Across the channel; I do not know exactly where, two rows of piles have been driven down and filled in with rubbish, leaving an opening large enough for the Anti-Blockaders to get in, as a gate to which they have an old hulk. On two shoals, also, they have driven in piles and sunk scows filled with bricks upon which foundation they have built heavy iron casements, mounting about 10 guns each. The shores of the bay, too, are lined with four batteries, mostly in barbette, as you approach the city.

The [Confederate] flotilla consists of one ram, ironclad, invulnerable and nearly immovable; of one river steamer, said to be fast and efficient; of two new well built gun boats, named *Gaines* and *Morgan* of ten guns each; of the steamer which ran in on the 4th inst. (which without doubt is the *Oreto*, as our accounts agree with others that she has ten Armstrong guns and excellent iron plating in her hold, now being put on. Whatever else they may bring to oppose us is rather insignificant.[122]

It is *understood* in these quarters that Farragut has orders not to attack Mobile until further advices. I am very confident that nothing will be done for a month or more yet. Gales are now so constant and so severe.[123]

The *Kennebec*, one of those "splendid," "efficient" gunboats came in yesterday morning from off Mobile having actually *rolled her whole smoke stack overboard* and snapped her main mast off. At the same time, the *Winona* came in from the same station, gaining an inch of water an hour with all her pumps going. What a navy we are blessed with.[124]

It is very stupid here indeed and we are looking anxiously to see if some proposals for peace won't soon be made, for I have been obliged to conclude that to whip the South back we never can.[125]

With love to all, very aff. yr
brother, Edward W. Bacon

[Cross-written on first page]

I am very anxious to know if the Dr. Bacon the N.Y. papers spoke of was at Harpers Ferry when Jackson was "around" and whether that Dr. Bacon was from New Haven. Whether, too, the Dr. in question went to Richmond with the 8 or 11 000.[126]

So ended Bacon's navy letters.

Evidently it was an abrupt departure from the Navy and one of his own choosing. Bacon's extant letters yield no information about his decision to resign. However, a letter from Captain Homer B. Sprague in Louisiana reveals that Bacon left the *Hartford* and went home to New Haven in October 1862. Given the slow transportation, he must have departed shortly after writing to Rebecca.[127]

Answering a letter from Bacon dated November 3, Sprague provided the only information available, as follows.

※

> H. Q. 13th C. V., Camp Stevens, near
> Thibodeaux, La., Nov. 25th, 1862

Edward W. Bacon, Esq.

My dear Sir:

Yours of the 3d inst. was duly received and read with much interest & pleasure, although it is a matter of regret to me that you should be so afflicted with sore eyes as to be compelled to leave the service of the Nation at such a time, unless, indeed, you leave the Navy for the Army, which I hope is the case.

※

While Sprague thought that perhaps Bacon resigned to join the army, it is more likely that bright sunlight sparkling on ocean waters finally proved too painful for Bacon's sensitive eyes. Perhaps, also, the debilitating effect of dengue fever lingered.

PART TWO ∼ THE HOSPITAL CLERK, 1863

BACON APPARENTLY BADE FAREWELL TO THE NAVY WITHOUT much regret and with scarcely a backward glance. Now he no longer feared dying "in the most unpleasant manner," as he had written a friend. Yet he could talk about "smoke and shell" as loudly as he pleased, because he had undergone his baptism of fire, risking life and limb more than once without visibly flinching.[1]

He seemingly adjusted readily to civilian life, even as the terrible struggle continued to rage. Since he was at home, he wrote few letters for sister Katherine to save. Consequently, little emerges about his leisure-time activities, health, or thoughts during the interlude year of 1863. However, external events, surmise, and reasonable deduction offer some clues.

Colonel Amos B. Eaton, a commissary officer in New York, soon offered Bacon a clerkship in the New Haven army hospital's subsistence department at the then good salary of seventy-five dollars a month. A reasonable assumption is that Bacon's father had a hand in securing this pleasant, safe position. Given his patriotic feelings and sense of duty, Bacon again had a way to continue serving the nation, however modestly. Considering his own lack of income and his father's usually awkward financial situation, he would also welcome the pay.[2]

Bacon accepted the job and soon held sway over his own small shop on the hospital grounds. His superior was Surgeon Pliny A. Jewett, the hospital director, a man Bacon learned to scorn and despise. He called him an "accomplished scoundrel" and rejoiced when Jewett eventually faced an official inquiry. The exact cause of this disdain is uncertain, and he refers to Jewett only briefly afterward, leaving much to conjecture.[3]

In that pivotal year of 1863 great events occurred on the home and battle fronts. First, on January 1, 1863, Lincoln issued his Emancipation Proclamation. Now perceived as a transcendental event, at the time it was not generally so regarded. Many Northerners, citizens and soldiers alike, deplored the proclamation as changing the war from a noble effort to save the Union to a low scheme to free the slaves. Soldiers especially rebelled at the idea of turning the struggle into a "nigger war." Except for the dedicated abolitionists and the Radicals in Congress, most Northerners rejected slavery's extermination as the war's aim. Prompted by a pervasive and often virulent prejudice, they rejected any suggestion of black equality. They also feared hordes of newly freed slaves would stream northward to pose an economic threat with their unskilled cheap labor.[4]

Some objected on legal grounds, and even Lincoln conceded that the proclamation had "no constitutional or legal justification except as a military measure." People argued that Lincoln's unilateral act was an outright violation of the constitution or protested that it was an unconscionable taking of private property without compensation. Some abolitionists cried that the proclamation did not go far enough, complaining that it exempted slaves held in the loyal Border States or that the president issued the order as a military measure to deprive the South of vital labor, rather than acting from a heartfelt sense of rudimentary justice.[5]

Leonard Bacon, whose thinking surely had some effect on son Edward, waited almost a month before he publicly spoke about the Proclamation. Then he "applauded his [Lincoln's] decision to base it upon military necessity." The senior Bacon also defended the president's edict against attacks by lawyers.[6]

North and South, the proclamation's immediate practical effect for slaves was limited (though slaves were immediately freed in parts of seven rebellious states occupied by the Federal army). Only the force of Federal arms would free those—the vast majority—still held in bondage in the South. But the negative results were instant and protracted. As predicted by Postmaster General Montgomery Blair, Lincoln's Republican Party registered severe losses in the fall elections after he issued the preliminary proclamation on September 22, 1862. Many soldiers deserted, protesting they fought to preserve the Union, not to free the slaves.[7]

With the Emancipation Proclamation Lincoln also authorized enlisting black soldiers in segregated units with white officers. That also angered people on both sides. An Indiana citizen called it "most degrading and miserably humiliating." Federal soldiers high and low objected because they wanted to keep the conflict a white man's war and saw a threat of enforced, de facto equality if blacks joined the fighting ranks; Confederates felt a visceral rage at the very idea of former slaves, creatures they deemed "hardly human," raising a hand against their masters.[8]

Still, there was a positive side for Southerners: their will to fight stiffened and enlistments surged. Happily, a Kentucky Confederate thought the proclamation at the least was "worth three hundred thousand soldiers" for the South.[9]

Another divisive act roiled the North when Lincoln signed the nation's first conscription law on March 3, mandating military service for able-bodied male citizens between the ages of twenty and forty-five. However, for three hundred dollars, a large sum in those days, a man could buy his way out of service. As a result, volunteer enlistments increased, but resistance to the act became widespread, culminating in the summer's deadly draft riots. The largely volunteer army lauded the draft but scorned conscripts or their substitutes, considering it shameful to be forced into the army.[10]

Both the draft law and the black soldiery innovation undoubtedly got Bacon's attention. He faced conscription and, early on, had argued for enlisting blacks in the army. During 1863 he obviously gave the matter some thought, perhaps long before Lincoln called for another three hundred thousand volunteers in October.[11]

On the fighting fronts, 1863 produced a mixed bag of victories and defeats for the Union. As 1862 ended, Federal troops fell by the thousands in repeated suicidal attacks on December 13 at Fredericksburg, Va. In the first days of the New Year, the Union suffered another costly defeat at Stone's River or Murfreesboro in Tennessee. A lull came when winter storms precluded movement by the armies, broken by Lee's splendid victory May 1–4 at Chancellorsville. In the West, Grant won battles when he advanced on Vicksburg, then besieged the bastion; southward at Port Hudson, Major General Nathan P. Banks, one of Lincoln's incompetent political generals, sacrificed his men, including black troops, in hopeless frontal attacks.[12]

These and all other battles paled before the symbolic importance and the real impact of two widely separated events in July's first days. In June, Lee had embarked upon an invasion of the North but lost the gambit when he retreated after three days of fighting, July 1–3 at Gettysburg, Pa.; in the West, Confederates surrendered Vicksburg and thirty thousand men to Grant on July 4, giving the Union control of the Mississippi and splitting the Confederacy into two unequal parts. Vicksburg's fall also meant that thousands of Confederate troops in Trans-Mississippi Texas, Arkansas, and Louisiana might as well be on the moon. Further, supplies moving in either direction would all but cease.

At the time, people North and South were uncertain about Gettysburg's significance. They knew it was important but exactly why or in what way, many were not prepared to say.[13]

Brimming with a different symbolism, a much smaller affair than either Gettysburg or Vicksburg took place on July 18 at Charleston, S.C. There the black 54th Massachusetts Infantry bravely led a doomed attack against Battery Wagner on Morris Island. Northern newspaper correspondents quickly praised their élan and courage. Newly organized black regiments had fought in earlier actions, but this was the first to receive extensive, firsthand coverage by newspapers in many Eastern population centers.[14]

During the year's last half, a drum roll of battles sounded East and West—Chickamauga, Bristoe Station, Chattanooga, Mine Run, Knoxville, among others. More and more men went away to the army, many to a soldier's grave, marked or unmarked. Some came back crippled, disfigured, or blinded, while others disappeared forever, missing in action.

During these tumultuous months, Bacon worked quietly as a clerk at the army hospital and his only battles were with Surgeon Jewett, the hospital chief. Although bloodless, these were clashes he could not easily win.[15]

Following are the 1863 letters. However limited in scope and number, still they inform about the clerkship, family matters, and his continuing efforts to become an army officer.

※

Office of Asst. Com. General Subsis.

New York, March 12th, 1863

Mr. Edward Bacon

The Subsistence Department is about to make arrangements for subsisting the Soldiers in the United States Hospital under the charge of Surgeon P. A, Jewett in New Haven, Conn.

I offer to you the position of Clerk in the Subsistence Department with the pay of ($75.00) seventy-five dollars per month; the duties exclusively as above indicated and in New Haven. Either I or some other officer who will be responsible for the duties will be in New Haven within a few days to arrange with Dr. Jewett in the matter. If you accept the position please at once make yourself acquainted with the present method of subsisting the men. Get the names of all the suppliers, the present prices of all the articles they furnish. Ascertain if Dr. Jewett can afford the Subsistence Department a sufficient Store room in or near the hospital in which to store our supplies as [and] also office room for the Commissary of Subsistence or Clerk in which to perform their duties. Ascertain how many men are now in hospital and what is the expectation as to their number in April.

Please drop me a line at once as to whether you will undertake the duties. If you do, show this letter to Dr. Jewett, and request him to give you the necessary facilities for getting the information I have indicated above. Go also to the principal dealers in the articles composing the Army ration and get from them the prices at which they will undertake to furnish the articles from time to time as they may be required delivered at the hospital, viz:—Pork, salt beef, fresh beef, flour, loaf bread, beans, rice, sugar, tea, vinegar, adamantine candles, soap, fine salt, also any other articles Dr. Jewett may name as such as he will require to be supplied.[16]

All must be of a quality to meet Dr. Jewett's views.

Very respectfully, your obedt.

Servt., A. B. Eaton

[To Colonel Amos B. Eaton, USA, Asst. Com. Substance, New York City]

New Haven, Conn., March 11, 1863

Sir,

I have the honor to acknowledge the receipt of your letter of the 12th inst. and have to reply that I accept the Clerkship in the Subsistence Department, to which you refer, and that I have ascertained as follows,

The present method of subsisting the men is by contract with the Hospital Society of Connecticut who furnish everything at $3.50 per week. The supplies are drawn from no regular sources and prices vary from week to week. I have ascertained that stores can be obtained from wholesale dealers here at but a slight advance on New York prices; it would be cheaper to purchase in New York.

Dr. Jewett can furnish office room but not storage room; should stores be sent in bulk, it would be necessary to construct one. Dr. Jewett also informs me that the present number of men is 350, but that in April it will increase to 600, that being the number of beds.

A slight delay in the mails will account for the tardiness of my answer.

I have the honor to be, Sir, very respectfully,

Your obdt. Servt., Edward W. Bacon

※

Bacon quickly found himself enmeshed in the involved mechanics of establishing the new subsistence department, including the construction of a twenty-two- by fifty-five-foot-long building to hold the foodstuffs.

An invoice dated March 31, 1863, from the New York Commissary office listed the initial stores shipment. This included 119 barrels of flour, 15 of "Prime Miss. Pork" and 16 of beef, 120 barrels of potatoes, 1,647 pounds of roasted and ground coffee, 158 of tea, 1,938 of rice, 14 bushels of salt, 840 pounds of soap, and 90 pounds of candles. One of the heaviest lots was 2,500 pounds of "hard bread" or crackers.

Before these many wagonloads arrived by ship on April 1, he wrote New York to say that Jewett did not want certain things, including a full supply of those adamantine candles, as follows,

". . . I have consulted with Surgeon Jewett, as desired, and . . . he does not wish for the full allowance of Hard bread, as he issues Soft Bread almost exclusively. Green and roasted coffee will be of no use at all, he therefore requests that none but ground be sent. The Hospital buildings are lighted by gas, use can therefore be made of only one quarter (1/4) the usual quantity of Candles. He has also no use for Dessicated [desiccated] Potatoes."[17]

Dealing with barrels, bottles, and bushels, hominy, vinegar, and molasses, likely proved unexciting work for a youth who had chased Confederate commerce raiders on the high seas and braved enemy fire on the Mississippi. Still, he stayed with it for most of 1863. From a letter written by sister Rebecca late in the year, however, it is clear that Bacon had tired of counting crackers.

%

[Extract: Rebecca to brother Frank from New Haven, Nov. 21, 1863]
Dear Frank,

Col. Homer B. Sprague—of some Colored Louisiana Reg—is [asking] Edward to be his Adjutant. He seems quite inclined to take the place, Dr. [Nathan B.] Ives having told him that if he were drafted, he would have to go or pay the money. If his present office [army hospital clerkship] exempted him from the draft, I think he would best stay where he is, but he thinks himself liable to be drafted. Father is going to see the Provost Marshall [sic] to-day to enquire about it. I think Father is not desirous of having him go, he feels so uncertain about his health.[18]

Aff. Your Sister R. T. B.[19]

Edward W. Bacon, the soldier.
American Antiquarian Society.

Leonard Bacon, the patriarch.
Yale University.

U.S. Steam Sloop of War "Iroquois" &
At Sea, Off Nantucket Shoals
July 17th 1861.

On Sunday, July 14th we left our
dock at the Navy Yard, Brooklyn and,
under the direction of the Pilot, steamed
down the East River, through New York
Bay and the Narrows into the Atlantic
Ocean   Just as we passed Sandy
Hook our Ship began to roll, for
it was a windy morning and
the "Iroquois" is apt to roll in a
very even sea.   Like all who
commence an ocean life, & of course
was made sea sick, but rather gloried
in that I did not yield until
one, at least, had led the way.
For two or three days I have been
very small in my own estimation
but my officers have "made a great
deal of me." Capt. Palmer, especially

First page from Bacon's diary, recording his first days in the Navy, relating, "On Sunday, July 14,
we left our dock at the Navy Yard, Brooklyn. . . ." American Antiquarian Society.

USS *Iroquois*, Bacon's first ship, a thousand-ton steamer, also carried sails during the Navy's transition from wind to steam. U.S. Naval Historical Center.

James S. Palmer (left), the *Iroquois'* captain, was "very kind" to Bacon (diary, July 17, 1861), while Bacon called Admiral David G. Farragut (right) a "very clever old salt" (letter, Sept. 6, 1862). U.S. Army Military History Institute.

Raphael Semmes, captain of the raiders *Sumter* and *Alabama*, was called a "pirate" by Yankees but lionized by Southerners. Alabama Department of Archives and History, Montgomery, Alabama.

Union Jack sending one of Jeff Davis' Pirates to "Davy Jones locker"—Serves 'em right.

Wartime pictorial envelope shows Confederate "pirate" meeting summary end, a fate that Northerners thought they richly deserved. PR 022-3-47-39, digital ID no. aj47039, Collection of the New-York Historical Society.

Entering the Mississippi, Bacon first saw mortar schooners, each mounting one huge thirteen-inch mortar (letter to father, April 30, 1862). From Miller's *Photographic History*.

While neither the artist nor Bacon was present when an enemy shell burst near an *Iroquois* gun crew, Bacon vividly described the event in his letter of April 30, 1862. From Leslie's *Famous Leaders*.

Bacon proudly related his role (May 20, 1862) in reclaiming the Baton Rouge powder arsenal that looks today as it did in 1862. Courtesy Louisiana Secretary of State Jay Dardenne.

Emerging from the Yazoo River above Vicksburg, the CSS *Arkansas* steamed through a surprised Federal fleet on July 15, 1862. Sepia wash drawing by R. G. Skerrett, U.S. Naval Historical Center.

Powder boys, like this youngster, bravely carried gunpowder to gun crews, but Bacon reported (July 16, 1862) that he pulled one terrified "miserable little powderboy" from a hiding place as Vicksburg's batteries raked their ship. Library of Congress.

USS *Hartford*, Bacon's second ship, served as Farragut's flagship during the initial fight for the Mississippi River. From Miller's *Photographic History*.

29th Connecticut Volunteer Infantry (Colored) officers and men stand at attention for dress parade at Beaufort, South Carolina. Bacon is presumably somewhere in this 1864 photograph. Library of Congress.

While some black troops relax behind the Petersburg-Richmond lines in 1864, others (left background) move up front with their rifles. Note the bombproofs (center foreground).

Stacked rifles keep the weapons clean, free soldiers for other tasks, or support makeshift awnings, as Bacon noted in letters (Oct. 8, 1864; June 25, 1865). Library of Congress.

Sometimes death and destruction took a holiday. Here Federal officers on the Petersburg-Richmond front stage a mock sword-and-bottle fight, though the man at the far right has other ideas. U.S. Army Military History Institute.

Brownsville's Levee Street in 1865, looking up the Rio Grande, contrasted to the prim order of Bacon's native New England. Lawrence T. Jones III Collection.

Edward W. Bacon, civilian.
American Antiquarian Society.

PART THREE ∿ THE SOLDIER, 1864–65

(1) 29TH CONNECTICUT VOLUNTEER INFANTRY (COLORED)

"HOW LONG, O GOD, HOW LONG MUST THIS CRUEL WAR DESOLATE our once fair and happy country," cried a twenty-eight-year-old Southern woman in late November 1863. Northerners echoed her lament. Though they had escaped the shortages, hard times, and destruction the war brought to the South, the mounting casualties afflicted both sections. As early as November 1862, a Michigan infantry officer had complained, "No one seems to have any heart for the war except Lincoln, some of the lower officers & the privates."[1]

Though war weariness gripped the North, by 1864 the struggle had tilted to favor the Union. Northern superiority in vital resources such as men, horses, manufacturing, and almost every material requirement had begun to tell. Most important was the Union's overwhelming advantage in manpower. Still available were hundreds of thousands while the South had all but exhausted its supply of able-bodied men. For example, on February 1, 1864, Lincoln called for five hundred thousand men to serve for three years or during the war and on March 14, he called for a draft of an additional two hundred thousand. Northern states largely filled their quotas under these draft calls, though most men volunteered rather than suffer the ignominy of conscription.[2]

Jefferson Davis and his generals could only dream about such reserves. Instead, they had to resort to patchwork solutions, such as abolishing substitutions and expanding conscription ages from eighteen through forty-five to seventeen through fifty for all white males. Social, cultural, political, and economic barriers precluded the mobilization of slaves as soldiers until the very end, when it was too late.[3]

In 1863 alone the North had turned tens of thousands of former slaves and free blacks into soldiers, much to the distress of many. However, practical considerations soon alleviated that dismay. Draft-eligible civilians reconsidered when state and national authorities counted black recruits in filling draft quotas, thus sparing an equal number of white men. Some soldiers, vehement in their initial opposition, reconsidered when they learned only white men would officer the new black units. That policy offered ordinary soldiers the chance to win commissioned rank with better pay and status and gave officers an opportunity to win quick promotion by transferring to black regiments.[4]

Bacon's travels and battles as a soldier. As an infantry officer, Bacon went from New Haven to South Carolina, then to the Virginia battlefields and finally south again to occupation duty in Texas. While these travels did not match his experience as a sailor, he was more often under fire. George Skoch.

Probably most effective in changing minds and hearts was the argument that blacks made superior cannon fodder. Elizabeth Blair Lee, sister of Lincoln's postmaster general and wife of a ranking naval officer, wrote that black soldiers "are however the best population to . . . be food for gun powder if it saves better men it is something gained." More graphic was Corporal James T. Miller, 111th Pennsylvania Infantry, who wrote home, "The more nigers they get, the better I will be suited for I would rather see a nigers head blowed off than a white mans." This philosophy gained ground with the publication of "Sambo's Right to Be Kilt," a humorous poem written by Charles G. Halpine, a Federal officer. Writing under the pseudonym of Private Miles O'Reilly, Halpine argued that it was right and proper if "Sambo's body should stop a ball/that was coming for me direct." In conclusion, he declared, "The right to be kilt we'll divide wid him/and give him the largest half!"[5]

In early 1864, Bacon began seeking a commission in a black unit. First, in Philadelphia he visited the Free Military School for Applicants for Commands of Colored Troops. Open to white males, schooling cost accepted students nothing for instruction and books. They paid only for their food and lodging, whether civilian or soldier. After intense instruction, students went before an examination board in Washington, D.C. Private Richard C. Phillips, 44th New York Infantry, said the examining officers, among other questions, asked him how to divide a fraction and what was the cooking time for beans. Phillips knew the answers and received a commission as a 2nd lieutenant.[6]

That school and the examining board represented an effort to provide good, qualified officers for the rapidly growing number of black units. Captain Augustus C. Brown, who served on the 5th Army Corps examining board, recalled that they eliminated many unsuitable applicants in the screening process for the school. But elsewhere, particularly in the West and South, commanders exercised less care, and many unqualified men became instant officers of Colored Troops.

Bacon sneered at the Philadelphia school and held its faculty and students in contempt after the briefest of visits. Then he went to the capital and directly approached Major General Silas Casey, the examining board's head. Casey also did not impress Bacon, and he urged his father not to recommend the Casey board to anyone else.[7]

Yet Bacon enjoyed special treatment from Casey, who immediately awarded him a captain's commission in the 29th Connecticut Infantry (Colored), jumping him ahead of men who had more military experience. Certainly his father's influence helped greatly, though Bacon still had to convince Casey that he met some requirements.

By that time, almost all black regiments were being organized by the national government. They were numbered consecutively as United States Colored

Troops, and Casey approved officers mostly for those units. Earlier, several states had organized black regiments and governors had appointed their officers. By May 1864, however, only the 54th and 55th Massachusetts Infantry (Colored) retained their state designations. Others, such as the 1st and 2nd Kansas Colored Infantry and the 14th Rhode Island Heavy Artillery (Colored), were redesignated and renumbered as USCT units. Exceptions to the rule were two regiments organized in early 1864—the 5th Massachusetts Cavalry (Colored) and the 29th Connecticut Infantry (Colored).[8]

Neither before nor after did Bacon or his family express concerns about the negative aspects of leading black troops. First, their white officers were in double jeopardy. In addition to the normal risk of death or wounds in battle, if captured they faced execution for instigating servile insurrection. Second, officers of white regiments were openly contemptuous of those leading black soldiers. Colonel Thomas J. Morgan, 14th U.S. Colored Infantry, said that they "were stigmatized as 'nigger officers'" and was himself insultingly called that at an 1864 New Year's party. A Polish-American angrily railed against the "spiteful feeling of volunteer officers" for officers of black units. That disdain was not confined to the army—a 55th Massachusetts captain wrote that even a troop ship's captain snubbed the regiment's officers.[9]

Petty snubs injured only feelings and egos, but the rage of Confederates infuriated by blacks daring to fight whites was lethal. Immediately it became their practice and de facto policy to kill captured or wounded black soldiers. While they might be "deluded victims" of the vile Yankees, as Confederate Secretary of War James A. Seddon and others often said, still death was the proper punishment for fighting their erstwhile owners. They considered the white officers particularly culpable as race traitors, deliberately inciting slave revolt. President Jefferson Davis and his Congress made this official with directives and joint resolutions. In the field, Southern soldiers summarily shot some such captured officers, and the threat was always there that they would execute more.[10]

This dire prospect for black soldiers and their officers was widely known in the North. In the spring of 1863, Sergeant Henry G. Marshall, 15th Connecticut, thought about a commission in a black regiment, although family members opposed it. He wrote, "I thought nothing of the extra danger, for in war I don't see much difference in the dangers. A man in the least dangerous spot may be killed & one in the most dangerous spot may not be." Marshall later became a 1st lieutenant in the 29th Connecticut, fully cognizant of the risks. Bacon could not but be equally aware.[11]

Recruiters began enlisting men for the 29th in the last quarter of 1863 and sent them to Fair Haven, then a suburb of New Haven. By January 1864 more than enough men had enlisted to form a standard infantry regiment of about one thousand men. Though more than required filled the ranks, the regiment only slowly attracted officers. While Bacon reported for duty on January 29, the officer shortage delayed formal acceptance into United States service until March 8. Not until four days later did the 29th acquire a commanding officer in the person of Colonel William B. Wooster, formerly the 20th Connecticut's second in command.[12]

On the day after the 29th mustered, a pivotal event advanced the Federal cause. Congress had revived the rank of lieutenant general and on March 9, 1864, Lincoln named Ulysses S. Grant to that grade and made him commander of all the armies. Grant soon planned coordinated spring offensives East and West.[13]

※

Washington, DC, Jan. 15, 1864

Dear Father,

Though I am not yet at the end of my business here, I am nevertheless far enough advanced to let you know about it.

We (Bennett is with me) stopped on Monday afternoon at Philadelphia to see what the "Military School" could do for us. But we found the pupils of it quite a lot of scrub and were content to go on our way after obtaining two examinations from Mr. Preceptor (Col. John H.) Taggart in which, though they were useful to us, we evidently suggested an idea or two to the mind of the principal, which may be of service to him.[14]

The "Supervisory Committee" are a set of rather small-bore men, who worship Philadelphia, Phelps and Pompey. You must not recommend the institution.[15]

Took Wednesday night's Owl train to W. and arrived Thursday a.m. at ten o'clock, some five hours late and no sleeping Car. Called at the Rooms of Casey's Board in the p.m. but found the Board had adjourned. Called at Casey's house in eve. but he was out. Thurs. a.m. left your letter at Dr. Parker's house. Spent yesterday pretty much at the Capitol. While in the Senate threw off my overcoat and must have lost from its pocket my correspondence with [Connecticut] Gov. [William A.] Buckingham and all my letters of introduction except Dr. P.'s before used. Saved, however, my permit & my recommendations.[16]

Presented my permit this a.m. [Friday] and called upon Dr. Parker, who insisted I should have him call with me upon Gen. C. So we went & from the Gen's evident character I am quite glad I lost my letters. He did not say he was glad to see me, but told me he would examine me to morrow a.m., while the majority of applicants have to wait until their regular turn. If I find the Gen. true to his word, I may start for home on Saturday afternoon.[17]

I never want to come to Washington again.

I'll add that Gen. C said that I must be ready on tactics & did not express a desire for anything else. I am at the Metropolitan Hotel.[18]

Yrs aff, Edward W. Bacon

※

Bacon's captain's commission was dated January 16, the day on which Casey examined him. Thomas G. Bennett, the New Haven friend, became only a 1st lieutenant, though he had fought as an infantry officer at Port Hudson.

Records show them both as mustered into the 29th Connecticut on January 29, 1864. Very plainly, however, some legerdemain occurred. A note on the back of Bacon's "Individual Muster-in Roll" advised, "This muster is dated back to take effect from January 29, 1864." So the date Bacon actually presented himself for duty with the regiment is unknown.[19]

A short note to Kate dated Feb. 13, 1864, from "Barracks, 29th C/ V." is the first extant from his new career as a rifle company commander. Bacon asks Kate to send him stockings, shirts, collars, boots, and pistol cartridges but does not reveal his arrival date. Other records show that the 29th remained at Fair Haven until mid-March. During that period, Bacon could go home and family members could visit him. That phase ended on March 20 when the regiment sailed away, bound for Annapolis, Md. They arrived on March 22 and learned that they must pitch their tents three miles from town, much to their chagrin. When they awakened the next morning, they stepped out into eight inches of snow.[20]

Here the disconnect between Bacon's comfortable, assured open white world and the uncertain lives of his black soldiers became increasingly apparent. But their aspirations and resentments would mostly remain beyond his ken. For instance, while in Maryland, a slave state, Sergeant Alexander H. Newton of the 29th recalled, "The colored people in this place were afraid to speak to us. Their masters looked upon us with contempt." If Bacon was ever aware of any of such undercurrents, he never mentioned it.[21]

Bacon was scarcely alone in his ignorance of black sensibilities and culture. Many white officers who led black troops were equally unenlightened. Worse, some despised their charges, "cuffed and knocked around" the men, and inflicted harsh punishments for minor infractions. However, not a few, high and low, understood black soldiers' hopes and grievances. That was particularly true regarding the discriminatory pay issue, of which more later. [22]

※

In Camp, 3 Miles from
Annapolis, April 6, 1864

Dear Kate,

Some time since I received a very nice letter from you with one from mother in the same enclosure and only yesterday the mail brought me still another from

Rebecca. I am so much crowded by first one sort of business & then another that I really have no time to answer each for itself, but my letters must be considered as belonging to the family. I have heard also from [friends] George & Danny who say that they saw [an account] of our departure in the *Congregationalist*—did Father write it? If so, please send a copy to me.[23]

We have details of the State election which are satisfactory except that I am sorry to see that Buckingham is growing in popularity. His sort of despotism in Military matters seems saddled as long as the war continues.

In this regiment almost all the officers have united in a petition to the Hon. Secy of War to change our title from "29th Conn. Vols." to any number he may select of U.S. Vols., which may insure some chance of justice in our promotions.[24]

We have begun our career by having our Sr. Captain jumped for the 2nd in rank, who is now Major [Henry C.] Ward (a very fine fellow & accomplished officer) but not superior enough to warrant the insult to [David] Torrance, a finer man than whom is not in the Regt. This leaves me 3rd in rank of Capts. & gives me the color company in line of battle, that is, changes the position of my company. If His Ex'cy does not follow us under the new appellation for which we have applied, I ought to have my leaves when I want them.[25]

I have been busy all day with Ordnance for we have had to receive & issue our arms, the newest pattern of the rifled Springfield musket, very light & most splendidly finished, which makes us the best armed regiment in this Corps. This is due to the energy & tact of Col. Wooster, for our Dutch uncle wanted to shove onto us a lot of old Enfields. We shall now be more busy than ever with careful instructions in the manual.[26]

There is also a prospect of our being paid off very soon, as I understand the pay rolls are now being made out at Washington.

I see no prospect of our expedition starting for full six weeks for none of the General officers of the Corps are here yet nor have we been assigned, while Gen'l Burnside seems to have nothing better to do than attend Sanitary parades.[27]

Our men break into camp life wonderfully well & though we had hardly had a full 24 hours clear sky since our arrival, our sick list does not increase. Could we only get rubber blankets I should have, for one, no [complaint?].[28]

My 1st Lieut. has been quite unwell but I am in the best of health & actually keep my weight down to 122 lbs.

Much love to all at home & regards to friends who inquire & believe me,

Your aff. brother, Edward W. Bacon

New Haven, April 20, 1864

My dear Son,

Mrs. Didymus, a very good old woman, as I believe, has called to see me several times about her two sons in your Regiment. She has just called again & having promised to write for her, I begin without losing any time. One of her sons, John, is in your company (I). The other, Samuel, is in Compy. A. She has heard nothing from either of them since they went away & she feels bad & discouraged, for they are her all. She wants me to inquire of you about them—whether they are alive & if so, how they are & whether they are doing well. She sent a box to them while the Regt. was at Annapolis but has never heard of its being received by them. The box seems to have been of considerable value; & she speaks of having put a letter or two into it, containing money. Tell those boys that they ought to remember their mother; & that they must not add anything to the anxiety which she cannot help feeling for them & which threatened to wear her out. Her message to them, repeated several times, is, "Tell them to give their hearts to God & be prepared to meet me in heaven, for I don't expect to see them in this world."

She spoke of another woman, the mother of [Jacob?] Prime, who has also sent a box to her son & fears that he has not received it. Perhaps John Didymus can tell or can find out. I think that Prime's box may not have reached Annapolis until after the departure of the Regiment. The [illegible] box, certainly *ought* to have been delivered.[29]

This message from an anxious & mourning mother reminds me of how great your opportunities are for doing good to the men under your command & (through them) to their families & friends. I pray that you may be a kind & faithful & wise friend to them. The more you can do to make themselves & for their families, to keep them from spending their wages undecorously or foolishly, to form in them a habit of soberly regarding the future instead of wasting every thing upon the present moment—the better will be it for them & for the country. It is said that the Ninth Regiment [Connecticut Infantry] had sent home more money for the families of the soldiers & for deposit in the Savings Banks than any other Regt. that went from New Haven. Let the colored soldiers do better than the Irish. Surely they can, if they will try.[30]

The soldier who sends money home regularly & liberally to his family or who sends money regularly to be deposited in a Savings Bank, so that he may be able to have a family & a house of his own when he returns has a higher & manlier interest in the country that he fights for than the soldier who spends all as he gets it & saves nothing. Such soldiers will be guarded against many temptations, will be more ready to learn every good thing & their minds will be more open to every truly religious influence. As much as possible, appeal to conscience & the fear of God in your men. Make them realize that they are to fight not only in the Service of a country which now acknowledges their manhood & in the Service & defense of their own race, but also in the service of the God of justice & love.

Commending you devoutly to the care of God,

I am affectionately, your father, Leonard Bacon

※

On April 9, 1864, the regiment sailed for Hilton Head, S.C., the headquarters of the Department of the South and, at that time, of the 10th Army Corps. On arrival, the 29th landed and camped at Beaufort.

Early in the war, the North had established mainland enclaves and seized South Carolina's Sea Islands. From these bases Federal forces attacked Charleston and raided along the coast to Florida. But no fighting involved the 29th. Officers and men busied themselves only with drill, guard, and picket duties.[31]

> Camp 29th Regt. Infy. C. V.,
> Beaufort S. C., April 26, 1864

Dear Kate,

I have several times within the last two weeks essayed to write to you, but the exceeding pressure of Company & other business which attends an officer in a colored regiment more than any other, has each time prevented my success.[32]

We are still employed in getting to rights our camp which promises to be a very nice one and in which I shall probably spend the next year of my life unless the Gen'l commanding takes a notion to send us farther South, which is of no consequence one way nor the other to me. I suppose the sand is as fine & sifting and the flies which live there as numerous & annoying at one post in our Department as at another &, as for general healthfulness, I believe, also, all are about equal.

We are having now weather which debilitates the newcomers into the Department very much & even I, who have seen as much of the same, am more of less influenced by the heat—however, after a few weeks I hope to become quite accustomed to the climate & able to do soon all of each day's hard duty without weariness. Indeed, since I reported for duty Jan. 29th, I have not had an hour's illness which relieved me from duty.

The excessive heat & the prospect of a permanent residence here almost induces me to ask you to pack up my white clothes, which are [confined?] in my old Navy outfit & forward them per express to my address, upon which I will pay all dues. Believe there are some white vests & pants as well as two white jackets and some white shirts fit for a little wear yet. Should we leave this, I could easily repack the same & leave them in safe keeping.

If the Bouquet society are now at work for the soldiers, present my Compliments to the managers with the information that one of their brave defenders is in much need of a pen wiper & ask Miss Theo Wheeler if she has finished the one I engaged of her at the State House fair last June. Also if any of the young ladies are bold enough to ask if I have any photographs to spare, I give you full authority to exchange as many as you can & charge to me as I would like to enlarge my collection & find the consultation of my albums almost as good as a walk through Chapel St.[33]

Our regiment will be mustered, of course, on Saturday the 30th and we hope to be paid within ten days of that time, which will be most beneficial, both as regards the spirits of the men & the pockets of the officers. Tell father that when that payment is made, I shall send him a remittance.[34]

When you send my clothes, which please do as soon as convenient, will you get and put in a narrow black silk neck tie of the very best silk—plain black, without any ornamentation. I have no objections if the silk have a rib in it but there must be no attempt at a figure. If you will send Chapman to Mason & Rockwell, they know enough to give him what I want & will charge it on my a/c.

I wish you would write me if Theodore sold his horse before he left [Hilton] Head. If he did not, I may still have a chance to sell him here, or in case I can get some lucky detail upon somebody's staff, buy him myself.[35]

Give much love to all & believe me in haste, your very aff.

Edward W. Bacon

P. S. May 4th Send also some leads for my pencil which are in a little white wooden box in my desk. Also the letters of recommendation from Capt. Palmer, Adm'l Farragut, Gen Russell which Rebecca can find in my desk. If you have some valuable reading, some cheap bound standard history, put it in. Tell Rebecca I have seen Didymus who says his mother has had all his bounty & that he has rec'd letters from & written to her.[36]

We are exceedingly busy so you must not expect to hear often as there's no news. EWB

[below was cross-written on first page]

I was surprised the other morning just after roll call to see Col. Eaton in the door of my tent who was kind enough to come out of his way at an early hour to call on me. He will report that I seemed to be in excellent condition.[37] EWB

※

Almost a year before the 29th's first payday, Ohio's Gov. David Tod had asked Secretary of War Edwin M. Stanton about pay for men of a black Ohio regiment. Tod wrote, "They are expecting the usual pay and bounty allowed white soldiers. Will they get it?" Stanton's short answer was "no." He said Congress had authorized only ten dollars a month for a black soldier, three dollars less than for a white recruit.

Citizens, soldiers, and legislators flatly refused to accept any semblance of black equality, even to soldiers' pay. So Congress had settled on a two-tier pay structure—one for whites, a lower rate for blacks. Stanton also knew he had ordered that of the ten dollars, "three dollars . . . may be in clothing" and that there was no "may be" about it. Army paymasters automatically deducted three dollars from each black soldier's mite, paying him just seven dollars, or about half the thirteen dollars paid then to a white private. Further, adding insult to injury, the seven dollars a month applied across the board to all, whether lowest private or regimental sergeant-major.[38]

Black soldiers bitterly resented the gross discrimination that defined them as second-class soldiers, and that rancor lingered for years. They denounced the inequity, and many refused the lower amount, going without pay for months on end. Private Isaac J. Hill, 29th Connecticut, said it was an insult and added that "I will . . . die before I accept that sum." Most believed the government had broken its contract with them. Accordingly, some reasoned that they need not fulfill their part and so deserted or refused orders. Those who led such protests often faced charges of mutiny and then went before a firing squad or met the hangman.[39]

Many of their officers thought it unjust, and some appealed for fairness. Colonel Robert G. Shaw, 54th Massachusetts (Colored), called it "a great piece of injustice," and Colonel James Montgomery, 2nd South Carolina Infantry (African Descent), wrote the chairman of the Senate's Military Affairs Committee to urge equal pay. In time, ordinary white soldiers also thought it wrong and said so. Bacon, however, reacted angrily when his men refused to take the inferior pay. To him, it was "obstinate & stupid." To some extent he apparently perceived the refusal as a personal affront, ignoring the anger and humiliation his men felt.[40]

%

In Camp, Beaufort S. C., May 14th, 1864

Dear Father,

After some twenty days delay, on Tuesday last our mails reached us, bringing us dates to the 4th & me some half dozen letters from different sources: two from Kate & two from Rebecca with yours enclosing the letter of introduction to Dr. Peck, though I had some time since introduced myself to him & took tea there a week ago; but the Dr. & his family have gone North this morning in the *Fulton* & our society in Beaufort is again quite limited, for the school teachers, as a rule, do not stand very high. Mrs. Senator Harlan & daughter are here now for their health but I have not met them.[41]

I am glad to hear of the water improvements In your house; if there were only some such arrangements in the field, Army life would be even more pleasant than it is. The *Journal* & *Courier* speaks of the mythical addition to the war of the church as if it were to become a fact. I should be pleased to hear it so.[42]

We are very pleasantly situated here indeed; have the best camp, I am told, that ever has been on the island. Details come very frequently &, when with the Company, my hands are exceedingly full of business, so that correspondence can only be attended to at intervals, & then in much haste & sometimes weariness.

Tomorrow—Sunday—I am detailed as "Field Officer of the Day," a duty which visits me every eighth day & which involves some tremendous riding & therefore suits me exactly while occasionally it is a little exciting.

We elected Rev. Mr. [Jacob] Eaton as Chaplain some time since but have heard of his appointment in the 7th. Will you send me the names of one or two proper men. No one here has any candidates & I don't want to recommend anyone unless he will satisfy the majority. A Theological Student named Jones is suggested by Capt. [Edwin A.] Thorp.[43]

As regards the matter in your letter of Didymus, Rebecca wrote me April 11th on this same subject & I saw Didymus & properly lectured him at once.

Our Regt. has never been paid & will not be before the 2nd week of June. Every one, therefore, is short of funds.

Two new officers reached us per *Fulton*[:] Capt. [George W.] Allen, Yale '65 & 1st Lieut. [John M.] Payne. Capt. A., who seems a fine fellow, has taken Co. E, which leaves Bennett the only Lieut. Commanding in the Regiment. Perhaps his Company will not soon be filled. If not, let me urge the propriety of his promotion. We reported at the same time & since then have both been in command constantly & it is bestowing a good deal of flattery upon my own shoulders when I say that our commands are neck & neck. There are Captains in the Regiment not so well qualified to wear two bars as Lt. Bennett.

If [Governor] Buckingham ever condescends to ask your advice, don't fail to say a word on his behalf—since the only Lieutenants who rank him are notoriously unfit for any commission at all.

We have not yet heard anything at all of a Lieutenant Colonel; the commander that we have is such as renders it most imperative that our second Field Officer shall be a man thoroughly posted in Tactics & Regulations; a graduate of Casey—not of Cincinnati—and a man of sound sense. If some sound young regular officer (I mean one who understands all the rules of Military decorum & etiquette & who recognizes the relative position & duty of all officers & is precise on all the little points) could be found, it would do more for the 29th Regt. than any other one possible thing that I can mention.[44]

It is quite late & the duty of to-morrow warns me to turn in.

With much love to all, Your affectionate
son, Edward W. Bacon

May 21 Have only time to add that I sent the Check on last Thurs via N. Y. for $250 & the Bounty checks of John Brown (1) Luther Harris (2) & Joseph Humphrey (3) which please collect & send Luther Harris back *at once*.[45]

I have told Marcus Lewis, a good boy who goes home sick to call if he wanted to & of course you will see him well treated his father [Stephen Lewis] is one of my best men—though rather old.[46]

Didymus refused to sign for $7—on which we were paid—though I used every argument. He has sent home $10 Bounty Check. He is very obstinate & stupid & I guess Mrs. D. Had better depend on the other son.

Most of the Regt. took their pay but a good many in my Comp. refused it. Jas. Sheldon's miserable influence.

Could I catch him in my Co. st. now, I would confine him.[47]

We have left the matter of our chaplain entirely to the Gov. Please write to him the names of some first class men of life—Mr. J. M. Morris style.[48]

We were paid the 20th. No news.

We had a mail a day or two since with news to the 14th. Hence our Countersign to-night is "Wilderness" & our parole "Burnside."

The batteries have all fired salutes on receipt of the news.[49]

Aff., Edw. W. Bacon

In Camp, Beaufort, S. C., May 30, 1864

Dear Kate,

Your very welcome letter of the 5th reached me some two weeks since & is my latest news from home, for I was almost the only one to whom the last *Fulton* did not bring letters from home. I have been so very busy ever since the receipt of your letter that I have had no time to answer it until now & the mail closes in a very few hours.

We had a little expedition here the other day against the Charleston and Savannah Rail Road but which proved a great failure with the loss only of 20 men and some 70 horses with a very fine transport. Indeed in this Department there is no use in trying to write letters except as they may keep one's friends informed as regards [one?], health etc.[50]

Sometime since I wrote home for a lot of thin clothing—my white jackets & white pants & shirts with sundry other articles. I hope the letter reached home for I am almost melting from the thickness of the clothing I have with me. If you have not sent the box, please do so as soon as possible, for I am in much need of it.

I shall send North, as soon as I can afford it, for a new sword & sash, the one which I have being worn out some time since. If the sash which Theodore bought be not sold &, in the opinion of good Judges, likely to wear well & not stretch, you might put it in the box, if not gone.

Tell Father I wish he would send me back the value of the Bounty Checks which I made payable to his order & sent in my last.

I was very sorry to observe the notice of Rebecca Bacon's death which I had been anticipating for some time. I hope it did not break Mrs. Bacon down.

Please send me some of those photographs, so easily collected at the "Bouquet," about which I wrote you some time since. That of yourself I can see some likeness in now—inasmuch as you distantly resemble Lu Thompson.

I understand that Rev. John Dudley is going to be imposed upon us. Tell Father he must stop such a proceeding, if possible. Mr. D. may be a very good man but he would not be cordially rec'd here.[51]

The climate begins to affect our Regt. Our sick list & losses by Discharges & Deaths are very large. We have, too, very few officers fit for duty so that those of us who are well have double work.[52]

Theodore's mare & colt & a colt belonging to Dr. Craven were sold to a Planter near Hilton Head for $250.[53]

Write me soon again & as far as able I will keep up my end of home correspondence; all others I am obliged to drop.

Love \to all at home and believe me, Your aff. brother

Edward W. Bacon

What from Frank & Theodore?

On Picket, Brick Kiln, P. R. [Port Royal] Island, June 4, 1864

Dear Father,

Your very welcome note came here to me this morning & I was astonished to discover my check therein. I had my hands as usual so full of Public business, in which one must needs be precise, that I chanced to forget the necessary endorsement. I return it now, properly filled.

My letter which I sent with the Bounty Checks I think sufficiently explained them. I had bought them up at par to accommodate certain of my men and would like you to return the money as convenient as I can readily see that before next pay day I may need funds again. My next payment will enable me to settle the Messers. Mason & Rockwell's a/c & yours also, thus leaving me square with something over.[54]

My company was detached on the 31st ult. for Picket duty on the extreme point. We marched out on the 1st & are living under shelters, though I have the remains of an old house, being commandant of the post. I have charge of the shore for some three miles & in the most exposed part of our whole line. The first night we turned out three times for a party of the enemy who had landed & were audacious enough to try to "gobble" one of my posts but they did not succeed.

I have applied for permission to make a raid upon one of the little islands near ours which the enemy usually occupy at night, my object being to capture a boat and some rebels—or better yet, knock them over in the scrimmage. So by next mail you may hear of us.[55]

My company will be relieved on the 10th when we will return to Beaufort. I should rather prefer to stay here all summer were it not for the flies and bugs which are most annoying. The heat, too, is usually very oppressive, though to day we have a fair breeze.

I am in receipt of Rebecca's letter informing me that my box had started & when I get back to camp I shall expect to find it there. With your letter comes also one from Mother which was very welcome, for it seemed to show that her health was better than usual. The extracts from Theodore's letter was very interesting & I hope you will send me more of them. The papers which we get give us no continuous news—for files are inaccessible—and I have no time to pick out items. Moreover, the 7th is not often mentioned.

If you would also send Theodore's address I would write him, if I found a chance, as also to Frank.[56]

Of course we have no news in this Department. The climate sadly affects our men who suffer worse than white men. In my company & mine is full as healthy as any, I can muster only 68 men for duty while I left New Haven with 100. Our officers too begin to give way & applications for sick leaves are tolerably numerous. My health, however, continues good, notwithstanding the heat which is very enervating.[57]

With much love to all at home, I am
affectionately, your son, Edward W. Bacon

In Camp, Beaufort, S. C., June 21st, 1864

Dear Kate,

Our last mail which arrived on Sunday brought me a letter from father of the 13th and one from you containing some account of the St. Paul which must have been very fine.[58]

The steamer before the last brought me also my expected box & immediately the weather, which had been exceedingly hot, became cold as our April days so that until day before yesterday I had really no opportunity to show myself in white. I enclose 25¢ [?] due expressage on the box.

The *Arago* brought us three officers: Capt. Lyon, Lt. Clarke, an old school mate of mine, and Lt. Kenyon, returned from sick leave. This relieves the commander & the few officers on duty in some measure.[59]

I have been for the last week very busily occupied as Recorder of a Court of Inquiry into certain alleged malfeasance in the administration of the Hospital Funds at this post, where there have been until lately, some 20 hospitals. It is a very important inquiry & one attracting much attention & will doubtless keep me fully occupied for the next two weeks.

When I last wrote, my Company was upon picket. We came in on the 11th inst. without having any chance to do any thing lively.

I infer that Theodore, since the capture of Maj. Sanford and Capt. Dennis, must command the 7th is it so? That Regt. must be pretty well demolished by this time.[60]

I have met a good many old settlers in this Dept. who speak in very high terms of Theodore & Frank. Surgeon Clymer, whom I am hauling over the coals just now in the most regardless manner, informs me that he was the President of the board which Frank passed for his U.S.V. But all hands persist in hating "Ad.," though they very much respect the General.[61]

Ask Miss Perkins, with my compliments, if she knows Capt. George W. Allen of '65, a Meriden man and a very fine fellow. He was inquiring about the Perkins the other day.

We hear nothing at all of our Lieutenant Colonel & I begin to hope he will be made by promotion in our own Regiment which should have me the second Captain in rank.[62]

When does Joe Thompson return to his regiment? Give my compliments to his sisters & inform them that I shall feel quite overjoyed when I receive the pictures which they promised me over a year ago.[63]

We have no news at all except that a "Camp of Instruction" is forming near us of some 6000 troops which might much better be in Virginia. Col. Baird's Regt. is expected here to join that camp. His Regt. (for all his high promises) is said to be the poorest in the Dept. & that is a good deal worse than medium. It is quite nonsensical

[continued in cross writing on first page] to suppose that a private, young at that, who has spent one of his two years in hospital should know enough to organize and discipline a new regiment of troops. A Colonel should be a military governor, is supposed to know all about military law—all about the vastly different sets of forms and business customs of the different military bureaus and to have pluck & quick decision of character enough to fill any emergency which may arise. This amount of knowledge is taken for granted and the field is a poor place to attain it. Casey's board are deficient if they think a quick perception of tactical problems is the only requirement for a Colonel.

But there is no use moralizing. If Col. B. Had only passed for one or two grades lower, it would have made him.[64]

I am pretty well—took a little cold in the rain we had last week from sleeping in wet blankets for we were pretty well soaked through, but am pretty well now.

I enclose some pictures which Bennett, Bristol and I had taken in a small walk down town one hot day two weeks ago. I hope you will think them artistic.[65]

Give much love to all my friends, your affectionate brother,

Edward W. Bacon

※

Very briefly, Bacon next described a failed amphibious assault in Charleston's harbor on July 1, 1864.

About five thousand Federal infantry, including the 26th U.S. Colored Infantry, some cavalry, and artillery, landed on James and Johns Islands.

From there they could threaten key Confederate positions, thus imperiling Charleston itself.[66]

On Johns Island, the 26th attacked two small Georgia infantry regiments, causing another bloody incident in the private no-quarter war between black soldiers and Confederates. William H. Andrews, a 1st Georgia sergeant, watched as blacks charged part of his line. In an instant, they overwhelmed an isolated detachment and fourteen of twenty Confederates fell dead or wounded. He wrote, "We saw the Negroes when they mounted our works and saw them as they jumped down (horror of horrors) and put the bayonet to the wounded. . . ." Andrews added, "It certainly caused my blood to run cold. I had faced death on many hard-fought fields, but had never faced the black flag before, where quarter would not be asked for or given."[67]

Fortunately for the outnumbered and hard-pressed Georgians, reinforcements arrived. Together they counterattacked, and then it was their turn for ruthlessness. They bayoneted wounded Federals, though officers reportedly saved some. Andrews said one black Yankee tried to surrender but ran when several Confederates urged everyone to shoot him. Many quickly fired, and he dropped dead with six bullets in his body.[68]

Just as unlucky was 2nd Lieutenant James C. Spry, who fell wounded. Perhaps he died of his wound, but it was just as likely that vengeful Confederates dispatched him. In any event, he was never heard of again.[69]

None of this appeared in the official reports. However, Bacon obviously obtained much information from those who took part. Though surely aware of the mutual murders and Spry's disappearance, he omitted the no-quarter aspects in his letter. Probably he did not want to worry his family.

※

In Camp, Beaufort, S. C., July 15, 1864

Dear Kate,

Your pleasant letter, giving some account of the enjoyment of Presentation Week, which reached me some time since, remains unanswered. I had hoped something would occur to ruffle the tiresome calm of the personal history of an officer in the 29th Regt. so that I could for once both have excitement myself and material for letter writing.[70]

Unfortunately, the Expedition of some 10,000 men to James and Johns' Islands did not include either my regiment nor myself and, still more unfortunately, though in keeping with previous local history, the record of the whole affair cannot be made to include any accomplishment of any object.

Foster's idea was to seize upon & destroy (for I think he could not have held) Charleston. He succeeded in seizing two brass 20 pounder smooth bore guns.

I am sorry, though, that the regiment was not there for our whole force was under fire pretty constantly and these new recruits would have had opportunity to see how few men out of a battalion are actually injured when under the severest fire of artillery and distant musketry.[71]

The troops taken from this post have now all of them returned—giving us more life—and rumors are current of another attempt at something. "Something"—what name these things ought to have I am at a loss to invent.

One of our officers went with the expedition as a volunteer surgeon—Lieut. Hyde, whom you doubtless recollect and who has lately been detailed in Beaufort as Post Treasurer. All reports mention the Lt. as having done most excellent service—which the *Journal* might have for an item.[72]

Gen'l Saxton and his bloody minded staff were there too and some of the poor fellows actually slept on the ground two nights without any mosquito bars! Gen'l Foster became indignant at an A. a. a. Gen'l & ordered him to his regiment & Saxton has had the sense to detail Hyde into the vacancy, a pretty good selection for the one and streak of luck for the latter.[73]

Collector Barney's son, a boy of nineteen and a good bit of an ass, had just been promoted to the Colonelcy of some New York regiment, for which I am sorry and thus is obliged to leave an excellent detail—Asst. Inspector Gen'l—vacant, an excellent chance for somebody. Not for me, however, for I have recovered from a Staff fever I once had when I first entered the service; for an officer who meant to remain in the service permanently had best, after all, if he can stand it, see the hard part first, and Company duties are more instructive as preliminary to greater commands in future, than any other work. The staff is rather the "Uptown" of the service, while the regiment are on their way—slow though it be—to reach that dignity.[74]

Our regiment grows disagreeably less. The deaths are not so frequent as they were but our officers begin to suffer. Two more applications for leave of absence on account of disability have gone in to-day and one 2nd Lieutenant, who stayed at home too long on sick certificate & when he could not dare stay longer returned, has been honorably discharged the service for disability. Capt. Dunlap is dismissed, but that is more gain than loss to us.[75]

It seems pretty well settled, in my mind, that my friend Bennett will have the next Captaincy, though it's best not to report the fact. Still another schoolmate of mine is expecting a commission with us, a fellow named Clinton, who will make the number six.[76]

The Court of Inquiry which has been so often mentioned in my letters is, I trust, drawing toward its close. We have about a day's work more before our first case will be sent in for approval and we have opened the prosecution in the second and last case—which promises to be much shorter than the other. Then I shall see my company once more, which, I fear, has rather depreciated under my "Country cousin" who commands in my absence and my 2nd is worthless.[77]

The *Fulton* arrived to day and some three days behind time, but brought me no news from home at all. I shall look anxiously for the next mail, for in some late paper I saw that "in the sickness of Capt. Bacon" (which could not mean me, for I am all right), the 7th Conn. was commanded by a Lieutenant.[78]

By the way, I summoned before our Court the other day Lt. Col. [Peter] Pineo, the Medical Inspector Dept. South, Virginia and North Carolina, late of the Dept. Gulf and formerly of the Army of the Potomac, who congratulated himself upon meeting the brother of so great a gentleman as Surgeon [Frank] Bacon, who had in New Orleans one of the best Hospitals—if not the best—that he ever inspected , and who was a model officer and Col. P. is a man of very large experience and mature judgment.

But it is growing later & my scanty epistolary material runs quite low, besides which I have my Ordnance Returns for the last quarter to complete.

With much love to all at home, where I hope it's pleasanter living than down here, believe me, Yr. aff. Brother, Edward W. Bacon

※

Bacon's father wrote next partly in reply to a letter from his son that is missing from the collection.

In commenting on the war, he provided some perspective for a son serving in a stalemated backwater. He related that people mostly followed events on the Petersburg-Richmond front and Sherman's drive toward Atlanta.

Grant, with George G. Meade's Army of the Potomac and Benjamin F. Butler's Army of the James, had settled down to trench warfare against Lee's Army of Northern Virginia. It was not entirely static. Grant constantly sought to extend his lines to further envelop Petersburg and attacked north of the James toward Richmond. Still, it was a war of attrition, one that Lee could not win because he lacked the human and materiel resources.

In the West, Sherman drove southward against General Joseph E. Johnston's Army of Tennessee. As Sherman neared Atlanta, Jefferson Davis relieved Johnston, replacing him with the aggressive General John B. Hood, stupendously inept as a field army commander. Atlanta fell on September 1–2, 1864, and by mid-December, Hood had succeeded in destroying his own army, proving once again that the North had no monopoly on incompetent generals.

According to Leonard Bacon, a Confederate raid into Maryland in early July did not divert attention from Grant and Sherman. Perhaps that was so in quiet New Haven but certainly not true for those in the path of Lieutenant General Jubal A. Early's troops. In medieval style, Confederates extorted cash payments from towns, burned Postmaster General Montgomery Blair's house, plundered others, and burned two-thirds of Chambersburg, Pa., when the townspeople did not pay a hefty ransom. Then Early attacked the capital's defenses, causing alarm and confusion. That forced Grant to send troops to Washington. Early withdrew from the capital's outskirts on July 12, but continued offensive operations in the Shenandoah Valley until forced to retreat in early August.[79]

Early's raid, the spring's staggering casualties, lack of impressive victories or an end in sight, and a cumulative war weariness all depressed Northern morale. While the Bacons steadfastly supported Lincoln and the war, that perseverance had weakened in many other citizens. In Washington, administration and Republican Party leaders recognized that the nation's sour mood posed a grave threat to Lincoln's reelection in the fall.

%

New Haven, July 19, 1864

My dear Son,

I was absent when your letter to Rebecca, enclosing two orders for state bounty money, was received. I send you herewith the *twenty dollars.*

The new movement against Charleston does not seem to have been very successful as yet, though the impression which I get from the latest reports is that it is still progress. At present, however, the interest of the war centered on Petersburg & Atlanta; & movements in other departments produce no great excitement here. Even the raid into Maryland hardly diminished the interest in Grant's & Sherman's operations.

Frank has consented to be a candidate for the professorship which Dr. Knight has just resigned in the Medical School & his election will be ratified at commencement next week.[80]

We have had no recent letters from Theodore. But we learn from men in the hospital who receive letters from their comrades that he is still in command of the regiment, or rather of what there is left of it since the fight near Fort Darling when Maj. Sanford, Capt. Dennis & so many more were taken prisoners. I don't look for his promotion. His chances in that direction were destroyed by the unadvised & [discourteous?] letter which Leonard wrote last winter to the Governor.

I greatly approve the principle which you lay down for yourself as to "gossip" about your "superiors." I only hope that you may be able to adhere to the spirit of it. One expression in your letter is such in its bearing on the man who (whatever errors he may have made in some of his appointments) is not excelled by any other governor in the United States—that I should be very unwilling to have any stranger ever see it & I have therefore taken the liberty of making it henceforth illegible.[81]

We hope that the end of this war is not far distant. May God permit us all to see the end & to rejoice together in the restoration of our country.

With much affection, your
father, Leonard Bacon

%

Bacon lamented the lack of mail while serving in the navy when delivery was uncertain. Now, while stationed in South Carolina at a fixed base, he received mail more reliably, but complained because friends failed to write. He was not alone in his longing for mail. Black soldiers, even if illiterate, also wished for mail. That struck one white Ohio corporal as odd, as if the blacks were like regular people.[82]

Without explanation, Bacon refers again to the black soldier pay inequity. In mid-June, Congress had partially rectified the blatant discrimination but made it retroactive only for those men who were free on April 19, 1861. To implement this, the army ordered black unit commanders to query each soldier as to his status in 1861, and, if free, to take an oath to that effect. That requirement excluded the great majority—those recruited in slave Border or Southern states. Bacon's 29th Connecticut, the Massachusetts regiments, the former 14th Rhode Island, and some others raised in the North benefited within a few months. But not until March 1865 did Congress belatedly relent and make full pay retroactive to the enlistment date for all black soldiers regardless of prior status. As noted earlier, pride and prejudice had spawned the egregious injustice in the first place.[83]

%

In Camp, Beaufort, S. C., July 24, 1864

Dear Kate,

Your letter of the 12th inst. reached me by the *Hermann Livingstone* on Wednesday and I am much obliged for it though it don't give me any news. Any sort of mail is so much better than none at all. Not that I mean to disparage your correspondence by such a remark, for it is always the most frequent that I have & most acceptable. But some how it seems as if I had been unlucky in my selection of correspondents for this absence, and if you would stir up to good deeds any one whom you think could be induced to write me some letters & who seems to you capable of such a task, I shall be very much obliged.[84]

Some officers—even those who are bachelors—are receiving half a dozen letters by each mail and I have, outside of home letters, received not one for nearly three months. Perhaps the explanation may be that whatever knack for letter writing I once had has left me, but be that as it may, if you will jog the memory of any of my friends who may call upon you & administer some of this reproof to each it may be of some advantage.

As usual, there is no news with us. My regiment is still upon picket. Major [Henry C.] Ward, by the *Livingstone*, secured his commission as Lieutenant Colonel and Captain [David] Torrance (senior captain) his commission as Major. These promotions give general satisfaction and quell my fears that some outsider might step in and fill the vacant Lt. Colonelcy. I am still 3rd ranking Captain, holding the right centre—(Color Company)—for Capt. [Edwin A.] Thorp, one of your favorites, I think—an individual who goes about town with his meals spread over his pants and with his blouse full of rents & who never wears a collar—has succeeded in being mustered back so as to rank me.[85]

Perhaps such a state of affairs as penned above should not be described by me, but it is most vexatious, to my mind, that an officer should not set his men a better example. And in this connection, just say to Rebecca that her views of the sword & sash matter are very nice, considered as a tribute to the "veterans" when she says "a sash that has seen service is more respectable than a new one" but that if such an argument were admitted once in my company: if I wear a ragged sash & a dirty coat or no gloves & my boots not polished, one hundred men or as many as are left of them, cannot be punished by me when they turn out with dirty clothes, ragged gloves, rusty pieces and unlaced shoes. I can teach my men any lesson sooner by example than I can by precept & for this—partly—I get the most pay—or used to; now the men have most. However, I think I'll darn up the old things & see about the matter when pay day comes but if the sash of Theodore's does not sell, I'll relieve him of it some day. The belt I don't want. Tell Rebecca, too, that if she means to describe old Pliny Jewett by calling him a "500 pounder." she should have added "Parrot[t]."[86]

I am glad to see that Colonel Eaton has gained a star. I presume he is established just where he wants to be and a very nice place he has. [87]

I am surprised that you never say any thing about Theodore. Perhaps you don't hear from him and, as I draw all my news from you, that would account for my not hearing. I saw some story in the paper about how Capt. Bacon was sick. Please keep me informed of your latest dates from the 7th.[88]

I am still busy with the Court of Inquiry, but we will adjourn soon for some six weeks in order to get testimony from the 10th Army Corps.

The regiment will probably be in from picket upon the 1st of August when we can begin drill again.

Upon my court is Lt. Col. Hall of the N. Y. Vol. Engineers, Provost Marshal Gen'l of the Dept., who was so very flattering the other day as he attempted to have me detailed as Asst. P. M., a very nice berth. I rather discouraged him of this purpose & this detail, partly too through other causes, was not made. I am vain enough, however, to consider the offer somewhat complimentary. It is not good policy for a young officer to take staff duty before he has fully made himself conversant with his duties in the line.[89]

Give my best regards to all my friends who may make inquiries about me. Please tell father that I hope to forward him a draft about Aug. 1st. as the Paymasters are not going to pay the black troops until they receive orders to make up the difference on back pay.[90]

My health continues as before, though to day I am writing with some headache. There are more officers sick in my regt. than ever before at one time.

> Much love to all at home & also to
> Julia Woodruff & believe me, Your
> aff brother, Edward W. Bacon[91]

I wish I could send you part of the magnificent Watermelon with which I am regaling myself.

※

While nurturing his career soldier ambitions, Bacon embraced several erroneous notions. Though he could not glimpse the future, evidence from the past and cold logic would have helped him to more realistic assessments. To explain necessitates moving ahead of the narrative a bit.

First he assumed the government would keep a "large body" of black troops in postwar service in which he could retain his present rank. Before the war, the army numbered about sixteen thousand officers and men, and there were no black units; after the war, the army expanded somewhat from its prewar strength. But there was a sharp reduction from the million or so enrolled in 1865, and the government organized just four new black regiments to fight Indians on the Frontier. That represented a considerable drop from the 150 such regiments Bacon wrongly thought existed as he wrote. With peace, the army rapidly demobilized white soldiers and the Northern black regiments.

Many officers decided they would like to remain in the army, so the competition became fierce among volunteer officers. Almost all who succeeded took a reduction in rank, a necessity even for West Point graduates. For instance, dashing Major General George A. Custer, a cavalry division commander during the war, afterward became a lieutenant colonel in the Indian-fighting 7th Cavalry. Bacon's 29th Connecticut lieutenant colonel, Frederick E. Camp, a volunteer officer, settled for a postwar 2nd lieutenant's commission.

Bacon also thought serving in a state regiment worked to his disadvantage. It was neither here nor there—all the wartime black regiments, state or Federal, vanished from the rolls, relegated to army archives and history.

Then he credited Washington authorities with an omniscience they had yet to display when he asked his father to ascertain postwar policy. Some broad tentative planning occurred, but no one knew when or how the conflict would end.

※

In Camp, Beaufort, S. C., July 29, 1864

Dear Father,

Your letter of the 9th inst. reached this [place] last night and I was happy to find you had received mine enclosing Bounty Checks. Since the date of that, on Monday of this week I sent to you a portion of my pay for May and June which I had just received. The Regt. will not be paid for sometime yet.

I am most happy to hear of Frank's sensible conclusion as regards the Chair of Surgery. He works so hard always & is so unable to stand hard field service that the Army don't seem to be the place for him, though I had hoped to see his leaves turn white before he left the service. Every one who has known him, among my acquaintance, speaks of him as an exceedingly good & promising officer.[92]

I am reminded by my date that it is just seven months to day since I reported for duty under my present commission and that the 9th inst. saw closed three years since I reported on board the *Iroquois*. From so full an experience of the World as I have had in those years, opinions may perhaps be formed which shall correctly influence my future actions.

When I went before Gen'l Casey's Examining Board, it was, as I think you are aware, with the intention, should I attain a Lieutenant's commission, and should I find myself adapted to the service and the service to me, to let that examination be the final one, graduating me into my profession.

From the seven months which have elapsed since then, and whose record has been that of earnest work with new men and with some time indifferent aid and some times none. I think I am prepared to say that I am the man for the service and I know of nothing to show why the service is not equally fitted to the man.

Plainly, if the Army will keep me, I intend to stand by it, my reasons being,

First, That my habits of study and confinement to set tasks were destroyed by my leaving there in 1861.

Secondly, That therefore my education being limited (Virgil in Latin, Xenophon in Greek, Algebra in Mathematics and some scattered impulsive reading being its fullest bounds), a Collegiate course succeeded by professional study is not to be considered.[93]

Thirdly, That my inexperience and entire distaste do not render success in any form of mercantile life probable.

Fourthly, there is then nothing which is reputable and honorable, nothing in which I could be assured of success but the Army. Naval life I have tried and found no abiding place therein, though it was very agreeable and to its Marine Corps there are strong objections. To exist as a clerk in some Bureau of a Department I trust is not for me.

In the Army success has joined hands with me at starting. It is my impression that even the negative and opposition testimony which could be obtained from the Head Quarters of this regiment would admit that so far as the management and discipline of my company are concerned, my record is satisfactory and there are officers high in rank who know me well who I think would afford better words than those.

The happy end of my adventure of my powers may pardon expressions which might seem self-satisfied.[94]

The object in writing the above was to follow here with the inquiry: What is the destiny of this regiment?

I believe it is the intention of the Government to retain in the service a large body of negro troops, converting them into the Regular Army on the peace footing—when we have one.

To my own conjecture it is improbable that any white volunteers or *state troops* will be thus finally included. This regiment, most unfortunately, is termed "Connecticut Volunteers," a respectable name but injurious, for where there exists a series from 1 to 150 regiments of "United States Colored Troops" I believe that in time the 54th and 55th Massachusetts and the 29th Connecticut, the only black regiments not in the regular series, will have leave to disband and their officers, however good or serviceable they may be, will, without much ceremony, be mustered out.[95]

This will be *my belief* until I have official notification to the contrary and after that a change may come over the official will.

I have to ask, then, if you will please ascertain from *Washington*, not Hartford, what the policy is to be and to find whether my appointment (by accommodation of Casey's Board last January) can be transferred without loss in Muster rank from a state to a United States organization. Of course I am in no immediate haste to leave so fine a Company as I command or so fine a regiment as ours, surrounded by my schoolmates and friends from near home, but by and by I shall probably need either that transfer or one to the Regular Army, where I should not want to go below my present rank.

Of course, could I enter some regiment of U.S.C.T. and at the same time "double my buttons," it would be a stroke of good fortune very seldom recorded. In about two years it will probably be my turn for a promotion here, which I understand, would be after I had passed examination for it, which is wise. However, the sooner such a thing happens, the better, though I can wait.[96]

If then you could ascertain in regard to these matters so that I could settle my mind & rest assured that some morning I shall not wake up to find myself coolly dropped out of the service to stay in which I trust I earned a right in the *Iroquois*, it would be of great service.

I have been quite plain and bold in these observations and in the hope that you will appreciate how I cling to the hope of my commission being or becoming a permanency as to the hope of living with success & happiness.

With much love to all, Believe me, Your aff. son,

Edward W. Bacon

(2) TRENCH FIGHTING, VIRGINIA

WITH LITTLE WARNING AND IN SECRECY, IN EARLY AUGUST THE
army shipped the 29th Connecticut and other black units from South Carolina
to Virginia.[1]

Much had happened there since Bacon left Maryland in early April. In May
Grant had launched his three-pronged spring offensive, with mixed results.
Advancing in the Shenandoah Valley, the ineffectual Major General Franz Sigel
had met defeat. Moving up from Fortress Monroe with his Army of the James,
Benjamin F. Butler proved again his ineptitude and got himself bottled up on
the Bermuda Hundred front, losing heavily at Drewry's Bluff, while his 18th
Corps commander had bungled an opportunity to capture Petersburg.

Grant himself had crossed the Rappahannock and hammered his way toward Richmond and Petersburg, losing fifty thousand men in just one month.
In June and July the armies had settled down to attritional trench warfare with
occasional attacks and counterattacks.

But on July 30, 1864, Federals exploded four tons of gunpowder beneath a
Confederate salient at Petersburg, blasting a big hole in Lee's lines, opening the
way to split Lee's army, capture Petersburg, and then to trap or destroy the rest
of the Army of Northern Virginia, perhaps shortening the war by months. Command failures turned the affair into a bloody fiasco, including the largest massacre
of black soldiers during the war when Confederates slew hundreds of them.[2]

While in South Carolina, the 29th's officers and men saw Northern newspapers and so knew something of events in Virginia. But they might not have
known that the private no-quarter war between Confederate and black soldiers
raged in full and merciless fury on the Petersburg-Richmond front. One of the
first news reports about this did not appear until mid-August. Then a black
correspondent for the Philadelphia *Press* who covered Butler's Army of the
James reported, "Between the negroes and the enemy it is war to the death. . . .
Those here have not the least idea of living after they fall into the hands of the
enemy and the rebels act very much as if they entertained similar sentiments
with reference to the blacks."[3]

On arrival in Virginia, the 29th Connecticut joined Butler's army where
no-quarter tales circulated around the campfires. Soon Bacon made his first
elliptical reference to this grim reality. Immediately, however, he denied it,
declaring "such is needless fear."[4]

%%

[Much of the following letter is missing because the writing has faded so much,
making accurate transcription impossible]

U.S. Transport *Trade Wind*, Off
Hatteras, Aug. 11, 1864

Dear Father,

Probably you do not expect to find a letter postmarked Fortress Monroe from the 29th Connecticut. Such is, however, the case.

At day break on Tuesday [August 9] we embarked for Hilton Head for our destination was withheld even from our Brig. Gen'l, so we were able to surmise that it was Md. All day Tuesday was spent in turning over our extra Camp & Garrison equipage & at 6 p.m. we were able fairly to start. Fortress Monroe will probably be reached tomorrow noon & then up the James & report to Butler for the 10th Army Corps. So we are really to be set to work.[5]

I cannot say that I am sorry for the change, though our work in Virginia will be excessively disagreeable, for the climate of South Carolina was beginning to wear upon us all. Indeed, I was quite astonished upon getting before a large mirror the other day to see how old I looked; the constant care of my large family having made wrinkles in my face, unless they were caused by thinness.

Our battalion is divided: on the *Trade Wind*—Col. Wooster, Cos. F, G. H, I, K; *James Green*—Maj. Torrance, Cos. E, A, B; *Beaufort*—Lt. Col. Ward, Cos. C & D and Co. B of the 7th U.S., Capt. [Lewis T.] Weld.[6]

We are part of a Brigade under Gen'l Birney (who will have a division, it is understood) consisting of the 7th, 8th & 9th U.S. & this Regt. Our going to the 10th Corps is because Maj. Gen'l [David B.] Birney, who commands it, is our Birney's brother. I hope, then, to overhaul the 7th C. V. some how or other & meet Theodore before he goes North. You may therefore address

 Capt. E. W. B
 29th Connecticut
 Birney's Brigade
 10th Army Corps[7]

The sending North of this Regt. was very sudden. It seems the choice lay between this & the 26th U.S. & we are complimented. Just before we rec'd our orders I had written in answer to Rebecca's letter of the Monday after Commencement which is the latest date I have. I hope Frank is by this time at home. Give him my congratulations upon his professorship. I wish his straps could fall upon my shoulders for I shall detest the tall marching which will be our lot in future. But, as I said, we do not grumble because we have seen our full share of a soldier's comforts in War times.[8]

If possible shall send home by express from Fortress Monroe a box containing my overcoat & some other articles of outfit too cumbersome for our campaigning which, I presume, will be in the lightest marching order.

I am sorry to hear of Joe Thompson's resignation after being in the service just long enough to gain an interest in & knowledge of it. One must naturally be very much provoked to have to leave it.[9]

Off Cape Hatteras, Aug. 12th

I am closing my letters now for we are about entering the Roads.

Letters from me must not be expected in future so regularly as before, though I always write as often as I can.

[The little remaining is largely illegible, but words and phrases readable show that he worried about correspondents getting his new address.]

Aff. yr son, Edward W. Bacon

New Haven, Aug. 26, 1864

My dear Son,

I have paid to Mason & Rockwell on your account the entire sum ($125—) which you remitted. The balance of their account will be, if I remember correctly, $23.25. They will make out their account in detail & when I receive it, I will send it to you.

I will take an early opportunity to answer your letter in which you speculate about what you think [to] do when the war is ended. At present I need only say that there is no hurry about deciding that question. Go on & do with your might the duty of to-day; and when that future comes (which I hope is not very far off) God will show you what he would have you do.

Meanwhile, may he keep you in perfect safety & in perfect peace!

Affectionately, Your father, Leonard Bacon

※

Bacon traded South Carolina's enervating heat for Virginia's lethal enemy fire.

Shortly after landing at Bermuda Hundred on August 14, the 29th Connecticut joined an attack toward Richmond at Deep Bottom, north of the James River. Grant had ordered the feint to keep Lee from reinforcing Jubal Early in the Shenandoah Valley. Entrenched Confederates repulsed the attacks of August 13–20, costing Grant's men almost three thousand casualties. The 29th played only a peripheral role and reported no losses.[10]

Soon, however, the regiment began to sustain casualties. Bullets, artillery shells, and mortar rounds took their daily toll. Soon, too, the inexperienced officers and men learned to keep their heads down, to avoid smoky cook fires, and to skirt places exposed to snipers or artillery shells.

In his first letter to Kate from a fighting front, Bacon exhibited traces of the romantic idealism so common in the war's early days. Then brave men did not take cover during combat but stood upright, defying enemy bullets, and troops fought in the open, scorning foxholes or shields of earth, stone, or logs.

Long since, veteran troops had learned better. Both sides dug in whenever they paused and, if caught in the open, had no qualms about fighting from behind a tree or prone on the ground. But Bacon said that "there is no difficulty in keeping about as much exposed as most men." He was either very lucky or quickly decided that he was worth more alive than dead.

He also considered a question pondered by officers of black troops. They repeatedly wondered whether their men would fight. No matter what positive answers came from other units, they wanted to know if their own men would face the enemy. In a diary entry for August 16, 1864, Sergeant Daniel Chisholm, 116th Pennsylvania Infantry, watched 10th Corps black troops and said that "theirs was the best line of battle I have ever seen go into action." Writing home that same day, Capt. Lewis T. Weld, 7th USCI, proudly declared, "The colored troops are very highly valued here. . . ."

Confederates had a different view. To explain blacks actually fighting their former masters, they usually said they were either primed with whisky, forced into action at bayonet point, or both. Thomas M. Chester, Philadelphia *Press* correspondent, said yet another pressure drove black soldiers. He reported, "Fully impressed that no quarter would be shown them if captured . . . they charged desperately upon the rebels."[11]

In the Trenches, Before Petersburg,
Va., August 30th, 1864

Dear Kate,

I wrote Rebecca on the 27th from the trenches giving some account of our Campaign thus far & of our situation then. That afternoon, after the letter had left my hands, the enemy got a range on our pits from the smoke of the little fires by which we boiled our coffee and shelled us quite energetically with a Battery of what I think are Brooke guns. The practice was very excellent & almost demolished my shelter at which the sharpshooters had been squibbing all day. I had a Corporal wounded and Co. B also had a man hurt.[12]

We were relieved at about nine o'clock after listening to a fine band which was discoursing music over in Petersburg and watching the beautiful practice of the batteries on both sides. I have been away from the firing of great guns for over a year & had no idea how great an advance I should find in the service of artillery & ordnance. The practice of the armies here is about twice as accurate and efficient as it was either at New Orleans or Vicksburg and as for small arms, our troops as well as those of the enemy have educated themselves to the utmost disregard of danger and put no thought in their minds of the value of life.

For instance, last night during a vigorous cannonade of an hour, in which a good many mortar shells—the least accurate of all—were thrown at us, every shell struck either in our trenches or just about them and one man was killed and six wounded in this one regiment. So long as we are in this work, we anticipate about this loss daily.[13]

But we are not now where we were at my last date. As I said about 9 p.m., the 117th New York marched in and relieved us & we made a detour of some four miles & entered the trenches again at a point some two miles to our left of our previous position. The works here are easier manned for we are protected by a grove of trees from the fire of the enemy's sharp shooters. In front of us are the 6th & 7th Connecticut as sharpshooters & they keep up a constant but not very destructive fire. About one man a day from each regiment gets knocked over. The enemy's shells are, however, more numerous than in our other place.

Either the Navy are much braver fighters than the Army or else my former experience has profited me greatly for there is no difficulty in keeping about as much exposed as most men.

On the whole I am pretty well satisfied with my men: they stand fire pretty well & are as a whole decently cool except when moving in line or column of attack against the enemy for which work they are not fit as yet. Behind works, I am wiling to fight my men against almost any troops & although there may be much more manageable & efficient armies than can be found in America, I think no where can be found more indomitable and ferocious fighting than in Lee's army. I have a respect for them, constantly growing greater[,] that a people under such appalling disadvantages as theirs could achieve such stupendous results as they have in withstanding us.[14]

We have no news here. Rumor says and the enemy say that we are pretty extensively engaged in mining. Some have the impression that active work is pretty much over, I have not.[15]

Grant has proved himself the most reckless of all our generals and will not fail to move some how & where, so long as the roads are passable & now they are quite good. I am charmed to hear so well of old Farragut. He ought to be made Vice Admiral to rank with Grant or, if Grant should drive Lee's Army to pieces, one should be Admiral & the other [full] General. Speaking of promotions, Gen'l [Alfred H.] Terry is in receipt of his Maj Gen'ls appointment. I consider it well deserved. I only hope that Ad won't get his Lt. Colonelcy. People do insist that the two bothers live like cats & dogs.[16]

Maj. [Daniel] Klein of the 6th did me the honor to call upon me expressly so soon as he found me in his neighborhood. His Regt. counts up 11 battles since April.

Col. Wooster—the opinion gained—is rather a "played out" man, very much broken down by malaria. Lt. Col. Ward is at Fortress Monroe, very much broken by his injuries, and Maj. Torrance now commands the Regt. If this state of affairs continues, there will be at least one promotion which Capt. [Frederick E.] Camp will get and deserve. Should one more be made, every one hopes Capt.

[Edwin A.] Thorp will be skipped as he is totally inefficient and exceedingly disagreeable to everyone in the command. Such a proceeding would bring my name next in the list of claimants.[17]

I regret exceedingly to hear of Dr. Knight's death. It has caused much sorrow in the regiment, especially among us from New Haven. Please give me some idea of what Mr. Street's notion is about the fine arts & what the other new buildings are to be & when to be built. Moreover, what "the general's lot" is on which Dan'l Eaton is to build a shanty of some sort.[18]

I had thought that I would not apply for any leave of absence during Campaign or during war service but these duties are so arduous & so fatiguing that I shall make an effort in November to go home to vote. Ask father to ascertain whether I can be made an elector in the field or not; I would like to hear of its impossibility.

[Lieutenant Eugene S.] Bristol is in receipt of a letter expressing considerable anxiety as regards the 29th regt. I may say that such is needless fear. Some of us—to be sure—are knocked over almost every day, but the duty of the 10th Corps just now is strictly to hold the trenches; all activity is on the left with the 5th and 9th Corps.[19]

We are at last assigned to a division & our address is

1st Brigade, 3rd Division, 10th Army Corps via Fortress Monroe, Va.

August 31st 1864

One of our 2nd Lts., McDonough, has been for a while on Genl Birney's staff. Night before last, I think, as he was visiting the front of our lines he disappeared & no one can hear any thing of him whatever.[20]

I hope to hear very frequently from home now for it don't take but two days for a letter to reach us from New Haven & they are more than welcome.

I meet a great many Connecticut men in this Corps, which is pleasant.

Send me a *Palladium* now and then.[21]

Aff. yr brother, Edw. W. Bacon

In the Trenches Before Petersburg,
Va., Sept. 18, 1864

Dear Kate,

Early this morning—a dismal cloudy one, too—I received two letters to cheer me, one being yours of the 15th, announcing Theodore's arrival home, the other from Isham. In one of your recent letters you congratulate yourself upon the fact that we can reach each other by the mails in two days. This is an error. No doubt the mail arrangements should be as you suppose, but the newest letter which has reached me was the first after our disembarkation, next which in shortness of transit is your last, through in three days. Most of my correspondence is detained to four and five days.[22]

A letter from Rebecca, arrived some days since, brings the answer to my inquiry about the manufacture of elections. I shall put in an application at the proper time for a leave of absence, but very likely it will be disapproved. If father will be so good as to speak to N. D. Sperry and state my case, a few words from the latter person to the managers at Washington will cause a leave to be sent to me. One of our Captains (Camp) who comes from that close city, Middleton, received when we were at Annapolis in April a leave direct from Washington for seven days which allowed him to go home and vote. The Capt. heard nothing of it until its receipt.[23]

I am much obliged for your description of the new buildings at College. It is a shame that so many pretentious piles of stone are to be crowded in such a little space. From all present prospects, I presume it will be some years before the completion of the project.

We are still upon this duty in the trenches, which has become monotonous. Of late it has been our good fortune to have had fewer casualties than at first, though occasionally a man gets chopped in some part of the brigade.

By the way, the 3rd Division which consisted of this Brigade and the 1st U.S., 22nd U.S. & 37th New Jersey (white) 100 days men in the 2nd Brigade, seems about to be broken up. The 1st U.S. has gone down the James, the 22nd to Dutch Gap & the 37th will in a few days be out of service. What will then become of us I don't know—but it is presumed that we will remain as an "independent brigade" to do the dirty work for the Corps.[24]

Yesterday we were inspected by Capt. [Lewis L.] Weld, Division Inspector. Rather to my surprise, my company is still found to be top of the heap; C, D & I holding the first place in the right.

Your letter opens pleasantly. Visions of grapes, pears & peaches are very pretty to contemplate but make one a little disgusted sometimes with the region about Petersburg. Occasionally, at a tariff of 5¢ each, we obtain a few withered peaches or gnarled and wormy apples, just to aid our imagination, but other than these, fruit is a scarce though necessary article with us.

But I am amazed at the account which you give of Lt. Thompson, which really has what we would call in the field rather a "dead bratish" look, though knowing the energetic character of that family, of course such a suspicion can not be entertained. As for me, I could not ask for a better post than Key West, unless New Orleans. The Key is clean—no danger of any marching and one's command can have more of a chance to perfect itself than that even in Beaufort. Its only objection is the prevalence of fever in the summer months.[25]

Gen'l Dix's staff is the best place in the Army just now (though I should prefer Grant's) but before taking duty there one should see the field. I observe my friend Lt. Goodrich of the 15th C.V. Is detailed as Provost Marshal in North Carolina.[26]

Col. Hawley's name appears in the New York papers as going home in command of the non-enlisting men of the 6th & 7th Conn. Are we to infer from that that he intends to quit the service or that he is merely home on leave? My impression is that his present muster holds to February.[27]

Col. Wooster is North—perhaps you are aware.

Rebecca asks in her letter if she shall not send me some shoes. It would be a very good idea. [illegible proper name], I think, has my measure & if you tell him to make a pair of "Marching shoes" just like the last I got of him, he will be able to give satisfaction. My last were made for Capt. Babcock of Gen'l Hunt's Staff & were satisfactory. The new ones must be of the best material and sewed.[28]

We came into the trenches last night and should go out Wednesday night. You do not mention the state of Theodore's health, so I presume he is not suffering much. I am glad Frank is getting settled. It seems rather queer to be the only representative of our family in the service & seems already to have had a good effect upon the number of letters I receive. My friend Bristol is a good instance of "only son in the Army." His friends were anxious at Beaufort, frantic now. Every now & then comes a box full of boiled hams etc, the last containing boxes of sardines & a dozen palm leaf fans because "the weather is so hot." So our mess keep right side upon the question of delicacies. As for Bennett & me, we are old soldiers & enjoy the joke greatly.[29]

It rained to night and is very disagreeable for the clay mud is very slippery and we have to live in it. When it clears off, I presume it will become Autumn. Heretofore, we have had very hot days & very cold nights which produce a great deal of sickness. It has been my good fortune to keep in pretty good health.

In haste, Aff. yr brother, Edward W. Bacon

Before Petersburg, Va., Sept. 26, 1864

Dear Kate,

I received this morning your's of the 19th inst., which was preceded by Rebecca's of the Monday after.

It is pleasant to hear of Theodore's arrival and of Frank's settlement at home; indeed, most people would envy them their comfort and security and perhaps even envy could be excited sometimes on my part, though it is the truth that there never was a soldier who more completely put to the rout all evil-prophesies than your representative in the 29th Connecticut. In the first place, I am more contented with the service than with any work which I had tried before it; I am blessed with the most flattering success in the management of my large and unruly family of adopted children (I think Capt. Weld's inspection report has been duly trumpeted like its predecessors) and am constantly increasing the interest which I have in them, and not least, the exposure and broken, jagged character of Army life thus far have, instead of ruining, confirmed my health.

Our Comisy [commissary] scales figure me at 120 lbs. and since the attack the Surgeons made upon me across the James, I have lost no tour of duty.[30]

Edwin Carrington came to see me yesterday morning &, as the 29th Conn. & 45th U.S. are camped in the Division camp—beside each other—I have seen a good deal of him. His visit was quite a surprise and very welcome, he coming so recently from home.

Unwelcome rumors—which, much to our regret, are founded well—are afloat to the effect that Lt. Col. Ward of our's is to be made Colonel of the 31st U.S. This will be a severe blow. I had much rather have even my promotion delayed than advanced by such a sacrifice. The transfer needs only Gen'l Butler's action—having been referred to him. As a probable result, Torrance & Camp will be advanced, leaving me 2nd Capt.[31]

At this rate my patient hard labor and care will be, before long, rewarded.

Sept. 27th

Speaking—where I left off last night—of promotions, we received a lot of them to night, Capt. Bennett, 1st Lt. Bristol being among them. They are now at Hd.Qrs being mustered. Bristol got another of his boxes today, so that around our Camp fire we are quite enthusiastic.[32]

On Saturday night we were very unexpectedly relieved in the trenches by the 2nd [Army] Corps, and marched immediately to the rear—bivouacking in this place about 8 o'clock on Sunday morning. So for a time, we are out of the front *before Petersburg.*

Deserters came in on our Picket line the last two nights we were at the front, & were quite terrified when they found they had thrown themselves into the hands of the avenging negro. As one of them passed through our inner trench on his way to the rear, a somewhat facetious darkey ventured to suggest, rather to the Deserter's chagrin, "Well, Johnny! We're all brothers now, aint we!" which made the whole line roar.[33]

Of course, the great question with you as with us is What next? We were ordered to Camp "As if for three days" & to-morrow morning then time is up. We have been working under orders at once to balance accounts with the U.S. Government to provide each man with two pairs of serviceable shoes and to mend our clothing for a campaign.

Probably before you receive this we will know what our task is to be—if we are not already engaged in its execution. Rumors speak of Wilmington, of Dutch Gap & Fort Darling and of the line of the Rapidan. The most popular says W.[34]

At any rate, prepare yourself for Grant's great move which shall be the climax of Atlanta & the Shenandoah and break Lee's army as Sheridan had scattered Early's. In this final blow of the campaign, my whole corps will be engaged with others which at present it is my duty not to mention and where so many such troops go, some noise must be made. When my next chance to write home comes (which may be some time hence), you may expect some particulars.[35]

This morning I received an unexpected call from Chas. Tomlinson on whom Army life has had its usual beneficial effect, though he is still C. T.[36]

Beyond the fact that we are going to get a chance to put a name on our colors, there is no news whatever. We get our New York papers two days old and our mails all sorts of ways. I am kept pretty well supplied with reading matter—(though I'd like the chance to read a few professional works)—and can not complain.

I am glad to hear that that accomplished scoundrel Surg. Jewett has been tripped up. Were I in New Haven, I should take great pains to elicit upon the Court Martial a few facts relating to the period during which I served there. There is no sort of goodness in the creature.[37]

I write in haste for I must get some sleep.

Aff. Yr brother, Edw. W. Bacon

P.S. Tell Father that I have written to N. D. Sperry about my voting & that a word to S. from him may do much good. EWB

※

Right after this letter was written, the 29th and other Army of the James troops took part in hard fighting. They attacked fiercely defended trench lines before Richmond in what are known as the New Market Heights battles of September 28–30, 1864. Federals captured Fort Harrison, an important position, but failed elsewhere, including a heroic but suicidal assault on Fort Gilmer.[38]

Losses were heavy. Black troops, though they comprised just a quarter of the attack force, reported 1,450 of the 3,327 total Federal casualties. Sergeant Edward K. Wightman, 3rd New York, observed that "the slaughtered negroes lay piled in heaps." A 5th U.S. Colored Infantry officer wrote that they entered the fight with 520 men and returned with only 200, though the official report listed just 236 casualties for that regiment. Another 5th USCI officer said he returned with only ten men of his fifty. Writing from a hospital, Capt. James H, Wickes topped that when he reported, "Only five of my company were left."

Such severe losses were not unusual for black troops. Most were inexperienced, so suffered greater casualties. Further, in this fighting they had to attack across wide, open spaces, exposing them longer to enemy missiles. Then, given the opportunity, Confederates concentrated their fire on their former slaves. Lastly, Butler wanted to show the world that his black soldiers could fight, which, in his view, required spilling large quantities of their blood. He said that "I did deliberately expose my men to the loss of greater numbers than I really believed" the results were worth.[39]

Black mortality rates increased when Confederates emerged from their trenches between attacks and killed the wounded. After a final successful rush forward, a Federal officer found one of his sergeants with both legs shattered but still alive. He had dragged himself away and hidden when he saw the enemy making short work of any blacks still breathing.[40]

Bacon told his family very little, though allusions in the following letter suggest at least one missive is missing and in that he may have provided a fuller account. During the two-day operation, the 29th was in reserve or guarded artillery units. Still, they counted nineteen casualties—one man killed and eighteen wounded, including four officers. Among those four were Bennett and Bristol, Bacon's close friends. They probably sustained only light wounds, because they soon returned to duty.[41]

While an account by Bacon is lacking, other 29th soldiers provided graphic descriptions of the "horrors of war," as Private I. J. Hill put it. Corporal Joseph O. Cross wrote his wife, "the Balles did whistle aroun our heads dreadfully. . . . wee all expected that it was our last time." He explained, "wee Could look ahead & see the men fall one after another." First Lieutenant Henry G. Marshall fervently prayed for protection and, when spared, concluded that God had saved him for some worthy purpose. Sergeant Alexander H. Newton came upon a "fearful sight" where surgeons worked. He recalled, "It was indeed sickening. There were arms and legs piled up like hogs' feet in a butcher shop."[42]

Then at dawn on October 7, Confederates counterattacked near Darbytown and New Market Roads to recapture ground lost a week earlier. Federals repulsed that effort, and quiet again prevailed. Bacon related some of this, though topography and the infantryman's circumscribed world limited his knowledge.

Before Richmond, Oct. 8, 1864

Dear Kate,

Your letter of Oct. 1st reached me on the night of the 6th & was duly enjoyed.

Yesterday we had quite a chase. We were roused a little after midnight by rumors of an attack from the enemy which passed over us & struck the 1st Division & Kautz' cavalry holding the right. Our line was deemed strong enough so we were relieved in the trenches by the 7th U.S. & sent into the woods to wash in an uninviting brook which there oozes through the mud.

Rejoicing in the opportunity, our men had stripped & those possessing shirts had put them into soak when down came two or three gunboat shell (100 pdr. rifles) amongst us & a general cannonade opened along the line. Of course, washing day was over. Slapping our wet clothes onto our backs, we moved back to the trenches in our old position, then we closed to the right, following a movement in that direction & finally, as we held the right of our Division, were detached & ordered to report to Gen'l Terry to reinforce the 1st Div., reported suffering badly. This involved a disagreeable tour through the close woods for about a mile & a half. The Gen'l took his usual pains to come & shake hands with me & cautioned me to take care of myself (about as possible a deed as to revive the dead). Capt. T too became affable & I gave some of the Staff some water. After resting by the road at the Hosp'l of the 10th Conn. & meeting some of the 7th C.V., who addressed me as Capt. Bacon, though I didn't know them, we threw out a company as skirmishers to feel for the enemy but failed to find them. This was on the New Market road.[43]

I was glad to notice that about half of the numerous wounded which here passed were of the enemy & wounded in the legs. They charged upon two regts. of Spencer rifles & were badly cut up, leaving their dead & wounded. We were, however,[two illegible words] Kautz's Cavalry running pretty much all over Virginia & deserting two Batteries which fell into the hands of the enemy. Our skirmishers could find no enemy & leaving them as a picket line, we were ordered back to Spring Hill, a spur in the range known as New Market Heights, commanding a wide extent of country & a superb view. We then set pickets here & bivouacked for the night when, in true military style, we were ordered back to our own Division. Accordingly back we marched, reaching the rear of Chapin's [Chafin's and also Chaffin's] Bluff at about 10 at night where we bivouacked. I slept on the ground until about 12 o'clock when the cooks brought up my blankets, very opportunely too, for it began soon after to grow very cold & windy.[44]

At day break we moved up & stacked arms in rear of the 45th U.S. where we now are, waiting for orders.[45]

Oct. 9th We remained behind our stacks all day yesterday & at nearly sundown I was detailed with about 50 men for picket in our front. So I am writing now where I can look right into the embrasures of the redoubt against which our division so handsomely charged on the 29th ult. & see the muzzle of a big gun which I think has been lately mounted.

The weather which changed so suddenly night before last has continued cold & last night watching was made almost painful by the high wind in our faces & by our being (of course) without fires. Indeed it has taken us until noon to get the chill off of us. I presume that the first cold snap cuts us more than the uniform temperature of winter.[46]

The general scare in regard to an attack which has prevailed for a few days past has, I think, pretty much blown over &, if Kautz can ever get his cavalry collected again so as to protect our right, there will be no cause for any anxiety. Nor need you be at all worried about the probabilities of our making any assaults; both parties have tested the impracticality of so doing when works are defended, as all in this vicinity appear to be, by any large force.[47]

We hear rumors of fighting at Petersburg day before yesterday & when Meade has driven the enemy from that point & cut effectively his lines of communication there, Butler may speak again; or rather Grant, for I have observed that when ever the Army of the James makes a demonstration, the Lt Gen'l is invariably with it.[48]

I am in receipt of a letter from Rebecca of the 4th. I am glad to be able to get my shoes by Chas. Tiffany when he comes; I only wish he were coming to this command. I shall look earnestly for him each day until he comes. Day before yesterday I was quite near his Regt., but they were engaged & we were on the march.[49]

There is a dearth of news with us. We have not yet taken Richmond but will do so eventually, perhaps before winter. I think we have made progress enough to sustain the government's worth from yesterday. Should active campaign continue, as for a week past, I probably will not go home. Lt. Col. [Llewellyn F.] Haskell of the 7th U.S. called on me day before yesterday to tell me that he had been to Orange & had seen George [?] [illegible] proceed [?] to call there but overpressured [?] by business.[50]

So occasionally I hear directly from those who have seen my friends. Adjt. {J. Lewis] Spaulding returned yesterday from sick leave.

Believe me, with much love to all, your aff. brother,

Edw. W. Bacon

P. S. Have heard from Bristol who is doing well. We are rebrigaded: 2nd Brigade, 3rd Division, 10th Army Corps

%%

Probably Bacon did not know why his regiment and other 10th Corps units moved out at 4 A.M. on October 13. Ordered to go, they went. Beforehand, troop commanders had received instructions from Butler to drive Confederates from fortifications they busily constructed on a new line near Richmond.[51]

Colonel Rutherford B. Hayes, 23rd Ohio, who later became the nineteenth president, once asked, "When will our generals learn not to attack an equal adversary in a fortified position?" Some, including Butler, never learned. Repeatedly, Butler ordered inferior forces to attack superior numbers behind strong trench lines and moated forts. His infantrymen, who paid the price for his incompetence, early on had quickly learned the costly lesson.[52]

As Grant reported, Butler's drive was repulsed with "heavy loss to us." The official casualty count was 396 men killed, wounded, and missing or captured.[53]

%%

Before Richmond, Oct. 14th, 1864

D[ea]r. Father,

We have been again in action & have 4 killed, 15 wounded (including Adjt. [J. Lewis] Spaulding, just returned from Conn.) & 2 missing. Of these, I lost 1 killed—Corp. Geo. W. Burr & two wounded.

I am safe but quite exhausted. I will write more to morrow.

In haste, Aff yr son, Edward W. Bacon

Kate's of 8th rec'd

※

Without explanation, Bacon mentions seeing captured 7th U.S. Colored Infantry soldiers working on Confederate fortifications. Probably he did not know the full story.

Those forced laborers were the survivors of the suicidal attack against Fort Gilmer. Reluctantly recognizing their bravery, Confederates took them prisoner rather than shooting them. Then they put the men to work digging trenches, granting extra rations and fair treatment.

Butler turned the matter into a minor cause célèbre, eventually involving Lee and Grant. Styling himself the black man's friend, Butler demanded Confederates stop exposing the men to friendly fire in such labor. In retaliation, he put Confederate prisoners to exposed work on his Dutch Gap canal, a pet project to bypass enemy batteries guarding the James River.

Lee soon ordered the blacks withdrawn, Grant removed the Confederate prisoners and Butler could claim victory. But for two-thirds of those hapless men, Butler's intervention proved a death sentence. They went to prisoner of war camps to suffer near-starvation and bad treatment.[54]

A 7th officer reported, "Fifty-five of the seventy-nine men captured died in prison within six months, either from wounds or privations. . . ." Only twenty-three of them survived, and another one, reclaimed by his former owner, returned in excellent condition when the war ended.[55]

※

Before Richmond, Va., Oct. 20, 1864

Dear Father,

Enclosed I am glad to be able to send you a check on the Asst. Treasurer of the U.S. for $152 (one hundred and fifty two dollars) from which please pay yourself the amount which I owe you, settle any other bills which I have contracted and not yet paid and deposit what ever may remain to my a/c in the Townsend Savings Bank, acknowledging the receipt of the check & informing me as to the division of the money. After the execution of the above request, I believe I owe no man any thing. I have never received the itemized bill of Mason & Rockwell, for which I asked. Perhaps now it had better be left until election is over.

We were paid on the 18th quite unexpectedly and on our August muster, so that now I have something more than $200 due me. I begin to feel as if I am supporting myself at last.

On Sunday we formally received from Col. [Ulysses] Doubleday, our Brigade commander, a new U.S. Color, which until now we never have carried. Unexpectedly, we had as witnesses of the presentation Maj. Gen'l Terry & Brig. Gen'l Hawley. Gen'l T called me from the line that I might see Mr. Henry Blake & Mr. Byington of Norwalk, who seemed to be in the front on political business. Upon my mentioning my hopes for leave these gentlemen took memoranda which they said they would present to the Sec'y of War in person.[56]

We have at length lost Col. Ward, much to the regret of all, though it places us nearer promotion. The other day he received a commission as Col. of the 11th Conn. which he wisely declined. Yesterday he received—unexpectedly to him—an appointment as Col. of the 45th U.S.C.T., of which Capt. Weld comes out as Major. With Col. W. I fear we lose also whatever *regularity* of discipline we have.[57]

Monday I received a visit tom Lt. Col. [Daniel] Klein of the 6th [Connecticut] and Mr. [Chaplain Charles C.] Tiffany, though they remained only a few moments. I was very glad to see Mr. T, coming as he did so recently from home. He appears to take kindly to campaigning.

There is no news with us. Bennett & I have just got in to a log house with a good chimney & with our shelter for a roof, so that last night we were able to sleep with part of our clothes off, which, except for about a week at Petersburg, we have not done in Virginia. How long we shall enjoy this luxury no one can guess, though appearances indicate for the winter.

I am pretty well, though these cold snaps stiffen one a little, a difficulty which I expect our log house will remove. The chance to make out my returns of Ordnance & [illegible] property is keeping me very busy, though only for a few days.

The enemy are very quiet but very industriously strengthening their works on which we can see our late comrades of the 7th U.S. shovelling the dirt about. Deserters continue to come in & report with great confidence that after Lincoln's reelection their numbers will be greatly multiplied. Indeed, the only shots fired on our front are from the enemy after deserters and no doubt they kill a good many.[58]

We amuse our spare time by climbing trees here abouts &, with a field glass, looking at the men & women walking the streets of Richmond. I have not yet been up but Bennett reports three lines of strong works and but few troops visible in our front.

Give much love to all at home & tell Kate I have rec'd her letter of the 14th inst.

Affectionately, your son, Edward W. Bacon

※

Bacon sought home leave so he could vote in the crucial November presidential election. That race between George B. McClellan and Lincoln had the attention of both North and South.

Northern people had tired of endless war, causing Lincoln to doubt his and the nation's future. In late August, Lincoln wrote that "it seems exceedingly probable that this Administration will not be re-elected." And he thought that if he lost, so was the Union.[59]

The Democrat peace plank, labeling the war a failure and calling for an armistice, seemingly negated all the death and maiming. Its publication was one of two events that helped reverse the public mood. The other came when Atlanta fell on September 2. People saw the capture of a major city in the Southern heartland as a turning point, not just another battlefield victory.[60]

Still, Lincoln's reelection was no sure thing. Many citizens deplored throwing more good money after bad, fresh blood after the rivers already spilled. Most soldiers favored Lincoln, fearing that all would be in vain if McClellan won. Summing it up, a New York lieutenant wrote, "In my opinion the question is union or disunion." But some opposed Lincoln, often because they resented his perceived bias toward blacks. For example, explaining his support of McClellan, a 22nd Massachusetts soldier wrote, "He is none of your old nigger heads like Lincoln."[61]

Acutely aware of such discontent and the country's war weariness, Lincoln loyalists campaigned hard for his reelection. Local politicians went to the front, and ranking officers left the lines to politick for him at home.

※

Before Richmond, Va., Oct. 23d, 1864

Dear Father,

On the 20th I wrote you enclosing a draft on the Asst. Treasurer at New York and stating the disposition which I wished made of it. Herewith I enclose a bounty check for $10, which I would like to have cashed and held by you until I need it.

Yesterday I received a note from Mr. Byington at Washington stating that his application on my behalf was refused (as I thought it might be) & intimation given that the 10th A. C. would be at election in active service. Mr. B., however, filed the application. All the names from other parts of the Army which Mr. B. presented were favorably received. Mr. Stanton evidently thinks because we are so near Richmond we are in danger of active service.

To us, however, every thing looks like a stay where we are. We are now engaged in building a chain of formidable redoubts along our front & those on our right flank were some time since completed. Our line is therefore to be a very strong one, though not so nearly approached to the enemy as before Petersburg.[62]

However, whether I go home or stay here, I have some satisfaction, if I remain, in the fact that the War Department sets a higher value upon my services than upon those of Col. Wooster, who, it appears, is as good a soldier as to be allowed to stump Connecticut and draw pay for stumping Virginia. I do not often allow myself to criticize my superiors but the feeling here is universal that if our Colonel cannot stay by us or do military duty when away, we dont want him back here. With Col. Ward's good influences withdrawn, we will soon become a miserable rabble of volunteers under his senior.[63]

When election is over, I shall send home quite an order for clothes for my present stock is well nigh exhausted.

Mr. [Chaplain Charles C.] Tiffany has been to see me several times &, though I am badly off to offer hospitalities, I am very glad to see any representative of civilization. He brought me the shoes for which I wrote some time since and for a week past whenever my eyes fell upon them, it was to sigh at their smallness: marching had so spread my feet that I could not get the shoes on. This morning, however, by one great effort, rather than lose so expensive an article, I got them on & now feel more happy & some what refined. I am particularly in need of stockings & handkerchiefs. However, I will give the whole list in a few days.

Gen'l Grant did me the honor to look at me as he passed my humble door yesterday noon and I of course felt better all the remainder of the day.[64]

We have no news. Gen. Hawley for a time commands our division.

With love to all, Aff. yr son, Edward W. Bacon

New Haven, Tuesd. Oct. 25, 1864

My dear Son,

Your letter of Oct. 20, enclosing a paymaster's check for $152, was rec'd yesterday, [two pages of financial data omitted]

Since writing the two preceding, I have happened to see Mr. Sperry & have learned that the last opportunity for you being made a voter for the coming election will be on Thursday (day after tomorrow) so that we must look for your arrival before that time or not at all. Yet I will send you this letter, for if it is lost, the loss will be trifling & if you don't come, you will be glad to receive it.

We are thankful for your frequent letters, always so cheerful, thankful that you are able to endure many hardships, thankful to God whose providence has so remarkably protected you. May He make you ever faithful in all trials & under all responsibilities.

Your loving father, Leonard Bacon

///

In late October Grant ordered the Army of the Potomac to seize the South Side Railroad below Petersburg and told Butler to send troops toward Richmond to keep Confederates busy there. While the railroad foray failed; Butler successfully busied Confederates by hurling his men against their entrenchments. As Grant said, Butler "failed of further results" because he once again blindly attacked strong fortifications.[65]

In that feint, known as Fair Oaks or Darbytown Road of October 27–28, 1864, the 29th Connecticut paid a price for Butler's relentless incompetence, losing eighty men. In the white 2nd Division, a 117th New York sergeant decried such futile assaults. He wrote, "But old Beast Butler ordered it, and it must be done."[66]

Here, for the first time, Bacon referred to the massacre of black and white Federals on April 12–13, 1864, at Fort Pillow, Tenn. There famed Major General Nathan B. Forrest's cavalrymen had overrun the isolated fort and then shot scores of the surrendered or helpless defenders. Unlike other Confederate atrocities, the Fort Pillow affair received wide publicity. Black troops reacted angrily to the massacre, taking it as their battle cry and vowing to retaliate in kind.

Bacon reported the enemy before them feared his vengeance-bent men, knowing that they "remembered Fort Pillow." He related this episode without explanation, suggesting that both he and the homefolks knew that black troops and their white officers could realistically expect only short shrift should they fall into Southern hands. Later, a 102nd U.S. Colored Infantry officer declared, "This was well understood by all of the colored people and their officers during the rebellion." After the October clashes, Henry G. Marshall, one of Bacon's fellow officers, wrote home reassuringly, "Those 29th missing all turned up one way or another, so you need not worry as if they were captured, for they are all right."[67]

Perhaps Bacon had decided not to dwell on unpleasant possibilities. Others, however, could not suppress their forebodings. For example, 1st Lieutenant Alonzo Rembaugh, 37th U.S. Colored Infantry, had nightmares that Confederates had caught him and prepared "to string him up." Horrified, he protested that he preferred "lead to hemp."[68]

///

Before Richmond, Oct. 28th, 1864

Dear Father,

The 10th Corps has again seen battle and again has failed to enter the works of the enemy.

The 2nd Division did the charging and were repulsed with severe loss. The 29th were advanced as Skirmishers in front of the left (3rd) Division with orders to drive the enemy into their works & keep them there, which we did, though they had well built gopher holes and a force equal, if not superior, to ours. In front of me were the 7th Georgia who stood until we saw their faces & when the "niggers" were close to them & ran up yelling in true savage style, they were afraid of revenge for we "remembered Fort Pillow."[69]

All day long, from sunrise until this morning we held our line—on the front of woods—under a severe fire of musketry and of grape and canister.

Our loss is heavy—nearly 100—but from all quarters we receive the highest praise & 29th stocks is above from the 8th to-day. I lost 7 men; Bennett, 7. We are both well & ready to go in again. I prefer this to a furlough. Capt. Camp commanded the Battalion & very handsomely, too, bringing credit to himself and us. Bennett & I are both very tired but not unwell, though drenched by the rain last night.[70]

We are now back at our old house and going to rest, we hope.

Grant has been moving all along the line and I hope has had more success than we were visited with. The name of the fight is the Kell or Chell House which they ought to put on our colors.[71]

Will write further by next mails.

Let the Bennetts know of the affair as Tom [Capt. Thomas G. Bennett] has no time to write.

Aff yr son, Edward W. Bacon

My wounded are
Morrison [William E. L.]
Stephenson [John Stevenson]
Wm Johnson
Theop. [Theopolis W.] Pinion
Thornton [Richard]
Sergt. Amos C. Brewster[72]

EWB

Before Richmond, Va., October 31st, 1864

Dear Kate,

I am in receipt of your letter of the 20th, Rebecca's of the 22nd and Father's of the 26th, all since I have written to you, save a note on the night of the 29th inst. to tell you that the 29th had been in & safely out of action once more.

Your letter contained an account of the County demonstration, which must have been a fine affair and the speaking at which I wish I could have heard. But if you had been here at day light on the morning of the 27th when we moved from camp to our right, you could have seen, not "seven or ten thousand," in imperfect order, but two whole Corps of as fine troops as there are in the country—20,000 men at least—every one in blue & under arms—moving with the utmost regularity, considerably faster than any political gathering I ever saw, in a dozen columns & without any interference.[73]

It was the grandest display of men I ever saw.

Moving in our proper place, we passed over much the same ground as when starting on our reconnaissance of the 13th and, when somewhat to our right of the Darbytown road, halted with our division—under Hawley.[74]

The 29th was quickly deployed as skirmishers, covering the division front—some 3/4 of a mile. We advanced slowly through a dense woods and a bad swamp for nearly a mile when we encountered the videttes of the enemy who promptly fired upon us—which revealed our force to some extent to the enemy. But here the line was halted—a bad break occurring in our left wing, no where near my Company which is right center. This adjusted, the line moved forward in excellent order but in a few moments received a severe fire from the gopher holes of the picket—which were very numerous and well built. I answered with my front rank and on we ran at full speed—for the land was more clear just then and when the men understood the design, they showed their appreciation of it by the most horrible howls—very similar to those with which the enemy love to charge—the gopher holes still sent out bullets into our faces until their inmates saw that we were black & close on them when they dropped all and ran. In front of me one of them fell with two holes in him—one of them which was made by a mere boy of a recruit who behaved so well that I have reported his name to Hd.Qrs. He—poor fellow—later in the day lost one of his legs by a grape shot.

We captured here several prisoners—from a South Carolina regiment—who were very badly scared lest the darkies should kill them. Indeed all the rebels who fell into my hands remind me strongly of the fugitives who used to call at our house for aid—except that now the master begs favors from the slave and gets them too. These on the 27th made haste onto their very knees and really craved for mercy and for life![75]

But we did not wait to soliloquize over any thing we met. Orders came to go on until we found works and the prevailing idea with my part of the line was to get there as soon as possible. A short half mile further through the meanest of under growth—slipping on the clayey ground wet by the last night's rain, dodging from the shrapnel which began to reach us now & from the branches which they were cutting from the bigger pines, wondering what we would find and how soon we would find it, on we went until at the edge of the woods we looked out upon a narrow strip of slashing, beyond it a cornfield, with a good many stumps in it, and a chain of redoubts connected in the usual manner by strong breast works. Into these the pickets which we had driven before us went pell-mell and as they rose to cross the works we took delight in hitting them. It was this display of strength which caused me to say in my last that the enemy were in more force than we.

We had no orders to go farther than up to the works of the enemy but as far as we got we had to stay. Of course the moment they saw us in front of the woods we received plenty of grape and canister—for which they had an excellent range.[76]

When the Company were posted to the best advantage—so that the gunners could not fire in security, Bennett and I chose an advantageous tree behind which were our headquarters for the day. We hoped so to annoy the battery men that they would let us rest in peace and for a while we succeeded—but after that the guns would suddenly disappear and in a moment as mysteriously come back and discharge their loads. This sharp practice of dragging the pieces down from the platforms to load them could not be stopped.[77]

This is about the whole story. The twenty hours we remained on our ground, even when the shells of the enemy caused the brigade in support to retire nearly a mile, and when toward dark the 2nd Division skirmishers saw fit to fall back, our line did not budge. At dusk the firing pretty much ceased and though on our part it was renewed with considerable life and continued through the night, the enemy did nothing but put out their fires. During the day, however, our position was disagreeable, for the line was somewhat thus,

so we could find but little shelter but by lying quite flat.

About dark we experienced much annoyance by the muskets becoming quite foul so that the bullets could not be rammed home; the men, however, coolly sat down, dismounted their pieces and cleaned them, after which they resumed firing. Some of my men—indeed, most of them—fired 200 rounds each.[78]

Day break of the 28th saw us still in line keeping up the fire. All night long a dismal rain had soaked us, but luckily not a very cold rain—for of course we had no fire. The darkness had been almost Egyptian so that it was difficult in visiting the line to find the men, but my orderlies got "fox-fire" and strewed it through the woods to keep us from wandering when we moved from place to place. There was nothing unsoldierly then in our desire to be relieved and in our delight when the 7th U.S. with part of the 9th [Colored Infantry regiments] advanced by the earliest light and we retired.[79]

Forming in the rear of our brigade, we remained at rest until afternoon when, with the whole Army, we drew back to camp. The retreat, though good enough—so far as it was undisturbed—was not by any measure so beautiful in its execution as that of the 13th.

The 29th was commanded by Captain Camp "skillfully and bravely," as our Brigadier's report says, Maj. Torrance being sick, Lt. Col. Ward having gone to the 41st U.S. and Col. Wooster any where but in the field. Gen'l Hawley was delighted with us because we were from Connecticut.[80]

Gen'l Birney—who returned on the 28th from his brother's funeral—has intimated that this demonstration—a total failure, I presume, because they won't tell us what happened—closed the campaign for the 10th Corps. At any rate, applications for "leaves" go forward now approved. The miserable dead beats who populate the hospitals at the rear are enjoying a vacation from their usual avocation and have gone home on 20 days leave, leaving all the work of the campaign to those to whom should come the honors of the privileged.[81]

To cap the climax, in the 8th a promotion has just come out for gallantry on the 27th Sept. while the officer at that date & long after was loafing at Old Point Comfort. If you see my name as among the "Heroes of the War" in any future edition of the *Tribune*, you may draw a deep sigh.[82]

Aff. your brother, Edward W. Bacon

P.S. I send by this mail to Mason & Rockwell for a new jacket and pantaloons to be done as soon as possible. I have told them to pack the articles in a large box & send them to 247 Church St. Will you please put into the package 4 pairs of blue woolen stockings—ribbed—for those I now have are nearly gone—my dress coat and the pair of white gloves which are in one of the pockets of my overcoat made of merino. I am also sadly in need of handkerchiefs & would like to get my shaving apparatus; razor-strop & brush. Also please buy for me an 1865 Pocket Diary & portmonnae bound to-gether. I have one now which opens somewhat like this [tiny sketch, showing folding writing portfolio] which I bought of Judd & Clark—size about an inch shorter than the envelop to this and one page to each day with a cash a/c at the end. Send me also some black sewing silk and an emery ball so that I can take the rust off my stock of needles which I have carried for nearly four years. Please in your next letter send me a supply of postage [stamps]—say $2 worth; & take pay from my last remittance.[83]

I am also greatly in need of towels; please send some good ones—like the last. Also a good tooth brush and some good dentifrice. I wish too you would buy me a plated dessert fork at Bromleys; have my name and rgt engraved on it, and send it with a stout knife of good steel about the same length as the fork. If not too expensive, add a dessert spoon. Then, if the box is not crammed, add a sponge and a piece of chamois skin. In case four or five days from the receipt of this do not bring the box with the clothes, please send a reminder to the tailor for I am anxious to get [last portion is missing].

From a tree near my
quarters in the action
of Oct. 27th, 1864
EWB

%

A letter to sister Rebecca is missing here. Apparently Bacon described his "brilliant prospects," a supposed change for the better.

But he does not explain the change in subsequent letters. Bacon and Captain Martin S. James, 3rd Rhode Island Heavy Artillery, temporarily assumed some special duty and perhaps thought they might consequently win quick promotion.

%

Signal Hill, Va., Nov. 7, 1864[84]

Dear Kate,

I wrote yesterday to Rebecca telling of my recent change, my pleasant situation and my brilliant prospects.

I want to add one or two items to my last long epistle to you & this is the reason why I snatch time to write so soon again.

Much to my grief in the suddenness of this last move those handsome slippers which you so thoughtfully worked for me and which have afforded me so much comfort during all the nine months since I left home were lost. Will you please get me a new pair at Prim's: I shall have to come down to leather again.

At the store of "Tomes, Melvain & Son," 16 Maiden Lane [,] New York [,] can be purchased shoulder straps like those upon my dress coat: embroidered upon sky blue *cloth* (not velvet), regulation size but a little raised (the embroidery) and of French manufacture, an imported strap. In February last the price pr. pair was, I think, $4.75 and now may be $6. Whatever it may be, please send it by some one who will *get the right* article and purchase two pairs of Captain's straps, one of which please have sewed upon my new jacket & put the other in the box. I want it for Capt. Bennett.[85]

I am to-day "Division Officer of the Day" and to night expect to be pretty wide awake all night for it is as certain as any thing military that our position will be attacked to morrow morning & I am the party responsible for a prompt alarm and vigorous resistance on the part of our pickets.[86]

Capt. James has been informed that this "is the key of our flank" and that it must not be given up. The Capt. is, so far as I have been able to observe him, one of the best officers, regular or volunteer, it has ever been my good fortune to meet and if we don't get our leaves to-morrow, it will be because the enemy don't attack us.

The Capt. desires to have me present his very best respects to all whom he met at home & speaks of his visit to New Haven with great jest. He says Gen'l Terry is uniformly attentive and kind and that it is due to him that the 3d R. I. is at this post.

Whether the James & Bacon copartnership military won't be too much is yet to be seen.

James seems unable to satisfy himself in attentions to my comfort & to-day—(a horrible one—very wet)—furnished me with a horse so I can make my rounds very expeditiously.[87]

Believe me, Very aff. yr. brother,

Edward W. Bacon

P. S. Hurry up the tailors—for being commandant of this Infantry demands new clothes.

EWB

New Market Heights, Va., Nov. 9th, 1864

Dear Father,

Enclosed is an informal note drawn by two colored men employed on the Steamer *City of Boston* plying between Norwich and New York. Henry Morris is a recruit in my company, received about a week ago. His story—a very common one—is that he did not know either Treadwell or Jordan until he met them at the recruiting station; that they (T & J) offered to keep $40 of Morris' bounty & to meet him & go with him to deposit it in some bank. He says that he never found time to call on them and that they still hold his money while he has this note (enclosed). These men, who may be honest (probably not, Morris knows nothing of them) can be seen whenever the *City of Boston* is in Norwich. It was therefore in my mind to address this note to Rev. Mr. Gulliver and ask him to aid a very worthy young man, who will—in good hands—make a very serviceable soldier, to get this amount—enough with what he now has to give him a comfortable footing in life.[88]

But I did not feel well enough acquainted with Mr. G to address him except through you. If you know any body patriotic enough to attend to the matter, which may be troublesome but will be a great obligation to me & still greater to this new member of my family please put the note in his hands.[89]

If the money can be obtained, please send it down here to Morris in my care; it would be well to send a little of it a time, lest the foolish fellow should lose it when it was on its way to him.

We are waiting in the greatest anxiety some tidings of the election and if Lincoln keeps his chair. I shall not regret that I lost my vote and visit home but will "fight it out on this line" without a leave.[90]

There is this morning very heavy artillery firing toward Petersburg, but strange to say & contrary to all military symptoms, we are left in perfect quiet.[91]

I shall send you in my next a plan of Camp "Ward"—as I call my post, &, if my opportunities had been improved, would try a sketch of this very little station with which I am quite delighted & which I propose to make a model for the Corps.

I am quite well.

With love to all at home, Aff. Yr.
Son, Edward W. Bacon

Signal Hill, Va., Nov. 25th, 1864

Dear Kate,

Your letter of the 21st inst. reached me yesterday and assured me of the departure of my box, which is somewhere on its way, I presume—at any rate, it has not yet reached this. I trust its fate may not be that of many boxes for Soldiers—for ever on their way.

Enclosed you will find a $10 bounty check which I wish Father would be so good as to collect and return.

Please ask Father, too, to send me $75 in small sums in a number of letters. My impression is that I have more than that amt. unappropriated.

Col. Wooster is in temporary command of the Brigade—Maj. Torrance [leads] the 9th U.S., so that for these few days I am in command of the Regiment.[92]

We rec'd this pm the promotions of Maj. Torrance to Lt. Col. and Capt. Camp to Major—eminently satisfactory. To day, too, (the day after the fair) came a confused mass of fowls, cakes, pies and elderly apples, valuable only because they showed how anxious people are to do something for the army. But why will people do such sort of kind deeds? If instead of $5 for a turkey, the half of that sum spent for good woolen stockings, mittens or under clothes, how much more good would have been done, how much money saved to each man's clothing a/c. But I must end this scrawl and turn in for I have had a hard day's work and am very tired.[93]

Love to all, Aff. yr brother, Edward W. Bacon

Note that in his next letter Bacon's enthusiasm for battle has diminished, a retreat from his earlier gung ho attitudes. When they next storm enemy fortifications, he would just as soon remain in his comfortable quarters.[94]

Signal Hill, New Market Heights,
Va., Nov. 27th, 1864

Dear Kate,

I wrote you on the evening of the 25th in rather a despondent frame of mind as to where in America my needed box might be.

This afternoon, however, my anxiety was relieved by its arrival in good order. Mason and Rockwell have done their prettiest and the fit and the material of their suit very much pleased me. Your black silk, which reached me a few days ago, added to the contents of the box, completes the heavy requisition which I made upon you and the family in general except that I have only one pair of shoulder straps when I asked for two because Capt. Bennett wanted some and did not know so well as I did the place or kind of them, and I had proposed to make him a present of them. Perhaps you will be able to send me another pair by mail.

Mason and Rockwell's a/c was enclosed in the box but none of the other bills. I shall have to make you so far a business agent as to ask you to obtain and send to me all accounts against me which I have not settled.

In the same mail with your last letter came one from Leonard enclosing an application from Rev. P. H. Hollister for the Chaplaincy of this regiment. I have referred both communications to Colonel Wooster and, if agreeable to him, we will, I think, elect Mr. Hollister without delay. We need a chaplain very much.[95]

I am beginning now school for non commissioned officers and promising privates in tactics (according to orders) and, of my own accord, in reading and writing. This is Chaplain's work and the necessary dignity and reserve of a Captain's position should forbid it in him. However, the exigency is so great that I could not refrain from the task, though I have plenty to do without it.

Capt. James and I were somewhat anticipating famous visitants to day, for His Excellency the President, Lieut Gen'l Grant and Maj. Gen'ls Hancock and Butler were last night all at Deep Bottom and a ride along the lines might probably be a part of their programme. So James had a mounted inspection of his most excellent battery and I put my little battalion through such a scorching ordeal of inspection as none but one who has stood on the Quarter Deck understands giving. But the distinguished visitors did not come, unless they came disguised in black faces.

However, had you been here I would have shown you some superb muskets, some handsome soldiers and the most comfortable and sensible quarters in the Army of the James, I believe. You could have seen, too, some very dirty men. In my detachment from several companies, which I name Company "Q," I have three pleasant creatures, who have every morning to report to the Sergeant of the Guard who takes them down to the brook and has a man scrub them thoroughly with sand, after which they are brought up for inspection. When I get through with them they will go back to their Companies tolerable soldiers but won't relish the time when the[y] come again to my detachment.

Grant's presence means action. If he be really here, you will have news from the Army of the James in less than two weeks. When, on about the 24th of October, I wrote that Grant had passed my door, I had to write on the 28th that we were just out of action, having lost heavily. This rule has been true in more cases.[96]

But should the army move (and there is but one direction for an offensive movement) it is to be trusted that we will be allowed to remain in the fortifications, as probably, indeed, will be the case.

Do not infer that I want to back out of a fight, but having just established ourselves comfortably, and having seen a good allowance of "glorious contest on the gory field," it would be too bad to turn us out and send us some where in the cold and mud to hew and build again, which would be the third time.[97]

Please write to me soon and send me now and then a New Haven paper. You seem to be too busy at school. Perhaps it is asking too much to expect such a Niagara of correspondence as mine seems to be answered at all.

But it is after taps—Monday brings me a long list of unaccomplished duties and I am going to open my picture books to guess how it would seem to be in civilized parts and then to turn in.[98]

> With much love to all at home, Your
> affectionate brother, Edward W. Bacon

%

If Bacon correctly dated his next letter, then he knew of a major change in army organization two days before its official announcement. On December 3, 1864, the War Department dissolved the 10th and 18th Army Corps and placed their white troops in a new 24th Corps. Black soldiers in thirty-two infantry regiments and a cavalry regiment formed the three divisions of a new 25th Corps. It was the first and the only black army corps in American military history.[99]

%

> Signal Hill, Va., Dec. 1st, 1864

Dear Kate,

The 10th Army Corps and the 18th Army Corps are dead.

The story about a colored corps, of such long standing that it grew old and untrustworthy, this morning proved unexpectedly true. The 3d Division of the Ninth Corps, the 3d Division of the Tenth Corps and the 3d Division of the 18th Corps constitute now the 25th Army Corps under command of Maj Gen'l Weitzel while the white portions of the 10th and 18th Corps form the 24th Corps under Maj. Gen'l Ord, who yesterday returned to duty, having been wounded Sept. 29th.[100]

I send this information so that you may know how we are situated.

Our new Division is not named yet, so that a letter addressed 29th Ct. 25th A.C., Army of the James, would be likely to reach me quite as soon as if sent by the old direction.

Within a day or two the 29th will have to turn over their quarters to some white relief and go to the vicinity of Dutch Gap and Fort Harrison.

When located I will write again.

Aff. yr. brother, Edward W. Bacon

※

Bacon bitterly derided the care provided a sergeant slightly wounded in the ankle. He charged that his soldier was "professionally murdered at the Colored Hospital" by a surgeon who wanted some experience at amputating legs.

However, in those days of rudimentary medical knowledge, such slight wounds often resulted in death for the patient, whether black sergeant or white general. Infection, including gangrene, set in and the patient slowly succumbed.[101]

While care and expertise varied considerably in the many army hospitals, black and white soldiers received about the same level of care, even if dismal by today's standards. Still, prejudice could affect treatment in the racially segregated army. Some surgeons spitefully maltreated black patients and occasionally experimented on the living or the dead.[102]

※

Chapin's Farm, Henrico Co.,
Va., December 18th, 1864

Dear Kate,

Your letter mailed Dec. 10th and Rebecca's of the 13th reached me last week. I am glad that every body and every thing at home is flourishing so nicely. It makes winter in the field more comfortable to know that at home all is well.

But I am very sorry to hear of the death of Dr. Terry of Chicago. Although I did not know him very well, I always liked his pleasant manner & his decease, too, must have a bad effect upon Mother's illness.

Mr. Henry Whitney called upon me the day I left Signal Hill and gave me the blanket you sent, for which I am much obliged. During the cold snap some days since, it afforded a great deal of comfort.[103]

I hear no more from the note which I sent home for Private Morris. He will begin to be anxious about it.

We are here all much as usual. After considerable perseverance over many obstacles, I am at last in comfortable quarters 15 feet by 9 and all by myself with a huge fire-place on one side. Finishing up my company accounts and arranging every thing in good shape for transfer, in addition to the ordinary routine of duty, keeps my time pretty well occupied while my force of sergeants is reduced to only two & my corporals to four; one of the former, the best in his control of men, who left me on the 13th of October slightly wounded in the ankle, having been professionally murdered at the Colored Hospital at Fortress

Monroe by some silly boy who wanted to cut off a leg. Mr. Brown, too, my valuable 1st Lieutenant, who has been since that same day Acting Adjutant, is now detached on Brigade Staff, so that, except by a temporary assignment, I see no prospect of relief.[104]

To-day we have been jubilant over the news from Gens. Thomas and Sherman. Next, in all probability, we shall hear of the occupation of the centre of communications at Branchville when, I doubt not, it will be the business of the Armies of the Potomac and James to accomplish something which shall rival the feats in Tennessee and Georgia.[105]

Yesterday Mr. Tiffany came to see me again, mounted on Mr. Eustis's horse which made our swamp look in his immediate neighborhood like some New Haven road.

The Rev. Mr. DeGoss Love also called here and took dinner on Friday. I was at first glad to see him, not knowing until I had experienced his obnoxious disregard of taste and discretion, what sort of a ranter he was. It is hoped he will not again be able to find my camp. Not that I object to ministerial visitations, but the ideas one received in the College part of New Haven are perhaps squeamish.[106]

You say nothing about my proposition that when Father is at Washington, he should take a week for a trip to the army. All hands hereabouts would be but delighted to see him and I've no doubt Gen'l Terry would detail an ambulance for his own use as long as he might remain.[107]

But there is no use writing so long a letter when we have no news and when we have to turn out each morning at four o'clock to remain in line of battle until day light.

Affectionately yr. Brother, Edward W. Bacon

(3) PROMOTION AND VICTORY

AS 1864 ENDED, MANY BELIEVED THAT THE SOUTH HAD RUN OUT of time, space, men, and materiel. Yet Confederates stubbornly continued the struggle, and most Federals expected that more hard fighting lay ahead.

Early in 1865 Colonel Robert W. Barnard, 101st U.S. Colored Infantry, wrote home, "I do not see how our Southern brethren are to stand another season, it seems to me their game is nearly up. How they hold on is a mystery, for endurance they certainly deserve great credit. I wish they had less of it." Realists among the shivering and hungry "brethren" in the trenches also wondered how they could survive another season. One of them, 1st Sergeant James E. Whitehorne, 12th Virginia Infantry, wrote that "I have fought, suffered, bled and almost died for nearly four years, but I fear the end is very near."

But William R. J. Pegram, one of Lee's colonels, insisted that their prospects were "growing brighter each day." Much more realistic was Lieutenant Colonel Walter S. Poor, 14th U.S. Colored Heavy Artillery, who said that "it is a question of resources between North and South and we can endure the longest."[1]

On the fighting fronts, Sherman had captured Savannah and prepared to push through the Carolinas; desertions thinned Lee's ranks during the winter stalemate on the Petersburg-Richmond lines; Major General Philip H. Sheridan had routed Confederate forces in the vital Shenandoah Valley; and Butler had bungled again in an attack upon Fort Fisher, N.C., a debacle that enabled Grant and Lincoln to get rid of him.[2]

Motivated by glowing ambition, Bacon transferred from the 29th Connecticut to the 117th U.S. Colored Infantry. With this move he abandoned friends and connections he enjoyed in the 29th. But by shifting to the 117th, Bacon acquired a major's commission while still just twenty-years-old. He also joined a United States regiment which he had always considered more desirable than a state regiment. Planning to make the army his career, he mistakenly believed wartime United States Colored Troops would become part of the postwar Regular Army.[3]

Exactly how the transfer and the promotion came about is uncertain. Probably Bacon heard about the vacancy in the newly organized 117th and applied for it, although not with his father's approval. While the number of black regiments steadily increased, it was always difficult to fill officer ranks. Many whites still regarded service with blacks as demeaning and believed that such service tarred them as second-class soldiers.

By that time recruiters also had trouble rounding up volunteers for new black regiments, and the 117th was no exception. They had begun enrolling Kentucky's slaves in July of 1864, but it took until the end of September to enlist enough men. Lacking volunteers, Federal press gangs scoured the countryside and shanghaied slaves from yard, road, and field. This practice became so widespread in Kentucky, a slave state with men in both armies, that a complaint about one overzealous recruiting officer reached Lincoln. The president telegraphed that he had heard "that you are forcing negroes into the military service, and even torturing them" and that such tactics must cease.[4]

After Bacon transferred, his father reprovingly declared that the switch to the 117th "puts you into a regiment made up of men less intelligent & less capable than those you have heretofore commanded." That common belief conflated ignorance and intellectual ability. Southern states prohibited schooling for slaves because whites believed learning would undermine the institution itself.

Northerners also thought that slavery had pulverized the thralls' spirit. A Federal naval officer wrote that "I supposed that every thing in the shape of spirit & self respect had been crushed out of them generations back." Virginia-born-

and-bred Major General George H. Thomas, Federal Army of the Cumberland commander, argued that "in the sudden transition from slavery to freedom it is perhaps better for the negro to become a soldier, and be gradually taught to depend on himself." Still, most regiments formed almost exclusively of ex-slaves performed just as well as those of free northern blacks.[5]

Bacon officially joined the 117th U.S. Colored Infantry on January 5, 1865, at Chaffin's Farm near Richmond.[6]

※

Camp 117th U.S.C.T., Henrico County,
Va., January 6th, 1864 [1865]

Dear Father,

At last I have torn myself away from the 29th Connecticut and am ensconced in an organization of United States Troops. Had the 29th borne the title, (as they should) there would have been, perhaps, some hesitation on my part about making this change, but the gold leaves & the chance (maybe the only chance too) of a permanency were inducements not to be sneered at.

So in future please address my letters to "Major E. W. B., 2nd Brig., 1st Div., 25th A. C."

As for my regiment, I must confess its inferiority to the 29th. It never formed a line of battle until its arrival at City Point in November last. It was enlisted in Kentucky and had only three or four men who can read and write, so that the administration of the command is much more difficult than where I have been before.[7]

Col. Louis [Lewis] G. Brown and I immediately became co-workers. Col. B. Is a young man—not more than 25 or 26 years of age, exceedingly prepossessing in appearance and manners and an excellent officer thoroughly posted in his duties. But he is almost alone in the Regiment. The Lt. Col. I have not seen; he is absent on recruiting service but he is an old man & Col. Brown does not speak favorably of him. There are a very few good, or passable, line officers, but the majority of them should be disposed of & the Col. says will be, though it will take time to do it. The arms are poor Enfields, but we are making an effort to change them for Springfields.[8]

If you know of any young men of suitable age and qualifications desirous of 2nd Lt. commissions, Col. B. will recommend their appointment upon receipt of their names. But a military turn of mind is indispensable, for not every man can make a good soldier, much less a good officer. We also need a Chaplain of any body almost—with education, common sense and good manners—who is also fit to be a minister can have the place in the same manner as 2nd Lts.

Rebecca's letter of the 31st ult. came to hand yesterday. I wish you had taken occasion to send me some money by Lt. {William H.} Bevin, of which I am sadly in need and have no chance of payment. Is it possible for you to draw upon my deposit in Townsend Bank? If so, I better have $250, which will leave me only a little remaining then. The conduct of the government in allowing its officers to become penniless & beggars cannot be too strongly condemned. Before I can think of any chance of being paid again, at least seven months wages will be due me! In these seven months I shall have completely changed uniforms & have purchased a horse—($225 for the latter & equipments)—and been obliged to borrow & beg for the money to pay.[9]

Whatever funds you send to me, you had better send per Adams Express, as I dare not trust our mails any longer.

So soon as I get my property fairly turned over and my papers squared up, I will be quite at leisure—a new notion for me, but a Major's business chiefly.

But I must end this lengthy epistle and seek some sort of rest before turning out in the morning.

I hope that you will really think seriously of visiting the "Army of the James" when you start for Washington. My promotion lessens the chance of my applying for a "leave" and you would find a hearty reception in many comfortable quarters on the front (not a dangerous one) while perhaps I might find that a visit from you would have a good effect on the Beast, so far as I am concerned.[10]

With much love to all at home,
Aff. yr. son, Edw. W. Bacon

New Haven, Jan. 14, 1865

My dear Son,

I am almost doubtful whether I ought to congratulate you on your promotion, inasmuch as it will separate you from the pleasant circle of friends & schoolmates with whom you have been associated in the 29th & as it puts you into a regiment made up of men less intelligent & less capable than those you have heretofore commanded. But I am sure that you will do with conscientious diligence all that can be done by a major to make the regiment as efficient as it is capable of becoming & to make the military apprenticeship of those emancipated Slaves useful to them as their preparation for the responsibilities of freedom.

[The rest of this letter concerns financial and bookkeeping matters, though the senior Bacon said he would try find a chaplain and lieutenants for the 117th]

Your affectionate father, Leonard Bacon

Camp 117th U.S.C.T., January 19, 1865

Dear Father,

Your letter of the 14th reached me yesterday with the draft for $100 enclosed.

I have only time to acknowledge its receipt and thank you for it. Just now I am quite busy winding up my Ordnance accounts & clearing myself of what little responsibility yet remains for property in possession of my old Company.

I called to-day upon Chaplain [Henry C.] Trumbull, 10th Conn., partly to express my gratitude for the excellent points he makes in his letters to New Haven papers. He told me that Leonard's engagement at Stamford had not been renewed and that he (Leonard) was expecting to go to some church in Brooklyn, N.Y. I hope that Leonard will not worry to remove from Stamford. It has always seemed to me just the place for him.[11]

I was in hopes to find my old class mate at Russell's (Capt. White of the 16th Conn) established at the Hd. Qrs. of the 10th and learned with regret that his appointment had been revoked.[12]

Give much love to all at home and believe me

Your aff son, Edward W. Bacon

%

Little occurred on the Petersburg-Richmond front in early 1865. Grant reported that "the winter had been one of heavy rains, and the roads were impassable." Moreover, bitter cold, mud, ice, and snow also deterred movement. So he had to wait for better weather before ordering offensive operations.

But summer or winter, night or day, death stalked the trenches. Daily men fell on both sides to mortar shells, snipers, and artillery fire. When a newly arrived surgeon visited Federal lines, a black soldier warned his party that they "better keep their eyes skeened for shells." A Michigan soldier complained that he "never knew when he went to sleep at night whether he would wake up dead in the morning." Snipers were more worrisome to a Confederate who wrote home in March, "We cannot hold our heads over the breastworks. We [have] steady firing on the line day and night."[13]

Federals endured the danger while well clothed and fed; many Confederates lived in dank underground bunkers, few had winter clothing, and almost none had enough to eat. They froze and starved in their wet, muddy trenches, where some caught and ate rats to ease their hunger. In sometimes risky work, they scavenged for lead and iron from Federal missiles to redeem for four cents a pound at ordnance depots. A 60th Alabama soldier said they did it to obtain "mess money." To escape such dire straits and a death or maiming they increasingly saw as pointless, ever more Confederates deserted, fully aware that a firing squad often awaited them if caught.[14]

Though Bacon said that early 1865 was a "very lazy" interlude for him, clearly it was a perilous time. However, Bacon and that precarious existence were strangers for part of that period. He enjoyed a four-week furlough, from January 23 to February 19, 1865. Apparently it was a sudden development, because he wrote home the day his leave began and never mentioned it.[15]

That leave explains the long gap in his letters between January 23 and March 9, 1865.

※

117th U.S.C. Troops, January 23d 1865

Dear Kate,

It is some time since I have written home, except a short business note to father acknowledging the receipt of $100 from him. Day before yesterday Rebecca's letter concerning Mr. Gulliver's success in obtaining some money for one of my men reached me. I have seen the man, who desired that for the present father will retain what ever amounts may be turned over to him. After some anticipated events have transpired, the youth will be better able to decide as to the final resting place of his bounty. Like enough that will be the Sutler's shop.

In a recent letter Rebecca said that Alfred wanted some Confederate Postage Stamps. Say to him that I have been on the look-out for some, but as yet have been unsuccessful. When we take Richmond I will be able to send any quantity of such matters North.[16]

I presume New Haven is in an uproar over Gen'l Terry. You will remember in commenting on the superb maneuvering upon the reconnaissance of Oct. 13th, I said that if Terry could always move troops in such splendid style, he was a general. I have had no occasion to change my opinion, an impartial one.

I was, however, some what startled to read that the Gen'l was rather of an "angel visitant" and cousin of a "sweet poetess." If my relations must suffer such personalities when I distinguish myself, I might almost desire that day postponed.[17]

Lt. Col. Torrance of the 29th started on 20 days leave yesterday morning. If Rebecca engaged a servant, I will arrange with Torrance to bring him on when he returns.[18]

Capt. Griswold and Lt. Marshall are now at home also. Bennett proposes an effort to reach home upon the return to duty of Griswold.[19]

I am having a very lazy sort of time just now. My little mare carried me every fair day over a good many miles, so that I am able to see some of my New Haven acquaintances camped far off. I called the other day upon Chaplain [Henry S.] DeForest of the 11th Conn, who was rejoiced to see me as he always is to see every-body. I also made the acquaintance of Col. [John E.] Ward of the 8th Conn, a very handsome and officer-like gentleman. I was very much taken with him.

The 29th are daily expecting the arrival out of Chaplain Hollister.[20]

I believe I have not acknowledged the package of Mr. Bevin. I thank the senders of it very much for it made one seem quite at home to see so many familiar views.

I have been some what worried as to how in the world the stiletto of a pencil works, but have at last succeeded in a way of my own, probably incorrect, in using it.[21]

I ought perhaps to write more but to-morrow I am "Division Officer of the Day" and besides, before turning in, must write other letters.

Love to all and believe me, Your aff. brother,

Edward W. Bacon

117th U.S.C.T., March 9, 1865

Dear Kate,

Your letter of the 3d instant reached me yesterday morning. I am very glad you did not accept Mr. Pease's offer since my bad luck with his package; I don't like to have "coals of fire" on me.[22]

My regular Sunday epistle home was interrupted this week by being obliged to congratulate both Stamford and [illegible] and by having an unusual pressure of business, for, though a Majority is considered as a sinecure, it is easy to find quite enough to do which, if the Major don't do, will not be accomplished.[23]

Col. Brown has applied for leave of absence for thirty days which will give me command of the regiment for that length of time. I am able to note considerable improvement in the command but much remains to be done before it reaches even tolerable proficiency. We are now below the minimum, 800, and can muster no new officers at present. Some arrangement of a so great a difficulty to progress will doubtless soon be made.

The Express bundle came duly to hand and in good order.

We have no news here—save what you have at home, too. Every thing looks very stupid & unlike a move—yet in the spring of the year a move may be ordered in a half an hour from the most confident prediction to the contrary.

The enemy were cheering last night about some thing, their first opportunity since they stole our beeves from below City Point last September.

We are well satisfied with Sheridan.[24]

Believe me, as ever, Your aff
brother, Edward W. Bacon

P.S. I enclose the order for our Corps badge. Perhaps you can get up some "square" which shall be prettier than a bit of red flannel. My color is red—1st Div.[25]

EWB

※

When Bacon mentioned "Dutch Gap" in his next letter, he referred to Butler's canal that cut across the bottom of a long hairpin loop in the James River near Richmond. That bypass would avoid Confederate batteries that blocked river traffic. But the canal was not operational until after the war and then Southerners thanked Butler for shaving almost five miles off the water route to Richmond.[26]

In a cynical mood, Bacon predicted "lots of promotions" would occur if they attacked the strong fortifications at the river loop. He believed many would fall, creating promotional opportunities for survivors.

%

117th U.S. Col'd Troops, March 16th, 1865

Dear Kate,

Your letter of Sunday last reached me this morning & I consider it wise on the whole to write a few words before I turn in, rather than wait for another chance, for never was I busier than now. The near prospect of a most vigorous campaign makes doubly valuable the little time yet left for study & for drill and to fully fit this regiment for successful and economical field service is a task worthy of a Hercules and a great devotion, yet this task precisely is what Col. Brown & I (assisted only by two good line officers) are expected to perform in about two weeks.

So if letters are few & brief you can easily tell the reason.

To day (and this is ominous of a move) Gen'l Grant, with an enormous staff, accompanied by Sec'y [of War Edwin M.] Stanton and any number of other persons of importance, reviewed our 2nd Division (Birney's) & afterwards the whole 24th Corps. I was present at both performances & stood within 120 paces of the Lt. Gen'l & the Hon. Sec., having a splendid chance to contemplate them for about half an hour. The 2nd Div. was reviewed on the drill ground of the 117th.

Last Sunday Grant & his Staff, with Ord & his Staff, rode through our camp. On both occasions large numbers of ladies were in the company.[27]

I imply that the Army of the James will be entitled to a whole page & a map in the papers in a very short time.

An immense squadron of ironclads is congregated at Dutch Gap which has 9 ft. of water all through & deepening. If we storm these works opposite in conjunction with the Navy, there will be lots of promotions. But I don't think Grant is a fool.

To night you are having the "Bouquet." I wish very much I could be at home to meet the society, though I've noticed that Yale men are much more polished than Army men & I feel much more at home with my battalion on the drill ground than I do with ladies in their parlors.[28]

Indeed, my home is with my regiment.

But I am exceedingly sorry to hear of Father's resignation, though I doubt not his wisdom is greater than mine. But the news was a very sudden blow to me & Bennett was highly indignant to think that such an event should ever be hinted at.[29]

But it grows quite late & I must not write any longer for we turn out early & I've a hard day's work to-morrow.

What is Leonard going to call his boy. Congratulate you upon your name-sake.[30]

> With much love to all, Aff yr
> brother, Edward W. Bacon

A nervous, restless energy rippled through Federal troops as winter waned and spring approached. They had endured trench warfare for more than nine months and they wanted movement.

Most felt confident of the result, though some worried about the recent Confederate decision to enlist slaves. Sergeant Edward King Wightman, 3rd New York Infantry, argued, "Don't think that the southern negroes will hesitate to fight for their masters . . . the spring will open for us with a brutal horrible phase of the war." Agreeing, John A. Wilder, a 2nd U.S. Colored Infantry officer, wrote that "I am afraid they will trouble us. The slaves will fight, & fight for them."[31]

Those concerns paled beside those of Southerners loyal to a Confederacy tumbling toward collapse. Preparing for that day, some soldiers adopted a pragmatic proposal: "Resolved, that in case our army is overwhelmed and broken up, we will bushwhack them; that is, some of us will." Others reached for rainbows of hope, half-believing preposterous rumors. They eagerly heard that a French fleet had captured New Orleans or that England and France had recognized the Confederacy. A Texas artillery captain thought the cause was lost but then heard that "England has notified Lincoln he is no longer president of the southern states. . . . If this is true it will place our success beyond a doubt and the war will not last very long."[32]

He was right only about the war's duration.

117th U.S. Col'd Troops, March 21st, 1865

Dear Kate,

Your letter of March 14, already answered, is my latest news from home and the latest paper I have seen is of the 16th. The mails & news agents seem to be far behind time.

In obedience to orders received to day to reduce baggage to the lowest possible limit, I shall send home per express a box containing my overcoat and perhaps some smaller items, which will probably leave this to-morrow or next day.

We are preparing for a great review of the whole Army on Friday, I think by the President and General Grant. The troops are in great shape & will do great credit to their [winter's?] work.

I called yesterday on Capt. James & on a friend of Theodore's, with whom I was on a Court at Beaufort, Brevet Brig. Gen'l, formerly Lt. Col., Hall of the Engineers.[33]

A large part of this Army is under marching orders; unfortunately for me, fortunately for this regiment, we are not as yet included.

Indeed the left of the 24th Corps struck tents yesterday before day light, but about noon, a rain storm arising, pitched again. So you probably lost news of a battle.

I am exceedingly impatient for some great move: it is now much easier marching and fighting than it will be in the summer. Indeed, we now have, in this bare wilderness which our Army has made, some days which make us long for shade or some green foliage to enliven the glistening of the white tents, yellow ground & red earthworks. Moreover, if we move now, it will probably be quite a long march—possibly—cutting loose from our base; the present fashion of a campaign—a shove at the right around Richmond to cut off Lynchburg. If we remain a great while longer, all we can do will be to carry the line which confronts us by an assault *in mass*, a military performance more agreeable in history than in the execution.[34]

But I am consuming considerable time in guessing at what even Gen'l Ord don't know & perhaps Grant himself may alter.

When my overcoat arrives, please let me know.

> With much love to all, Aff. yr.
> brother, Edward W. Bacon

※

The Confederate attack against Fort Stedman, noted by Bacon, was a last desperate effort to salvage their cause. Major General John B. Gordon, who planned the assault, said that "the purpose . . . was not simply the capture of Fort Stedman. . . . The tremendous possibility was the disintegration of the whole left wing of the Federal army . . . enabling us to withdraw from Petersburg and join [General Joseph E.] Johnston in North Carolina."

Gordon's men swiftly overwhelmed Stedman's garrison but could not exploit their initial success. They withdrew through a "furnace of fire" and Gordon later called it the "expiring struggle of the Confederate giant."

That convulsion cost Lee about 3,500 men while the Federals lost about 2,000.[35]

※

117th U.S. Col'd Troops, March 31st, 1865

Dear Kate,

Your letter of March 27th inst. reached me last night. Of late our mails reach us one day sooner than they used. Why I don't know but it is quite a satisfactory change.

The Spring Campaign has opened, a little sooner than Grant intended, by two days. On Saturday the enemy took and left Fort Stedman, which I helped build last September, and where we lay for more than a month, and on the evening of that day the 2nd Division of our Corps, under Gen'l Birney, was withdrawn from our line & bivouacked in the rear. We supposed they must have marched the same night, but Sunday morning disclosed them behind us.

About ten o'clock that morning, by the way, I went down to Aiken's Landing to see Capt. Clitz of the Navy and was just turning back disappointed when I observed a detachment of exchanged prisoners, who proved to be in great part the 15th Connecticut. So I spent about an hour with them.[36]

Returning by way of Butler's Monument (Dutch Gap), I had time to dine before the 2nd Division formed for review by the President. Our Division, which had been quite fully drilling in movements on the double-quick, which were to be displayed for the benefit of his Excellency, was left on the line.[37]

The affair was very creditable indeed, though the 24th Corps, which was reviewed immediately after, far surpasses any marching or any display of negro troops which I have seen. Colored troops demand the best of officers.

Gen'l Butler, in whose care we have been so long, gave, almost invariably, the worst. I have no doubt that negro troops can be made equal to any. There is no doubt that now they are inferior. As a rule their discipline is good but there the goodness ends.

When will the War Department find that it is but one man in five hundred who can make any thing of an officer.[38]

But I have made a diversion of two pages.

Monday at Sundown, Birney marched as also did the whole of the 24th Corps, leaving the Richmond line to be held by two divisions only—one white and one black.[39]

As to what has been to this date done, you know quite as well as I do. Whatever else may be the object of the move, I have the best authority in the Department for saying—confidentially—that Richmond ought to be evacuated.

At any rate you may congratulate yourself that this Division did not go to Petersburg, for from the really wonderful cannonading which every day takes place there now it is easy to draw that some body is going to be hurt. So far as anyone can foretell, we here are, fortunately for our heads, pretty sure of an easy time until Richmond is occupied by our forces.

My regiment has, at last, a Lieutenant Colonel. Gen'l Ord has appointed John A. Kress, a West Point man, a Lieutenant of Regulars, and a man who entirely satisfied me, not only because he is an officer but because he has been detached at once upon the Corps Staff as Inspector General, so that in case Col. Brown at any time steps aside, the command devolves upon me.[40]

We have also a Surgeon in place of the old one cashiered and a new Asst. Surg., *vice* one discharged. But I am writing too long a letter.

Aff. yr. brother, Edward W. Bacon

%%

Petersburg and Richmond had fallen when Bacon next wrote home. Confederate troops had evacuated the cities, hoping to join Johnston in North Carolina. Instead, Federals encircled them near Appomattox Courthouse in Virginia and Lee then surrendered his Army of Northern Virginia on April 9, 1865.

Though General Edmund Kirby Smith did not surrender his isolated Trans-Mississippi troops until May 26, Confederate commanders east of the Mississippi soon followed Lee's lead. So four years of civil war ended.

No letters from Bacon describe Richmond's fall. Either he did not write about the momentous events or, more likely, a letter or letters have vanished.

His brigade, which included his old 29th Connecticut (Colored), raced for Richmond on April 3, 1865, and was the first to reach the city's outskirts. But there high authorities halted them, wanting white troops, they who had borne the brunt of the struggle, to first enter the Confederacy's capital. However, events spun out of control and 5th Massachusetts Cavalry (Colored) troopers were among the first to reach the city's center.[41]

War correspondents saw the black soldiers in the burning city and reported, "The city . . . was taken by colored troops." Later dispatches correctly related that the white 24th Army Corps had taken Richmond.

However, the initial reports often prevailed. A Maine infantry major wrote that "the pride of the Great Southern metropolis has been humbled by the black man." Richmond's inhabitants reinforced the first accounts. Sallie A. Putnam, a Richmond resident, recalled, "Long lines of negro cavalry swept by . . . brandishing their swords and uttering savage cheers." John B. Jones, a Confederate bureaucrat strolled to Capitol Square about noon and noted that "The street was filled with negro troops, cavalry and infantry."[42]

While Bacon left no extant accounts, Captain Henry G. Marshall, 29th Connecticut, gave a full description of Richmond's fall. He reported a city afire "and the bursting shells in the flame sounded like a fierce battle raging." He concluded, "Thus falls the proud city in one grand drunk and conflageration and Uncle Abe's niggers have come and occupy the land."[43]

Bacon's first letter after Richmond's surrender, dated April 8, was a brief request (not included here) to his father for money. Next is a longer letter to Kate in which he wrote as if she would be aware of certain things, suggesting earlier but missing correspondence. While this is dated April 9, the day Lee surrendered, Bacon apparently did not know that yet.

※

117th U.S. Col'd Troops, Richmond,
Va. April 9th, 1865

Dear Kate,

Your letter of the 5th reached me this morning.

I have just returned from town where I attended St. Paul's Church, where last Sunday afternoon Mr. Davis received his startling telegram.[44]

These Richmond people behave themselves remarkably well—such a contrast to the New Orleans citizens when we landed there. St. Paul's seemed to have much the same audience as ever, save some Northern clothes & some blue uniforms. No inhabitant of the Confederacy (with a few exceptions) wears either good or new clothes.

We are settling down very quickly. I have built me very nice summer quarters & am enjoying Richmond hugely. Met on Friday Capt. Geo. B. Sanford of Gen Casey's Staff & on yesterday Capt. Foote, who is assigned to Gen'l Kautz of our Division, but who is fearful little ninny, no matter what his ancestry may have been.[45]

I have got me a servant at last. A house servant of a sick old fellow named Griffin who lives near by.

I send you a number of relics of the Confederacy. Of most touching interest are the "Rules & Regulations" which I tore from a post in Room "No. 9, Castle Thunder." They seem to have been adopted as some sort of self preservation from the horrors of that inferno.

I never wanted to fight so much as when I finished my very careful & minute exploration of that place, even to the little hole cut for escape of the inmates on the morning of the 3d April & the rope of tattered blankets reaching from a fourth story window to the pavement of the yard of execution.[46]

Perhaps Father might like to send the paper to the College Library, stating that I took it down only a little while after the place was vacated by the prisoners.

I send also an unpublished letter to Gov. [Joseph E.] Brown of Georgia which I obtained at the "President's Room, C.S.A." where the Cabinet meetings used to be held. From its style I infer that Mr. Davis may be the author. I would like to have the hand writing compared with Mr. D's autograph. I also send some certificates of election which I found in the Records of the C.S. House of Reps.

& some postage Stamps for Alfred who wanted some I think. The 10¢ ones were on an envelop addressed to J. Davis.

But I could send bushels of matter equally interesting & yet not begin to mention what fell in to any ones hands who would gather up the spoils.

By all means induce Father to come to Richmond. It is the most beautiful city I have seen & at least in the south. Had it not been burned it would rival New Haven. It is blessed with excellent drainage, gravelly soil, capital water, good society, delightful drives. Is easy of access & of intense interest to the visitor.

Aside from the great interest, such a visit would be to father, his presence would most likely be of advantage to me. And Rebecca would doubtless be as much pleased as any one.

But I suspect you are not right in speaking of Gov. Pierponts inauguration at Richmond. I thought him Governor of West Virginia.[47]

Richmond is full of Northern civilians of distinction. Mrs. Lincoln is here.[48]

Upon consideration I leave out some of the matter I mention as sending because they may make too bulky a bundle

> With much love to all, Aff. yr.
> brother, Edward W. Bacon

P.S. Room No. 9 was the best & most comfortable in Castle Thunder.

%%

Shock, grief and anger abruptly replaced the North's joy just five days after Lee's surrender. On April 14, John Wilkes Booth, a fanatical Southern loyalist, shot Lincoln at Ford's Theater in Washington. Mary Todd Lincoln said that her husband never even quivered when the bullet crashed into his brain. Early on April 15, Lincoln died and a stunned North shuddered and mourned.

Southerners had mixed reactions, some rejoicing while others regretted both act and possible consequences. Madge Preston of Maryland, a Southern sympathizer, initially called it "joyful" and "good news" but quickly had second thoughts, fearing great trouble as a result. From Tennessee a Federal soldier wrote, "They [citizens] all seem to regret the death of President Lyncoln they fear Johnson more than they did Lyncoln."[49]

Vice President Andrew Johnson became the nation's leader and promptly charged that Jefferson Davis and other high Confederates had concocted the assassination.

Those accusations further inflamed already seething emotions. In Virginia, a 141st Pennsylvania soldier reported, "The feelings of the army is excited to a high degree" and a Maine infantryman advised, "Revenge is the cry in the army & by all." One of Sherman's generals thought that "if active operations were to commence again it would be impossible to restrain the troops from great outrages." But passions subsided when searchers killed Booth, Davis was captured in early May, and remaining Confederate forces surrendered.[50]

%

New Haven, April 20, 1865

My dear Son,

The awful & stunning event of last Friday night has caused two days suspension of all business, Saturday & yesterday & the duty of preaching appropriately Sunday morning & of conducting the funeral services in one Church yesterday (simultaneous with the funeral at Washington) with so continued a strain upon the mind & feelings has almost exhausted me.

But I have not quite forgotten your call for money. I enclose a draft payable to your order on the Continental Bank, New York, for one hundred dollars. This leaves your credit in the Townsend Savings Bank only the little interest which has received & been added to your deposits, $7.54. I will take care of whatever bills may be sent in prior to the next visit of your paymaster. None has come in as yet (I believe) except T. P. Morrison and Co.s for $7.00.

God has ordered the course of events that the terrible crime which has overwhelmed the nation with sorrow, cannot arrest for an hour the grand [succession?] of our victories. But it will make the treason of this rebellion more abhorred than ever. The whole world will cry out for justice, not only on the wretched assassin & his immediate accomplices but on all the leading authors of the treason which attempted to destroy the life of the nation. I think there will be a much more thorough purgation of the South than there would have been but for the murder of the President. The keeping up of large military force in order to the complete civilization & pacification of the South will seem to be an absolute necessity & I trust that no officer who, having been educated at West Point, has borne arms against his country will ever be entrusted again with even the slightest military command.[51]

You have heard that I have some thought of going to Richmond. I am not very confident about it, but if I find that I can leave here when the opportunity comes, I will go. I need not say how much pleasure it will give me to see you there. Meanwhile, I commend you [illegible word] to the protection & blessing of God.

Very affectionately, Your father, Leonard Bacon

%

Bacon asserted there was "no news at all" in his next letter and then reported many events, including atrocities allegedly committed by black troops in Richmond.

Defeated but scarcely submissive, Richmond's citizens fiercely objected to the "impertinence and insults" of black soldiers and flooded Federal authorities with endless complaints. Though they had labeled all Yankees as "negro-equalizing Abolitionists" during the war, they now acted on the contrary notion that those same Yankees would promptly restore order based on the inequality of the races.[52]

Major General Henry W. Halleck, the former chief of staff who commanded in Richmond, immediately began to agitate for the 25th Army Corps' removal. Always crafty and cunning, Halleck's motive is unclear when he made false or grossly exaggerated charges. He told Grant, "General [Edward O. C.] Ord represents that want of discipline and good officers in the Twenty-fifth Corps renders it a very improper force . . . a number of cases of atrocious rape by these men have already occurred."[53]

Major General Godfrey Weitzel, 25th Corps commander, denied that his black troops had rampaged through the city, committing atrocious rape or any other kind of rape. He said that "nearly all the irregularities complained of were committed by black and white cavalry" who either did not belong to his corps or had served with it only briefly.[54]

However, plans for the black troops were already afoot. Grant soon ordered the 25th Corps to Texas to help reclaim the Trans-Mississippi and to demonstrate against the French occupation forces in Mexico. A major reason for that decision was simple necessity. Many black regiments had formed late in the war and enlistments would not expire until long after those of most white units. In the spring, the army had a million troops, but that included 123,000 black soldiers, the most in service at any one time. Rapid demobilization reduced the army to about 227,000 men by September 1865. Of that number, 83,000—more than 36 percent—were black.[55]

Still, it was also true that Northern and Southern racial attitudes converged. Conqueror and conquered agreed that black soldiers belonged someplace else, anywhere out of sight and mind. Many Yankees, moreover, did not want blacks moving North. But often black Federals hesitated about returning to Southern homes, fearing reprisals.[56]

Bacon realized winds of change swirled, but knew not where they would take him.

117th U.S. Col'd Troops, Near
Petersburg, Va., April 26th, 1865

Dear Kate,

The last news I have had from home is Father's very welcome letter enclosing the draft on New York which I have so much needed. I have also Rebecca's letter of the 17th & your's of the 18th since I last wrote to you, so I cannot grumble.

There is no news here at all. Just a week ago to day we changed camp, leaving our position on the Weldon Railway in the winter quarters of the Sixth Corps for new ground on the South side Road, just four miles out of Petersburg.

On the 18th the 29th Conn. left our Corps and is now, I understand, at Point Lookout in Maryland, so that Col. Wooster wont have to sicken this summer. Since their departure I have been very homesick or 29th sick, for going to the 117th did not separate my chums & me very far.

It looks now very much as if the 25th Army Corps, in its organization a mistake, was going to break up. Our 3d Div. Is assigned to Terry's new 10th Corps and parts of the 1st and 2nd Divs. have been detached. Weitzel and Butler were Siamese prodigies: separated they die.[57]

I have seen Carrington, though he has not returned my call, he probably will obtain leave of absence for a few days. My Colonel, twice unsuccessful, has again applied for 30 days leave and I hope he may obtain it.[58]

Gen'l Birney was relieved of his command (2nd Div.) during the late campaign for mismanagement of various sorts: too much eagerness to shove into danger & for stopping Gen. Meade's Head Quarters Train. Rumor says, however, that he will soon return. His division marched sixty miles in thirty two hours (60 ÷ 32), cutting Lee's last line of retreat & completing the campaign.[59]

Col. Ward's Regt., the 31st U.S., held Grant's extreme left in the last line of battle.

It is wonderfully comfortable to let down the tension of one's powers, to turn in with the absolute certainty that it is for all night, to have absolutely no hostile pickets. One cannot realize war until he changed back to peace.

I went the other day to the Hare House—"Fort Stedman"—& strolled all about the works which we helped build & into the bomb-proof which I had occupied, walking up right through covered ways in which we used to stoop right low and I confess myself astonished to behold all the trials & dangers we really endured.[60]

I visited also the old bomb-proof under the hill in the bank of the road side where Bennett & I lived so long but found only its ruins. Crossing into the rebel lines I found our fire quite as accurate as ever theirs was, for I think over the same extent of ground they have left many more graves than we, though ours are too thick. The lay of the land, however, was in their favor & quite against us.

We are getting a camp built. I have an A tent of Confederate manufacture stockaded, with a fly in front which makes me very nice quarters about 12 x 12 in my room & the same under the fly.[61]

Will you do me the favor of presenting my compliments to Miss Perkins and say that almost no item in my [illegible] outfit has been so useful as the twine which she wound for me; indeed that I used the last of it this afternoon sewing up a rent in the aforesaid rebel tent; (in which operation, too) I broke the last of the two crowbar needles which you provided.[62]

If the supposed end of the War has not put it out of the province of young ladies to work for young veterans, perhaps Miss P., as a favor to you will consent to replenish my stock, for which trouble I shall feel deeply indebted, and if you will send on another supply of cast steel bars, the expense of freightage shall be mine.

In a few days, when the disposal of us for the summer seems settled, I shall send on for some thin clothing. The surrender of Moseby's gang seems to block active Campaigning & unless they send us to Texas, we must either remain here or go into garrison. I don't care what.[63]

We are recruiting here at the rate of 25 men per day and if we continue a week longer, we shall be full to the maximum. The class of men is good, though rather small. Negroes do not attain the size of whites & keep proportionate strength.

I think the end of hostilities is going to end the service of many incapable officers. Some of ours have discovered an affection for peaceful pursuits and an unfitness for military command sufficient to induce their resignations. I wish very much our Colored Service could be put through a sieve.

The atrocities which disgraced the Corps at Richmond (not so numerous, happily, to amount to a rule} were due chiefly to the fact that our officers are as a rule not officer-like enough to teach their men or "boys," as some demagogues libel them, their place or discipline them into a proper respect for those entitled to it or worthy of it.[64]

Notwithstanding my admissions in this respect, I think the sending the 1st Division 25th A.C. away from Richmond in a manner so offensive as that of Ord's was to Weitzel an unmerited severity—properly noticed by the War Department when they relieved Ord.[65]

I wrote some account of how we feel here over the latest development of chivalry—but did not send it. When we get into another fight, there will be *no quarter*. So every body swears.[66]

With love to all, Aff yr brother,

Edward W. Bacon

Bacon began to grasp that a big difference existed between a peacetime and a wartime army. He observed that "playing soldier" was not the same as the real thing. Nevertheless, he still wanted to be a career officer, trusting that his regiment would remain part of the postwar regular army.

At this juncture his pay was eight months over due. While such lapses were not unusual during the war, the arrears probably resulted from his transfer to the 117th, thereby causing bureaucratic delays.

117th U.S. Col'd Troops, April 30th, 1865

Dear Kate,

I wrote last some few days since & I don't know that I can add anything more now than I then said but as this is Sunday I have nothing better to do but fall into my custom of writing home.

Gen. Grant, having finished his glorious campaign, seems to be at a loss what to do with his immense armies. We are kept here but we know not for how long. It cant be a great while, however. Rumor already sends us back to Richmond this week sometime. I hope we will not move until we go into permanent garrison or leave the service, which latter I trust for us will never come, though playing soldier isn't so much of a business as fighting.[67]

I send you some mementoes of memorable localities.

The blue violets are from the South Side Railway, near our present camp and the butter cup I got from one halting place for breakfast just outside of Petersburg, one of the prettiest country Seats I have ever seen, its principal feature being a fine lawn covered with some of the largest & most venerable cedars I have met. A real Virginian residence.

I have applied for permission to proceed to Norfolk for the purpose of drawing the 8 months pay now due but do not think Gen'l Weitzel will grant it.

I heard of your visit to New York from Capt. [Charles F.] Ulrich of the 31st (Col. [Henry C.] Ward), a very nice fellow & excellent officer, who says that Miss McCready wrote she had met you & that you had told them of my writing home that Col. W's regt. had gone across the James.[68]

But I am going to [ride?]. It is exceedingly dull here & no news.

Love to all, in haste, yr aff
brother, Edward W. Bacon

※

White soldiers fretted at demobilization's slow pace while black troops, particularly 25th Corps men, feared treachery.

Reality and rumor reinforced each other, stirring disaffection and unrest among black soldiers in Virginia. In May, Major General Ord abruptly and secretly stopped rations for their dependents and the soldiers heard that they would sail for Texas. Without the rations, the men thought their families would starve and they saw the Texas story as a ruse. Many believed the persistent rumor that the government would ship them to Cuba and sell them on the slave market to pay for the costly struggle.[69]

Probably the Cuba story's endurance made it easier to accept. Southerners originally concocted the tale to discourage slaves from fleeing to the Yankees. As early as July 1861, a Confederate Congressman warned slaves of their fate if they defected and, in January 1862, a future president noted in his diary, "They

[Southerners] tell slaves that the Yankees cut off arms of some negroes to make them worthless and sell the rest in Cuba for twenty-five hundred dollars each to pay cost of war." Quickly the chilling tales gained wide circulation among blacks. Finally the stories circled back to Southerners who accepted it as gospel or said they did.[70]

Alone or in combination, the reenslavement rumor, the family ration stoppage, and the sometimes harsh discipline imposed by racist officers caused black soldiers to rebel. Having little reason to trust whites, it is not surprising that they acted to defend their freedom. Mutinies erupted in black regiments from Virginia to Florida. Officers quelled the uprisings with strong measures, sometimes with summary executions. Ringleaders often suffered severe punishment, including death sentences.[71]

Unfortunately for Bacon, his 117th soldiers were among the first to defy authority and rebel. Further, he had no inkling that trouble brewed.

%%

> Hd. Qrs. 117th U.S.C.T., Camp
> Lincoln, Va. May 16th, 1865

Dear Kate,

Your letter of the 5th and 8th of May is my last date from home except Frank's unexpected visit, which came on Sunday.

I had almost finished a most tiresome inspection—lasting three hours—on the men and their arms alone & was looking forward to another siege of a couple of hours on quarters when Frank rode up. I could not adjourn the inspection, though I naturally shortened it. At 3 o'clock, however, there was a Division Dress Parade, so if Frank intended a long visit, he must have been disappointed: I lost him on parade which was a long affair & where we had some medals presented.

I had some hopes of being able to go down to City Point while Frank is there, but yesterday I was Officer of the Day and I am very busy. Am looking for Father during this week.[72]

I have had quite a lively time since Friday when I had the regret of seeing a mutiny & the satisfaction of so squelching it that so long as & whenever I am in command of the Regt. that I can do with it whatever I please.

Since the Colonel left I have put on the screws after my own mind & by correcting one or two standing evils in the command obtained at once the hearty co-operation of all the officers.

Some of the men would not stand this. Specially one who had been 1st Sergt. but whom I reduced for being tardy one day at Guard Mount. Accordingly, the disaffected ones formed a plot. At Midnight of the 12th, the Companies were to quickly turn out under arms, march up to the Guard House, over awe the Guard

& tear down the prisoner's cell, releasing the prisoners. Capt. [Henry C.] Wood of Co. K was to be informed that his style of discipline could be dispensed with & a similar call was to be made at my tent.

But sheer discipline saved me from such disgrace. Ignorant as an infant of the scheme & at Dress Parade having a Company too restless to look well, I directed them to remain in line after Parade was dismissed, and afterward, their restlessness continuing, increased the time they were to stay. This excited the Mutineers [to] hasty action. Just at dusk they quickly armed themselves, to the number of about 200, & moved by a distant route to the Parade, surrounded the Company under discipline ("H") & ran them into camp with a yell.

I saw in a wink what was up, sounded the "Assembly," formed the Battalion at the double-quick before the men thought of the trap, formed Square on the Center, faced the men in and put my officers, few in number, around the outside. I then notified the men that any man who left the Square would be shot dead & proceeded to gather up stragglers & search Camp for weapons, drawing in some 2 dozen pistols.

I then offered heavy rewards for the detection of the ring leader & informed the command that all allowances would be withheld until the whole matter was settled. Two men, who "did not think they would do" thus & so I had bucked & gagged in the Center of the Square.[73]

Still no body had any thing to say. It was growing dark & when night favored, there were strong probabilities that the men would break my frail line of officers & accomplish their pleasure. I accordingly sent a request to my next neighbor of the 9th U.S. (Col. [Thomas] Bayley, temporarily in command of the Division) for a Guard of 200 men; but he stupidly said "it was a serious matter: he did not desire to act rashly, but he would take the request into consideration." Leaving him to his meditations upon mutiny, my officer went direct to Weitzel.[74]

Weitzel expressed himself in certain words probably not used when calling on Mrs. W—said he approved all that was done & ordered out more troops than I needed.

By one o'clock at night I had twenty-two ring leaders in limbo. Yesterday I sent up charges against one officer (my 2nd ranking Captain) & 24 men for aiding and inciting Mutiny, mutiny and violation of 6th, 7th, & 8th Articles of War.[75]

I have had the satisfaction of receiving the congratulations of Gen. Weitzel & a number of lesser stars for efficient & prompt action.

My regiment has improved. Inspectors have ceased to libel it since the Colonel left and are hammering at my neighbors.

I have just given the Sutler 24 hours to leave camp & forbidden the collection of all debts by him, having found out that he has been making from 300 to 500 per cent profits.[76]

Meantime, I have been and are so much occupied that I can't write much.

Please send me in Mason & Rockwell box a sponge and a hair brush with *very stiff* bristles. Some Brown Windsor or scented soap and some Cologne. I also have some linen drawers and some thin undershirts of which I shall soon stand in much need. Please put them in.[77]

When you see the Thompsons, say to Miss Mary that I acknowledge her demand for my Carte and shall supply it soon.[78]

Have received Rebecca's of the 13th.

Aff. yr brother, Edw. W. Bacon

%

General Edmund Kirby Smith's surrender in the Trans-Mississippi on May 26 closed the war. Bacon lamented the end of chances for glory and rapid promotion, but welcomed the "new lease of life" for himself and others. He knew his division would sail southward, though he was ignorant of their final destination.

%

Camp 117th U.S.C.T., May 30th, 1865

Dear Kate,

I received last night your letter of the 25th and 26th, welcome as usual. I am sorry that my express package did not leave New Haven until so late a date as the 24th, I fear that now I shall miss it. There is, however, a possibility that just as we sail, the box may arrive. I hope so, for my winter clothing has already become oppressive about mid-day. I watch the Express Agency narrowly.

Col. Brown returned yesterday, a day behind time. He finds his regiment—I warrant—much better than he left it. So his Brigadier tells him anyhow. I am exceedingly satisfied upon receiving the history of the 25 days &, if the 117th is doomed to have always a bad name, I've saved my reputation.

Very much to my delight the 29th Conn. turned up at City Point yesterday—returned to our brigade. Though all of them are much disappointed (Point Lookout being a very nice place), the effect upon me was quite the contrary. I've been very homesick without them.[79]

Two Brigades of our Division, the 1st & 3rd, moved down to the Point this a.m., but we do not go until to-morrow. After the embarkation we stop at Fortress Monroe for payment & then go on South.

Kirby Smith, it seems, has gone up & with him all chance for Brevets & promotion. However, its satisfactory to those in the service to think that the end of the War gives, in its way, a new lease of life.

May 31st Transportation being short, the 2nd Brigade still remains in Camp, but expect to move each day until we go. I don't know if we are better off thus than we would be at Fortress Monroe, but the situation is marvelously stupid.

You don't say to whom Miss [D?] Ray and Miss Charnley are to be married. Why do you spell Fort Hale *"hail"*?[80]

Please tell Chapman the next time you see him that with the exception of a letter for which you mentioned his asking you the address, but which has not reached me & the additional exception of your mention of [illegible] parties & the Bouquet, etc., I have not heard of him since I last shook hands with him. "Thankful for past favors," I hope he isn't going to stop writing to me.[81]

June 1st We are not off yet. Transportation seems very limited indeed.

Our mails stop now at Fortress Monroe, so that I hope to receive quite a batch of letters there before we start.

Give much love to all & believe me, Your aff. brother,

Edward W. Bacon

117th U.S.C.T., on Board *Star of the South*, June 10th, 1865[82]

Dear Kate,

I wrote home just as we were leaving Fortress Monroe, enclosing a draft on New York for $200. As might be inferred from that, we were paid at Norfolk down to the first of May.

We went to Norfolk on a tug Saturday noon and were detained there until Monday noon. It is a stupid place, but better than remaining aboard ship. I met there several old acquaintances, among them an old shipmate from the *Hartford* and Lt. Johnson of the 15th Conn.[83]

We have thus far made a very fine passage. The weather has been very smooth & I have had no sea sickness at all, though some of our officers have lost a good many meals.

We are now off the coast of Florida (east) and due off Key West some time to-morrow. It is in hopes of a chance to mail this there that I am induced to write to-day—for, as you may judge by the style of the penmanship, the jar of the machinery makes the task a tedious one.

We disembark at Fort Morgan or Fort Gaines, probably on Wednesday next and we have orders to cleanse up—refresh the men and refit—that done, to reembark and await orders.[84]

You will observe that we are to remain in the same state of tantalizing uncertainty which has possessed us for the last six weeks until near the fourth of July, if not much later. So the prospect is not very [pleasing].

Lt. Col. John A. Kress, who was appointed here in order to give him a staff appointment & who never has served with the command, resigned to take effect June 1st. As soon as the Corps become settled down again, I presume I shall be examined for the vacancy—though I have some doubt as to my ability to pass the board. I do not know, either, whether Col. Brown will be anxious to recommend me since I have ascertained that in dismissing the Sutler of the regt. (which I did for general bad conduct & swindling), I cut off not only the Sutler's but part of the Colonel's income.[85]

It is somewhat of a satisfaction to know that no recommendation adverse to my claim will be entertained at higher Head Quarters. I prefer that the vacancy be not mentioned until the examination is passed.

But this letter is getting too long for interest.

I presume Joe Thompson is not at Key West now, or I should—if we stop—try to see him. Possibly his regt. may be added to the 25th Corps. We need some troops to compose our 3rd Division. Terry took our original 3rd into his 10th Corps.[86]

This is all the news—except that I did not get my Express box at Fortress Monroe—as I wrote I expected I might. I hope you took a receipt for it when you sent it.

> With much love to all, Your
> aff. brother, Edward W.

> 117th U.S. Col'd Troops,
> On board tnspt *Star of the South*.
> Between Forts Morgan & Gaines,
> June 15th, 1865

Dear Kate,

The four lines which I have consumed by my heading pretty much give you the contents of this letter, mainly that we are thus & so.

Sunday last I put a letter aboard of the Key West pilot-boat, as we pulled off the [illegible]. From that we steered the direct course for Mobile Bay, coming in with day light of yesterday, 14th.

We found the Second Division of our Corps had already departed for the mouth of the Rio Grande, about which interesting locality they are to perform duty while the First Division, in all probability, will be sent farther up the river, still on the Western boundary. This arrangement, if carried out, will be highly satisfactory—since, I presume, the farther back from the Coast one gets, the more healthy he will find the climate. As I write Gen. Weitzel has arrived and our destination will be known definitely during the day. It seems likely that we will have to visit New Orleans for coal, but that, too, is undecided.

Yesterday afternoon a party from this ship went ashore at Fort Morgan. I was surprised to find it so important a work: Much stronger than I had supposed. It is pretty much knocked to pieces, however, by the late bombardment, The approaches before the surrender had reached nearly as close as some of ours before Richmond and Petersburg. I project a visit to Fort Gaines after dinner, though it is some distance from the Ship across.[87]

We look for some letters by the transport arriving now—after which it will be a long time ere we hear from home again. When we get comfortably established in some interior Texan town we may hope for at least regular, if not frequent communication with the North.

I am in excellent health. Some of the Officers are more or less affected by the hot climate, but I consider myself used to it.

There is no news, our latest dates are to the 3rd inst.[88]

With much love to all, Your affectionate
brother, Edward W. Bacon

(4) OCCUPATION DUTY, TEXAS

BLACK TROOPS HAD FAST BECOME UNWELCOME IN THE SOUTH and Border States. Strongly prejudiced, President Andrew Johnson set the tone when he denounced them as insolent, undisciplined, domineering, depredatory, and disorderly. He also charged they would likely aid black insurrections and that they drove white people away. Personally, he found it "humiliating in the extreme" that they had taken over his house in Greenville, Tennessee, and turned it into a "common negro brothel . . . a sink of pollution." Johnson fumed, "It was bad enough [when] . . . converted into a rebel hospital, but a negro whore house is infinitely worse."[1]

Yet the government needed troops to maintain order in the shattered South and to demonstrate on the Mexican border to encourage the French to withdraw. Under Major General Philip H. Sheridan's command, about fifty thousand Federals went to Texas and finally the French army went home in May 1866.

Meanwhile, Federal armies demobilized and the veterans, including some black soldiers from the North, returned to their homes. Black troops in Texas, however, had joined the army late in the war and their enlistments would not expire for another two years. So the 25th Army Corps stayed there, subject to bad food, unhealthy climes, illness, dreary terrain, and endless tedium.

Very quickly, Bacon decided that Texas was not his cup of tea, calling it a "heated Siberia."

※

117th U.S. Col'd Troops, June 25, 1865

Dear Kate,

We were at Mobile Bay, from which point I last wrote home on the 15th inst.

We did not visit New Orleans as I surmised we might & as the other transports did (getting severely snubbed by Gen'l Sheridan) but proceeded direct to Matagorda Bay. We found ourselves drawing five feet too much water to cross the bar (which affords only nine feet), so Col. Brown and three other officers, including myself, ran in on a yawl boat as far as Lavaca, some 30 miles up the bay, bringing out three blockade runners secreted there, which we proposed to use as lighters, but by the time of our return, after two days absence, on the 21st, we found Weitzel had passed down on the coast & left orders for us to proceed to Brazos de Santiago and disembark, which we did—arriving on the 22nd & immediately disembarked.[2]

That wretched sand bar surpassed any desert I have yet encountered. Not a drop of fresh water is obtained save from condensers (since our departure out of order), hardly a blade of grass to be seen nor a break in the flatness of the drift. The whiteness of the sand is, however, not so dazzling as on Santa Rosa where I spoiled my [illegible] and a fine breeze from the Gulf carried off all mosquitoes.

We found at this lag end of the Union two brigades of the Second Division and one of the First. We found not a stick of wood big enough to pitch a shelter tent upon & the regiment spent the day under the line of Stacks with tents & blankets hung on them & the night under the Stars. We had fine surf bathing. I, with good fortune, was captured by Gen'l Armstrong of 2nd Brig. 2nd Div. & Col. of 8th U.S., an acquaintance at Beaufort, but claiming to be under particular obligation to Frank for vacating rooms for him at Richmond. The Gen'l provided quite a sumptuous repast & a comfortable bunk for which I was very grateful. I also met Lt. Pease, who was well. That Brigade, Doubleday's, of which Carrington's regt. formed a part, remained at Brazos.[3]

Next day, at about 5 P.M., we marched for our present location on the Rio Grande some four or five miles from Bagdad. We were followed yesterday by the remainder of the Corps—Hd Qrs. & Doubleday's Brigade excepted. I have seen Col. [Henry C.] Ward & Capt. [Charles F.} Ulrich (who, by the way, on his return from leave brought me the jolliest little pocket lantern imaginable & very handy—).

The 9th & 29th have not arrived nor has Brigade Hd. Qrs. Our new Divi. Comdr., Gen'l Giles A. Smith, remains for the present at Brazos. Our horses have not yet reached us: most of those brought down thus far disembark mere skeletons & worthless for use at present. So our ten mile march the other night reminded me very much of my Captain's duty in Virginia.[4]

Indeed Texas—so far as have seen it—does not at all make a good impression on my mind. I have not seen a tree in the whole state—There was considerable grass at Lavaca (where we got very fine beef with green corn, new potatoes & fresh milk, butter & eggs[)].

The people are very anxious to have our forces to occupy the state but are much afraid of the negro troops & don't want to see them. Everybody "has always been Union" but everybody, too, has been in the service of Mr. Davis.

I found Col. Hamilton [as] much respected as a mere politician ever can be. Every one described Col. Ashbel Smith as "real secesh" &, previous to Kirby Smith's surrender, he was a candidate for Governor of the State.[5]

Specie is the only currency & has been for some eighteen months: it is tolerably plentiful. Indeed, the state has not suffered from the War. Col. Ward described Galveston, where he stopped, as rather broken down.[6]

A line drawn on the map through Palo Alto & Resaca de la Palma to the Rio Grande strikes our present bivouac, which is on the field of the last action of the War where too about a year or so since four armies—two on each side the river—were seen in action at the same time. It is a wretched land "which yields us no supply" and we are near the point of starvation, not having teams enough to haul rations.[7]

I look anxiously for the orders which shall convey our objectionable corps to its place of exile—each Regiment & Brigade to its permanent prison in this heated Siberia. I presume there are but few officers beside myself who, could they afford the journey home, would not immediately resign.

Perhaps, however, we may happen into some desirable locality. Texas is valued as an important acquisition to the United States: its land so far as heard from where I have been brings at highest prices about two cents per acre & likely to depreciate as civilization increases.

If Mexico is no more inviting than this place, I trust that Maximilian may be left in uninterrupted possession.[8]

But I am writing a very long letter.

My health is good.

I hope to see the 29th here in a day or two.

No news from home since we got our last mail at City Point—about the 25th of May.

> With much love to all, Your aff.
> brother, Edward W. Bacon

P.S. I shall send for another box soon in which I want—if you can get it, the best map of Texas, showing wagon roads, watering places, etc. Perhaps you can mail it. EWB

I may need the map for practical & official use, so make sure is the best.

Court Martial Chamber, Brownsville, Texas, July 5th, 1865

Dear Kate,

I last wrote home from our former bivouac at White's Ranch, a few miles above the mouth of the Rio Grande, at which place we remained, I think, four days. From that doleful desert we marched directly for Brownsville. The weather, which had been very warm, was fortunately cloudy, but the mud and water were so deep that we could make on the first day only ten miles and that at the loss of all the men's shoes which stuck fast in the bottom of the mud. Reaching a little rise of ground we bivouacked for the night and at four next morning started again and after crossing Palo Alto battle ground, had pretty good marching for some eight miles when we reached a body of clear water which stretched before us knee deep for a good mile. There was only one thing to be done: wade. Having gotten over the pond we again bivouacked at a place called Jackass Prairie, barren ground, save the growth of Prickly Pear & Chapparal, which only served to make the place more dismal. Moreover, rattle snakes, moccasins, Scorpions, centipedes, tarantulas and all manner of more insignificant torments made existence miserable & several officers were severely bitten by them.[9]

Jackass Prarie [Prairie] was our home for two nights but not the same spot for by sundown of the first day—after a heavy rain—the water from the pond before mentioned had encroached so as to be ankle deep in camp and still rising. We accordingly moved off about two miles nearer Brownsville & abode until morning where we made camp some two miles above the town, passing around it.

All this wretched marching was made more disagreeable by the fact that our horses had not arrived and all the field officers were on foot.

Brownsville is rather the best place I have seen in all of Texas thus far and even the most wretched hamlet, our most miserable districts at the north would be perfection compared to this place. The whole country, for long miles in every direction, is a miserable dead level with but little vegetable growth upon it. Vegetables are at present unknown & when can they be obtained, if not at this season? Beef seems tolerably plenty, but I can count the bones in every specimen of stock thus far seen. Eggs are a dollar per dozen and milk twenty-five cents per quart. Bananas sell readily at ten cents each.

Matamoros is generally esteemed—nicer place—than Brownsville; it is larger and every thing but food is cheaper there than here.[10]

I spent yesterday afternoon in that place & was much pleased with the French troops whom I do not desire to fight with our wretched negroes who as soldiers under the present system are almost a failure, sent into the desert to be hidden from their friends. If I supposed myself competent to be any thing but a soldier, I should immediately quit the organization.[11]

Indeed, resignations are constantly going in by the multitudes & a very unhealthy spirit of disquiet is alive throughout the army which it is extremely difficult to combat.

I just learn from an officer arrived from below that our Brigade Head Quarters the 9th U.S. and the 29th Conn. are a few miles below town en route. This is good news for probably they have some rumors from home. No letters have reached [us] since the last week in May and our latest New York dates are June 10th.

I hear nothing of the Express matter of summer clothes which missed me at City Point & money is so scarce that I am still sweltering in woolens. It is my impression that Adams Express does not [serve?] west of Galveston. The loss of the box will be considerable.

I was detached upon Gen'l Court Martial some few days since & we are now very busy trying cases long delayed. I expect to be on this duty for some weeks. I am told by an officer direct from Weitzel's Head Quarters that Corps Head Quarters will be here in a few days and that when this Division is scattered, the Second Brigade will remain in Brownsville. It is immaterial to me, though I had hoped to gain the interior which is said to be better; it cannot be worse than this section.

I will write again when we get more news.

Aff yr brother, Edward W. Bacon

Address via: New Orleans, La.

P.S. I send you to-days newspaper—price 15 cents.

Court Martial Chamber, Brownsville,
Texas, July 10th, 1865

Dear Kate,

Your letter of the 10th ultimo reached me yesterday, just as we were sitting down to dinner. It is my latest date, though some are so fortunate as to receive letters of the 20th.

I am much awed by the multitude of marriages in New Haven. What can the people mean or is this one of the results of the end of the war?

We have no such gossip in Texas. Indeed there are no inhabitants here, so far as I can ascertain, who are of good enough society for me to associate with. Even the limited stock of respectable people with which Brownsville was supplied before the War is now pretty much weeded out. Four ladies came out with the 29th Conn, the wives of Lt. Col. [David] Torrance, Capt. [Charles] Griswold, Lt. [Martin L.] Leonard & Adjt [J. Lewis] Spalding [Spaulding]. A Capt. Smith of the Brigade Staff has his wife here also & an Asst Surg of the 114th. But the women must be having a horrible time living at a mean hotel with board at the modest price of $16 per week. Query: how long an officer on subalterns pay can support himself & wife at such rates. Then, too, considering the neighborly gossip, jealousies and spats in the little circle, I am disposed to congratulate myself that my wife is not with me.[12]

Imagine a city girl upon the horrible march from Brazos de Santiago to Brownsville; yet we had three ladies through all that mud, at which every body swore, which must horribly have shocked their feelings. Until we settle comfortably into garrison, ladies should stay at home. The troops now are quite as much under privation & suffering (save that of action) as they usually were in

Virginia. Scurvy is beginning to manifest itself among the men, still the Sub-sistence Department has no anti scorbutics and the Medical Department has nothing at all. Men sent from Camp to Hospital lie on a hard brick floor until they die or get well, while the Satellites of the different Head Quarters keep constantly corned in whisky and mixed drinks. Indeed it is my belief that the Hd Qrt 25th Corps have not been sober since the evacuation of Richmond. In every department of the Corps—except that of Subsistence—there appears to be most criminal incompetency.[13]

Of course these remarks are highly improper and must not be repeated un-less you wish me dismissed the service.

We have no news at all. Some sort of negotiations seem to be going on with both Cortina and the imperialists across the river, but nothing is said as to the subject or nature. Every body sees the folly of plunging the Country into a Mexican War and all hands plead that we may not have one.

It is stated this morning that the wagons and artillery which Kirby Smith sold to Maximilian have been returned to Gen'l G. A. Smith, comdy U.S. Forces. The wagons have been parked conspicuously just this side of Matamoros city ever since our arrival here.[14]

Chaplain [Philander H.] Hollister of the 29th has resigned & goes home in a day or two. I have asked him to call when he visits New Haven, & if I have a chance, may pick up something to send by him.

I am still in some hopes of getting my Express box, though I really cannot inquire how it is to come here.

My horse arrived day before yesterday in very tolerable condition. Two horses in the regiment were lost.

Give much love to all at home and believe me ever,

Your affectionate brother, Edward W. Bacon

Gen'l Court Martial Chambers,
Brownsville, Texas, July 18th, 1865

Dear Kate,

I last wrote to you shortly after my arrival here & my detail upon this Court.

We are doing a good deal of business in Mutiny cases chiefly & if the revis-ing authorities do not spoil the cases doubtless a stop will be put to the highly disorderly proceedings which have disgraced the Corps ever since we started for Richmond.

Believing that the real evil lies in inefficient & "negro-worshipping" officers, I have now before the Court one of the 117th Captains for inciting and failing to suppress mutiny. His case will be followed by those of several enlisted men. A challenge in this case was sustained and I am consequently now at leisure for to day & to-morrow.[15]

There is literally no news, we have rumors of the execution of some of the Assassination Conspirators at Washington on the 7th inst, but my latest date from home is the 10th ult.[16]

Brownsville and its whole vicinity is now almost invisible to the naked eye, being obscured by dense clouds of fine dust which penetrate every thing & every where. Indeed washing is almost foolishness, so soon is one buried again.

Matamoros, "the Heroic City," as it styles itself, is even worse.

We have one bit of news, the frequent repetition of which may make trouble. That prince of cutthroats and out-laws, Cortina, than whom a greater vagabond does not remain unhung, captured last week a Mexican steamer, the *Camargo*, plying on the upper Rio Grande and, after pillaging her, tied her up to our bank of the river that she might escape recapture. I do not think our Government advanced the interest of civilization by lending any sort of countenance to this guerrilla.[17]

It is rumored this afternoon that our Brigade is to move up the river some seven miles where there is less dust.

We are very anxiously looking for a mail.

The Second Division, in which I have many friends, Col. Ward, Capt Ulrich & others, left here on Sunday for their Stations from Edinburg to Roma, a march of from 150 to 300 miles through this horrible country.

The 1st Division remains in this neighborhood.

Col. [William B.] Wooster has resigned, I know not from what immediate cause, but he has had many difficulties with his officers.[18]

Give much love to all at home and believe me
in haste, Your aff. Brother, Edward W. Bacon

P.S. There is a great deal of sickness & some suffering among the troops, the principal troubles being Scurvy and Broken Bone fever. With the exception of the Subsistence Department, we have no supplies, our horses are on half rations & there are no anti scorbutics. Corps Head Quarters seem to be having a pretty jolly life of it and for the matter of providing for the troops, no one seems to care a penny. Do not, however, allow any such statements to be made in connection with my name. My health is good.[19]

※

After almost four years of service, Bacon had reached a critical juncture. While still wishing to stay in the regular army, he doubted he could pass a retention examination. Also, he urgently wanted to see the last of Texas and a detested Brownsville. Henry G. Marshall, Bacon's friend in the 29th Connecticut, said the town was "a regular whore house and gambling shop outdoors."[20]

Bacon still thought it would be pleasant to serve in some "civilized" place, perhaps on some prestigious staff or with some interesting new board. Bacon forgot that after such an agreeable post, he might next endure unremitting boredom at an isolated fort in very hostile territory.

If he left the army, Bacon had no idea what to do as he had no civilian occupation. So again he turned to his father for guidance, and also asked him to pull a few strings and get him out of exile in Texas, ever his heated Siberia.

%

Private   Brownsville, Texas, August 5th, 1865

Dear Father,

I am in very much of a quandary what to do with myself.

There is a Circular out from Corps Head Quarters desiring the names of all those who wish to leave the service. Those who do not desire to leave (it is given to be understood) are to be subjected to a severe examination, one which I do not feel competent to pass.[21]

It has, as you know, been my intention, if I could obtain a position in the Regular Service, to remain in the Army, but I have pretty much given up that idea as impossible of fulfillment.

My reasons for this were, chiefly, because I know how to soldier better than I understand anything else and that in leaving the service, I should be obliged to take up something entirely new, to have a new business. But now there seems to be a probability that I shall have no choice in the matter.

If I do not resign and am sent to an Examination which I can not pass, shall I not have cause to regret that I did not resign?

Indeed, so strongly am I impressed with the probabilities of the case that if I could get the three months extra pay by resigning and knew of any congenial opening at the North, I think I should immediately leave the service. As matters now are, however, I shall remain as I am until I hear from you, which should be in about forty or fifty days from now. (Letters reach me in about twenty days from home.)

I believe that the very best thing which could be done would be to send me from the War Department the same sort of order which Adjt. Carrington received just as the Corps reached Brazos de Santiago, namely to report in person to the War Department for orders.

Such orders would bring me North on full pay where I could consult with you in regard to what my course had better be and, if deemed proper and possible to remain in the service, would open the way for duty in some civilized place where would be chance for improvement and in a climate which would be healthier than this, the effect of which is very enfeebling.

Should I have to leave the service here there is a very expensive journey North, even though transportation were furnished, for the simple Mess bill coming down reached over $60.[22]

I wish very much, therefore, that though our M.Cs., Gen'l Eaton, or some such quarter, you would make an effort to have such orders sent to me as soon as possible. There are many matters which I ought to discuss with my friends at home, and which a couple of hours conversation would settle, but which at this distance correspondence is insufficient to master.[23]

It is apparent—being a surplus Field Officer—that my services are not imperative with my regiment. I am now detached from it and my Colonel is not anxious for my return. There are many places at the North where, would I be kept in service, I might be of use to the Government at duty on some of the new Staff now organizing or on some of the boards appointed to investigate and pass upon accounts of retiring officers or perhaps, specially, in Gen'l Howard's new bureau.[24]

It has not been my custom to ask favors of the Government or of any Head Quarters. I never before asked one that I remember. I think my record in the service is officer-like enough to warrant such a proceeding on the part of the Department.

Duty in the Army of the Rio Grande, I am convinced, is not advantageous in any point of view, either that of health, of improvement in military knowledge, nor in the influence of respectable society, which are to one who has suffered exile from them for the War, of great value.

I really wish you would give this subject your full consideration.

Leaves of absence can not be obtained here and are too expensive luxuries when bestowed.

With much love to all at home

Ever your affectionate son,

P.S. Probably Senator Foster would be just the party to assist in the case.[25]

Brownsville, Texas, August 10th, 1865

Dear Kate,

My last date from home is July 14th from Rebecca containing, as she says, but little news. We are looking now for another mail which left Brazos de Santiago four days ago and which from the top of our Court House had been in sight for a day and a half, but the "Grand River of the North" is so tortuous and so rapid and the steamboat can raise so little steam that it is questionable exactly when we receive the great boon of news from home.

When it comes my dates ought to be to the 20th of July or perhaps to the first days of Commencement Week. It seems strange here—after the excellent mail facilities of the glorious Potomac Army—to have to remain so constantly behind the times to know that at the least there must be twenty days elapsed about which we know nothing, stranger than it did in my West Indian cruise to wait for seven months without the first rumor from home. However, in the West Indies and the Spanish Main there was so much that was pleasant, so much that was delightful constantly occurring that time passed rapidly while here there is absolutely nothing pleasurable and no news, so that if one writes at all, it must be in such stupid reflection as this.

I went again to Matamoros the other day with Lt. [Eugene S.] Bristol, a proceeding which nearly laid me up again, but which gave a little variety to our life here. We made some few purchases and enjoyed a dinner with potatoes, which in Matamoros are obtainable at $25 in specie per bbl. We also came across the oddest animal I think I ever saw, an armadillo.[26]

There is quite an excitement in the Corps now over the subject of resignations. In the 29th, Col. Wooster, Dr. Hyde, Capts. Allen & Sweetland and 1st Lts. Bristol and Bevin insist upon their immediate discharge under existing orders. In my regt. only two Captains desire to leave, though pretty much all hands talked strongly of resigning until the opportunity offered.[27]

I am still busy on Court Martial. We are now on the sixteenth day of a very long case, which will probably occupy ten days longer.

Boards of Examination are ordered for the examination of all officers. That for Colonels is announced. What one I shall go before I do not know yet as it is not announced. I presume it will be my lot to be examined twice, once for promotion and once for retention until the expiration of our term.

But I think perhaps it is as well to pause here until something else occurs to help fill this envelop. It really is an effort to write a letter.

Sunday August 13th

Your letter of the 10th and the 18th of July and Rebecca's of the 5th of July reached me yesterday morning—the slow steamer having at last arrived.

I don't understand what you say about Bob Styles and the assassination conspiracy, you have not mentioned any thing of the sort in previous letters received. The news in Rebecca's of the 5th was anticipated by the receipt in the previous mail of another letter from her of the 15th ultimo.[28]

We still have no news at all. Nothing ever happens here and our dates from the North are very irregular and unsatisfactory—a New York Herald or a Times costs 30¢ and the New Orleans papers are no cheaper.

We are still living without vegetables and the men are still dying of Scurvy—and the scant supply of tomatoes, which has in some way prevented an increase of scurvy, is now exhausted. The mortality among the troops is very large and the months for the largest mortality is yet to come. As I have several times before stated, the total sinful incompetency of the several departments is plainer than I ever thought it would appear. Only a few articles of clothing have been issued for more than three months and the men do not even get vinegar, without which the salt food of the ration is not palatable. This state of affairs exists at a time when profound peace is supposed to exist and when the Government is making vast sales of military stores at ruinous prices. It cannot be wondered at then, that an officer who understands his business, who understands and anticipates the wants of his troops and who appreciates a soldiers rights and privileges should be indignant. But it is none of my business, I suppose, and I ought not to wish I were serving in a department where some at least of the officials know and do their duty.[29]

I had pretty much given up all hopes of seeing my box of clothing but Major [name unclear], our Division Adjt Gen'l, got a box last night which had followed the Corps to some point, [then] returned to New York and from there been forwarded to New Orleans where a friend of the Major found it and sent it to him. I have accordingly written to the Company at New Orleans and anxiously await their answer.

Saturday August 26th
I must confess to some neglect in not before now dispatching this letter, but I really have hesitated to write without some excuse for news. But one might wait for that till dooms-day and not hear of it.

Since my last date I have received a letter from Rebecca and you down to the end of Commencement Week and one mail has come with nothing in it for me.

I am very sorry to hear of George's loss. I was quite in hopes sometime to be able to see his child as well as Leonard's youngest, both of which were born since I left home the last time.

The Gen'l Court Martial, of which I am a member, is still busily in session and still has some 30 cases yet to try. If charges continue to be sent to us as fast as we can work them off, our work may well be considered interminable. However, I prefer it to Regimental duty.

Adams Express Company have opened an office here at last and their Agent informed me that in a few days he expects all the stuff for the 1st Division to arrive here. I shall then be at rest.

There are rumors that none but Colored Troops are to occupy Texas, which may put us out of this horrible desert into some civilization but I can trace them to no source worth considering.[30]

Your letter directed to Washington came very promptly. Perhaps that is a better way than to send them to New Orleans.

With love to all, Your aff.
Brother, Edward W. Bacon

(5) HOMEWARD

BACON'S PLEA FOR RESCUE PRODUCED RESULTS. SISTER REBECCA read, then immediately forwarded the letter to their father, away on vacation. She conveyed a sense of urgency in a cover letter that was probably written in late August 1865.[1]

Leonard Bacon wrote both Amos B. Eaton, now the army's commissary general, and U.S. Senator Lafayette S. Foster, asking each to intercede on his son's behalf. But he cautioned his son that he had "no great hope" of action. Perhaps he was truly pessimistic or simply sought to avoid stirring unwarranted hope in his son.

However, Senator Foster, the Senate's president pro tempore, promptly asked Secretary of War Edwin M. Stanton to grant a twenty-day leave of absence for Major Edward W. Bacon, with that officer to report to the War Department in Washington for orders when his leave expired.[2]

Foster's intercession was effective, though the army acted at its own glacial pace.

Meanwhile, Bacon felt increasingly isolated and exhibited greater disaffection, alienation, even anomie. His father's reply offered no luminous life goal for him, but sensibly advised deferring any such decision until he returned home.

///

Colebrook, Sept. 2, 1865

My Dear Son,

Your letter of Aug. 5 came to hand last evening, having been forwarded from New Haven by Rebecca. I have written to Gen. Eaton and Senator Foster asking from each of them a word on your behalf at the War Department. I have, however, no great hope that anything will come of it. Should the Secretary or Assistant Secretary be inclined to send the orders you desire, you will be likely to receive the order before I know anything about the success of my efforts in that direction. Ex-adjutant [Edwin] Carrington suggests that if you receive such orders & can choose your own way of coming to Washington, it may be better for you to transport yourself & receive an allowance for mileage than to accept "transportation" from the government.

I am fully of [the] opinion that now the war is virtually (though not yet formally) ended, there are many ways in which you can serve God in your generation more effectively & acceptably than by remaining in the army. Even if the most desirable prospects of employment in the military profession were open before you, I should not hesitate to advise your resignation of your commission in order to engage in peaceful pursuits. I am not now prepared to say what sort of employment would be best for you. Much will depend on your own feelings & aspirations & much on the openings which may be made for you in the providence of God. I will only say that I dont think you are too old to prepare yourself for even a learned profession, and that the training you have had since the beginning of the war will be of use to you in almost any employment.

My advice is, in brief, that you come North, at any rate, as soon as you can, leaving all questions about the future to be decided after your arrival here.

By the way, if you came on finding conveyance for yourself, your journey will be more expeditious than if you receive "transportation"; & should you bring a servant with you (which may be expedient if practicable), you can be allowed half-mileage for him, so Edwin informed me.

Mond. Morning Sep 4. I expect to go home tomorrow, with the little girls. Your mother will probably remain here a week or two longer. May God give you a safe & prosperous journey homeward!

Affectionately, your father, Leonard Bacon

Brownsville, Texas, Sept. 8th, 1865

Dear Kate,

The latest news I have from you is your letter of August 2nd from Garrison's and I have nothing at all from home but dates heretofore acknowledged.[3]

I am afraid that my descriptions of this wretched country have made too deep an impression. I have described the country as it is—not as we make it—for one can oblige himself to get along decently even in the greatest discomfort. With-in this month the wants of the troops (and it was in their behalf that I complained—not mine), have been provided for, so that we are able now to have [illegible] and the Scurvy is not so prevalent as it was because the men have potatoes.

But the fact that we can live now makes the blame of previous neglect and suffering all the more severe.

There is no news with us. The reduction of the force of white troops in this Department would seem to look toward the transfer of some of the 25th Corps to the interior of the state. I can only hope for such a result; I have seen quite enough of the border.

We are to be paid on Tuesday next—the 12th inst. The men get six months pay to June 30th and I look for four months—to Aug. 31st. There is a faint promise that hereafter we will be paid regularly every two months but government promises are very queer matters.

Hoping that when we move we will be allowed proper transportation, I have run the risk of buying me a trunk in Matamoros and I only await the arrival of my box with thin clothing to fill it up. That forlorn box, however, I have as yet heard nothing of. After the arrival of the next batch of Expressage, I shall give it up as lost. Thin clothing, which you seem to think I will so much need, I have to some extent supplied my-self with in the Matamoros market.

The Gen'l Court Martial still holds its own, though the business is pretty much over. I have moved out to camp and am quartered in some degree of comfort, though just now it is very windy and dusty. The last rain nearly drowned every body out and this is its reverse—almost burying us in.

When the Court is dissolved, which will doubtless happen within a month, I do not expect to return to Regimental duty but shall obtain some detachment. Col. Brown's conduct has been so inconsiderate, unchivalrous and untruthful that in honor I can not serve under him again.[4]

Should any news turn up, I will write again.

With much love to all, Your aff. Brother

Brownsville, Texas, September 24th, 1865

Dear Kate,

Your letter of the 25th and Rebecca's of the 29th ultimo reached me in the last mail, three or four days ago.

I begin to answer them now, not that there is any news, for here such an article is unknown, but so that word of me shall be ready for the mail when it goes.

The same steamer brought Prof. Shepherd who kindly sought me out that same morning. He is going to have a very interesting expedition up the river. With him is a Judge Watrous of Galveston, who mentioned having known Frank. They are remaining in Brownsville about a week & I have tried to be polite to Prof. S. but he does not seem to take kindly to camp life. I am in hopes of seeing him at a Brigade dress parade to night.[5]

The same steamer brought also Lt. Bristol's box, through in about twenty days. Capt. Bennett had some things sent in it, and I am very sorry that you did not either put in some of my things or, better, send on a whole box to me. Before now you must have my letter telling you that Adams Express have opened an office in Brownsville, and I have still some hopes of getting some thing from home. Rebecca says she does not know what to send. By all means, the blouse which I had made last May and for want of which my dress coat is nearly thread-bare for the Matamoros clothes don't do when worn as "uniform." Indeed, I think that clothing in the original box would [not] be much avail now, unless, perhaps, the white jackets, rather expensive luxuries when washing costs $2.60 per dozen.

I send you a little memorial of my present quarters. The other night I woke up about twelve o'clock with a pricking sensation on my left wrist &, half awake, grabbed for the pin, as I supposed it. Imagine how pleasant to find the object in my sleeve wriggling in my fingers. As I pinched, he grew hot, almost too hot to hold. When his struggles ceased, I, now thoroughly awake, lighted my candle and found the enclosed scorpion. He had not bitten me because my sleeve fitted too close to give room for the blow with which the sting is given. He had crawled into the sleeve in the day time & had only been disturbed by some movement of mine in my sleep.[6]

Heretofore my quarters have been particularly fortunate. Only mosquitoes, Scorpions, lizards, ants and toads have infested them, with now and then a mouse, while some officers have killed tarantulas and snakes seen in their beds. I assure you that this is the Italy of America, indeed.

I have succeeded in getting Motley's Dutch Republic, quite a treasure in a land of no books and for only $1, sold low because nobody down here wants to read such a work.[7]

The Court Martial still holds its own, with a fair prospect of continuance for the remainder of the season. We have now got another interesting case before us, one Dr. Potts, who has been charged with trying experiments upon his men, hardly justified by the generally accepted idea of integrity.[8]

The 29th Conn have been for a few days past in great excitement with regard to going home; rumor being quite positive that orders for their Muster-out are in the Department. Indeed, the Army & Navy Journal, than which there is no more valuable paper in the land, seems in its last number to infer that all of the colored troops will soon be mustered out. That is contrary to the anticipation of all hands, for there have lately come many officers from white regiments to the 25th Corps hoping to obtain commissions for life. Perhaps they are mistaken. I am induced to hope not.[9]

Sept. 25th

I am expecting in a few days to be ordered before the Board of Examination to be dissected as to character and education by gentlemen, the majority of whom can ask more questions than they can answer, and if I keep my temper & give them satisfaction, to be recommended for promotion one grade. I don't much expect to give them satisfaction, for long continued Court Martial duty has rusted my tactics and my school-boy knowledge of the Classics and particularly of mathematics, insufficient of itself for so August a Board, has at least not been brightened by four years and over in the service. So even performance of duty is made prejudicial to one's interests. But details of Examining Boards are worth more to those interested than to you at home.[10]

Please do not forget to send in each letter which you write a few stamps. My supply is running very low indeed, and the Post Office Department don't take care of Brownsville.

In case I receive orders to appear for Examination, all my spare time will be occupied in reviewing such works as have within reach, mainly Revised Regulations U.S.A. and the thin volume of Casey's Tactics, so in case my correspondence should seem irregular, you will know how to account for the fact.[11]

I presume College is together by this time.[12]

When any friends of mine call, remember to say that I inquire after them. Tell Chapman—specifically—that I have answered his last epistle and await another with anxiety.

But my sheet is nearly full.

With much love to all, Believe me, Your
aff. Brother, Edward W. Bacon

※

That was Bacon's last extant letter from Texas.

Perhaps he wrote additional letters describing his next moves. If so, they have disappeared. As it is, only his relatively thick Compiled Military Service Record with the 117th U.S. Colored Infantry reveals subsequent events.

First, Bacon declined to take the examination for promotion to lieutenant colonel and the regiment's senior captain did and passed. Then he got permission on October 3, 1865, to travel to headquarters at Ringgold, Texas, to obtain home leave.

Next he went home. How he got there is unknown, but Bacon arrived in New Haven sometime toward the end of October. There he began considering his future and, at the same time, sought extensions of his leave. At one point, he was declared absent without leave, but that difficulty was resolved.[13]

Rather quickly he learned that not much call existed in civil life for the skills he had acquired while serving his country since 1861. So, like many other young men who had already lived a lifetime, he was at a loss as to what to do with himself as a civilian. Though but twenty-two-years-old, Bacon poignantly conveyed his sense of estrangement from the normal, peacetime world he had known ages earlier.

※

New Haven, Conn., October 28, 1865

Dear Father,

When I was in Rochester, on my way home, Theodore promised me a letter of introduction from Gov. Selden to Secretary Stanton.[14]

In the early part of November, I propose—armed with that—to visit Washington and see how matters look there. If, during your present visit, you can at all pave the way for me in any quarter at the Capital, I shall be very much obliged.

It being probable that my regiment will not long remain in service, it is doubtless wise for me to leave the service while on leave. If you can ascertain any thing in regard to the muster out of more troops on the Rio Grande, particularly the 117th U.S.C.T., raised in Kentucky, it will be of assistance to me.[15]

I have been looking about since my return and there seems to be nothing in the world for an ex-soldier to do.

Aff. your son, Edward W. Bacon

EPILOGUE

EDWARD W. BACON RESIGNED FROM THE ARMY ON NOVEMBER 20, 1865, and was honorably discharged by the Military Division of the Gulf on January 8, 1866.[1]

Footloose and uncertain for a while, he soon ventured upon a new career. Almost certainly his father influenced the choice and also helped him to overcome his concerns that he was too old to return to university classrooms. Probably few were surprised when Bacon entered Yale Divinity School. Two older brothers, Leonard and George, had entered the ministry and, of course, father Leonard Bacon enjoyed high standing as a Congregational clergyman.[2]

In 1868 Edward Bacon earned his Bachelor of Divinity degree at Yale, and then married Mary E. Staples, granddaughter of Jonathan Knight, former head of the Yale Medical School. Soon they had their first child, George W., born in 1869.

Also in 1869 he became the minister of a church in Wolcottville, now part of Torrington, Conn. But soon Bacon moved his wife and son to Flint, Michigan, as pastor of another Congregational church and there a second son was born in March 1873, followed by a daughter in December 1874. A Flint history's church section reported that he belonged to the "celebrated Bacon family of Connecticut" and that the new minister was "conspicuous for his rare gift of preaching."[3]

Next Bacon shifted to a church in Springfield, Ohio. After a short time with that gathering, he learned of a vacancy closer to his roots and family. The First Congregational Church of New London, Conn., needed a minister and he took that post in 1877. Church members described him as a "scholarly preacher and able pastor."[4]

Seemingly, all was well. Bacon had adjusted to civilian life. He took time off in 1876 to accompany his father and several brothers on a sentimental journey to the senior Bacon's beginnings in Ohio. However, that year was shadowed by the death of sister Rebecca, the family stalwart. Apparently he spent little time looking back on his war service, though he retained some interest in military matters. He belonged to the Army and Navy Club and for a time served as a chaplain for the 3rd Connecticut National Guard regiment. One source declared that he "was a great favorite with the members of the command." Then in 1879 he addressed the New London Historical Society with a paper entitled "New London and the War of 1812."[5]

Yet all was not well. As a lad and as a youthful sailor and soldier, Bacon's family had always worried about his health and believed that he had a frail constitution. Bacon himself spoke of afflictions during his service and likely the years in the armed forces had hastened the advance of his illness.[6]

At any rate, "consumptive tendencies" appeared in the early 1880s. In modern terminology, that meant he showed symptoms of active tuberculosis. His mother had died of the disease in 1844, just a year after his birth, and an older brother, Benjamin, had succumbed to it in 1848. At the time, no antibiotics existed to kill or suppress the responsible bacteria. Then the only treatment for the contagious disease—and that only newly recognized—was for the patient to seek a cure in a better climate or in a sanatorium.[7]

Sorrow joined worry when Bacon and his wife lost their oldest son, George. Described as a "bright boy," the thirteen- or fourteen-year-old died in New London in 1883.

Though the New London church listed Bacon as serving there until 1886, he took his family West sometime in 1884 in an effort to restore his health. He served briefly in 1884–85 at the First Congregational Church of Santa Barbara, California, but "unwisely" returned to New London when he felt better. But consumption also returned with a vengeance and Bacon then went back to California. There he was a minister at the First Congregational Church of Berkeley. It was in San Francisco, across the bay, that his wife gave birth to their last child, Rebecca, born in 1886.[8]

In a last desperate effort to reverse the course of his illness, Bacon entered a sanatorium in Santa Clara County, just south of San Francisco. It was too late. He died in June 1887 at the age of forty-four.[9]

Mary Staples Bacon, his widow, was left with three children, but then death struck again. Rebecca, their last born, died in 1889 when about three years old. Bacon's father had died in 1881 at the age of seventy-nine and the surviving sons, including Edward, had acted as pallbearers.

Sister Kate (Katherine), Bacon's steadfast correspondent during the war, married in 1872 when about twenty-four, then bore two boys and two girls, in that order. She lived until 1915, dying at the age of sixty-seven.[10]

Fortune favored some senior navy and army officers who figured in Bacon's Civil War, but untimely deaths took several. Andrew H. Foote, the abolitionist naval officer who steered Bacon to his captain's clerk berth, was wounded twice at Fort Donelson and won promotion to rear admiral in 1862, but then died in New York City in December 1863 at the age of fifty-seven.[11]

Jams S. Palmer, captain of the *Iroquois* and the *Hartford*, continued to rise in rank. In July 1866 he became a rear admiral. Then in those same waters where he had hunted and lost the CSS *Sumter*, he contracted yellow fever and died in 1867 at St. Thomas, Virgin Islands, also at the age of fifty-seven.[12]

Raphael Semmes, the nemesis of Palmer and the U.S. Navy when he commanded the *Sumter* and *Alabama*, finally came to grief when he fought the USS *Kearsarge* on June 19, 1864, off Cherbourg, France. Semmes lost that battle and jumped from his sinking ship into the ocean where an English yacht rescued him. But victorious Federals arrested him in December 1865 for violating the rules of war because he did not swim to the *Kearsarge* to give himself up as a prisoner. Released after almost four months in prison, he became a professor, newspaper editor, and then practiced law in Mobile, Ala. He died in 1877.[13]

David G. Farragut, sometimes criticized but usually admired by Bacon, advanced to rear admiral in July 1862, then to vice admiral after winning the battle of Mobile Bay on August 5, 1864. He won promotion to full admiral in 1866, the first in the American navy. But in a few years he became ill and succumbed to a stroke in 1870. He was sixty-nine.[14]

Amos B. Eaton, who gave the hospital clerk job to Bacon, became the army's commissary general in 1864 and held that post for the next ten years. Breveted major general for his war service, he was forced to retire in 1874 after forty-five years in the army. He then made his home in New Haven, dying in 1877.[15]

William B. Wooster, colonel of the 29th Connecticut Infantry (Colored), drew Bacon's ire when he frequently absented himself from the regiment. Wooster, an 1846 Yale Law School graduate and prewar Republican legislator, returned to Connecticut and established a law practice. However, he did not receive the customary brevet promotion after he resigned from the army in 1865.[16]

Lewis G. Brown, Bacon's last commanding officer, first enlisted in the 11th Ohio Infantry and rose to captain before shifting to the 117th U.S. Colored Infantry as its colonel. Initially, Bacon praised him, then grew disenchanted. But Brown received a brevet promotion to brigadier general and commanded a brigade in the 25th Army Corps. He returned to Ohio and killed himself in 1889 when forty-seven-years-old.[17]

Homer B. Sprague, who encouraged Bacon's desire to serve in the army, wrote the 13th Connecticut's history in 1867 and in 1887 became the University of North Dakota's second president. An academic, he wrote and lectured on Milton and Shakespeare. Born in 1829, he lived until 1918.[18]

Many black soldiers, like those Bacon had commanded in the 117th U.S. Colored Infantry, often had no home or family to which they could return. They belonged to regiments organized in slave states and filled with former slaves. In the great displacement of blacks caused by the war, sons and parents became separated, sometimes forever. Some tried to reconnect by placing ads in black newspapers. Those forlorn pleas continued to appear long after Lee's surrender.[19]

ABBREVIATIONS USED IN NOTES AND BIBLIOGRAPHY
NOTES
BIBLIOGRAPHY
INDEX

ABBREVIATIONS USED IN NOTES AND BIBLIOGRAPHY

AAS	American Antiquarian Society
AG	Adjutant General
AGO	Adjutant General's Office
APS	American Philosophical Society
B&L	*Battles and Leaders*
CDC	Centers for Disease Control and Prevention
CHS	Cincinnati Historical Society
CMSR	Compiled Military Service Record
CDAB	*Concise Dictionary of American Biography*
ConnHS	Connecticut Historical Society
CWH	*Civil War History*
CWP	*Civil War Papers*
CWSS	Civil War Soldiers and Sailors System
CWTI	*Civil War Times Illustrated*
DANFS	*Dictionary of American Naval Fighting Ships*
EWB	Edward Woolsey Bacon
GHQ	*Georgia Historical Quarterly*
HEH	Henry E. Huntington Library, San Marino, Calif.
HNOC	Historic New Orleans Collection
IMH	*Indiana Magazine of History*
KSHS	Kansas State Historical Society
LSU	Louisiana State University
MOLLUS	Military Order of the Loyal Legion of the United States
MHS	Montana Historical Society
NA	National Archives and Records Administration
NPS	National Park Service
NHC	Naval Historical Center
NHM&HS	New Haven Museum & Historical Society
NYHSQ	*New-York Historical Society Quarterly*
NYPL	New York City Public Library
OR	*The War of the Rebellion: A Compilation of the Official Records of the Union and Confederate Armies*

ORN	*Official Records of the Union and Confederate Navies*
PCMS	*Proceedings Connecticut Medical Society*
PN	*Personal Narratives*
RG	Record Group
RISSHS	Rhode Island Soldiers and Sailors Historical Society
SHSP	*Southern Historical Society Papers*
UM	University of Michigan, Ann Arbor
UNC	University of North Carolina, Chapel Hill
USC	University of South Carolina
USCI	United States Colored Infantry
USCT	United States Colored Troops
YU	Yale University

NOTES

United States and Confederate States vessel specifications derive from the *Dictionary of American Naval Fighting Ships,* a Naval Historical Center online resource at www.history.navy.mil/danfs/index.html. After the first descriptive identification, most subsequent ship entries will not repeat the citation *DANFS,* NHC.

INTRODUCTION

1. Fox, *Regimental Losses,* 62.

2. On dual service, see Everson, ed., "Service Afield and Afloat," 47; Gould, ed., *Diary,* 188, 156; Milligan, ed., *Fresh-Water Navy,* 19.

3. H. Davis, *Leonard Bacon,* 194–97; Basler, ed., *Collected Works,* 7:281.

4. AG, *Record,* 3, 19.

5. Ringle, *Life in Mr. Lincoln's Navy,* 37–39, 74–77.

6. Livingston, ed., *Civil War Marine,* 67; Swift, ed., "Letters from a Sailor," 59.

7. Ringle, *Life in Mr. Lincoln's Navy,* 113–20; Gould, *Diary,* 194; Huch, ed., "Civil War Letters," 24; EWB to Skiddy, July 16, 1862, AAS.

8. EWB diary, Oct. 26, 1861, AAS; [Homer B. Sprague], from camp of 13th Connecticut Volunteers, to EWB, Nov. 15, 1862, AAS.

9. Davis, *Leonard Bacon,* 50–73; Burkhardt, *Confederate Rage,* chap. 1, "Emancipation and Black Soldiers."

10. Mickley, *Forty-Third Regiment,* 85; Blight, ed., *When This Cruel War Is Over,* 316; Howe, ed., *Home Letters,* 252–53; Hunter, ed., *One Flag One Country,* 59; Romeyn, "With Colored Troops," 14–15.

11. AG, *Record,* 293, 310.

12. Davis, *Leonard Bacon,* 178–79.

13. Kellogg, ed., *Army Life,* 165; Rebecca T. Bacon to Frank, Nov. 21, 1863, Bacon Family Papers, YU.

14. See Davis, *Leonard Bacon,* 179, for Rebecca's reaction to father's debt burden.

15. EWB to Kate, Aug. 1, 1862, AAS.

16. EWB to Kate, March 31, 1865, AAS; Thorpe, *Fifteenth Connecticut,* 201; Wash Vosburgh to Ella, Aug. 22, 1864, UM; Bowditch, "War Letters," 424, 469.

17. Henry H. Brown diary, vol. 7, pasted letter from EWB to Acting Adjutant H. H. Brown [29th Connecticut], Oct. 29, 1864, Henry Harrison Brown Papers, ConnHS; EWB to Kate, April 26, 1864, Sept. 8, 1865, and to Father, Nov. 9, 1864.

18. EWB to Father, Aug. 11, 1864, AAS; Redkey, ed., *Grand Army,* 262.

19. Randall, *Civil War,* 51, 77; Davis, *Leonard Bacon,* 58–59.

20. Bennett, *Union Jacks,* 12; Quarles, *Negro,* 230.

21. For the USS *Hartford,* see *DANFS,* NHC.

22. On free blacks as better soldiers, also see Bowditch, "War Letters," 468; Henry G. Marshall to Folks at Home, Sept. 6, 1864, Schoff Coll., UM.

23. Besides EWB's letters and diary, other captain's clerk accounts are Morrow, ed., *Journal of Leslie G. Morrow*; Osbon, *Sailor of Fortune*; Albert D. Bache's diary, APS; and Scheller, ed., *Under the Blue Pennant*.

24. For naval strengths, see Bennett, *Union Jacks*, 5; Tucker, *Blue & Gray Navies*, 9.

25. On riverine warfare, also see Gary D. Joiner, *Mr. Lincoln's Brown Water Navy: The Mississippi Squadron* (Lanham, Md.: Rowman & Littlefield, 2007).

26. Anderson, *By Sea*, 303; Tucker, *Blue & Gray Navies*, 361, 365.

PART ONE. THE SAILOR, 1861–62

1. High Seas Hunt

1. Everson and Simpson, eds., *"Far, Far from Home,"* 4; Kakuske, ed., *A Civil War Drama*, 18; Dunlap, ed., *"Your Affectionate Husband,"* 3; Milligan, *Fresh-Water Navy*, 13, 167; Durham, ed., *"'Dear Rebecca,'"* 183; Roberson, ed., *Weep Not for Me*, 93.

2. Elias Davis to Mother, running letter, Dec. 10–18, 1863, UNC; Wash Vosburgh to Ella, March 29, 1864, UM; J. T. Kern to Mother, J. T. Kern Papers, #2526, UNC; Weigley, *Quartermaster General*, 287.

3. Laas, ed., *Wartime Washington*, 187n5, for derisive reference to abolitionists; Davis, *Leonard Bacon*, 188–89.

4. G. R. Sherman, "Negro as a Soldier," 9; Silber and Sievens, eds., *Yankee Correspondence*, 111, Edward F. Hall.

5. Basler, *Collected Works*, 4:331–32.

6. Livingston, ed., *Civil War Marine*, 67; Swift, "Letters," 52, 55, 59.

7. Evans, *Sailor's Log*, 65; "Anti Shoddy" to editor, New York *Herald*, Jan. 25, 1862, complaining about shoddy pea jackets; EWB to George, Sept. 28, 1862, AAS.

8. Swift, "Letters," 52–53; Evans, *Sailor's Log*, 61; Basile, ed., "Harry Stanley's Mess Book," 72–73; Gould, *Diary*, 110.

9. Bennett, *Union Jacks*, 13–15, 182–85 192–95; "Casualties: U. S. Navy," NHC electronic; Coleman, "A July Morning," 6; E. W. Goble to Joseph B. Boyd, Feb. 11, 1862, Joseph B. Boyd Papers, CHS; Evans, *Sailor's Log*, 67, 74–75; Bartholomew Diggins, "Recollections of the War Cruise of the U. S. Flag Ship Hartford," handscript ms., NYPL, 264; Huch, "Civil War Letters," 18; Gould, *Diary*, 121, 131, 153, 162, 164, 167, 176, 188, 203; Daly, ed., *Aboard the USS Florida*, 175.

10. Livingston, *Civil War Marine*, 106; Milligan, *Fresh-Water Navy*, 111; Bennett, *Union Jacks*, 30, citing William Mason Bright journal, Aug. 1, 1864, George Adams Bright Coll., HEH; Swift, "Letters," 55, 59.

11. Michael J. Crawford, Head, Early History Branch, NHC, to editor, Oct. 29, 2004; "Regulations for . . . Navy, 1865," 4, para. 249; "The Captain's Clerk," for "fair hand" requirement, www.polkcounty.org/timonier/clerk/clerk.html (access Nov. 30, 2008).

12. Foote, born 1806 in New Haven, joined the navy as a midshipman in 1822 and helped end the daily grog ration in 1862, NHC and www.historyofwar.org/articles/people_foote_ah.html (access Nov. 30, 2008); A. H. Foote to Leonard Bacon, June 10, 1861, EWB Papers, AAS.

13. James S. Palmer, born 1810 in New Jersey, became a midshipman at age fifteen, commanded a ship during the Mexican War, and became the *Iroquois'* captain at her commissioning, NHC; USS *Iroquois,* a thousand-ton steam sloop, was launched at the

New York Navy Yard in 1859; Lincoln had proclaimed a blockade of Southern ports on April 19, 1861, Basler, *Collected Works*, 4:338–39.

14. The "decent fellow" was possibly Midshipman Bartlett J. Cromwell, a career naval officer who became an acting master in September 1861 and rear admiral in 1899, NHC; Hamersly, *Records*, 88.

15. Hampton Roads, Va., was an important Federal naval base; the letters mentioned, among others, are missing from the collection.

16. When Theodore or any man recruited a company or regiment, he usually became its leader; Oyster Point was at the river's mouth, near the oyster grounds; Gerard Hallock built a fine house there, E. M. Brown, *New Haven*, 40; Adrian Terry of New Haven did become the quartermaster but in a few months transferred to a rifle company as a 1st lieutenant, AG, *Record*, 293, 304.

17. Sherman W. Knevals was a tailor in New Haven, census, Ancestry.com.

18. A. Jones, *Civil War Command*, 142; Daly, *Aboard the USS Florida*, 20, letter to Anna, April 11, 1863; Diggins, "Recollections," 244, NYPL; Milligan, *Fresh-Water Navy*, 153. For a comprehensive analysis of the blockade and its effectiveness, see Anderson, *By Sea*, 215–32.

19. Anderson, *By Sea*, 9, 12; Carrison, *Navy*, 4, 9; Dalzell, *Flight from the Flag*, 249.

20. Anderson, *By Sea*, 44–45; Dalzell, *Flight from the Flag*, 237–62; J. A. Butler, *Sailing on Friday*, 100–101.

21. Basler, *Collected Works*, 4:338–39; Welles, *Diary*, 1:216; Evans, *Sailor's Log*, 59; EWB to George, Oct. 17, 31, and diary entries Oct. 1, 26, 1861; Anderson, *By Sea*, 45; Davis, *Rise and Fall*, 2:10–12.

22. Nash, *Naval History*, 293–99; Carrison, *Navy*, 140–43; Anderson, *By Sea*, 43–44, 196–206, 213; Evans, *Sailor's Log*, 55, 58, 60, 63–64, 70; Livingston, *Civil War Marine*, 88–89; *Official Records of the . . . Navies (ORN)*, 1:20, 22, 240, 576, 2:234.

23. Anderson, *By Sea*, 180–81, 185–91; Nash, *Naval History*, 275.

24. Gosnell, ed., *Rebel Raider*, 3–4, 11–16; Campbell, ed., *Stainless Banner*, 41–45.

25. The *Jeff Davis*, a full-rigged brig, began as a slaver and ended as a privateer, capturing nine Yankee vessels in seven weeks in the summer of 1861, "causing consternation on the coast from Maine to Delaware," *DANFS*, NHC.

26. William Skiddy, then sixteen or seventeen, the son of a retired sea captain, was probably a former classmate, census, Ancestry.com.

27. *St. Lawrence*, a 1,700-ton fifty-gun vessel with a crew of 480, first sailed in 1848; "banked fires" meant keeping a low fire under the boilers which could be quickly brought to full blast; the side-wheel steamer *Harriet Lane* originally served as a Treasury Department revenue cutter but transferred to the navy as war loomed; Silas H. Stringham, born in 1798, commanded the North Atlantic Blockading Squadron and retired Dec. 21, 1861, but continued to serve at the Boston Navy Yard, Hamersly, *Records*, 20–21; the *Minnesota*, a wooden steam frigate, served as squadron flagship.

28. EWB repeatedly wrote "Sumpter," an incorrect spelling for "Sumter"; Denmark then owned St. Thomas and other Virgin Islands.

29. Lieutenant David B. Harmony, mentioned several times, remained in the navy after the war, becoming a rear admiral in 1889, NHC; *New York Times*, June 24, 1891, 8.

30. Originally a seafaring family, the Trowbridges were well established in New Haven. Edward H. Trowbridge, native of the city (b. 1824), protected American interests in the Caribbean during the war and died in Barbados in 1877 at the age of fifty-three,

e-mail to editor, July 19, 2007, from Megan G. Sheils, librarian, Ralph J. Bunche Library, State Department, Washington, D.C.

31. George, an older brother (b. 1836), was first a reporter, then a minister.

32. EWB apparently heard a story that confused place and event. At Paramaribo on Aug. 19, 1861, the Dutch authorities readily supplied the *Sumter* with coal; but at Curaçao in mid-July, another Dutch island, officials initially refused the raider entry into the port, whereupon Lieutenant Robert T. Chapman, the *Sumter's* envoy, advised the Dutch that if refused, he "could not be responsible for what might happen to Dutch vessels at sea," Campbell, *Stainless Banner,* 49–50; William P. Brooks, handscript recollections in scrapbook, 11 (MS 961), Georgia Historical Society.

33. *Sumter* left Maranhan on Sept. 15, captured the brigantine *Joseph Parke* 450 miles northeast of the Amazon River on Sept. 25 and took the schooner *Daniel Trowbridge* 300 miles east of Guadeloupe on Oct. 27, 1861, so she was far more than 100 miles from the *Iroquois,* Campbell, *Stainless Banner,* 53–54; Gosnell, *Rebel Raider,* 208–9.

34. Dasent's father had served the Crown in the British West Indies island of St. Vincent as attorney general; H.B.M.S.—Her Britannic Majesty's Ship, usually just HMS, Her (or His) Majesty's Ship; the *Cadmus* was a screw-driven corvette of twenty-one guns, Peter Davis, "Mid-Victorian RN Vessels," access at www.pdavis.nl (Feb. 17, 2009).

35. David Dixon Porter commanded the USS *Powhatan,* a 2,400-ton side-wheel steamer with a speed of eleven knots, and had hunted the *Sumter* in the West Indies from August to October 1861; Charles Wilkes had recently returned from Africa with the USS *San Jacinto,* a 1,500-ton ship, one of the navy's first propeller-driven vessels.

36. The Cornet was a signal flag, in this instance used to recall crew members on shore, letter from Michael J. Crawford, Head, Early History Branch, NHC, to editor, Oct. 29, 2004; capstan bars were wooden bars of uniform length inserted into the upright, rotating capstan mechanism which, when turned by hand, lifted the heavy anchor. Note that *Ed, Wd, Nd, Sd* are EWB's abbreviations for *eastward, westward, northward,* and *southward.*

37. Eye surgeons consulted for this work report that a form of tuberculosis can cause acute eye sensitivity to bright light. The Bixbes and Mentz cannot be further identified.

38. "*S*" is the *Sumter.*

39. Bacon's "under fire" comment is unexplained, as neither he nor Capt. Palmer mention any such incident. Possibly a shore battery lobbed a shell at the *Iroquois* while on blockade duty.

40. La Guaira is the port for Caracas; USS *Macedonian,* a thirty-six--gun frigate with a crew of 489, entered service in 1836.

41. The Dragon's Mouths or Bocas del Dragón are a series of straits along the coast; Porto Cabello, Venezuela, lies north west of La Guaira.

42. Both merchantmen and navy vessels often sailed under false colors, but warships had to show their true colors before taking action.

43. A corvette launched in 1836, the *Acheron* took its name from Greek mythology and meant "river of woe," *Dictionnaire des bâtiments,* www.netmarine.net/dico/tome1-a-pdf (access Nov. 18, 2008).

44. Clitz soon won promotion to commander and his own ship, Hamersly, *Records,* 72; USS *Dacotah* was a steam sloop with a speed of eleven knots.

45. Anagada Passage is the risky reef-ridden way between the British Virgin Islands and St. Martin, the Dutch-French island.

46. "Half a cable length"—a cable length is 720 feet, so the *Sumter* steamed northward about 360 feet from shore.

47. *ORN* 1:209–10.

48. Gosnell, *Rebel Raider,* 130–33; Campbell, *Stainless Banner,* 58–59.

49. *ORN* 1:213–14, 645, reports of Palmer and Semmes; Gosnell, *Rebel Raider,* 133, 136–39.

50. Now EWB spells the raider's name correctly.

51. Federals unsuccessfully besieged Charleston until Feb. 18, 1865, when Confederates abandoned the battered city.

52. Terry later commanded an Army Corps; EWB had a long wait—Fort Sumter resisted attacks almost to the end.

53. Campbell, *Stainless Banner,* 59–61; Brooks recollections, 13, Georgia Historical Society.

54. Campbell, *Stainless Banner,* 63–65, 70–71.

55. Palmer's request for a formal inquiry is at *ORN* 1:215.

56. EWB here refers to the *Trent* Affair, an Anglo-American crisis caused by Charles Wilkes, commanding USS *San Jacinto.* He forcibly removed two Confederate envoys from the British steamer *Trent* on Nov. 8, 1861. U.S. officials returned the pair to British custody on January 1, 1862, and wrote a conciliatory letter to the British, for which see Anderson, *By Sea,* 181–85; Fairfax, "Captain Wilkes's" in Johnson and Buel, eds., *Battles and Leaders of the Civil War,* 2:135–42 (hereafter cited as *B&L*); Basler, *Collected Works,* 5:62–64, 82–83.

57. USS *Quaker City,* a 13-knot side-wheel gunboat and a blockader, also had joined the search for CSS *Sumter.*

2. Riverine Warfare

1. *ORN* 1:215; Gosnell, *Rebel Raider,* 133, 146, 208–9; *New York Times,* Dec. 12, 14, 15, 16; *Philadelphia Inquirer,* Dec. 14, 16, 1861.

2. Rebecca A. Livingston, Old Military and Civil Records, NA, to editor, April 17, 2006, described Palmer's hearing and Welles's letter, available on Microfilm Publication M149, NA, while retirement board proceedings are in Judge Advocate General records, RG 125, NA; EWB diary, April 3, 1862, AAS.

3. On sickness and poor medical care, see EWB to Kate, July 11, 1862; E. W. Goble to Joseph B. Boyd, USS *Forest Rose,* July 1, 1863, Joseph B. Boyd Papers, CHS; Huch, "Civil War Letters," 24.

4. Jones, *Civil War Command,* 162–64, argued that Vicksburg's loss in July 1863 had little "strategic importance" to the Confederacy, though it was of great political significance. However, it is indisputable that Vicksburg's fall ended major movements of Confederate supplies or troops across the river.

5. Porter, "Opening," *B&L* 2:22–54; Meredith, "Farragut's Capture of New Orleans," *B&L* 2:70–73; "Opposing Forces . . . at New Orleans," *B&L* 2:73–75; Diggins, "Recollections," 82–90, NYPL; Silber and Sievens, *Yankee Correspondence,* 30–32, W. H. Robert to Wife, April 28, 1862; Massa, "Fire and Brimstone," transcribed by Terry Foenander, www.TFoenander.com/massa.htm (access Nov. 20, 2008); Albert D. Bache diary, April 18, 1862, APS.

6. Walke, "Gun-boats" and "Western Flotilla," both *B&L* 1:358–67, 430–52; Ballard, *Vicksburg,* 27–29.

7. For an excellent study of the lengthy campaign, see Ballard's *Vicksburg*; EWB to George, Sept. 28, 1862.

8. For EWB's reactions under fire, see his poignant passages in letters to Isham, July 5, 1862, and to George P. Brinley, Sept. 28, 1862.

9. USS *Rhode Island* was a civilian steamer when the navy bought the 1,500-ton side-wheeler in 1861 and initially used her as a fleet supply ship.

10. The *Merrimac* (CSS *Virginia*) and the USS *Monitor* fought their epic duel at Hampton Roads on March 9, the first between ironclad ships; Federals besieged York-town, Va., during the Peninsular Campaign, and it fell when Confederates retreated on May 3, 1862.

11. Major General Ambrose E. Burnside attacked North Carolina coastal strong-points in February, then Beaufort on April 11, capturing the place on April 26, 1862, Burnside, "Burnside Expedition, *B&L*, 1:660–69.

12. The USS *Cambridge* was an 868-ton screw steamer, converted to navy use in August 1861.

13. Both the *Monticello*, captained by Lieutenant Daniel L. Braine, and the *Mt. Vernon* proved adept at capturing blockade runners, but the *Jamestown* was equally successful; brothers Francis (Frank) and Theodore, both 7th Connecticut Infantry, took part in the successful attack on Fort Pulaski, Ga.

14. South West Pass was an entrance to the Mississippi River from the Gulf of Mexico.

15. Commander David D. Porter had assembled a small fleet of schooners, each mounting a heavy thirteen-inch mortar, to bombard the forts guarding New Orleans.

16. EWB altered the name, making it illegible.

17. CSS *Nashville*, a fast 1,200-ton side-wheel steamer outfitted as a commerce raider, slipped in and out of Georgetown, S.C., embarrassing Federal blockaders.

18. Major General Mansfield Lovell, CSA, withdrew his four thousand troops from New Orleans and civil authorities surrendered the city on April 29, 1862, see Kautz, "Incidents of the Occupation," and Baker, "Farragut's Demands," both *B&L* 2:91–94, 95–99.

19. EWB's version is also skewed. Porter had gathered nineteen schooners, each with one huge thirteen-inch mortar, with which he thought he could demolish the forts, *ORN* 18:356–446; high water had also moved the chain obstructions stretched across the river; Commodore George N. Hollins, CSN, helped organize New Orleans defenses; CSS *Manassas,* an ironclad resembling a half-submerged floating cigar, blew up after the fight but did not sink the *USS Varuna,* a propeller-gunboat sunk by two other Confederate ships, *DANFS*, NHC; Read, "Reminiscences," 342–43; Warley, "Ram Manassas," *B&L* 2:89–91.

20. The 13th Connecticut left New Haven March 17, 1862, and arrived in Louisiana April 13, AG, *Record*, 510.

21. Sailors draped heavy chains over ships' sides to deflect enemy projectiles; the cutwater is the bow's leading edge as the ship slices through water and the bow sprit is a spar projecting outward from a ship's bow; *Iroquois* sustained damage and casualties in passing the guardian forts, *ORN* 18:221–22; Massa, "Fire and Brimstone," electronic.

22. Tar was a nickname for sailors, derived from their practice of waterproofing clothing with tar.

23. The meaning of "New York custom" is uncertain, unless he refers to pushy habits; launched in 1843, the USS *Portsmouth* was a wooden sail sloop, and apparently older brother George (b. 1836) had sailed on her.

24. The *Manassas*'s namesake reference is unclear. If the first battle of Manassas, or Bull Run, in July 1861, that was a Confederate victory; barbette guns are those mounted on a platform within a fort.

25. Distance from the sea to New Orleans was about ninety miles.

26. The fifty thousand figure is more than ten times the number of Confederate troops available to defend New Orleans, "The Opposing Forces . . . at New Orleans, La.," *B&L* 2:75.

27. Regarding the "Memphis Packet Landing" sign, EWB suggested that traffic will soon move freely on the Mississippi to Memphis, Tenn.; Tehamitipee House was probably a small hotel or guest house, e-mail from John T. Magill, curator and head of Research Services, HNOC, to editor, Feb. 15, 2006; *fillibusters* [filibusters] referred to New Orleans' reputation as a base for Americans bent on fomenting insurrections in Latin America.

28. Benjamin F. Butler (b. 1818), an influential and crafty politician but an incompetent general, reigned as military governor of New Orleans, where he earned the nickname "Spoons" for allegedly stealing citizens' silverware. He ruled harshly, issuing his famous "Woman Order," directing that women who insulted his troops be treated as common prostitutes.

29. Charles Longfellow (b. 1844), the son of noted poet Henry Wadsworth Longfellow, reached Ship Island three weeks before EWB arrived and later also became a Federal army officer, Charles Longfellow to father, journal letter beginning April 4, 1862, Houghton Library, HU; Calhoun, *Longfellow*, 222–24.

30. The St. Charles Hotel was "a grand establishment and one of the first luxury hotels in the world," but a rebuilt version was demolished in the 1970s, giving way to a fifty-six-story office building, although the Custom House still stands, e-mail from John T. Magill, curator, HNOC, to editor, Feb. 16, 2006.

31. Relatively new in the 1860s but long gone now, the Marine Hospital was then on the city's fringe; their "stroll" was more than a two-mile walk past the shop of Moses Greenwood, a Massachusetts native EWB thought he knew, information again courtesy of John T. Magill, curator and head of Research Services, HNOC, in e-mail to editor, Feb. 16, 2006. The phrase "just come out from under a featherbed" probably meant that the people spoke in a muffled voice, fearing retaliation by Southern sympathizers, e-mails from Professor Laurence Horn, YU, and other members of the American Dialect Society, to editor, May 23, 2006.

32. When slaveowners feared losing valuable chattels to advancing Federals, they often moved their slaves to safer areas, Hughes, ed., *Liddell's Record*, 118, 164; Laas, *Wartime Washington*, 122; slaves often were bought and sold while held in slave pens.

33. Prior pillaging in Virginia is not recorded.

34. Shinplasters were privately issued paper currencies, varying in worth, in whole or fractional denominations, common during the war; Butler was still securing the city.

35. Round shot was a solid cannon ball; the official tally was nine men killed, *ORN* 18:221–22; obviously, some exaggeration colored the tale about the heroic master's mate.

36. EWB missed Farragut's attack on Mobile Bay on Aug. 5, 1864, more than two years later; while it was not impossible that "old" Commander John De Camp, fifty, was "drunk all the time," it was most unlikely. He retired as a rear admiral in 1870.

37. John W. DeForrest, another New Haven man, served until Dec. 2, 1864, in the 12th Connecticut Volunteer Infantry, a unit organized in late 1861 that fought in Louisiana and Virginia's Shenandoah Valley, AG, *Record*, 493, 471–73.

38. Tom was Thomas Rutherford Bacon, a younger brother born in 1850, also called "Ruddy," Davis, *Leonard Bacon*, 147–48; genealogy chart, Bacon Family Papers, YU; John V. Isham, a student from Hartford, probably boarded with Dr. William J. Whiting in New Haven, census, Ancestry.com.

39. USS *Brooklyn*, launched in 1858, was a wooden screw sloop of 2,070 tons, first commanded by Farragut, and she was the blockader that the CSS *Sumter* eluded when the raider escaped into the Gulf of Mexico; Andre B. Roman, who opposed secession, served two terms as Louisiana's governor, 1831–35 and 1839–43; Donelsonville is a variant spelling of Donaldsonville, Louisiana's capital from January 1830 to January 1831.

40. *Sesesh* (usually spelled *secesh*) refers to secessionists, another term for Southerners who sought to secede from the Union; Yorktown, Va., was a Union victory on May 3, 1862; Butler popularized the term "Contrabands" as the word for former slaves who entered Federal lines; yellow jack is another name for yellow fever, a virus transmitted by mosquitoes, often fatal in those days, and Southerners hoped the disease would cripple Yankee forces.

41. Mid-watch is from midnight to 4 A.M.

42. Constructed in 1838 with four-and-a-half-foot-thick building walls and surrounded by an exterior ten-foot-high, thick blast wall with just one entry gate, the arsenal manufactured gunpowder, Louisiana Secretary of State, www.sos.louisiana.gov/tabid/244/default.asps/ (access Nov. 30, 2008).

43. For the official account of Baton Rouge's surrender, see *ORN* 18:473–76.

44. The last sentence refers to Farragut's fight at New Orleans' Forts Jackson and St. Philip.

45. *ORN* 18:489–91, for Natchez episode.

46. Not until three years later did Southerners return to their original allegiance, and that not gladly. If Foote, commanding the navy's flotilla higher up on the Tennessee and Mississippi Rivers, and Farragut, pushing north from the lower Mississippi, shook hands at Memphis, then Farragut would have passed Vicksburg's batteries.

47. Federals happily confiscated chickens and sheep from Davis's estate, but the Confederacy's president had stored his household goods on another plantation, which Federals later found and plundered, for which see Bache diary, May 20, 1862, APS; *The War of the Rebellion: A Compilation of the Official Records*, 10, 2:45 (*OR* citations are from Series 1, unless otherwise noted, and indicate volume, part, and page in that order, using Arabic numerals, rather than the original Roman, for volume and part); Robert Melvin to Davis, July 22, 1863, Jefferson Davis Papers, Duke University; "the reception of the news" apparently refers to Confederates abandoning Fort Pillow June 3–4 and Foote's destruction of an outclassed enemy flotilla at Memphis on June 6, thus clearing the river as far south as Vicksburg. Ballard, *Vicksburg*, 29.

48. Letter to Mother is missing; *Itasca* and *Katahdin* were small wooden screw steamers with crews of seventy-eighty men, constructed under the "90-day gunboat" crash program; Federal gunboats shelled Grand Gulf on June 9 when a shore battery fired on them, wounding and killing sailors and damaging warships, *ORN* 18:545.

49. On June 10–11, Federal ships again bombarded Grand Gulf, then landing parties burned the town, *ORN* 18:547.

50. EWB presumed wrongly—little was made of Grand Gulf's burning; "whole cloth" means pure fabrication.

51. Brigadier General Thomas Williams, an 1837 graduate of West Point, either

changed his mind or had it changed for him, for on June 25 his troops struck Grand Gulf from the rear and finished the arson work, *ORN* 18:711.

52. Some would call the USS *Sciota*, a ninety-day gunboat, a hard-luck ship because she was twice sunk, once after colliding with another vessel in July 1863 and then, after the navy raised and returned her to service, when she hit a mine in Mobile Bay on April 14, 1865, finally ending her career.

53. Ballard, *Vicksburg*, 46; Coggins, *Arms & Equipment*, 96; Lockett, "Defense of Vicksburg," *B&L* 3:483.

54. *ORN* 18:640; *OR* 15:8; Bache diary, May 20, 1862, APS.

55. *ORN* 18:641, 588, 590.

56. The letter to John V. Isham, June 28, 1862, a friend in New Haven, is missing.

57. USS *Oneida*, a three-masted screw sloop of almost 1,500 tons, could make twelve knots, so she was merely slow in moving into position to pass the batteries.

58. Pivots were guns mounted on turning platforms, usually in bow and stern, which allowed wider range of fire; the poop was a partial deck in the stern, higher than the main deck.

59. Launched in 1860, the USS *Richmond*, a 2,600-ton screw sloop, carried twenty nine-inch Dahlgren smoothbore guns for her main armament, ten on each side, each firing a seventy-pound projectile—so a broadside salvo would weigh seven hundred pounds, not one thousand, Coggins, *Arms & Equipment*, 142, 145.

60. Rifled cannons, those with a twist of lands and grooves inside the barrel to give projectiles a spin in flight, were more accurate, though smoothbores could be fired faster. The "no. 6" battery is missing from Bacon's diagram.

61. Neither *Iroquois* nor *Hartford*, a 2,900-ton wooden screw sloop serving as Farragut's flagship, or any other Federal warships could elevate their guns enough to hit Confederate batteries emplaced high on the river bluffs.

62. Mizzen mast is the last sternward mast of a three-masted ship; mainstays support the main mast; windsails funneled air into lower decks for ventilation, and halyards or lines held windsails in place.

63. Shifting from command of the *Iroquois*, a thousand-ton steam sloop, to the *Wissahickon*, a small five-hundred-ton gunboat, may have sobered John De Camp, see EWB to Father, journal letter May 5, 1862.

64. *Brooklyn, Katahdin*, and *Kennebec*, a new gunboat, inexplicably remained below, contrary to Farragut's orders, and while an adequate land force might then have captured Vicksburg, there was no such force available, *ORN* 18:588–90; Lewis, *David Glasgow Farragut*, 98, 101–2.

65. A full year passed before Vicksburg fell.

66. Of Williams's 3,200 men, fevers and death had reduced his effective strength to 800; disease had also killed or disabled the hundreds of contrabands working on the one-and-a-quarter-mile-long canal; most importantly, Flag Officer Charles H. Davis reported that the river had fallen so low that the project was hopeless and Williams soon abandoned the work, *ORN* 19:55, 18:625.

67. Farragut captured the *Tennessee*, a former Confederate side-wheel steamer, at New Orleans.

68. EWB is self-deprecating with "lucubrations," meaning pretentious or studied writing; the Rev. Homer Wilbur, a fictional character, figured prominently in abolitionist James Russell Lowell's popular *The Biglow Papers*, humorous but biting satire that

first opposed the Mexican-American War and then, in the second series published in the *Atlantic Monthly,* supported the Union during the Civil War.

69. Flag Officer Charles H. Davis joined Farragut from upriver on July 1, 1862, bringing with him boats each mounting a single thirteen-inch mortar. These boats, anchored behind high land points, fired their heavy explosive shells in a high trajectory into Vicksburg; "big rifles" meant Confederates' large rifled cannon.

70. As noted above, Williams had begun digging the canal to cross a narrow loop in the river below Vicksburg; the "upper army" was the Federal force near Corinth, Miss.

71. Lieutenant Colonel William R. Palmer, Topographical Engineers, died of "disease caused by exposure" on June 18, 1862, during the Peninsula Campaign in Virginia, *OR* 11, 1:154.

72. Farragut's fleet celebrated the Fourth of July with a brisk bombardment of Vicksburg, Ballard, *Vicksburg,* 54; Federals had occupied James Island at Charleston, S.C., then withdrew, *OR* 14:2, 109.

3. Turning Point

1. Silver, ed., "Diary of Robert A. Moore," 247; Berlin, ed., *Confederate Nurse,* 165; Jerome Bussey to Robert Crouse, July 4, 1862, Crouse Coll., UM; Throne, ed., "Iowa Doctor in Blue," 126.

2. Basler, *Collected Works,* 5:296–97; EWB to George, Sept. 28, 1862.

3. Farragut had upbraided Craven for failing to pass Vicksburg's batteries, and Craven, greatly offended, went home to defend his record, Lewis, *Farragut,* 101–2; at 2,900 tons, the *Hartford* was longer, broader, and heavier than the 1,016-ton *Iroquois* and mounted more than three times as many cannons.

4. EWB, born May 5, 1843, is now two months into his twentieth year.

5. The "sad defeat" at Martinique was the *Sumter's* escape; contrast EWB's optimism with that of many Northerners who believed the South was ahead in the war's first two years, e.g., Samito, ed., *Commanding Boston's Irish Ninth,* 161, Guiney to wife, Jan. 6, 1863, "I hope for success. I fear defeat."

6. Concern for EWB's uncertain health influenced family thinking, though their view that shipboard life was salubrious had proved erroneous.

7. Again EWB had sought his father's guidance, though the patriarch could know little about the war's realities on the Mississippi River.

8. Rumors swirled through the divided nation during the war, some quite preposterous, and almost always wish-fulfilling for those who heard or repeated them—for examples see Berlin, *A Confederate Nurse,* 158; Levstik, ed., "Diary," 71. Richmond resisted until April 1865, and Vicksburg held out for another year; Lincoln named Halleck general in chief several days later and urgently ordered him to Washington, Basler, *Collected Works,* 6:312–13, 325.

9. As noted above, Craven had requested relief from command and Farragut obliged. Near the war's end, Craven, commanding the USS *Niagara,* turned away from a fight with the stronger raider CSS *Stonewall.* For that break with tradition, he faced a court-martial, and Farragut was one of the judges. Though found guilty, he was later exonerated and promoted to rear admiral, Lewis, *Farragut,* 101–3; Gould, *Diary,* 219. Commander Henry H. Bell (b. 1808, North Carolina) was Farragut's fleet captain and later commanded the West Gulf Blockading Squadron, NHC.

10. EWB's brothers Frank (Francis) and Theodore served in the 7th Connecticut Infantry during the capture of Fort Pulaski, Ga., on April 11, 1862.

11. It was more than annoying—earlier a shell decapitated one woman and people lived in caves for shelter, Ballard, *Vicksburg*, 46, 51–52.

12. Caused by a lack of ascorbic acid, found in fruit and vegetables, often missing in their diet, scurvy afflicted many Civil War soldiers, sailors, and, especially, prisoners of war.

13. As noted above, Halleck was not coming, and neither were any troops. In any event, Farragut sorely wanted to return to the open seas.

14. Postmaster General Montgomery Blair's first wife was Caroline Buckner Blair. However, she died in 1844, so Dr. Buckner was a past brother-in-law, Blair Family Papers, Library of Congress.

15. Chicago newspapers relied on unfounded rumor in reporting Vicksburg's fall.

16. Confederates repulsed Major General George B. McClellan's drive to Richmond in the Seven Days battles, June 25–July 1, 1862; newspapers mostly reported a defeat, though some sugarcoated it as a "strategic retreat," Andrews, *North Reports,* 209–17; New Englanders were probably disappointed with the general, Silber and Sievens, *Yankee Correspondence,* 37–38, Charles E. Jewett to siblings, July 18, 1862.

17. Congressman Charles A. Wickliffe of Kentucky, a Peace Democrat, spurred the House to inquire whether Major General David Hunter had organized a regiment of "fugitive slaves" in South Carolina. Hunter flippantly replied that he had formed a "fine regiment of persons whose late masters were 'fugitive rebels'" and that the regiment would soon fight their late "fugacious and traitorous" owners, *OR* Ser. 2, 1:820–22.

18. On July 4, 1862, Farragut reported the river had fallen sixteen feet, dropping faster than the canal diggers could dig, *ORN* 18:624.

19. Sickness, including dysentery, diarrhea, and dengue and malaria fevers, beset the fleet, with sixty-eight of the *Brooklyn's* 380 men on the sick list, and with few medicines, including quinine, on hand, *ORN* 18:634, Farragut to Welles, July 11, 1862. Time did not improve matters—a year later aboard the USS *Forest Rose*, eleven of thirteen officers and half the sixty-man crew were incapacitated, "all down with the break bone [dengue] fever the same as I had last summer," E. W. Goble to Joseph B. Boyd, July 1, 1863, Boyd Papers, CHS.

20. USS *Richmond* was a large ship of 2,600 tons and a crew of 259 and had also hunted for CSS *Sumter.*

21. Halleck, a good administrator but a poor field commander, had taken Corinth and Memphis but repeatedly said he could not send any troops to Vicksburg, *ORN* 18:593, 636, July 2, 15, 1862.

22. On July 1, 1862, Lincoln had called for another three hundred thousand three-year volunteers, Basler, *Collected Works,* 5:296–97; *OR* Ser. 3, 2:187–88. That would increase the army's paper strength to one million men, and actually 421,000 volunteers answered the call, Phisterer, *Statistical Record,* 4–6. However, deaths, wounds, illness, accidents, discharges, and desertions sharply reduced the number present for duty, so the actual effective strength was much less than 1.1 million.

23. Northerners feared that France or England might intervene, while Southerners hoped they would, Henry A. Potter to Father, May 3, 1864, http://freepages.genealogy. rootsweb.ancestry.com/~mruddy/letters5.htm (access Nov. 16, 2008); LeConte, *When the World Ended,* 19, 75; Barnwell, ed., "Civil War Letters," 227. Both expectations de-

rived from European government and upper-class sympathy for the South, the need for Southern cotton and some Northern bumbling, such as the *Trent* affair. But Lincoln's Emancipation Proclamation of Jan. 1, 1863, made it difficult thereafter for Europe to recognize the slaveholding Confederacy.

24. Frank, a surgeon with the 7th Connecticut Infantry, had returned from arduous service in South Carolina; older sister Rebecca probably was a volunteer worker at the New Haven army hospital; Brockway, thirty-two, daughter of a former Whig Congressman, lived in Ellington, north of New Haven, Ancestry.com; Katy was Katherine, Kate to EWB; Mrs. Phillips is not identified.

25. Skiddy was the Stamford friend.

26. EWB may have invented the "Bloodthirsty Bake" sobriquet; "muss" was slang for a confused battle.

27. *Carondelet,* a 512-ton ironclad river gunboat was built in 1861 for the army at St. Louis, Mo., but transferred to navy control on October 1, 1862. She had taken part in capturing Forts Henry and Donelson on the Cumberland and Tennessee Rivers, then passed Confederate guns at Island No. 10 on the Mississippi, February-April 1862, for which see *DANFS,* NHC.

28. Bache diary, May 19, 1862, APS; *ORN* 18:675, 19:133, from papers of Acting Master's Mate John A. Wilson, CSS *Arkansas.*

29. I. N. Brown, "Arkansas," *B&L* 3:572.

30. *ORN* 18:729, *Hartford* log.

31. *ORN* 19:37–41, 68–69; I. N. Brown, "Arkansas," *B&L* 3:574–75, and Note, 580; Coleman, "A July Morning," 9–10.

32. Milligan, *Fresh-Water Navy,* 107; *ORN* 19:747; I. N. Brown, "Arkansas," *B&L* 3:576; Sylvester Doss to W. D. Crandall, Oct. 8, 1894, Warren D. Crandall Collection, Missouri Historical Society.

33. Edward M. Galligan, diary, July 15, 1862, typescript copy, MHS; I. N. Brown, "Arkansas," 576; *ORN* 19:133.

34. *ORN* 19:5, 39, 41, 69.

35. *Ibid.,* 4, 15, 36.

36. USS *Benton* was a thousand-ton ironclad; the former USS *Merrimac,* converted to an ironclad and renamed CSS *Virginia,* by Confederates, had rampaged through a Federal fleet at Hampton Roads, Va., on March 8, 1862, and fought the iron USS *Monitor* the next day, inaugurating a revolution in naval shipbuilding and warfare. In external appearance the *Arkansas* resembled the *Merrimac.*

37. Another fifteen or so gunboats and rams belonged to Lieutenant Colonel Alfred W. Ellet's army fleet; the "blown up" ram was the *Lancaster.*

38. Shell was a fused exploding projectile; fused shrapnel contained musket balls, dispersed when the projectile exploded; grape held iron balls about 1½ inches in diameter, canister held musket balls, and both acted like giant shotgun blasts; solid shot hammered other ships, shore batteries, and forts, Coggins, *Arms & Equipment,* 67. 78.

39. A six-pounder, caliber 3.67 inches, was the lightest field piece in use, throwing a 6.10-pound projectile, Coggins, *Arms & Equipment,* 66; EWB did not see new paint reflecting gun flashes, because the *Arkansas* bore an old coat of dull brown paint, *ORN* 19:133, Wilson papers; a Federal warship had "sent a 160 pound wrought-iron bolt" crashing through the *Arkansas'* armor, disabling engines and ship, I. N. Brown, "Arkansas," 577.

40. The journals fitted into engine bearings.

41. Just five ships reported casualties, *ORN* 19:4, 5; Acting Master Charles E. Jack blew up his grounded mortar schooner after some confusion about shouted orders, a scenario at odds with EWB's hearsay version, though Jack was sent home in disgrace, *ORN* 19:29–33.

42. Both sides reported the ignored warning story, *ORN* 19:56; I. N. Brown, "Arkansas," 573. Commander Robert F. Pinkney, CSN, ordered two Confederate gunboats burned when a lone Federal vessel ventured up the Yazoo River and the burning boats fired the side-wheel ram *General Earl Van Dorn*, for which "cowardly work" the area army commander recommended that Pinkney "should be tried by court-martial," Read, "Reminiscences," 350–51; *ORN* 18:652, 714; Lieutenant Isaac N. Brown commanded the *Arkansas*; USS *Niagara* was a steam frigate of 5,500 tons, launched in 1855.

43. EWB had contracted dengue fever, also called break-bone or bone-crusher, a mosquito-borne viral disease that may result in severe joint pain, high fever, and a bright red rash, Centers for Disease Control (CDC), www.cdc.gov/ncidod/dvbid/dengue (access Nov. 30, 2008); the near epidemic sickness and the debilitating climate told severely on the fleet, and Farragut so reported, *ORN* 18:634.

44. Flag Officer Charles H. Davis commanded the ships above Vicksburg; USS *Oneida*, a 1,500-ton sloop, was supposedly second in line; EWB persists in thinking he saw a "freshly painted" *Arkansas* when many, including Farragut, could not see the dark-hued *Arkansas* against the river bank in the growing darkness, *ORN* 19:8.

45. EWB apparently missed the vigorous response of the enemy ram—*Arkansas* gunners could easily see the Union ships and fired at them as they passed, *ORN* 19:134, Wilson papers; I. N. Brown, "Arkansas," *B&L* 3:577.

46. While there was no breakdown of Federal casualties for the passage, Flag Officer Charles H. Davis reported that the "loss of life . . . is wonderfully small," *ORN* 19:6; the *Arkansas* lost eight men killed and eleven wounded, *ORN* 19:134 and Read, "Reminiscences," 356.

47. Farragut and Davis blamed each other for the failure to destroy the *Arkansas*, *ORN* 19:56–58.

48. A powderboy or powder monkey, some younger than twelve years old as regulations stipulated, carried powder from ships' magazines to gun crews, Ringle, *Life in Mr. Lincoln's Navy*, 40.

49. Again EWB repeated a flawed version of this incident, for which see *ORN* 19:29–33.

50. *ORN* 19:10–11, 44, 60. The army bought the *Essex*, a prewar river ferry, and transformed her into a 159-foot-long ironclad gunboat of 614 tons with a crew of 124 and five cannon, and the *Queen of the West* was a wooden side-wheel river steamer of 406 tons converted into a ram.

51. Galligan diary, July 22, 1862, MHS; *ORN* 19:60, Porter report; Diggins, "Recollections," 156, NYPL.

52. *ORN* 19:46, 50, 61–62; Galligan diary, July 22, 1862, MHS; I. N. Brown, "Arkansas," *B&L* 3:577–78; Read, "Reminiscences," 358.

53. *ORN* 19:46, 61, 62; Galligan diary, July 22, 1862, MHS; I. N. Brown, "Arkansas," 578.

54. *Iroquois*' propeller stopped during the first attack on the *Arkansas*, and the survey was to examine her machinery; *Oneida*'s "rifle" refers to her rifled cannon; apparently they blamed Davis for the *Arkansas*' escape from the Yazoo River.

55. Lieutenant John L. Worden commanded the USS *Monitor* during her famous duel with the CSS *Virginia,* known as the *Merrimac,* on March 9, 1862; Brown later wrote that Porter could have boarded and captured *Arkansas* with just fifty men, given that half his crew of twenty-eight men were killed or wounded during the affray, I. N. Brown, "Arkansas," *B&L* 3:578.

56. Except for the inability of the *Essex* to steam upriver, the story is essentially correct; "deliverance" came when Navy Secretary Welles told Farragut to go sea, *ORN* 19:19.

57. Mustered on Jan. 4, 1862, the 30th Massachusetts Infantry soon joined Brigadier General Thomas Williams's troops at Vicksburg; the 30th lost sixty-one men in battle, while 343 died of disease during the war, Dyer, *Compendium,* 1259.

58. Temperatures could climb to 150 degrees in the engine room, I. N. Brown, "Arkansas," *B&L* 3:575; Ringle, *Life in Mr. Lincoln's Navy,* 37, 50–51.

59. Flag Officer Davis reported on July 23, 1862, that Confederate field artillery fired upon mail boats from upriver Cairo, reportedly burning one, and a week later confirmed that a mail boat had sunk, *ORN* 19:49, 64. No hospital boats were lost.

60. Loyalty oaths required swearing fidelity to the United States, and those refusing could suffer various penalties; oath violators faced severe punishment. For a comment by Lincoln on the sometimes complex oath question, see Basler, *Collected Works,* 7:169–70.

61. The newspaper was probably the St. Louis *Missouri Democrat.*

62. More than fifteen hundred troops held New Orleans, though the exact number is uncertain, *OR* 15:548–49, Butler to Stanton, Aug. 14, 1862.

63. EWB had resisted shifting to the flagship, the USS *Hartford,* EWB to Father, July 5, 1862.

64. The 13th soon left New Orleans for active campaigning.

65. Chaplain Salter departed in June because he and Captain Sprague, an abolitionist, disobeyed orders by sheltering a slave girl. Sprague argued his way out of trouble but Salter, the instigator, could not, Sprague, *13th Connecticut,* 261, 341–47.

66. EWB thought Butler "too timid" because he ostensibly heeded Washington's still conservative rules on slaves; for this and the regiment of loyal white men, see *OR* 15:548–49; Butler, *Private and Official Correspondence,* 2:270–71; Sprague, *13th Connecticut,* 59–62. White slaves resulted when slaveholders used slave women to relieve sexual needs, to save stud fees, or to "improve" the slave stock, thereby fetching higher prices at slave auctions, Woodward, ed., *Mary Chestnut's Civil War,* 29, 31, 168–69; Ella Thomas diary, Jan. 2, 1858, Duke University; Rawick, ed., *American Slave,* Ser. 1, 7:49, Ser. 2, 19:216.

67. The "boy" was a runaway slave, perhaps a full-grown man.

68. The 7th Connecticut stayed near Charleston, S.C., not shifting to Virginia until April 1864, AG, *Record,* 291.

69. The *Creole* was safe.

70. Captain Charles D. Blinn later became the 13th's colonel, AG, *Record,* 511; George was an older brother.

71. EWB thought letters from home were lost when Confederates sank a mail boat from Cairo.

72. The steamer *Roanoke* was another mail boat.

73. In caulking a wooden ship, sailors pounded oakum (tarred rope) between plank seams to make the ship watertight, Noel and Beach, *Naval Terms,* 61, 211. Butler cred-

ited most rumors about imminent attacks on New Orleans, though none materialized. Confederate Major General John C. Breckinridge did attack Baton Rouge on Aug. 5, but was repulsed, and the *Arkansas,* which had sought to join the attack, was destroyed by her crew when her engines failed, *OR* 15:51–54, 76–81; Galligan diary, Aug. 6, 1862, MHS; I. N. Brown, "Arkansas," 3:579; Read, "Reminiscences,"358–61.

74. Lincoln had called for three hundred thousand three-year volunteers on July 1, 1862, Basler, *Collected Works,* 5:296–97; *OR* Ser. 3, 2:187–88.

75. Shepherd was friend George Shepherd.

76. "Shipped men" were the enlisted crew, the ordinary sailors, given to billingsgate, or coarse, foul language; salt horse was pickled beef preserved in brine, and hardtack was a water-and-flour biscuit, sometimes so hard that men broke teeth trying to eat it. By "boat-legs," EWB means that officers ate salt horse and hardtack only as a last resort.

77. Both the army and navy rated hospital stewards as high-ranking enlisted men, but army stewards apparently had more duties and greater responsibilities, www.geocities.com/hospital_steward (access May 18, 2007). Though not an exact quote, "All the ills. . . ." is from Shakespeare's *Hamlet,* act 3, scene 1, Hamlet's soliloquy.

78. Minor was probably Alfred Minor, twenty, of Hebron, Conn.; USS *Sumpter,* a small propeller-steamer, served on Atlantic blockade duty and sank June 24, 1863, after colliding with a transport, *DANFS,* NHC. A Medical Cadet belonged to the obscure Medical Cadet Corps, a program authorized by Congress in 1861 to enlist men with medical educations as battlefield aid men or hospital operating-room assistants. Though they wore an officer's shoulder straps, they officially ranked as senior noncommissioned officers and received thirty dollars a month, Dunkelman, "George Bosley," 15–16.

79. Genteel folk lived on New York's Fifth Avenue, while the city's riffraff inhabited the notorious Five Points, a center of vice around Foley Square in nineteenth-century Manhattan, http://r2gsa.gov/fivept/wifp.htm or simply search online for "Five Points."

80. The "wounded from Richmond" referred to the casualties from the Seven Days Battles in Virginia, ending July 1, 1862.

81. Farragut did not attack Mobile until Aug. 5, 1864.

82. Farragut sent a naval force to capture Galveston, Texas, on Oct. 5, 1862, but Confederates recaptured the port in a surprise attack on Jan. 1, 1863, Soley, "Gulf Operations," *B&L* 3:571.

83. Preble, *Chase*; *ORN* 1:431–32; Basler, *Collected Works,* 5:102.

84. Sailors installed iron plates to protect vulnerable parts such as boilers.

85. Many others, including Lincoln, also harbored doubts about McClellan, who had failed in the summer's Peninsular Campaign and who again hesitated after the battle of Antietam in mid-September, whereupon the president removed the general from command.

86. CSS *Manassas,* an ironclad ram of "radically modern design," slammed into the USS *Brooklyn* during Farragut's passage by the forts below New Orleans on April 24, 1862, for which see *DANFS,* NHC.

87. USS *Mississippi,* a 3,220-ton side-wheel steamer, commissioned in 1841, ran the CSS *Manassas* aground at New Orleans but grounded while passing Port Hudson's guns, and her crew destroyed her to prevent capture; on the ship's loss, see Dewey, *Autobiography,* 85–95. USS *Susquehanna,* a 2,400-ton side-wheeler and another veteran of the prewar navy, stayed in the Gulf until spring of 1863 despite needing repairs, *ORN*

19:648. Apparently the New York *Herald* engaged in some editorial bluster, perhaps because English shipyards had recently launched the commerce raiders CSS *Florida* and CSS *Alabama*.

88. The USS *Rhode Island* and the *Connecticut*, on which Blackman (not identified) sailed, were both side-wheelers serving then as fleet supply ships from New York to the Gulf.

89. Launched in 1822 but not commissioned until 1831, the sail frigate USS *Potomac* became a stores ship for the West Gulf Blockading Squadron.

90. Davis, *Leonard Bacon*, 120–21; "Questions and Answers about TB," CDC site at www.cdc.gov/nchstp/tb/faqs/qa.htm (access Nov. 30, 2008).

91. EWB diary, Oct. 26, 1862, and letter fragment, [Homer B. Sprague] to EWB, Nov. 25, 1862.

92. [Sprague] to EWB, Nov. 25, 1862; AG, *Record*, 510; Sprague, *13th Connecticut*, 95.

93. Colebrook was a small village on the state's northern edge.

94. Leonard Bacon's long letter of July 17, 1862, is in the collection, so EWB eventually received it.

95. Leonard Bacon erred—individual risk was greater in the army; older brother Theodore, a 7th Connecticut Infantry captain, had returned to duty near Charleston after an absence, AG, *Record*, 291, 310.

96. Russell, a Connecticut militia major general, was a former state legislator who headed the Collegiate and Commercial Institute, the C.C.I., in New Haven, Osborn, ed., *Men of Mark*, 2:420–22; Shumway and Hegel, *New Haven*, 98. Ruddie or Ruddy was EWB's younger half-brother Thomas Rutherford Bacon, born 1850, genealogy chart, Bacon family Papers, YU.

97. Alfred H. Terry, a volunteer officer from New Haven, had won promotion to brigadier general in April 1862, AG, *Record*, 293; Major General David Hunter led the Department of the South until late August, but made little progress in the effort to capture Charleston, Warner, *Generals in Blue*, 244.

98. Frank (Francis) Bacon, on detached service from the 7th Connecticut Infantry, worked for Major General Silas Casey, who trained troops around Washington.

99. Mother was Catherine Elizabeth (Terry) Bacon, EWB's stepmother, who "perhaps suffered from a chronic arthritic condition," Davis, *Leonard Bacon*, 251; Katy was sister Katherine, EWB's correspondent, while Ruddie, Alfred, Ellen, and Alice were EWB's younger half brothers and sisters. Fanny Bostwick was probably Frances H. Bostwick, daughter of William Bostwick, a wealthy retired New Haven merchant, while Rebecca G. Bacon was the daughter of Daniel Bacon, another New Haven resident, census, Ancestry.com.

100. EWB had written about diseases in the area.

101. Confederates had pushed to within about seven miles of Cincinnati, and Lee had launched the Antietam Campaign, reaching Hagerstown, Md.

102. Blackman remains unidentified.

103. Mason & Rockwell were tailors at a prime location and likely "a pretty upscale store," and James H. Hall was a "shoe jobber," e-mail from James W. Campbell, curator, NHM&HS, to editor, Aug. 15, 2006; Congress gaiters are ankle-high shoes with elastic gussets in the sides, still made and sold at this writing; by today's standards, EWB's shoe size was rather small but was not unusually so then; Wallace B. Fenn was a New Haven merchant, Ancestry.com.

104. Note that earlier (EWB to Father, July 5, 1862), EWB had criticized the *Hartford* as "very much crowded" but here uttered no complaints.

105. "Baryon" collars were probably brand-name detachable paper or linen collars worn with collarless shirts by navy and army officers and even ordinary Army of the Potomac soldiers. Clergy and actors still buy and use them today.

106. Oxford ties were shoe laces.

107. On Sept. 15, when EWB began his letter, Confederates took Harper's Ferry and about twelve thousand prisoners, and also reached the Ohio River across from Cincinnati. On the seventeenth, one of the war's bloodiest battles took place along Antietam Creek in Maryland. Lee withdrew the next day, as did Confederates at Cincinnati.

108. This George was George P. Brinley of Hartford, probably a Yale classmate.

109. Lincoln had suspended the writ of habeas corpus, political prisoners crowded jails, and military commissions tried citizens, while generals arbitrarily jailed dissenters, closed newspapers, and threatened or imposed summary punishments upon civilians—all of which excited strong criticism, Basler, *Collected Works*, 5:436–37; *OR* Ser. 2, 4:271; Holzer, *Dear Mr. Lincoln*, 163–64, 167–68; Gould, *Diary*, 188.

110. Many initially believed the conflict would end quickly, hence no need existed for a massive mobilization, Silber and Sievens, *Yankee Correspondence*, 111, Edward F. Hall to Susan, Sept. 16, 1862; Randall, *Civil War*, 339, quoting Jefferson Davis. As to the 150,000 "intelligent and willing negroes," only about 238,000 free blacks of all ages and both sexes lived in the North in 1860, and so it was impossible to enlist that many black men in the beginning, Randall, *Civil War*, 51. Even if Congress had passed "a rigid Confiscation Act" at the time, that would not have immediately provided 150,000 black soldiers, Basler, *Collected Works*, 5:48, 435. When Lincoln issued the final Emancipation Proclamation and authorized black enlistments on Jan. 1, 1863, both measures met much opposition among Northern soldiers and citizens, Burkhardt, *Confederate Rage*, chap. 1, "Emancipation and Black Soldiers." As for a "strict blockade," EWB knew full well many blockade runners evaded blockaders and not until the Union captured the last open Southern port would the traffic end. Finally, severe shortages had already appeared in the South. However, his appraisal of Southern determination and bravery was correct.

111. The South was far from monolithic and harbored many Unionists, for which see Current, *Lincoln's Loyalists*.

112. The biblical quote is "The glory has departed from Israel," 1 Samuel 4:22.

113. Richard Wainwright (b. 1817), commanding the *Hartford*, died of fever on Aug. 10, 1862, *ORN* 19:144; Brinley's adverse opinion of Palmer probably stemmed from reports about the *Sumter*'s escape.

114. EWB was not joking about arrest—when Lincoln suspended habeas corpus, he also ordered that "all persons discouraging volunteer enlistments . . . shall be liable to trial and punishment by Courts Martial or Military Commission," Basler, *Collected Works*, 5:437. As noted above, though the *Susquehanna* required repairs, she stayed in the Gulf until the spring of 1863, *ORN* 19:648.

115. USS *Winona*, a side-wheel gunboat, leaked so much that she barely managed to stay afloat, *ORN* 19:243. People with delirium tremens, which is caused by sustained heavy drinking, often suffer hallucinations and tremors, but EWB's diagnosis likely came from shipboard gossip; when the CSS *Florida* evaded blockaders at Mobile, *Winona*'s captain was F. A. Roe, and Navy Secretary Welles ordered an inquiry into his actions during that incident, *ORN* 19:237.

116. Midshipmen study and train to be naval officers; master's mates were high-ranking enlisted men, "Enlisted Ratings in U.S. Navy, 1775–1969," NHC.

117. On idleness under fire, a *Hartford* sailor concurred, writing, "One has nothing to do to occupy the mind[;] the mind runs on the great uncertainty about to take place," Diggins, "Recollections," 82, NYPL.

118. Dr. Ireland is not identified.

119. Thieves pilfered military mails, so Federal soldiers and sailors used private express services or homeward-bound comrades to send money or valuables. Southern soldiers often relied upon couriers for all mail, Lemke, ed., *Letters,* letter 13; McClure, ed., *Confederate from East Texas,* 16–17, 24.

120. On Sept. 17, 1862, the battle of Antietam, Md., resulted in horrendous casualties, and McClellan failed to pursue the retreating Confederates.

121. EWB explained that much of Mobile Bay's entrance was too shallow for many Federal ships, while the deep-water channel ran too close to the guardian forts.

122. To defend Mobile, Confederates had a formidable ironclad ram, CSS *Tennessee,* and three side-wheel gunboats, "The Opposing Forces at Mobile," *B&L* 4:400. Never part of the defenses, the *Oreto* was the CSS *Florida,* and she would again slip by blockaders in January 1863 to begin a successful raiding career, Lewis, *Farragut,* 160–61. Armstrong guns were excellent English rifled cannon, made in both breech- and muzzle-loading models, Coggins, *Arms & Equipment,* 84.

123. Navy Secretary Welles indeed had ordered Farragut to postpone plans to attack Mobile, *ORN* 19:161–62.

124. *Kennebec* and *Winona,* both launched in late 1861, were 158-foot-long, narrow-beamed (28 feet) gunboats of about five hundred tons.

125. During the first two years, many Northerners despaired while Southerners grew confident, but after Gettysburg and Vicksburg's fall in July 1863, those sentiments were reversed, Bright, ed., "Yankees in Arms," 202; Jackson, ed., *Three Rebels Write Home,* 81, 85, 87, 89; John C. Birdwell to wife, Oct. 27, 1862, Whitaker-Fenley Papers, Austin State University; Allen, "Civil War Letters," 376, 382–83; Crandall and Newell, *History of the Ram Fleet,* 353–54.

126. Stonewall Jackson captured about twelve thousand Federals at Harper's Ferry on Sept. 15, 1862, but the Dr. Bacon mentioned was not brother Frank.

127. Sprague's letter fragment is from EWB Papers, AAS.

PART TWO. THE HOSPITAL CLERK, 1863

1. EWB to George, Sept. 28, 1862.

2. Amos B. Eaton to EWB, March 12, 1863, AAS; for father's finances, see Davis, *Leonard Bacon,* 178–79, 219.

3. EWB to Kate, Sept. 26, 1864; Barnes, "Pliny A. Jewett," *PCMS,* 170.

4. Laas, *Wartime Washington,* 186–87; John Vliet to Mr. Boge, Feb. 2, 1863, Thomas W. Sweeny Papers, HEH; Klaas, ed., *Portrait of Elnathan Keeler,* 44; Kroll and Moran, eds., "White Papers," *Massachusetts Review,* 257–58; Trask, ed., *Fire Within,* 134–43.

5. Basler, *Collected Works,* 6:428, Lincoln to Chase, Sept. 2, 1863; Disbrow, ed., "Lincoln's Policies,"360–64; Behm, "Emancipation: A Soldier's View,"46–47; Humphreys, *Field, Camp,* 1; Douglass, *Life and Times,* 354, 352.

6. Davis, *Leonard Bacon,* 199.

7. Nicolay and Hay, eds., *Complete Works,* 6:127; Basler, *Collected Works,* 5:433–36;

Randall, *Civil War*, 599–603. For Federal desertions, see David M. Ray to Mother, Jan. 28, 1863, University of Texas, Austin; George F. Chittenden to Wife, Feb. 8, 1863, Indiana State Library; Lord, ed., *Fremantle Diary*, 70.

8. Brooks, *Washington in Lincoln's Time*, 103; M. W. Rodman to Congressman James A. Cravens, March 1, 1863, James Addison Cravens Papers, Indiana University; Howe, *Home Letters*, 252; Winther, ed., *With Sherman*, 149; Wagandt, ed., "Civil War Journal," 137, 139.

9. Henry L. Stone to father, Feb. 13, 1863, KyHS.

10. Randall, *Civil War*, 410–18; Phelan, ed., *Tramping Out the Vintage*, 113; Jackson and O'Donnell, eds., *Back Home in Oneida*, 66–67, 94; Bernstein, *New York City Draft Riots*.

11. EWB to Kate, Aug. 1, 1862, and to George, Sept. 28, 1862.

12. Lincoln's political generals, most glaringly inept as military leaders, supposedly advanced the war effort through their influence with voters. Banks and Butler were prime examples, though both were finally relieved and returned to politicking, where they belonged.

13. For reactions, see Ellsworth D. S. Goodyear, diary, July 19, 1863, Goodyear Family Papers, YU; Marszalek, ed., *Diary*, 281; Everson and Simpson, "Far, Far from Home," 257; Harrison, *Recollections Grave and Gay*, 141.

14. Black soldiers first fought on Oct. 28, 1862, at Island Mounds, Mo. In the first half of 1863, they fought at Port Hudson and Milliken's Bend, both in Louisiana, and in South Carolina, Georgia, and Florida.

15. Pliny A. Jewett (b. 1816), an 1839 Yale Medical School graduate, become wartime chief surgeon and major commandant at the New Haven army hospital where the "born autocrat" ran afoul of superior army autocrats, Barnes, "Pliny A. Jewett," *PCMS*, 169–70.

16. Adamantine candles were long-burning stiff candles made of commercially processed animal fats, superior to drooping tallow candles and less expensive than the best of beeswax.

17. Hard bread was another name for hard tack, a thick long-lasting baked cracker made of flour, water, and salt; desiccated potatoes (and other vegetables) were dehydrated, cooked by placing in water.

18. The Federal Enrollment Act of March 3, 1863, made all male citizens between the ages of twenty and thirty-five subject to military service, unless physically or mentally disqualified or exempt because of occupation or other reasons. However, a drafted man could hire a substitute or pay a commutation fee of three hundred dollars, OR Ser. 3, 3:88–90. EWB probably faced conscription, hospital job and health notwithstanding; army provost marshals supervised the draft in each city or area.

19. Rebecca Taylor Bacon to Frank, Nov. 21, 1863, Bacon family Papers, YU.

PART THREE. THE SOLDIER, 1864–65

1. 29th Connecticut Volunteer Infantry (Colored)

1. Martin, ed., *Courageous Journey*, 34; Sears, ed., *For Country*, 288.

2. Basler, *Collected Works*, 7:164, 245; Phisterer, *Statistical Record*, 6.

3. OR Ser. 4, 2:1065, 3:178; Oates, *War*, 494–506; DuBose, *General Joseph Wheeler*, 259; Buck, "Negroes in Our Army," 215–28. For a full study, see Levine, *Confederate Emancipation*.

4. John F. Slaver to Rosanna, Aug. 17, 1864, Ness Coll., UM; Brooks, *Washington in Lincoln's Time,* 105–6; Browne, *Four Years in Secessia,* 438.

5. Laas, *Wartime Washington,* 237; James T. Miller to siblings, April 25, 1864, Schoff Coll., UM; Miller, ed., *Photographic History,* 9:176, 178, for full text of "Sambo's Right to Be Kilt."

6. Binder, "Philadelphia's Free Military School," 287; Supervisory Committee, *Free Military School*; Phillips and Parsegian, eds., *Richard and Rhoda,* 40.

7. Binder, "Philadelphia's Free Military School," 290; A. C. Brown, *Diary,* 25–28; EWB to Father, Jan. 15, 1864.

8. Edward W. Bacon's CMSR, AGO, RG 94, NA; Ross, *Tabular Analysis,* 19–27.

9. Morgan, "Reminiscences of Service,"20–21; Levstik, "Diary," 35; Bowditch, "War Letters," 426.

10. *OR* 14:599; *OR* Ser. 2, 5:795–97; Cornish, *Sable Arm,* 159–62. For murderous practice, see Burkhardt, *Confederate Rage,* and Urwin, ed., *Black Flag*; Hollandsworth, "Execution of White Officers," 475–89. For "deluded" labels, see *OR* Ser. 2, 6:115; Rosenburg, ed.,"*For the Sake of My Country,* 101; Park, "Diary," 371.

11. Mary A. Marshall to Henry G. Marshall, April 29, 1863, and Henry G. Marshall to Folks at Home, May 3, 1863, Schoff Coll., UM.

12. AG, *Record,* 559; EWB CMSR, NA.

13. Basler, *Collected Works,* 7:234, 236.

14. Thomas G. Bennett, also of New Haven, served as a 2nd lieutenant with the 28th Connecticut, the state's last nine-month regiment; mustered out Aug. 28, 1863, he then sought another commission, Bennett CMSR, AGO, RG 94, NA; AG, *Record,* 856. A three-story row house at 1210 Chestnut St. housed the Free Military School with its average daily attendance of 194 students in the spring of 1864, Binder, "Philadelphia's Free Military School," 289.

15. Among those "small bore men" were Colonel John H. Taggart, commended for battles in 1861 and 1862, *OR* 5:475, 11, 2:387, and Thomas Webster, committee chairman, an influential man who had helped raise three black regiments, *OR* Ser. 3, 3:376. "Philadelphia, Phelps and Pompey" disparaged militant abolitionism—Philadelphia as a center of it; Phelps perhaps was Amos A. Phelps, a Boston abolitionists who had criticized father Leonard Bacon, Davis, *Leonard Bacon,* 128, 130; and Pompey might refer to any one of several activists.

16. That Owl train took ten to twelve hours to traverse the 135 miles or so to Washington, D.C., traveling at twenty-five to thirty miles per hour, a respectable speed at the time. EWB then called on Major General Silas Casey, the Supervisory Committee's leader. Parker was surely Dr. Peter Parker (b. 1804), a Yale graduate and a clergyman and surgeon, who had served as a medical missionary in China, Peter Parker Coll., YU.

17. The permit probably came from the New Haven provost marshal.

18. Casey wrote the two-volume *System of Infantry Tactics,* adopted by the U.S. Army in 1862 and also used by Confederates; the 160-room Metropolitan Hotel, built in 1855, was on Pennsylvania Ave., within walking distance of the Capitol, 1912 postcard description at www.CardCow.com.

19. EWB CMSR, NA; AG, *Record,* 859.

20. EWB to Kate, Feb. 13, 1864, EWB Papers, AAS; AG, *Record,* 859; Hill, *Sketch of the 29th,* 8–9.

21. Newton, *Out of the Briars,* 36.

22. Redkey, *Grand Army*, 261, 260, letter from "Private," 43rd USCI, and "B. W.," 32nd USCI; Bowditch, "War Letters," 464; Duren, "Occupation of Jacksonville," 283, 285; James Montgomery to Henry S. Wilson, Jan. 22, 1864, Montgomery Coll., KSHS.

23. George was probably George P. Brinley of Hartford, but Danny is unidentified; the *Congregationalist* was a church newspaper for which Leonard Bacon wrote during the war years, Davis, *Leonard Bacon*, 187.

24. Dislike of Buckingham apparently stemmed from the governor's right to appoint officers and approve promotions in state regiments, a wartime cornucopia of political patronage; if controlled by the War Department, EWB believed appointments would be based on merit. He and fellow officers signed their petition in vain—the 29th Connecticut always kept its state designation.

25. EWB mistakenly assumed that the government would make the 29th a Federal regiment and that Buckingham, "His Ex'cy," would lose control of officer appointments, in which case the ambitious, newly minted captain thought he would win promotion to major whenever it suited him.

26. The 29th was unarmed until issued the Springfield rifled musket, an accurate .58 caliber single shot muzzle-loading weapon considered superior to the earlier Enfields. With eighteen-inch bayonet attached, it weighed about nine and three-quarters pounds and measured seventy-four inches in length, AG, *Record*, 859; Boatner, *Civil War Dictionary*, 861. "Manual" meant the manual of arms, the various movements and positions the soldier assumes with his rifle.

27. Major General Ambrose E. Burnside, West Point graduate, veteran of Mexican and Indian wars, inventor of a breech-loading carbine, ably led the 9th Army Corps to which the 29th Connecticut belonged, Warner, *Generals in Blue*, 57–58.

28. Waterproof rubber blankets, placed on the ground underneath cloth blankets, kept soldiers dry during inclement weather.

29. John and Samuel Didymus survived the war unscathed, AG, *Record*, 862, 877. Three men named Prime served in the 29th, but the particular one cannot be identified.

30. The 9th Connecticut Volunteer Infantry "was composed mainly of men of Irish birth" and early in their service had sent home "almost their entire pay," AG, *Record*, 359.

31. AG, *Record*, 859.

32. Officers could not easily delegate clerical duties to black enlisted men because most lacked the schooling necessary for such work.

33. Probably the Bouquet Society was a young women's informal social group that left no record of meetings; Chapel St., known to most New Haven residents, borders the New Haven Green and passes by the old Yale campus, e-mail from James W. Campbell, curator, NHM&HS, to editor, Aug. 8, 2006; Wheeler was probably Theodocia N. Wheeler, about seventeen, whose mother was rather prosperous, census, Ancestry.com.

34. The army had not yet paid the 29th.

35. Chapman was a friend but eludes further identification; Brother Theodore, 7th Connecticut Infantry, left a horse behind when his regiment went to Virginia on April 13, 1864.

36. EWB's father wrote about the Didymus family on April 20, 1864.

37. Eaton, the New York commissary officer, had given the hospital clerkship to EWB in early 1863.

38. Steiner, *Life of Reverdy Johnson*, 76; OR Ser. 3. 3:419–20, 252.

39. Redkey, *Grand Army,* 229–48; A. S. Fisher to Dear Friend and Strange Acuaintance, March 14, 1864, Gettysburg College; Hill, *Sketch of the 29th,* 12; Nolin, ed., "Civil War Letters," 234; William H. Simons to Sister, [c. June 1864]; Lewis H. Douglass to R. G. Hinton, May 1, 1895, KSHS; "List of U.S. Soldiers Executed," 4–5, 8–11.

40. Duncan, ed., *Blue-Eyed,* 367n4; James Montgomery to Henry S. Wilson, Jan. 22, 1864, KSHS; Emil Rosenblatt and Ruth Rosenblatt, eds., *Hard Marching,* 231; EWB to Father, May 14, 1864. Note that the 2nd South Carolina became the 34th U.S. Colored Infantry shortly after Montgomery wrote Wilson, Ross, *Tabular Analysis,* 11.

41. The Rev. Dr. Solomon Peck was an Andover classmate of Leonard Bacon and active in Baptist Missionary and Colonization Society work, Davis, *Leonard Bacon,* 35–36; Sen. James Harlan was a Republican from Iowa. While EWB found Northern schoolteachers beneath him, others, including Boston Brahmin Colonel Robert G. Shaw, 54th Massachusetts (Colored), had a contrary opinion, Duncan, *Blue-Eyed,* 372, 375 n1. The *Fulton,* a mail packet and transport, sailed back and forth from the North.

42. Presumably "water improvement" refers to some better delivery of water inside the home; many Northern church groups had defended slavery or were indifferent to it, Randall, *Civil War,* 105–7.

43. Jacob Eaton, the missing chaplain, had initially served as a 1st lieutenant with the 8th Connecticut but was wounded at Antietam Sept 17, 1862, and soon resigned. After a lengthy absence, he became the 7th Connecticut's chaplain on May 30, 1864, but apparently did not notify the 29th, AG, *Record,* 333, 293. Meanwhile, Governor Buckingham had recommended Eaton as major or lieutenant colonel of the 29th, Buckingham to Charles W. Foster, Dec. 26, 1863, ConnHS. Theological student Jones is unidentified.

44. Major Henry C. Ward won promotion to lieutenant colonel in July; note that now EWB values Casey and his school, an about face.

45. These men were all privates in EWB's Company I, and he asked his father to cash their checks, something which neither he nor the men could do on the isolated Sea Island.

46. Father and son, both of Thompson, Conn., served in EWB's company, the father throughout, while son Marcus Lewis soon received a disability discharge.

47. Clearly, EWB had no sympathy for black soldiers' rejection of their discriminatory pay; other 29th officers told the men they would receive full pay the next time, so they "quieted . . . passions" and most took the $7, Newton, *Out of the Briars,* 26. Sheldon cannot be identified.

48. J. M. Morris was likely John M. Morris of New Haven, formerly the 8th Connecticut's chaplain.

49. Grant pushed through Virginia's Wilderness in hard fighting May 6–7, 1864, with both sides sustaining heavy casualties, OR 3, 4:261; Livermore, *Numbers and Losses,* 110–11.

50. Two transports carrying the 9th U.S. Colored Infantry mistakenly steamed eight miles past their objective on the Ashepoo River, whereupon one transport ran aground, an easy target for Confederate artillery, resulting in the loss of the ship, eighty-three horses, thirteen or more soldiers, and the court-martial of the 9th's colonel, who was acquitted, OR 35, 1:8, 10–11.

51. This Rebecca Bacon was not EWB's sister but another Bacon; Thompson was probably Lucy Thompson, daughter of Joseph P. Thompson, a Connecticut clergyman who moved to New York and there associated with EWB's father in publishing the

Independent, an antislavery newspaper, Davis, *Leonard Bacon,* 141–42; the Rev. John Dudley of New Haven was also district secretary for the National Freedman's Relief Association, but why EWB rejected him is unknown.

52. Like most Civil War regiments, white or black, the 29th lost more men to disease than to enemy action—178 died of disease and 103 received disability discharges, while 42 were killed or mortally wounded in action, AG, *Record,* 969.

53. Given wartime inflation and shortages of horses, the mare and colts sold for a low price; Dr. John J. Craven, a staff surgeon, transferred from the District of Hilton Head to the 10th Army Corps, and postwar attended an imprisoned Jefferson Davis, OR 35, 2:79; Craven, *Prison Life of Jefferson.*

54. Like a good officer, EWB had troubled himself and his father on behalf of his men and paid face value for their checks.

55. "Gobble" was army slang for "to capture" or "be captured"; even if EWB made the raid, such minor affrays often went unreported in the press.

56. The box contained the requested summer-weight clothing; brother Theodore still served as a captain with the 7th Connecticut, while brother Frank (Francis) had earned promotion to brigade surgeon almost two years earlier.

57. Three schools of thought existed about black soldiers' ability to weather Southern climes. EWB asserted white men fared better, but he considered only Northern blacks and conceded that white officers had begun to succumb to the oppressive heat. Others argued that Southern blacks were acclimated, while another school believed whites and blacks were equally susceptible to miasmatic conditions. Bad sanitation practices, disease, and primitive medical care had much to do with the high mortality rates, so thousands of Southern blacks died from disease while serving in their native sections, Fox, *Regimental Losses,* 49.

58. Kate described an event at St. Paul's Episcopal Church, built in 1829, Shumway and Hegel, *New Haven,* 136.

59. Originally a Coast Survey schooner, *Arago* serviced the South Atlantic Blockading Squadron and also carried military passengers. Arriving officers, all former enlisted men in Connecticut regiments, were Captain Daniel A. Lyon, 1st Lieutenant Clarence M. Clarke, and 2nd Lieutenant Ransom Kenyon.

60. Superiors apparently rejected EWB's proposed raid; Major Oliver S. Sanford and Captain John B. Dennis were captured June 2, 1864, in Virginia, though both eventually escaped; very likely Theodore led the 7th for a time, as line officers "virtually commanded" during the summer of 1864, AG, *Record,* 293, 316, 291.

61. Surgeon Meredith Clymer later was medical director, Department of the South; "Ad." was Adrian Terry, a staff officer and younger brother of Brigadier General Alfred H. Terry; Frank probably appeared before a medical examining board to qualify as brigade surgeon, to which post he won promotion on Aug. 14, 1862, AG, *Record,* 293.

62. Perkins was probably Frances Perkins, daughter of George W. Perkins, a clergyman active in the antislavery movement, Davis, *Leonard Bacon,* 128–29; census, Ancestry.com. Captain George W. Allen had joined the 29th on April 5, 1864; Major Henry C. Ward, formerly a 29th company commander, advanced to lieutenant colonel a month later.

63. Thompson was Lieutenant Joseph P. Thompson, 2nd U.S. Colored Infantry, the son of Joseph P. Thompson, New York clergyman and cofounder of the *Independent,* an antislavery newspaper in New York, Davis, *Leonard Bacon,* 141–43; CWSS, NPS, online database at www.itd.nps.gov/cwss (access Dec. 1, 2008).

64. Major General John G. Foster, department commander, had ordered school-ing "for those colored regiments that required drill and discipline," *OR* 35, 1:9; Pri-vate George W. Baird, 1st Connecticut Light Battery and Veterans Reserve Corps, on March 18, 1864, won promotion to colonel of the 32nd U.S. Colored Infantry, a regiment formed at Camp William Penn, Philadelphia, February-March 1864, AG, *Record*, 101; Dyer, *Compendium*, 1729; Ross, *Tabular Analysis*, 21. Neither Baird's leap in rank nor EWB's envy and resentment were uncommon.

65. Bennett and 2nd Lieutenant Eugene S. Bristol, another New Haven man, were EWB's close friends.

66. *OR* 35, 1:14, 120–22, 124; Johnson, *Defense of Charleston*, 214–15.

67. McMurry, ed., *Footprints*, 105, 205n13.

68. McMurry, *Footprints*, 141–43; Burkhardt, *Confederate Rage*, 157–58.

69. Hollandsworth, "Execution of White Officers," 488–89.

70. Presentation Week at Yale, a literary fete, was one of two "high festivals" during the summer term, Ward, "Presentation Week at Yale," 497–501.

71. As noted above, just five thousand troops formed the expedition; those "few . . . actually injured" might have had a different perspective than EWB, who had not yet experienced ground combat.

72. 2nd Lieutenant Joel W. Hyde, Co. A, apparently had some medical training. In September 1864, he became the regiment's new assistant surgeon, not an unusual event at a time when formal medical training was brief and knowledge limited, AG, *Record*, 861; Lowry and Welsh, *Tarnished Scalpels*, Intro, 18–21.

73. Rufus Saxton, promoted overnight from captain to brigadier general, had or-ganized a revived 1st South Carolina Infantry, African Descent, as the first officially sanctioned black regiment, Nicolay and Hay, *Complete Works*, 6:444–45; Ross, *Tabu-lar Analysis*, 8. Whatever EWB thought of Saxton, black soldiers respected him, Hill, *Sketch of the 29th*, 12; Newton, *Out of the Briars*, 39. "A. a. a. Gen'l" translates as acting assistant adjutant general.

74. Collector Barney was Hiram Barney, a controversial figure whom Lincoln had appointed collector of customs in New York City. The son was Lewis T. Barney, who first enlisted as a private in the 7th New York and next became a 1st lieutenant in the 68th New York, then in late 1864 joined Saxton's staff. But on June 21, 1864, he resigned to accept a commission as colonel of the 106th New York but was never so mustered. Near the war's end, Barney was breveted both brigadier and major general for "meri-torious service," e-mail from Olga Tsapina, Norris Foundation curator, American His-torical Manuscripts, HEH, to editor, Sept. 22, 2006; CWSS, NPS.

75. The 2nd lieutenant who overstayed his sick leave eludes identification; Thomas Dunlap, commanding Co. F, was cashiered for drunkenness on June 23, 1864, Henry H. Brown diary, July 2, 1864, ConnHS.

76. Clinton is not among listed officers.

77. Probably 1st lieutenant Henry H. Brown led the company during EWB's absence and he was from Thompson, a small village in the northeast corner of Connecticut; EWB was right about his "worthless" 2nd lieutenant, because that officer, William P. Brooks, was cashiered before the war ended, AG, *Record*, 877.

78. Brother Theodore still served in the 7th Connecticut as a captain.

79. Early, "Early's March," *B&L* 4:492–99; Laas, *Wartime Washington*, 403; Grant, *Personal Memoirs*, 2:304–6; Andrews, *North Reports*, 589–95.

80. Jonathan Knight (1789–1864) had led Yale Medical School, http://info.med.yale.edu/library/exhibits/hospitals/knighthosp.html (access Dec. 1, 2008).

81. Unlike many regiments, Theodore's 7th Connecticut listed more battle casualties than the number lost to disease, AG, *Record*, 290–92, 326. Probably Leonard Woolsey Bacon, an older brother (b. 1830) wrote the ill-advised letter. But Connecticut's Governor William A. Buckingham also may have tired of pressure from father Leonard Bacon, who had "frequently" urged Buckingham and the 7th's commanding officer to promote Theodore, Davis, *Leonard Bacon*, 192. Likely EWB criticized Buckingham, thus earning his father's censure.

82. Morse, ed., *Civil War Diaries*, 195.

83. OR Ser. 3, 4:564–65, for Circular 60 on retroactive back pay; Cornish, *Sable Arm*, 181–96 for a full account of the pay issue.

84. A large steamer, the *Hermann Livingston* transported troops and mail, and exchanged prisoners, OR 44:554; OR 46, 3:1206.

85. Before the 29th had fully organized, Buckingham had urged an outsider's appointment as a field grade officer, Buckingham to Charles W. Foster, Dec. 26, 1863, ConnHS. Thorp, from North Haven, had a muster date of Jan. 27, 1864—two days before EWB's, making Thorp senior. EWB forgot that his own muster was also backdated, EWB's CMSR, NA.

86. "Rusty pieces" referred to his soldiers' rifles; all officers received more pay than any enlisted man, unless EWB referred to the one-time retroactive adjustment for black soldiers; the quip about Jewett refers to Parrott rifled cannon, immediately recognizable by its bulky breech, though the largest was the three-hundred-pound siege gun.

87. Eaton, EWB's patron for the hospital clerk job, became the army's commissary general and a brigadier general on June 29, 1864, Warner, *Generals in Blue*, 136–37.

88. A battered 7th Connecticut fought at Bermuda Hundred, Va., in May, losing 205 men; in June, listing 124 casualties; and in July, "with frequent casualties." AG, *Record*, 291.

89. Lieutenant Colonel James F. Hall served with the 1st New York Volunteer Engineers, one of the few engineer units organized during the war.

90. EWB referred to the retroactive pay due black troops in making their pay equal to that of whites.

91. During the 29th's twenty-one months of service, just one officer died of disease, Dyer, *Compendium*, 1016; Julia Woodruff (b. 1807) was his aunt, a younger sister of father Leonard Bacon.

92. As a major, Frank wore gold oak leaves but would advance to silver or "white" leaves as a lieutenant colonel.

93. Vergil or Virgil (70–19 B.C.), a great Roman poet, wrote the grand epic *Aeneid* and other works; Xenophon (c. 430–c. 355 B.C.), noted Greek historian, whose *Anabasis* relates the story of a Greek expeditionary force's heroic retreat.

94. In sum, EWB declared that any self-praise was warranted.

95. Never was there completed "a series from 1 to 150 regiments" of United States Colored Troops, Ross, *Tabular Analysis;* Dyer, *Compendium*, 1720–40. The Massachusetts and Connecticut black regiments disbanded, but not until the general demobilization after the war.

96. "Double my buttons" meant to advance to field grade rank (major, lieutenant colonel, colonel) and derived from army regulations stipulating a single row of nine

buttons on frock coats for lieutenants and captains, but a double row of seven buttons for field grades, *Revised Regulations . . . 1861,* Article 51, paras. 1446–47.

2. Trench Fighting, Virginia

1. EWB to Father, Aug. 11, 1864, AAS.

2. Grant, *Memoirs,* 2:147, 238; Joint Committee, *Attack on Petersburg,* 123; Govan and Livingood, eds., *Haskell Memoirs,* 77; William J. Pegram to Jenny, Aug. 1, 1864, Pegram-Johnson-McIntosh Papers, Virginia Historical Society; Robert G. Fitzgerald, 5th Massachusetts Cavalry (Colored), diary entry May 16, 1864, Microfilm #4177, Southern Historical Collection, UNC.

3. Yacovone, *Voice of Thunder* (Urbana, Ill., 1997), 316; Blackett, *Thomas Morris Chester,* 109–10, dispatch of Aug. 22, 1864.

4. EWB to Kate, Aug. 30, 1864.

5. Fortress (or Fort) Monroe, Hampton, Va., commanded entrances to the James River and Chesapeake Bay, www.monroe.army.mil (access Nov. 20, 2008).

6. Grant had ordered the black troops shifted to Virginia, *OR* 40, 3:422; the three transports were all propeller steamers, *OR* 35, 2:125.

7. Brigadier General William Birney on Aug. 27, 1864, took command of the 3rd Division, 10th Army Corps, and later led the 2nd Division in the all-black, 25th Corps; brother Theodore, also in 10th Army Corps, was not discharged until Sept. 12, 1864.

8. EWB's wished for Frank's rank of major, because then he could ride rather than walk. Infantry field grade officers, majors to colonels, were entitled to horses.

9. Either Thompson's resignation was rejected or he withdrew it, as he continued to serve with the 2nd U.S. Colored infantry, NPS, CWSS.

10. Hill, *Sketch of the 29th,* 15–17; Grant, *Memoirs,* 2:321–22; *OR* 42, 1:120.

11. Romeyn, "With Colored Troops," 14; Carter, "Fourteen Months' Service," 159; Menge and Shimrak, eds., *Civil War Notebook,* 33; Lewis T. Weld to Mother, Aug. 17–19, 1864, Lewis Weld Family Papers, YU; Polley, *Hood's Texas Brigade,* 251; Blackett, *Thomas Morris Chester,* 113.

12. The letter to Rebecca is missing; Brooke guns, named after their Confederate inventor, John M. Brooke, were very accurate rifled cannon, Coggins, *Arms & Equipment,* 76. Also see Brooke, ed., *Ironclads and Big Guns.*

13. Squat smoothbore mortars fired explosive shells in high arcs so that they dropped from the sky at a steep angle, Coggins, *Arms & Equipment,* 94, 96. Some Confederates called the universally detested mortars "the top-filader," a pun and play on the word *enfilade,* or "fire to the side," Chamberlayne, ed., *Ham Chamberlayne,* 286.

14. By then most Federals had a healthy respect for Confederate fighting ability and tenacity. On Jan 4, 1863, a surgeon in the West wrote, "We are bound to succeed finally but it will be a long struggle," and, two years later, a black regiment's colonel acknowledged Southern determination and endurance, Wheaton, ed., *Surgeon on Horseback,* 208; Robert W. Barnard to Dora, March 19, 1865, Historical Society of Washington, D.C.

15. Rumors had both sides busily digging shafts for mines, Turner, ed., *Allen Family,* 84; Simon, ed., *Papers,* 12:53, 54, 95, 296, 322. Confederates exploded a small mine on Aug. 5, 1864, but gained nothing, *OR* 42, 2:64; Harrill, *Reminiscences,* 29.

16. Farragut won the battle of Mobile Bay on Aug. 5, 1864, and promotion to vice admiral in December, Lewis, *Farragut,* 273–82, 315; Terry did not become a full rank major general until January 1865, Warner, *Generals in Blue,* 498; Ad (Major Adrian

Terry), the general's younger brother, was not promoted until after the war and then only by brevet, AG, *Record,* 304.

17. Of these 29th Connecticut officers, Wooster remained in nominal command until he resigned in August 1865; Ward became colonel of the 31st USCT in November 1864; Camp then rose to major in November; Thorp stayed a captain, AG, *Record,* 851.

18. Jonathan Knight (1789–1864), smooth-shaven in a time of beards, led Yale Medical School until shortly before his death. Cushing/Whitney Medical Library, YU, electronic; Augustus R. Street was a noted Yale benefactor and helped endow the School of Fine Arts, Kelley, *Yale,* 190–1; *CDAB,* 1023, Daniel C. Eaton (1834–1895), botanist and scientific author, became a professor of botany at Yale in 1864, *CDAB,* 260.

19. Bristol's letter probably expressed some justified concern about Confederates' murderous ways with black soldiers.

20. Louis H. McDonough likely took a wrong turn in the darkness and was captured Aug. 26, 1864.

21. The *Palladium* was a Congregational church newspaper.

22. Captain Theodore Bacon was discharged Sept. 12, 1864; Isham was EWB's friend.

23. By manufacture of elections, EWB meant the process of holding an election; Nehemiah Day Sperry, Connecticut's Republican Party boss, also served as New Haven's postmaster and handled elections, *CDAB,* 988; EWB here puts in motion his plan to finagle home leave.

24. By 1864 authorities formed few one-hundred-day regiments like the 37th New Jersey.

25. Joseph P. Thompson's 2nd U.S. Colored Infantry had moved to Key West in February 1864, Dyer, *Compendium,* 1723; the nature of his "dead bratish" behavior is unknown.

26. Major General John A. Dix commanded the Department of the East, which included the New England states, with headquarters in New York, so it would be a cushy staff job; 1st Lieutenant William Goodrich Jr. also of New Haven was at Newbern, N.C., where a yellow fever outbreak crippled his regiment in August, AG, *Record,* 588.

27. Joseph R. Hawley, 7th Connecticut, a 10th Corps brigade commander, won his brigadier general's star on Sept. 13, 1864, and stayed in the army until late 1865, Warner, *Generals in Blue,* 219–20.

28. Hunt was probably Lewis C. Hunt, who earlier in the war commanded the draft depot in New Haven, but Babcock is not identified; EWB wants shoes made from a last or shoe pattern originally shaped for Babcock.

29. Troops in the Petersburg-Richmond trenches were relieved at intervals; officers and men cooked their own meals, forming small mess or eating groups; Beaufort was a backwater while Virginia meant constant fighting.

30. The "attack of the surgeons" was apparently a humorous reference to an encounter with army doctors.

31. 1st Lieutenant Edwin T. Carrington was the 45th U.S. Colored Infantry's adjutant, NPS, CWSS; Henry C. Ward later led a 25th Corps brigade; Major David Torrance became the 29th's lieutenant colonel, and Captain Frederick E. Camp advanced to major.

32. Friends Bennett and Bristol each advanced one grade.

33. EWB's 1st lieutenant also reported this incident, Henry H. Brown diaries, vol. 7, Sept. 21, 1864, ConnHS. When deserting Confederates stumbled into trenches held by black soldiers, they feared instant retaliatory execution, though EWB did not make that clear.

34. Wilmington, N.C., was one of the Confederacy's last open ports, and Grant wanted to capture its guardian, Fort Fisher; other possible tasks mentioned were all in Virginia.

35. Sherman took Atlanta on Sept. 2, 1864, and, on Sept. 19, Sheridan defeated Early at Winchester in Virginia's Shenandoah Valley. But the "final blow" was still more than six months and many casualties distant.

36. Charles Tomlinson was an assistant surgeon, 14th Connecticut, AG, *Record,* 552.

37. Jewett briefly "was lodged a prisoner in Fort Lafayette [in New York harbor]" and faced a court-martial, but then Dix, the department commander, restored him to duty, much to the disgust of some New Haven observers, Barnes, "Pliny A. Jewett," *PCMS,* 170; John A. Porter to Secretary of War Edwin M. Stanton, Jan. 18, 1866, RG 94, NA; T. Juliette Arai. Old Military and Civil Records, NA, to editor, Oct. 17, 2006.

38. Grant, *Memoirs,* 2:332–34.

39. *OR* 42, 1:134, 136; Livermore, *Numbers and Losses,* 128; Longacre, ed., *From Antietam to Fort Fisher,* 209; Elliott F. Grabill to Anna, Sept. 30, 1864, Oberlin College; Synnestvedt, ed., "Earth Shook," 34; James Henry Wickes to Father, Oct. 4, 1864, Boston Public Library; Butler, *Autobiography,* 742.

40. Grabill to Anna, Sept. 30, 1864, Oberlin College; Goulding, "Colored Troops," 150–51; Blackett, *Thomas Morris Chester,* 147.

41. *OR* 42, 1:134, 778; AG, *Record,* 866, for Bennett and Bristol wounds.

42. Hill, *Sketch of the 29th,* 18; Nolin, "Civil War Letters," 220, Cross to Wife, Oct. 4 [1864]; Henry G. Marshall to Folks at Home, Oct. 2, 1864, Schoff Coll., UM; Newton, *Out of the Briars,* 50.

43. A lean six-footer, Brigadier General Alfred H. Terry had attended Yale, then worked as a court clerk in New Haven from 1854 to 1860 and apparently knew the Bacon family, Warner, *Generals in Blue,* 497–98; Captain T is surely Edwin A. Thorp, described earlier as rude and uncongenial.

44. Christopher M. Spencer of Manchester, Conn., invented the .52 caliber repeating breech-loading carbine named after him, a weapon that shattered the Confederate attack on 10th Corps infantry, though Lee's troops succeeded in routing Brigadier General August V. Kautz's cavalry at New Market Road, *CDAB,* 987; Coggins, *Arms & Equipment,* 35; Gallagher, ed., *Fighting for the Confederacy,* 483–84. Confederates could not long use captured Spencers, because they were unable to manufacture its self-contained copper cartridge, George Kryder to Wife, March 15, 1863, Bowling Green State University.

45. "Stacking arms" meant standing rifles upright together to form a pyramid.

46. The absence of fires deprived the enemy of identifiable pinpoint targets.

47. As noted, ordinary soldiers knew the futility of attacking strongly entrenched positions, but some generals never learned, Cockrell and Ballard, eds., *Mississippi Rebel,* 299; Ambrose, ed., *Wisconsin Boy in Dixie,* 1961, 148.

48. EWB heard a false rumor—only a small reconnaissance took place on the Petersburg front on Oct. 7, 1864, *OR* 42, 1:2, 75.

49. Charles C. Tiffany of New Haven joined the 6th Connecticut as chaplain on Oct. 12, 1864, AG, *Record,* 260.

50. Orange, a small town, was close to New Haven.

51. *OR* 41, 1:776–78; Grant, *Memoirs,* 2:341.

52. Hayes, *Diary and Letters,* 2:377.

53. Grant, *Memoirs,* 2:341; *OR* 42, 1:147.

54. Sommers, "Dutch Gap Affair," 51–64; Sparks, ed., *Inside Lincoln's Army,* 417, 429.

55. Sherman, "Assault on Fort Gilmer," 12–13.

56. Colonel Ulysses Doubleday, brother of Major General Abner Doubleday, later became a brigadier general by brevet; Henry Blake was a lawyer in New Haven, and Byington was A. H. Byington, an editor and war correspondent of the Norwalk (Conn.) *Gazette,* census, Ancestry.com.

57. Why Ward "wisely" declined promotion to the 11th Connecticut is uncertain, unless he viewed it as a hard luck unit because it had lost half its officers and four hundred men just since May 1, 1864, AG, *Record,* 432.

58. William Birney, the black brigade's leader, had ordered four small 7th USCI companies to make a suicidal attack upon Fort Gilmer with entirely predictable results, *OR* 42, 1:772; Califf, *Seventh Regiment,* 41–42; Sherman, "Assault on Fort Gilmer," 6–7. The "virus of desertion," as historian Ella Lonn termed it, had become epidemic in Confederate armies by the autumn of 1864; sentries stopped a few, but hundreds crossed to Union lines, Lonn, *Desertion,* 21, 27; Henry G. Marshall to Folks, Oct. 2, 1864, UM.

59. Basler, *Collected Works,* 7:514.

60. Randall, *Civil War,* 614–21.

61. Roth, ed., *Well Mary,* 92, 95; Walton, ed., *Civil War Courtship,* 115; White, "White Papers," 265–66.

62. Opposing trenches at Petersburg in some places were only four hundred feet or so apart, and even shorter distances separated the picket holes or sentry posts between the lines, *OR* 40, 1:559.

63. Ward now led the 31st USCI.

64. A star-struck EWB was easily honored.

65. Grant, *Memoirs,* 2:341–42.

66. *OR* 42, 1:149–50; Jackson and O'Donnell, *Back Home in Oneida,* 174.

67. For Fort Pillow, see Burkhardt, *Confederate Rage,* 105–17; Cimprich, *Fort Pillow;* Ward. *River Run Red.* Mitchell, *Badge of Gallantry,* 160; Marshall to Hattie, Nov. 19, 1864, Schoff. Coll., UM.

68. Alonzo Rembaugh to Captain, Feb. 28, 1864, Loomis-Wilder Papers, YU.

69. "Gopher holes" was the Civil War term for today's foxholes; the battle cry "Remember Fort Pillow" was also understood to mean no quarter given or asked, take-no-prisoners, Dayton E. Flint to Father, June 20, 1864, United States Army Military History Institute; Jones, *Civil War Memoirs,* 127.

70. The official count listed eighty killed and wounded in the 29th, *OR* 42, 1:150; Captain Frederick E. Camp led the 29th as the senior officer present for duty.

71. As noted earlier, Grant's attack south of Petersburg also failed; that at the Kell House was but one action in the 10th Corps' push up Darbytown Road.

72. Private Morrison died of his wound Nov. 12, 1864, AG, *Record,* 877.

73. The county demonstration was probably a patriotic rally; Butler's 10th and 18th Army Corps took part in the Fair Oaks or Darbytown Road diversion of Oct. 27–28, 1864.

74. EWB referred to the action of Oct. 13, 1864, on the Darbytown Road when the 29th lost nineteen men, *OR* 42, 1:778; Hawley, once the 7th Connecticut's leader, temporarily commanded 3rd Division, 10th Corps.

75. EWB again referred to the private war between black Federals and Confederates when he reported the enemy fled when they saw black soldiers and that prisoners expected summary execution, though apparently these captives survived, unlike many others taken by black troops. The brave recruit who lost a leg was Private Richard Thornton, for which see *OR* 42, 1:779.

76. Grape shot and canister were like giant shotgun loads—grape usually had nine large balls and canister had many small cast iron or lead balls encased in a can that scattered upon firing, Boatner, *Civil War Dictionary*, 354; Coggins, *Arms & Equipment*, 67.

77. Calling the disappearing cannon a "sharp practice" meant that he considered it too clever, akin to cheating.

78. Black powder, then in use, plugged or fouled barrels after prolonged firing.

79. "Darkness . . . almost Egyptian" means total darkness and came from the Bible, *Wisdom* 17; "fox fire" is the phosphorescent light from decaying wood, caused by a luminous fungus that makes the wood glow.

80. For brigade report, see *OR* 42, 1:777; Ward went to the 31st rather than the 41st USCI; Wooster's record of nonservice possibly cost him the usual brevet promotion to brigadier general at war's end; Hawley, though born in North Carolina, had lived in Connecticut since boyhood, Warner, *Generals in Blue*, 219.

81. Birney had attended the funeral of his younger brother, Major General David B. Birney, 10th Corps commander, who died of malaria Oct. 18, 1864, Warner, *Generals in Blue*, 34–35. As noted, both main attack and Butler's demonstration had failed; Brevet Major General Godfrey Weitzel, leading the 18th Corps, said the diversion resulted in a "more lively demonstration than was intended" and cost Federals 118 killed, 787 wounded, and 698 missing or captured, while Confederates counted 451 casualties, for which see *OR* 42, 1:795–97; Dyer *Compendium*, 957; Phisterer, *Statistical Record*, 218.

82. The 8th was the 8th USCI; Old Point Comfort at Hampton Roads, Va., near Fortress Monroe, had been a bathing and fishing resort since the 1830s.

83. An emery ball or bag was a small pouch tightly filled with emery powder through which metal needles were pushed to remove rust; a portmannae or large wallet held a small pocket diary with a flap holding the combination closed.

84. Signal Hill probably was the site of a Confederate signal station taken by Federals, who used it and referred to it as New Market Hill, *OR* 41, 1:650, 654.

85. Prim's, or any variation of the name, is not found in the New Haven City Directory for those years, James W. Campbell and Amy L. Trout, curators, NHM&HS, e-mails and letter to editor, Aug. 2, 22, 2007; as usual, EWB was a fastidious shopper by proxy.

86. Officer of the Day was a rotating position among line and staff officers.

87. Martin S. James joined the 3rd Rhode Island Heavy Artillery as a 2nd lieutenant, commanded a company by late 1864 and survived the war, NPS, CWSS. When EWB wrote that James "speaks of his visit to New Haven with great jest," he meant that his new friend expressed great pleasure or enthusiasm.

88. Henry Morris of Putnam, Conn., joined the 29th on Oct. 24, 1864, and was mustered out a year later, AG, *Record*, 878.

89. John P. Gulliver was a Congregational minister in Norwich, Conn., census, Ancestry.com.

90. Lincoln and his Republican Party won the election held on Nov. 8, 1864, with

Lincoln winning 212 electoral college votes to McClellan's 21 and 55 percent of the popular vote, Paludan, *Presidency*, 290; "fight it out on this line" is from Grant's famous vow made during the spring offensive, *OR* 36,1:4 or Grant, *Memoirs*, 2:226.

91. No significant action occurred at Petersburg to explain the artillery firing, but sometimes such bombardments thundered simply to annoy the enemy. Grant once asked the cause of a barrage and a general replied, "I suppose it means the same this morning as yesterday and the day before. Previous to the first the rebels . . . called out to our men that they were going to shell Burnsides niggers and they must not mind it—they have shelled us every morning since," Simon, *Papers*, 12:54.

92. Wooster, the 29th's colonel, had returned from stumping for Lincoln.

93. Lincoln had made Thanksgiving a national holiday in 1863, setting November's final Thursday as the day. In 1864, it fell on Nov. 24, the day before EWB's letter. When he refers to the *fair*, he apparently meant the holiday.

94. For earlier enthusiasm, see his letters of June 4 and Aug. 30, 1864.

95. Leonard Woolsey Bacon was an older brother, born in 1830; the Rev. Philander H. Hollister joined the regiment on Jan. 29, 1865, but resigned on May 20, less than four months later, AG, *Record*, 861.

96. No significant action occurred in the next two weeks north of the James; on the south, Army of the Potomac troops struck the Weldon Railroad, tearing up twenty miles of tracks December 7–12, 1864, *OR* 42, 1:443–46.

97. Apparently EWB incorrectly recalled the quotation for it resists tracing; both black and white troops complained that they were shifted elsewhere as soon as they built a good camp, whereupon another unit occupied their site, Greiner, Coryell, and Smither, eds., *Surgeon's Civil War*, 213; Redkey, *Grand Army*, 49.

98. Taps is the bugle call for day's end, lights out.

99. *OR* 42, 1:113–14.

100. Major General Edward O. C. Ord was badly wounded at Fort Harrison, Warner, *Generals in Blue*, 350.

101. For example, Brigadier General Samuel A. Rice, wounded in the ankle on April 30, 1864, died two months later of that minor wound, Warner, *Generals in Blue*, 402.

102. Redkey, *Grand Army*, 50, 256–57; Hill, *Sketch of the 29th*, 20; Levstik, "Diary of Colonel Albert Rogall," 43; Lowry and Welsh, *Tarnished Scalpels*, 41–47, 68–75.

103. Dr. Adrian Russell Terry (b. 1808) died in Chicago Dec. 3, 1864, http://famousamericans.net/adrianrussellterry; EWB's stepmother, Catherine Terry Bacon, "perhaps suffered from a chronic arthritic condition . . . often bedridden," Davis, *Leonard Bacon*, 251; Whitney is not identified.

104. Sergeant James Evans of Newtown, slightly wounded in the ankle Oct. 13 at Darbytown Road, died Nov. 19, 1864; Brown transferred to 1st USCI as a captain on Jan. 1, 1865, both AG, *Record*, 877.

105. Branchville, S.C., was an important junction on the South Carolina Railroad between Charleston and Augusta, Ga., one that Confederates still held in February 1865, *OR* 53:400.

106. Tiffany was the 6th Connecticut's chaplain, but Love is unidentified; William T. Eustis, aged about forty-two, was a Congregational clergyman in New Haven, Ancestry.com; "squeamish" here meant fastidious or scrupulous in conduct or belief.

107. Army ambulances often had springs, providing a more comfortable ride.

3. Promotion and Victory

1. Robert W. Barnard to Dora, March 19, 1865, Robert Barnard Family Papers (Ms 541), Historical Society of Washington, D.C.; Elmore, ed., *Diary,* 60; Robertson, ed., "'Boy Artillerist,'" 248; Heslin, ed., "Yankee Soldier," *NYHSQ,* 125.

2. Sherman, *Memoirs,* 2:231; Redkey, ed., "Rocked in the Cradle," 70–79; Basler, *Collected Works,* 8:187, 207; *OR* 46, 2:52, 60; Longacre, ed., "Task before Them," 36–43.

3. EWB CMSR, NA; Ross, *Tabular Analysis,* 19–27.

4. Beale, ed., *Diary,* 352; Penn, *Rattling Spurs,* 9–11; Dyer, *Compendium,* 1739; Rowell, *Yankee Cavalrymen,* 139, William Thomas diary; Basler, *Collected Works,* 8:266, 268.

5. Leonard Bacon to Son, Jan. 14, 1865, AAS; Daly, *Aboard the USS Florida,* 60; Cleaves, *Rock of Chickamauga,* 204.

6. EWB's CMSR for 117th USCT, AGO, RG 94, NA.

7. Illiterate ex-slaves filled the 117th, organized Sept. 27, 1864, at Covington, Ky., Dyer, *Compendium,* 1739.

8. Brown began his war service as a 1st Lieutenant with the 11th Ohio Infantry; some thought Enfields more accurate than the newer Springfields, but the 117th might have received worn Enfields, Coggins, *Arms & Equipment,* 32.

9. 2nd Lieutenant Bevin, who enlisted in August 1862, served in Co. E, 29th Connecticut, AG, *Record,* 869; infantry field grade officers, majors to colonels, were entitled to ride horses but they had to buy their own and if the animal was killed or stolen, it was their loss; as a major, he would receive $169 monthly, up from a captain's $115, but the promotion put him in debt, Boatner, *Civil War Dictionary,* 624; as noted earlier, officers and men often went six or eight months without pay, Bowditch, "War Letters," 431, 443, 464.

10. The "Beast" was Benjamin F. Butler, a pejorative first applied by Confederates, then adopted by irreverent Federals. Southerners called him that for his harsh rule of New Orleans.

11. Older brother Leonard had graduated from Andover Theological Seminary after attending Yale and became a minister at several churches in the East, Davis, *Leonard Bacon,* 147, 178.

12. Russell's was a reference to the Collegiate and Commercial Institute in New Haven; White is not identified.

13. Grant, *Memoirs,* 2:427; David Warman diary, Aug. 18, 1864, www.homepages.dsu.edu/janke/civilwar/warman.htm (access Oct. 27, 2006); Charles G. Merrill to Mother, Sept. 8, 1864, Charles G. Merrill Papers, YU; Mulholland, *Story of the 116th,* 249; Turner, *Allen Family,* 81.

14. Allen, *Forty-Six Months,* 293–300; Harmon, ed., "Letters," 303; Shaver, *History of the Sixtieth Alabama,* 77; Turner, *Allen Family,* 81–82; Jocelyn, *Mostly Alkali,* 44.

15. EWB CMSR, 117th USCT.

16. The Rev. John P. Gulliver, a Congregational minister in Norwich, recovered money for one of EWB's soldiers, as requested by EWB to father on Nov. 9, 1864; Alfred Terry Bacon was EWB's youngest half-brother, born 1852.

17. Terry captured Fort Fisher, N.C., on Jan. 15, 1865, thereby closing Wilmington, the Confederacy's last major open port; describing Terry as an "angel visitant" suggested he had supernatural powers, but the "sweet poetess" allusion is uncertain.

18. EWB sought to hire a servant in Connecticut, though most officers hired one locally, either a contraband or a soldier.

19. Charles Griswold, Henry G. Marshall and Thomas G. Bennett all returned and stayed with the 29th Connecticut.

20. As noted earlier, the Rev. Philander H. Hollister joined the 29th on Jan. 29, 1865, but resigned in May.

21. Bevin was probably 2nd Lieutenant William H. Bevin, 29th Connecticut, or a family member; the worry apparently concerned a mechanical pencil's operation.

22. Pease was Thomas H. Pease, forty-nine, a bookseller in New Haven, Ancestry. com; "coals of fire," a biblical reference, is from a homily at Proverbs 25:21, 22, urging kindness to enemies, but EWB said he does not want any more such good deeds from Pease.

23. Stamford eludes identification.

24. Why Confederates cheered is unknown; "stole our beeves" referred to the Confederate capture of 2,500 cattle from behind Federal lines on Sept. 16, 1864, *OR* 42, 1:25–30; a few days earlier, Sheridan had scattered the last Confederate force in the Shenandoah Valley, *OR* 46, 1:476.

25. Major General Joseph Hooker, who briefly led the Army of the Potomac in 1863, had ordered soldiers to wear distinctive cloth badges on their caps identifying their division and corps, *OR* 25, 2:152. EWB wanted a badge of a lozenge on a square in red, showing that he belonged to the 1st Division, 25th Corps, *OR, Atlas,* plate 175, for corps badges

26. Michie, "Dutch Gap Canal," *B&L* 4:575; Nichols, *Perry's Saints,* 254; Pickett, *Heart of a Soldier,* 160; Wallace, ed., *Under the Stars and Bars,* 238.

27. Ord had led the 24th Corps and then the Army of the James and the Department of Virginia; ladies often attended reviews and inspections in Virginia.

28. As noted earlier, the Bouquet Society was a young ladies' social group.

29. On his 63rd birthday in February 1865, the senior Bacon had decided that his life neared an end and that he had outlived his usefulness as a pastor in New Haven and so announced his resignation in March, Davis, *Leonard Bacon,* 205.

30. Older brother Leonard and his wife had just had a child and someone had named a newborn after Kate.

31. Wightman, *From Antietam,* 215; Bright, "Yankees in Arms," 213.

32. Moore, *Story of a Cannoneer,* 271; Childs, ed., *Private Journal,* 228; McGee and Lander, eds., *Rebel Came Home,* 75; Douglas, ed., *Douglas's Texas Battery,* 153, 156.

33. Lincoln visited the Petersburg lines on Saturday, March 25, 1864; James was likely Martin S. James, 3rd Rhode Island Heavy Artillery; James F. Hall became colonel, 1st New York Volunteer Engineers, on March 20, the day before EWB's letter, Boatner, *Civil War Dictionary,* 366.

34. In his musings about strategy, EWB mostly missed the mark—Grant planned to strike the Petersburg lines to the south, Grant, *Memoirs,* 2:436–53.

35. Gordon, *Reminiscences,* 398, 403, 407–11, 412; Kilmer, "Gordon's Attack," *B&L* 4:579–83; Day, *True History,* 94–96; Fox, *Regimental Losses,* 548.

36. Captain Clitz was Commander John M. B. Clitz, a regular navy officer who had served on the USS *Iroquois, ORN* 6:163; Organized in New Haven in August 1862, the 15th Connecticut spent most of 1864 in North Carolina where the exchanged men were captured, AG, *Record,* 588–89; *OR* 47, 1:977.

37. "Butler's Monument" referred to the failed Dutch Gap Canal project.

38. EWB charged that Butler "invariably" assigned bad officers to black units.

39. William Birney at that time commanded the 2nd Division, 25th Corps.

40. Kress was a lieutenant throughout the war until his last minute promotion, *OR* 46, 2:242.

41. *OR* 46, 1:596, 1211, 1227–28; Prescott, "Capture of Richmond," 64–70; Blackett, *Thomas Morris Chester*, 289–92, 303; Ford, ed., *Cycle of Adams Letters*, 2:261–62.

42. Pollard, *Southern History*, 2:490–96; Boston *Daily Evening Transcript*, April 3, 1865; *Baltimore American*, April 4, 1865; Chicago *Tribune*, April 6, 1865; *New York Times*, April 6, 1865; Racine, "*Unspoiled Heart,*"265; Gates, ed., *Colton Letters*, 322; Putnam, *Richmond during the War* (reprint, Alexandria, Va., 1983), 367; Swiggett, ed., *Rebel War Clerk's Diary*, 2:468–69.

43. Harrison, *Recollections Grave and Gay*, 214; Putnam. *Richmond during the War*, 366; Blackett, *Thomas Morris Chester*, 292–92; Henry G. Marshall to Folks at Home, April 3, 1865, Schoff Coll., UM.

44. Davis was attending church services when he received General Robert E. Lee's telegram advising that he could no longer hold the Petersburg-Richmond lines, Dowdey and Manarin, eds., *Wartime Papers*, Doc. 985, telegram to Davis, April 2, 1865.

45. Casey still presided over the board examining officer candidates for black troops; the ninny's ancestry may refer to Rear Admiral Andrew H. Foote, who had helped EWB begin his navy career, but there were several prominent Footes; August V. Kautz led the 1st Division, 25th Army Corps.

46. Castle Thunder, a converted tobacco warehouse, housed Federal captives but also criminals, political prisoners, military offenders, male and female spies, and deserters from both armies; some escaped when Confederates evacuated the city, Michael D. Gorman, "Civil War Richmond," www.mdgorman.com (access Aug. 30, 2007).

47. Francis H. Pierpont served as pro-Union governor (1861–1863) of the "Reorganized Government of Virginia" at Wheeling, Va., and later moved his office to Alexandria, Va., ruling a puppet-state in Union-controlled parts of Virginia; at war's end, he shifted to Richmond, *CDAB*, 790; see also Ambler, *Francis H. Pierpont*. West Virginia split from Virginia, gaining admission to the Union in 1863, and Arthur I. Boreman served as governor 1863–1869, Boreman obituary, West Virginia Archives & History, electronic.

48. Lincoln toured fallen Richmond on April 4, welcomed by cheering throngs of exhilarated blacks; other luminaries also hastened to visit the shattered city, exulting in victory and the war's end, Redkey, *Grand Army*, 177.

49. Horatio N. Taft, diary, April 30, 1865, Library of Congress; Adelbert Baughman, diary, typescript copy, April 15, 1865, UM; Laas, *Wartime Washington*, 499; Beauchamp, ed., *Private War*, 184; Woodward, *Mary Chestnut's Civil War*, 791; Amasa K. Richards to Mary, April 27, 1865, Mary E. Richards and Family Papers, Minnesota Historical Society.

50. *OR* 49, 2:566–67; Clay-Copton, *Belle of the Fifties*, 248; Robert A. Driver and Gloria S. Driver, eds., *Letters Home*, 102; Bird, ed., *Quill of the Wild Goose*, 257; Kallgren and Crouthamel, eds., "*Dear Friend Anna,*" 124; *OR* 47, 1:937.

51. Johnson extended amnesty to thousands of Confederates, but ex-Confederate West Point graduates were not welcomed back into the army, Dorris, *Pardon and Amnesty*, 344.

52. Lewis, ed., *My Dear Parents*, 134; Ford, *Cycle of Adams Letters*, 2:267–69; Smith and Mullins, eds., "Diary of H. C. Medford," 220.

53. *OR* 46, 3:891, 990, 1005–6.

54. Ibid., 1160–61.

55. *OR* 48, 2:476, 525; for numbers, see *OR* Ser. 3, 4:1283, 5:113, 138; on Mexico, see Thomas and Hyman, *Stanton*, 437.

56. *OR* 49, 2:1108–12; Thomas and Hyman, *Stanton*, 440, 479; Bearss, ed., *Louisiana Confederate*, 243; Yacovone, *Voice of Thunder*, 87–89; Offenberg and Parsonage, eds., *War Letters*, 161; Higginson, *Army Life*, 205.

57. The black 25th Corps never fought as a unit, but went to Texas minus only its third division; Butler and Weitzel, the "Siamese" twins, became separated when Grant and Lincoln dismissed Butler.

58. Carrington was a New Haven man and the nearby 45th U.S. Colored Infantry's adjutant.

59. Birney, brevetted major general, mustered out in August 1865.

60. Bomb-proof—a hut covered with heavy logs or a cave dug into the side of a ravine, hill or bluff, with openings always facing away from enemy fire. The "bomb" part referred to explosive mortar or artillery shells and the "proof" was always the hope but not necessarily the reality. Covered way—Civil War terminology for a communications trench that concealed soldiers moving to and from the main trench line, though it was not actually covered or roofed.

61. He enjoyed a large tent, apparently girded by wooden sides and end.

62. Crowbar needles, still in use today for quilting, leather work, and other tasks, are long, heavy needles curved at their pointed end.

63. "Moseby's gang" was the 43rd Battalion Virginia Cavalry or Colonel John S. Mosby's Partisan Rangers, who had sorely troubled Federals in Virginia or "Mosby's Confederacy." Many partisans surrendered on April 21, 1865, and others followed suit in May and June, Wert, *Mosby's Rangers*, 287–90.

64. Colonel Charles F. Adams, scion of the famous presidential family, disagreed somewhat with EWB. Adams led the 5th Massachusetts Cavalry (Colored) when he was arrested for allowing his men to "straggle and maraud." He blamed himself, but only for thinking it possible to make good horse soldiers of blacks, Ford, *Cycle of Adams Letters*, 2:267–69; Adams, *Charles Francis Adams*, 166.

65. Likely EWB was unaware of Halleck's machinations and perhaps also the efforts of Richmond's citizens to oust the 25th Corps; Ord merely shifted from one command to another.

66. Evidently the unsent letter was in reaction to Lincoln's assassination. "Chivalry" was an ironic, sarcastic reference to Southerners' purported knightly conduct, Henry Ketzle, diary, April 1865, www.ketzle.com/diary/rightpane.html (access Dec. 1, 2008); Robert W. Barnard to Mother, Aug. 5, 1864, Robert Barnard Family Papers (Ms 541), Historical Society of Washington, D.C.; *OR* 22, 2:735, W. P. Leeper. Lincoln's murder caused Federal soldiers to cry for retribution and Sherman warned that "there is but one dread result" to expect from such an act, Jones, *Reminiscences*, 98; *OR* 47, 3:238–39. "No quarter" meant that they would take no prisoners, Swift, "Letters," 62; Kallgren and Crouthamel, *"Dear Friend Anna,"* 124; Driver and Driver, *Letters Home*, 102.

67. Some uncertainty existed at this juncture. Lee and Johnston had surrendered but Richard Taylor's forces in Louisiana, Mississippi, and Alabama and Edmund Kirby Smith's troops in the Trans-Mississippi had not yet yielded.

68. McCready is not identified.

69. Berlin, *Freedom,* Ser. 2:721–24; Newton, *Out of the Briars,* 70; Hill, *Sketch of the 29th,* 29.

70. Wiley, ed., *Letters of Warren Akin,* 21; Williams, ed., *Diary and Letters,* 2:175; Thomas and Sauers, eds., *Civil War Letters,* 42; Hughes, *Liddell's Record,* 118 n1. See also Wiley, *Southern Negroes,* 13–14.

71. Browne, "My Service,"11–12; Newton, *Out of the Briars,* 70; James Shaw, "Our Last Campaign,"38; Califf, *Seventh Regiment,* 79; *New York Times,* Nov. 17, 26, Dec. 25, 1865.

72. Brother Frank [Francis] had resigned as a brigade surgeon on Aug. 25, 1864, and visited EWB in a private capacity. Even during the war, civilians visited the front lines.

73. "Bucked & gagged"—an unpleasant punishment, effected by gagging the soldier, binding feet and hands, seating the man, then passing a rod or bayonet between drawn up knees and arms looped over knees, rendering the offender immobile in a contorted position.

74. Weitzel led the all-black 25th Army Corps, which included the 117th USCI.

75. Here "limbo" meant a place of confinement; the *Articles of War* were the codified rules for governing the army and officers read the *Articles* to the troops at intervals. Articles 7 and 8 allowed a death sentence for mutiny or failure to inform superiors of pending mutiny; Article 6 forbade disrespectful behavior toward superiors. Confederates used the same Articles of War, see 1862 Articles of War at www.usregulars.com/articles_of_war.html (access Dec. 1, 2008).

76. A sutler was a civilian merchant with a permit to sell food and sundries to a unit or garrison, often accompanying troops with a horse- or mule-drawn sales van.

77. Here "Brown Windsor" is an herbal soap, not the English meat soup of the same name.

78. Mary Thompson was another daughter of Joseph P. Thompson, the New York clergyman, Ancestry.com; by Carte, EWB meant the widely popular card-sized photograph or Carte de Visite.

79. The 29th had guarded Confederate prisoners at Point Lookout, Md., where the Potomac River joins Chesapeake Bay. Built for ten thousand, at that time the camp reportedly held fifteen thousand men, Nolin, "Civil War Letters," 232.

80. Charmley, twenty-four, of New Haven, was the daughter of a bank president, Ancestry.com; Ray, one of many Rays, is unidentified; Fort Hale, built in 1863 to protect New Haven's harbor from Confederate raiders, was named after Nathan Hale, a Connecticut Revolutionary War patriot.

81. "Thankful for past favors" was and is a common expression; again, Chapman cannot be identified among the many Chapmans in the area.

82. *Star of the South* was an army steamer, transporting horses as well as men.

83. While the old shipmate is unidentified, 2nd Lieutenant Henry P. Johnson also lived in New Haven.

84. Forts Morgan and Gaines guarded the Gulf entrance to Mobile Bay and there Farragut had defeated a Confederate squadron on Aug. 5, 1864; Fort Morgan, the last to hold out, yielded on Aug. 23, Lewis, *Farragut,* 263–90.

85. Kress served on Ord's staff, went on leave April 17, 1865, and then resigned, *OR* 46, 3:816.

86. Thompson, by then a captain, and his 2nd U.S. Colored Infantry remained in Florida until mustered out in January 1866, NPS, CWSS; Terry, who earlier had led the 2nd and 7th Connecticut, commanded the 10th Army Corps.

87. Army and naval cannon had pounded Fort Morgan, siege trenches had pushed close and the fort surrendered Aug. 23, 1864; Fort Gaines, some distance away, had yielded Aug. 8, 1864. after a perfunctory resistance, *OR* 39, 404, 417. Note that dinner was usually the noon meal.

88. By dates, he refers again to the most recent newspapers.

4. Occupation Duty, Texas

1. Thomas and Hyman, *Stanton*, 440; *OR* 49, 2:1108, 1110–11.

2. Major General Philip H. Sheridan was in New Orleans; Lavaca was near the top of Matagorda Bay; Brazos de Santiago was a coastal island a bit north of where the Rio Grande entered the Gulf of Mexico.

3. "Stacks" were the stacked rifles upon which they stretched tents and blankets; Samuel C. Armstrong was a brigadier general by brevet only and Brevet Brigadier General Ulysses Doubleday led 2nd brigade, 2nd division, 25th Army Corps, Boatner, *Civil War Dictionary*, 26, 244; Pease was 1st Lieutenant William B. Pease, a New Haven man with the 8th U.S. Colored Infantry, Ancestry.com; NPS, CWSS. Carrington still belonged to the 45th U.S. Colored Infantry.

4. Bagdad was almost directly south of Brazos Island; his pocket lantern probably used a candle, though some had kerosene tanks; Brigadier General Giles A. Smith began the war as a captain in the 8th Missouri, fought in the West, and rose to major general in November 1865, Warner, *Generals in Blue,* 456–57. As a captain, EWB walked; as a major, he rode—if he had a horse.

5. Colonel Hamilton was likely Andrew J. Hamilton, a Texas Unionist politician, appointed brigadier general by Lincoln, Warner, *Generals in Blue,* 198; Ashbel Smith, born in Hartford, Conn., was a physician, diplomat, agriculturist, and politician before leading the 2nd Texas Infantry during the war, *CDAB,* 967.

6. Specie was and is money in gold or silver.

7. The last action refers to an engagement on May 13, 1865, at Palmetto [also Palmito] Rancho when Confederates defeated Federals, *OR* 48, 1:266; Conyer, "Last Battle of the War," 309–15. Four different armies fighting undoubtedly referred to fighting between French and allied troops and Mexican insurgents on one side of the river and between Federals and Confederates on the other, but the specific event is uncertain. EWB quoted a hymn that begins, "Lord what a wretched land is this/ That yields us no supply/ No cheering fruits, nor wholesome trees. . . ."

8. France's Napoleon III had installed Austrian Archduke Maximilian as emperor of Mexico in 1864, but his reign was brief. Captured by Republican troops, he went before a firing squad on June 19, 1867, Boatner, *Civil War Dictionary,* 521.

9. Palo Alto, five miles from Brownsville, was the site of the first major battle in the Mexican-American War, ending in a draw on May 8, 1846; the prickly pear cactus, common to southwestern deserts, has large flat edible leaves covered with sharp spines; chaparral is dense shrub and stunted tree growth.

10. Matamoros lies across from Brownsville on Mexico's side of the Rio Grande.

11. EWB's disenchantment with his black soldiers is clear, but exactly what he means by "under the present system" is not.

12. A board and room bill of $16 a week would take more than half a captain's or a lieutenant's monthly pay; the self-congratulations were mocking humor—EWB had no wife.

13. Scurvy, caused by a want of fruit and vegetables, more commonly appeared among sailors and prisoners of war than soldiers in the field; the meaning of corned or preserved in whisky is obvious, but the charge that the 25th Corps headquarters staff stayed drunk for more than three months strains belief.

14. General Juan N. Cortina, Mexican folk hero whose mother owned much land around Matamoros and Brownsville, mostly fought on the Republican side; the Imperialists were the French and conservative Mexican forces. Kirby Smith did not sell the wagons and artillery, but another Confederate general did. For more on this simmering dispute, see Thompson and Jones, *Civil War and Revolution,* 100–101.

15. Many mutiny cases originated in the disturbances in Virginia as black troops boarded transports, though trial and punishment waited until arrival in Texas, "List of U.S. Soldiers Executed," 8–11. The court-martialed officer was probably Captain Franklin G. Daggett, who was dismissed from the service Sept. 27, 1865, American Civil War Research Database, www.civilwardata.com (access Dec. 1, 2008).

16. Those rumors were correct—four convicted in Lincoln's assassination, including Mary Surratt, went to the gallows on July 7, 1865.

17. Cortina defended Mexican-America property rights, aided the Union during the war, and fought French intervention, but also robbed and pillaged, Goldfinch and Canales, *Juan N. Cortina.* For the Camargo incident, see Thompson and Jones, *Civil War and Revolution,* 103.

18. Ward and Ulrich belonged to the 31st U.S. Colored Infantry; Wooster led the 29th Connecticut, EWB's old regiment.

19. Broken Bone fever (break bone, bone crusher fever) or dengue is an infectious mosquito-borne viral disease, the illness that afflicted EWB on the Mississippi River.

20. Henry G. Marshall to Folks at Home from Brownsville, Aug. 7, 1865, Schoff Coll., UM; Redkey, *Grand Army,* 198.

21. The circular went to officers, for only they could resign; enlisted men had to serve for the length of their enlistment term.

22. Officers paid for their food.

23. "M.Cs" meant Members of Congress; Amos B. Eaton was then the army's commissary general.

24. Brigadier General Oliver O. Howard headed the newly established Freedman's Bureau as part of the War Department, but soon charges of corruption embroiled subordinates, Warner, *Generals in Blue,* 237–38.

25. A powerful politician, Lafayette S. Foster of Connecticut, a Republican, was the Senate's president pro tempore and then next in line to the presidency should the president die or become incapacitated.

26. A nocturnal creature, the armor-plated armadillo was probably in a cage.

27. Of the 28th Connecticut officers, Wooster managed to resign on Aug. 21, but the others had to wait until Oct. 24 for their "immediate" discharges; enlisted men mustered out on Nov. 25, 1865, at Hartford, Conn., AG, *Record,* 860–61.

28. Styles is unidentified, but any connection to the Lincoln assassination conspiracy or the trial in May-June 1865, was probably remote.

29. More than twice as many soldiers succumbed to disease as died in battle. For example, the 29th Connecticut listed forty-two killed and mortally wounded in action while disease killed 178 men, Fox, *Regimental Losses,* 50; AG, *Record,* 881. For more on terrible conditions in Texas, see Glatthaar, *Forged in Battle,* 218–20.

30. The rumor was false—white troops remained in Texas.

5. Homeward

1. Rebecca Bacon to Father, undated but late August 1865, EWB Papers AAS.

2. Lafayette S. Foster to Leonard Bacon, Sept. 5, 1865, EWB Papers, AAS.

3. Several Garrison families lived in the area and Kate's hosts cannot be identified.

4. Contrast this denunciation of Brown with the warm praise in EWB's letter to Father, Jan. 6, 1865.

5. Shepherd was probably Forrest Shepherd of New Haven, a geological explorer, who wrote Lincoln in 1864 about using an incapacitating gas against Confederates, Smart, "Chemical & Biological Warfare," 11. Judge Watrous was John C. Watrous, Republic of Texas attorney general and the first Federal district judge in Texas, who left when the state seceded; brother Frank had first practiced medicine in Galveston where Judge Watrous presided before the war, Davis, *Leonard Bacon,* 178.

6. To clarify, EWB sent his sister the dead scorpion.

7. The "Italy of America" comparison was obviously not complimentary; John L. Motley's *The Rise of the Dutch Republic: A History,* a three volume work, was first published in 1855, then reprinted in 1861 by Harper & Brothers in New York.

8. Surgeon George C. Potts, 23rd U.S. Colored Infantry, was twice found guilty of frivolously removing a dead soldier's innards and then decapitating the corpse, Lowry and Welsh, *Tarnished Scalpels,* 68–75.

9. Northern black units quickly demobilized. The two Massachusetts black infantry regiments had already gone home in late August and the 29th sailed from Texas in mid-October. But, as noted earlier, the U.S. Colored Troop units often stayed until 1867. For example, the 117th mustered out on Aug. 10, 1867, Ross, *Tabular Analysis,* 19–27.

10. EWB's low emotional and mental state is clear here.

11. Silas Casey wrote the two-volume *System of Infantry Tactics* in 1861, used by both armies; in 1863 he added *Infantry Tactics for Colored Troops* and probably it was this "thin" book that EWB would study.

12. A new term started at Yale.

13. EWB CMSR for 117th U.S. Colored Infantry, NA.

14. Henry R. Selden served as New York's lieutenant governor (1857–58) and was a prominent figure in the Republican Party, www.politicalgraveyard.com/bio/selden. html (access Dec. 1, 2008).

15. Bacon's miscalculations about the 117th's destiny resulted in part from the uncertainty prevalent in the immediate postwar era.

EPILOGUE

1. EWB CMSR for 117th U.S. Colored Infantry, NA.

2. See EWB to Father, July 5, 1862, where the nineteen-year-old believed he was too old to return to school.

3. Baldwin, *Michael Bacon,* 327; for Flint tenure, see online Deb and Clayton Holice's "History of Genesee, MI," (Religious Organizations, Part II), www.usgennet.org/usa/mi/county/lapeer/gen (access Dec. 1, 2008).

4. Baldwin, *Michael Bacon,* 327; New London details at web site "First Congregational Church—New London, Connecticut."

5. Printed obituary for EWB, unknown publication, Edward W. Bacon Papers, AAS; Willmantic (Conn.) *Chronicle,* Aug. 27, 1884; Edward W. Bacon, *New London and the War of 1812* (New London: By the Society, 1890).

6. Rebecca Bacon to brother Frank, Nov. 21, 1863, Bacon Family Papers, YU.

7. Davis, *Leonard Bacon,* 120–21; University of Medicine, "A History of Tuberculosis Treatment," www.umdnj.edu/globaltb/tbhistory.htm (access Feb. 19, 2007).

8. EWB obituary, AAS; email from Beth Palmer, First Congregational Church of Santa Barbara to editor, Aug. 28, 2006; Baldwin, *Michael Bacon,* 327.

9. EWB obituary, AAS.

10. Baldwin, *Michael Bacon,* 327; Davis, *Leonard Bacon,* 252; facts about Kate came from family trees and census data, Ancestry.com.

11. Tucker, *Blue & Gray Navies,* 129; Musicant, *Divided Waters,* 398.

12. NHC; *New York Times,* obituaries p. 4, Dec. 17, 1867.

13. Tucker, *Blue & Gray Navies,* 286–93; *New York Times,* Dec. 27, 1865; Semmes, *Memoirs of Service,* 324–33.

14. Lewis, *Farragut,* 269, 315, 331, 372–75.

15. Warner, *Generals in Blue,* 136–7.

16. EWB to Father, Oct. 23, 1864; Spalding, *Illustrated Popular Biography.*

17. EWB to Father, Jan. 6, 1864, and to Kate, Sept. 8, 1865; for Brown's career and death, see www.findagrave.com (access Dec. 1, 2008).

18. AG, *Record,* 510–12; Homer B. Sprague Papers, Chester Fritz Library, University of North Dakota.

19. *Anglo-African,* Sept. 9, 16, 1865.

BIBLIOGRAPHY

UNPUBLISHED DOCUMENTS AND COLLECTIONS

American Antiquarian Society, Worcester, Massachusetts. Edward Woolsey Bacon Papers.

American Philosophical Society, Philadelphia, Pennsylvania. Albert D. Bache diary.

Austin State University, East Texas Research Center. John C. Birdwell in Whitaker-Fenley Collection.

Boston Public Library. James Henry Wickes letters.

Bowling Green State University. George Kryder letters.

Cincinnati Historical Society. E. W. Goble in Joseph B. Boyd Collection.

Connecticut Historical Society. Papers of Henry H. Brown, William A. Buckingham.

Duke University. Robert Melvin in Jefferson Davis Collection, Hubert Saunders, Ella Gertrude Clanton Thomas.

Georgia Department of Archives and History. James M. Jordan in "letters from Confederate soldiers, 1860–1865."

Georgia Historical Society. William P. Brooks recollections.

Gettysburg College. A. S. Fisher letters.

Harvard University, Houghton Library. Charles Longfellow Papers.

Henry E. Huntington Library. Papers of Thomas W. Sweeny, Delos Van Deusen, John Vliet.

Indiana State Library. George F. Chittenden letters.

Kansas State Historical Society. Papers of R. G. Hinton, James Montgomery.

Kentucky Historical Society. Henry L. Stone letters.

Library of Congress. Blair Family Papers, Horatio N. Taft diary.

Minnesota Historical Society. Amasa K. Richards in Mary E. Richards and Family Collection.

Missouri Historical Society. Sylvester Doss in Warren D. Crandell Collection.

Montana Historical Society. Edward M. Galligan diary.

New York City Public Library. Bartholomew Diggins recollections.

New York State Library. Francis G. Barnes and Dealton Cooper Papers.

Oberlin College. Elliott F. Grabill letters.

United States Army Military History Institute. Dayton E. Flint Papers.

University of Michigan, Ann Arbor. Papers of Adelbert Baughman, Jerome Bussey, Henry Grimes Marshall in Schoff Collection; James T. Miller, John F. Slaver, Wash Vosburgh.

University of North Carolina, Chapel Hill. Elias Davis letters, Robert G. Fitzgerald diary.

University of South Carolina. Calvin Shedd letters.
University of Texas, Austin. David M. Ray letters.
Virginia Historical Society. William J. Pegram in Pegram-Johnson-McIntosh Collection.
Washington, D.C., Historical Society. Robert W. Barnard letters.
Yale University. Papers of Bacon Family, Ellsworth D. S. Goodyear, Charles G. Merrill,
    Peter Parker, Alonzo Rembaugh, Lewis T. Weld.

ELECTRONIC SOURCES

Boreman, Arthur, obituary. www.wvculture.org./history/statehood/boremanarthur01.
    html (Nov. 20, 2008).
"Casualties: U. S. Navy and Marine Corps Personnel Killed and Wounded in Wars,
    Conflicts . . ." NHC. Access at www.history.navy.mil/faqs/faq56 (Nov. 20, 2008).
Civil War Soldiers and Sailors System (CWSS), NPS. Access at www.itd.nps.gov/cwss
    (Feb. 23, 2009).
Gorman, Michael D. "Civil War Richmond—Prisons." Access at www.mdgorman.com
    (Nov. 20, 2008).
Kemp, Daniel F. "Civil War Reminiscences, Aboard the USS *Cincinnati*, 1862–1863," cour-
    tesy Barbara Covello, http://sunsite.utk.edu/civil-war/kemp.html (Nov. 20, 2008).
Ketzle, Henry. Diary. Access at www.ketzle.com/diary/rightpane.html (Nov. 20, 2008).
Knight, Jonathan, biography. http://info.med.yale.edu/library/exhibits/hospitals/
    knighthosp.html (Nov. 20, 2008).
Massa, Samuel. "Fire and Brimstone—Aboard the USS *Cayuga* at Forts Jackson & St.
    Philip: Excerpts from the Journal of Paymaster's Clerk Samuel Massa." Tran-
    scribed by Terry Foenander. Access at http://Foenander.com/massa.htm (Nov.
    20, 2008; search for "Samuel Massa").
Potter, Henry A., to Father, May 3, 1864. Access at http://freepages.genealogy. rootsweb.
    ancestry.com/~mruddy/letters5.htm (Nov. 20, 2008; search for "Henry A. Potter").
Spalding, J. A. *Illustrated Popular Biography of Connecticut*. Hartford: Case, Lockwood
    and Brainard, 1891. Access at http://all-biographies.com/soldiers/william_burr_
    wooster.htm (Nov. 20, 2008).
Warman, David. Diary. Access at www.homepages.dsu.edu/janke/civilwar/warman.
    htm (Nov. 20, 2008; search for "Diary of Dr. Warman").

PUBLIC DOCUMENTS

Adjutant General, Connecticut. *Record of Connecticut Men in the Army and Navy of
    the United States during the War of the Rebellion*. Hartford: Case, Lockwood &
    Brainard, 1880. Reprint. Salem, Mass.: Higginson, n.d.
History of Fort Monroe. Access at www.monroe.army.mil (Nov. 20, 2008).
List of U.S. Soldiers Executed by United States Military Authorities during the Late
    War. AGO, RG 153, NA. Washington: Aug. 1, 1885.
Official Records of the Union and Confederate Navies in the War of the Rebellion. 30 vols.
    Washington, D.C.: GPO, 1894–1922.
"Questions and Answers about TB." CDC, www.cdc.gov/nchstp/tb/faqs/qa.htm (Nov.
    20, 2008).
"Regulations for the Government of the United States Navy, 1865." Washington, D.C.:
    GPO, 1865.

Report of the Joint Committee on the Conduct of the War on the Attack on Petersburg on the 30th Day of July, 1864. 38th Congress, 2d Session. Rep. Com. 114. Washington, D.C.: GPO, 1865.

Report of the Joint Committee on the Conduct of the War on the Fort Pillow Massacre and on Returned Prisoners. 38th Congress, 1st Session. Rep. Com. 63 and 68. Washington, D.C.: GPO, 1864.

Revised Regulations for the Army of the United States, 1861. Philadelphia: George W. Childs, 1862.

Ross, Joseph B. *Tabular Analysis of the Records of the U.S. Colored Troops and Their Predecessor Units in the National Archives of the United States.* Special List No. 33. Washington, D.C.: GPO, 1973. Reprint. 1985.

Supervisory Committee for Recruiting Colored Regiments. *Free Military School for Applicants for Commands of Colored Troops.* Philadelphia: King & Baird, 1863.

———. *Report of the Supervisory Committee for Recruiting Colored Regiments.* Philadelphia: King & Baird, 1864.

War of the Rebellion, The: Atlas to Accompany the Official Records of the Union and Confederate Armies. Washington, D.C.: GPO, 1891–1895. Reprint. *Official Atlas of the Civil War.* New York: Thomas Yoseloff, 1958.

War of the Rebellion, The: A Compilation of the Official Records of the Union and Confederate Armies. 128 vols. Washington, D.C.: GPO, 1880–1901.

PRIMARY SOURCES: BOOKS

Adams, Charles Francis, Jr. *Charles Francis Adams, 1835–1915: An Autobiography.* Boston: Houghton Mifflin, 1916.

Adams, Virginia M., ed. *On the Altar of Freedom: A Black Soldier's Civil War Letters from the Front—Corporal James Henry Gooding.* Amherst: University of Massachusetts Press, 1991.

Allen, George H. *Forty-Six Months with the Fourth R. I. Volunteers, in the War of 1861 to 1865.* Providence: J. A. & R. A. Reid, 1887.

Ambrose, Stephen E., ed. *A Wisconsin Boy in Dixie: The Selected Letters of James K. Newton.* Madison: University of Wisconsin Press, 1961.

Basler, Roy P., ed. *The Collected Works of Abraham Lincoln.* 9 vols. New Brunswick, N.J.: Rutgers University Press, 1955.

Beale, Howard K., ed. *The Diary of Edward Bates.* Washington, D.C.: Originally published as Vol. 4, *Annual Report*, American Historical Association, 1930. Reprint. New York: Da Capo, 1971.

Bearss, Edwin C., ed. *A Louisiana Confederate: The Diary of Felix Pierre Poché.* Translated from the French by Eugenie W. Somdal. Natchitoches: Louisiana Studies Institute, Northwestern State University of Louisiana, 1972.

Beauchamp, Virginia W., ed. *A Private War: Letters and Diaries of Madge Preston, 1862–1867.* New Brunswick, N.J.: Rutgers University Press, 1987.

Berlin, Ira, Joseph P. Reidy, and Leslie S. Rowland, eds. *Freedom: A Documentary History of Emancipation, 1861–1867.* Series 2: *The Black Military Experience.* New York: Cambridge University Press, 1982.

Berlin, Jean V., ed. *A Confederate Nurse: The Diary of Ada W. Bacot, 1860–1863.* Columbia: USC Press, 1994.

Bird, Kermit Molyneux. *Quill of the Wild Goose: Civil War Letters and Diaries of Joel Molyneux*. Annandale, Va.: Privately printed, 1996.

Blackett, R. J. M., ed. *Thomas Morris Chester, Black Civil War Correspondent; His Dispatches from the Virginia Front*. Baton Rouge: LSU Press, 1989.

Blight, David W., ed. *When This Cruel War Is Over: The Civil War Letters of Charles Harvey Brewster*. Amherst: University of Massachusetts Press, 1992.

Bouton, Edward. *Events of the Civil War*. Los Angeles: Kingsley, Moles and Collins, [1906].

Brooke, George M., Jr., ed. *Ironclads and Big Guns of the Confederacy: The Journal and Letters of John M. Brooke*. Columbia: USC Press, 2002.

Brooks, Noah. *Washington in Lincoln's Time*. New York: Century, 1895. Reprint. New York: Rinehart, 1958.

Brown, Augustus C. *Diary of a Line Officer*. New York: privately printed, [1906].

Butler, Benjamin Franklin. *Autobiography and Personal Reminiscences of Major-General Benj. F. Butler: Butler's Book*. Boston: A. M. Thayer, 1892.

———. *The Private and Official Correspondence of General Benjamin F. Butler during the Period of the Civil War*. 5 vols. Norwood, Mass.: Plimpton Press, 1917.

Califf, Joseph M. *Record of the Services of the Seventh Regiment, U. S. Colored Troops*. Providence, R.I.: E. L. Freeman, 1878. Reprint. Freeport, N.Y.: Books for Libraries, 1971.

Campbell, R. Thomas, ed. *Beneath the Stainless Banner: With selections from his* Recollections of a Naval Life. By John McIntosh Kell. Washington, D.C.: Neale, 1900. Reprint. Shippensburg, Pa.: Burd Street Press, 1999.

Chamberlayne, C. G., ed. *Ham Chamberlayne—Virginian; Letters and Papers of an Artillery Officer in the War for Southern Independence, 1861–1865*. Richmond: Dietz, 1932.

Childs, Arney R., ed. *The Private Journal of Henry William Ravenel, 1859–1887*. Columbia: USC Press, 1947.

Church, James P., and Edward F. Keuchel, eds. *Civil War Marine: A Diary of the Red River Expedition, 1864*. Washington, D.C.: History and Museums Division, USMC, 1975.

Clay-Copton, Virginia. *A Belle of the Fifties*. New York: Doubleday, Page & Co., 1905. UNC electronic ed., 1998, http://docsouth.unc.edu/fpn/clay/clay.html (access June 27, 2007).

Cockrell, Thomas D., and Michael B. Ballard, eds. *A Mississippi Rebel in the Army of Northern Virginia: The Civil War Memoirs of Private David Holt*. Baton Rouge: LSU Press, 1995.

Crandall, Warren D., and Isaac D. Newell. *History of the Ram Fleet and the Mississippi Marine Brigade . . . the Ellets and their Men*. St. Louis, Mo.: Buschart Bros., 1907.

Craven, John Joseph. *Prison Life of Jefferson Davis*. New York: Carleton Press, 1866.

Daly, Robert W., ed. *Aboard the USS* Florida: *1863–65*. Annapolis: United States Naval Institute, 1968.

Davis, Jefferson. *The Rise and Fall of the Confederate Government*. 2 vols. New York: Appleton, 1881. Reprint. New York: Thomas Yoseloff, 1958.

Day, William A. *A True History of Company I, 49th Regiment North Carolina Troops, in the Great Civil War between the North and South*. Newton, N.C.: Enterprise Job Office, 1893.

Dewey, George. *Autobiography of George Dewey, Admiral of the Navy*. New York: Scribner, 1913. Reprint. Annapolis: Naval Institute Press, 1987.

Douglas, Lucia R., ed. *Douglas's Texas Battery, CSA*. Tyler, Tex.: Smith County Historical Society, 1966.

Douglass, Frederick. *Life and Times of Frederick Douglass*. Reprint. New York: Bonanza, 1962.

Dowdey, Clifford, and Louis H. Manarin, eds. *The Wartime Papers of R. E. Lee*. Boston: Little, Brown, 1961.

Driver, Robert A., and Gloria S. Driver, eds. *Letters Home: The Personal Side of the American Civil War*. Roseburg, Ore.: Robert A. and Gloria S. Driver, 1993.

DuBose, John W. *General Joseph Wheeler and the Army of Tennessee*. New York: Neale, 1912.

Duncan, Russell, ed. *Blue-Eyed Child of Fortune: The Civil War Letters of Colonel Robert Gould Shaw*. Athens: University of Georgia Press, 1992.

Dunlap, Leslie W., ed. *"Your Affectionate Husband, J. F. Culver": Letters Written during the Civil War*. Iowa City: Friends of University of Iowa Libraries, 1978.

Elmore, Fletcher L., Jr., ed. *Diary of J. E. Whitehorne, 1st Sergt. Co. "F" 12th Va. Infantry, A. P. Hill's 3rd Corps, A. N. Va.* Utica, Ky.: McDowell, 1995.

Emilio, Luis F. *A Brave Black Regiment: History of the Fifty-Fourth Regiment of Massachusetts Volunteer Infantry, 1863–1865*. 2d ed. Boston: Boston Book, 1894.

Evans, Clement A., ed. *Confederate Military History*. 12 vols. Atlanta: Confederate Publishing, 1899.

Evans, Robley D. *A Sailor's Log: Recollections of Forty Years of Naval Life*. New York: Appleton, 1901.

Everson, Guy R., and Edward H. Simpson, Jr., eds. *"Far, Far from Home": The Wartime Letters of Dick and Tally Simpson, Third South Carolina Volunteers*. New York: Oxford University Press, 1994.

Fisk University, Social Science Institute. *The Unwritten History of Slavery: Autobiographical Accounts of Negro Ex-Slaves*. Comp. Ophelia Settle Egypt. Nashville: Fisk University, 1945.

Ford, Worthington C., ed. *A Cycle of Adams Letters, 1861–1865*. 2 vols. Boston: Houghton Mifflin, 1920.

Gallagher, Gary W., ed. *Fighting for the Confederacy: The Personal Recollections of General Edward Porter Alexander*. Chapel Hill: UNC Press, 1989.

Gates, Betsey, ed. *The Colton Letters: Civil War Period, 1861–1865*. Scottsdale, Ariz.: McLane Publications, 1993.

Gordon, John B. *Reminiscences of the Civil War*. New York: Scribner, 1904. Reprint. Gettysburg, Pa.: Civil War Times, 1974.

Gosnell, Harpur A., ed. *Rebel Raider: Being an Account of Raphael Semmes's Cruise in the CSS Sumter*. Chapel Hill: UNC Press, 1948.

Gould, William B., IV, ed. *Diary of a Contraband: The Civil War Passage of a Black Sailor*. Stanford: Stanford University Press, 2002.

Govan, Gilbert E., and James W. Livingood, eds. *The Haskell Memoirs*. New York: Putnam, 1960.

Grant, Ulysses S. *Personal Memoirs of U.S. Grant*. 2 vols. New York: Charles L. Webster, 1885.

Greiner, James M., Janet L. Coryell, and James R. Smither, eds. *A Surgeon's Civil War: The Letters and Diary of Daniel M. Holt., M.D.* Kent, Ohio: Kent State University Press, 1994.

Harrill, Lawson. *Reminiscences, 1861–1865.* Statesville, N.C.: Brady, 1910.

Grimsley, Mark, and Todd D. Miller, eds. *The Union Must Stand: The Civil War Diary of John Quincy Adams Campbell, Fifth Iowa Volunteer Infantry.* Knoxville: University of Tennessee Press, 2000.

Harrison, Constance. *Recollections Grave and Gay.* New York: Scribner, 1911.

Hayes, John D., ed. *Samuel Francis Du Pont: A Selection from His Civil War Letters.* 3 vols. Ithaca, N.Y.: Eleutherian Mills Historical Library, by Cornell University Press, 1969.

Higginson, Thomas Wentworth. *Army Life in a Black Regiment.* Boston: Fields, Osgood, 1870. Reprint. East Lansing: Michigan State University Press, 1960.

Hill, I. J. *A Sketch of the 29th Regiment of Connecticut Colored Troops.* Baltimore: Daugherty, McGuire, 1867.

Hill, Jim Dan, ed. *The Civil War Sketchbook of Charles Ellery Stedman, Surgeon, United States Navy.* San Rafael, Calif.: Presidio Press, 1976.

Holzer, Harold, comp. and ed. *Dear Mr. Lincoln: Letters to the President.* Reading, Mass.: Addison-Wesley, 1993.

Hoole, W. Stanley, ed. *The Logs of the C.S.S.* Alabama *and C.S.S.* Tuscaloosa, *1862–1863.* University, Ala.: Confederate Publishing, 1972.

Howe, M. A. DeWolfe, ed. *Home Letters of General Sherman.* New York: Scribner, 1909.

Hughes, Nathaniel C., ed. *Liddell's Record: St. John Richardson Liddell, Brigadier General, C.S.A.* Dayton, Ohio: Morningside, 1985.

Humphreys, Charles A. *Field, Camp, Hospital and Prison in the Civil War.* Boston: Press of George H. Ellis, 1918.

Hunter, Edna J. Shank, ed. *One Flag One Country and Thirteen Greenbacks a Month: Letters from a Civil War Private and His Colonel.* San Diego: Hunter, 1980.

Jackson, Edgar, ed. *Three Rebels Write Home, Including the Letters of Edgar Allan Jackson, James Fenton Bryant, Irvin Cross Wills and Miscellaneous Items.* Franklin, Va.: News Publishing, 1955.

Jackson, Harry F., and Thomas F. O'Donnell, eds. *Back Home in Oneida: Hermon Clarke and His Letters.* Syracuse, N.Y.: Syracuse University Press, 1965.

Jocelyn, Stephen P. *Mostly Alkali.* Caldwell, Idaho: Caxton, 1953.

Johnson, John. *The Defense of Charleston Harbor, Including Fort Sumter and the Adjacent Islands, 1863–1865.* Charleston: Walker, Evans & Cogswell, 1890.

Johnson, Robert U., and Clarence C. Buel, eds. *Battles and Leaders of the Civil War.* 4 vols. New York: Century, 1884–88.

Jones, Samuel C. *Reminiscences of the Twenty-Second Iowa Volunteer Infantry.* Iowa City: 1907. Reprint, Iowa City: Camp Pope Bookshop, 1993.

Jones, Terry L. *Civil War Memoirs of Captain William J. Seymour: Reminiscences of a Louisiana Tiger.* Baton Rouge: LSU Press, 1991.

Kakuske, Herbert P., ed. *A Civil War Drama.* Trans. from the German. New York: Carlton, 1970.

Kallgren, Beverly Hayes, and James L. Crouthamel, eds. *"Dear Friend Anna": The Civil War Letters of a Common Soldier from Maine.* Orono: University of Maine Press, 1992.

Kellogg, Mary E., ed. and comp. *Army Life of an Illinois Soldier, Including a Day by Day Record of Sherman's March to the Sea: Letters and Diaries of the Late Charles W. Wills.* Washington, D.C.: Globe, 1906.

Klaas, Helen, ed. *Portrait of Elnathan Keeler, a Union Soldier.* Wappingers Falls, N.Y.: Goldlief Reproductions, 1977.

Laas, Virginia Jeans, ed. *Wartime Washington: The Civil War Letters of Elizabeth Blair Lee.* Urbana: University of Illinois Press, 1991.

Lemke, W. J., ed. *The Letters of Albert O. McCollom, Confederate Soldier.* Fayetteville, Ark.: Washington County Historical Society, 1961.

Lewis, A. S., ed. *My Dear Parents.* New York: Harcourt Brace Jovanovich, 1982.

Livingston, Mary P., ed. *A Civil War Marine at Sea: The Diary of Medal of Honor Recipient Miles M. Oviatt.* Shippensburg, Pa.: White Mane Books, 1998.

Longacre, Edward G., ed. *From Antietam to Fort Fisher: The Civil War Letters of Edward King Wightman, 1862–1865.* Rutherford, N.J.: Fairleigh Dickinson University Press, 1985.

Lord, Walter, ed. *The Fremantle Diary, Being the Journal of Lieutenant Colonel Arthur James Lyon Fremantle, Coldstream Guards, on His Three months in the Southern States.* New York: J. Bradburn, 1864. Reprint. Boston: Little, Brown, 1954.

Main, Edwin M. *The Story of the Marches, Battles and Incidents of the Third United States Colored Cavalry.* Louisville, Ky.: Globe, 1908.

McClure, Judy Watson, ed. *Confederate from East Texas: The Civil War Letters of James Monroe Watson.* Quanah, Tex.: Nortex Press, 1976.

McGee, Charles M., Jr., and Ernest M. Lander, eds. *A Rebel Came Home: The Diary of Floride Clemson.* Columbia: USC Press, 1961.

McMurry, Richard M., ed. *Footprints of a Regiment: A Recollection of the 1st Georgia Regulars, 1861–1865.* Atlanta: Long Street Press, 1992.

McPherson, James M., and Patricia R. McPherson, eds. *Lamson of the Gettysburg: The Civil War Letters of Lieutenant Roswell H. Lamson, U.S. Navy.* New York: Oxford University Press, 1997.

Marszalek. John F., ed. *The Diary of Miss Emma Holmes, 1861–1866.* Baton Rouge: LSU Press, 1979.

Martin, Florence A., ed. *Courageous Journey: The Civil War Journal of Laetitia Lafon Ashmore Nutt.* Miami, Fla.: E. A. Seeman, 1975.

Menge, W. Springer, and J. August Shimrak, eds. *The Civil War Notebook of Daniel Chisholm.* New York: Orion Books, 1989.

Mickley, Jeremiah M. *The Forty-Third Regiment United States Colored Troops.* Gettysburg, Pa.: J. E. Wible, 1866.

Milligan, John D., ed. *From the Fresh-Water Navy, 1861–64: The Letters of Acting Master's Mate Henry R. Browne and Acting Ensign Symmes E. Browne.* Annapolis: Naval Institute Press, 1970.

Mitchell, Joseph B. *The Badge of Gallantry: Recollections of Civil War Congressional Medal of Honor Winners. Letters from the Charles Kohen Collection.* New York: Macmillan, 1968.

Moore, Edward A. *The Story of a Cannoneer under Stonewall Jackson.* New York: Neale, 1907. Reprint. Alexandria, Va.: Time-Life Books, 1983.

Morrow, Albert P., ed. *Journal of Leslie G. Morrow, Captain's Clerk of the U. S. Steamer Galena.* Yorba Linda, Calif.: A. P. Morrow, 1988.

Morse, Loren J., ed. *Civil War Diaries & Letters of Bliss Morse*. Tahlequah, Okla.: Heritage Printing, 1985.

Mulholland, St. Clair A. *The Story of the 116th Regiment, Pennsylvania Infantry*. Philadelphia: McManus, 1899.

Newton, Alexander H. *Out of the Briars: An Autobiography and Sketch of the Twenty-Ninth Regiment Connecticut Volunteers*. Philadelphia: A.M.E. Book Concern, [1910]. Reprint. Miami: Mnemosyne, 1969.

Nichols, James M. *Perry's Saints or the Fighting Parson's Regiment in the War of the Rebellion*. Boston: Lothrop, 1886.

Nicolay, John G., and John Hay, eds. *Complete Works of Abraham Lincoln*. 12 vols. Harrogate, Tenn.: Lincoln Memorial University, 1894.

Oates, William C. *The War between the Union and the Confederacy and Its Lost Opportunities, with a History of the 15th Alabama Regiment*. New York: Neale, 1905.

Offenberg, Richard S., and Robert Rue Parsonage, eds. *The War Letters of Duren F. Kelley, 1862–1865*. New York: Pageant, 1967.

Osbon. Bradley S. *A Sailor of Fortune; Personal Memoirs of Captain B. S. Osbon*. New York: McClure, Phillips, 1906.

Phelan, Helene C., ed. *Tramping Out the Vintage, 1861–1864: The Civil War Diaries and Letters of Eugene Kingman*. Almond, N.Y.: Helene C. Phelan, 1983.

Phillips, Marion G., and Valerie P. Parsegian, eds. *Richard and Rhoda: Letters from the Civil War*. Washington, D.C.: Legation Press, 1981.

Pickett, George E. *The Heart of a Soldier, as Revealed in the Intimate Letters of Genl George E. Pickett, CSA*. New York: Seth Moyle, 1913.

Pollard, Edward A. *Southern History of the War*. 2 vols. in 1. New York: C. B. Richardson, 1866. Reprint. New York: Fairfax, 1990.

Polley, Joseph B. *Hood's Texas Brigade: Its Marches, Its Battles, Its Achievements*. New York: Neale, 1910.

Porter, David D. *Incidents and Anecdotes of the Civil War*. New York: Appleton, 1885.

Preble, George H. *The Chase of the Rebel Steamer of War* Oreto, *Commander J. N. Moffit, C.S.N., into the Bay of Mobile by the United States Steam Sloop Oneida, Commander Geo. Henry Preble, U.S.N., September 4, 1862*. Cambridge, Mass.: Allen and Farnham, 1862.

Putnam, Sallie B. *Richmond during the War; Four Years of Personal Observation*. New York: G. W. Carleton, 1867. Reprint. Alexandria, Va.: Time-Life Books, 1983.

Racine, Philip N., ed. *"Unspoiled Heart": The Journal of Charles Mattocks of the 17th Maine*. Knoxville: University of Tennessee Press, 1994.

Rawick, George P., ed. *The American Slave: A Composite Autobiography*. Ser. 1 & 2, 19 vols. Comp. 1936–37 by Federal Writers' Project, WPA. Pub. 1941. Reprint. Westport, Conn.: Greenwood, 1972.

Redkey, Edwin S., ed. *A Grand Army of Black Men: Letters from African-American Soldiers in the Union Army, 1861–1865*. New York: Cambridge University Press, 1992.

Roberson, Elizabeth W., ed. *Weep Not for Me Dear Mother*. Gretna, La.: Pelican, 1996.

Rosenblatt, Emil, and Ruth Rosenblatt, eds. *Hard Marching Every Day*. Originally pub. as *Anti-rebel: The Civil War Letters of Wilbur Fisk*. Croton-on-Hudson, N.Y.: Rosenblatt, 1983. Reprint. Lawrence: University Press of Kansas, 1992.

Rosenburg, R. B., ed. *"For the Sake of My Country": The Diary of Col. W. W. Ward, 9th Tennessee Cavalry, Morgan's Brigade, C.S.A.* Murfreesboro, Tenn.: Southern Heritage Press, 1992.

Roth, Margaret Brobst, ed. *Well Mary: The Civil War Letters of a Wisconsin Soldier.* Madison: University of Wisconsin Press, 1960.

Samito, Christian G., ed. *Commanding Boston's Irish Ninth: The Civil War Letters of Colonel Patrick R. Guiney, Ninth Massachusetts Volunteer Infantry.* New York: Fordham University Press, 1998.

Scheller, Robert J., ed. *Under the Blue Pennant; or, Notes of a Naval Officer, 1863–1865.* New York: Wiley, 1999.

Sears, Stephen W., ed. *For Country, Cause and Leader: The Civil War Journal of Charles B. Haydon.* New York: Ticknor and Fields, 1993.

Selfridge, Thomas O. *What Finer Tradition: The Memoirs of Thomas O. Selfridge, Jr., Rear Admiral, U.S.N.* New York: Knickbocker Press, 1924. Reprint. Columbia: USC Press, 1987.

Semmes, Raphael. *Memoirs of Service Afloat during the War between the States.* Baltimore: Kelly, Piet, 1869.

Shaver, Lewellyn A. *A History of the Sixtieth Alabama Regiment, Gracie's Alabama Brigade.* Montgomery: Barrett & Brown, 1867. Reprint. Gaithersburg, Md.: Butternut Press, n. d.

Sherman, William T. *Memoirs of General William T. Sherman.* 2 vols. New York: Appleton, 1875. Reprint. 2 vols. in 1, paperback. New York: Da Capo, 1984.

Silber, Nina, and Mary Beth Sievens, eds. *Yankee Correspondence: Civil War Letters between New England Soldiers and the Home Front.* Charlottesville: University Press of Virginia, 1996.

Simon, John Y., ed. *The Papers of Ulysses S. Grant.* 30 vols. Carbondale: Southern Illinois University Press, 1967–.

Sparks, David S. ed. *Inside Lincoln's Army: The Diary of Marsena Rudolph Patrick, Provost Marshal General, Army of the Potomac.* New York: Thomas Yoseloff, 1964.

Sprague, Homer B. *History of the 13th Infantry Regiment of Connecticut Volunteers, during the Great Rebellion.* Hartford, Conn.: Case, Lockwood, 1867.

Swiggett, Howard, ed. *A Rebel War Clerk's Diary at the Confederate States Capital.* 2 vols. Reprint. New York: Old Hickory Bookshop, 1935.

Thomas, Mary W., and Richard A. Sauers, eds. *The Civil War Letters of First Lieutenant James B. Thomas, Adjutant, 107th Pennsylvania Volunteers.* Baltimore: Butternut and Blue, 1995.

Thorpe, Sheldon B. *The History of the Fifteenth Connecticut Volunteers in the War for the Defense of the Union.* New Haven: Price, Lee & Adkins, 1893.

Trask, Kerry A., ed. *Fire Within: A Civil War Narrative from Wisconsin.* Kent, Ohio: Kent State University Press, 1995.

Turner, Charles W., ed. *The Allen Family of Amherst County, Virginia: Civil War Letters.* Berryville, Va.: Rockbridge, 1995.

Walkley, Stephen. *History of the Seventh Connecticut Volunteer Infantry, Hawley's Brigade, Terry's Division, Tenth Army Corps, 1861–1865.* Hartford: n.p., [1905].

Wallace, Lee A., Jr., ed. *Under the Stars and Bars: A History of the Surrey Light Artillery.* Richmond, Va.: Waddy, 1909. Reprint. Dayton, Ohio: Morningside, 1975.

Walton, William, ed. *A Civil War Courtship*. Garden City, N.Y.: Doubleday, 1980.

Welles, Gideon. *Diary of Gideon Welles*. 3 vols. Boston: Houghton Mifflin, 1911.

Wheaton, James W., ed. *Surgeon on Horseback: The Missouri and Arkansas Journal and Letters of Dr. Charles Brackett of Rochester, Indiana, 1861–1863*. Carmel, Ind.: Guild Press of Indiana, 1998.

Wiley, Bell Irvin, ed. *Letters of Warren Akin, Confederate Congressman*. Athens: University of Georgia Press, 1959.

Williams, Charles R., ed. *Diary and Letters of Rutherford Birchard Hayes, Nineteenth President of the United States*. 5 vols. Columbus: Archaeological and Historical Society, 1922. Reprint. New York: Kraus, 1971.

Wilson, Joseph T. *The Black Phalanx: A History of Negro Soldiers of the United States in the Wars of 1775–1812, 1861-'65*. Hartford: American, 1890. Reprint. New York: Arno, 1968.

Winther, Oscar Osborn, ed. *With Sherman to the Sea: The Civil War Letters, Diaries & Reminiscences of Theodore F. Upson*. Bloomington: Indiana University Press, 1958. Reprint. New York: Kraus, 1969.

Woodward, C. Vann, ed. *Mary Chestnut's Civil War*. Originally published as *A Diary from Dixie*. New York: Appleton, 1905. Rev. ed. New Haven: YU Press, 1981.

Yacovone, Donald, ed. *A Voice of Thunder: The Civil War Letters of George E. Stephens*. Urbana: University of Illinois Press, 1997.

PRIMARY SOURCES: ARTICLES

Allen, Amory K. "Civil War Letters of Amory K. Allen." *IMH* 31, no. 4 (December 1935): 338–86.

Baker, Marion A. "Farragut's Demands for the Surrender of New Orleans," *B&L* 2: 95–99.

Barnwell, John. "Civil War Letters of Lieutenant John Elliott." *GHQ* 65 (fall 1981): 203–39.

Basile, Leon, ed. "Harry Stanley's Mess Book: Offenses and Punishments aboard the *Ethan Allen*." *CWH* 23, no. 1 (March 1977): 69–79.

Behm, Jacob. "Emancipation: A Soldier's View." *CWTI* 21, no. 10 (February 1983): 46–47.

Bowditch, Charles P. "War Letters of Charles P. Bowditch, 1861–1864." *Proceedings of the Massachusetts Historical Society* 57 (May 1924): 414–95.

Bright, Thomas R., ed. "Yankees in Arms: The Civil War as a Personal Experience." *CWH* 19, no. 3 (September 1973): 197–218.

Brown, Isaac N. "The Confederate Gun-Boat *Arkansas*," *B&L* 3: 572–580.

Browne, Frederick W. "My Service in the U.S. Colored Cavalry." *Paper of Frederick W. Browne, Second Lieut. 1st U.S. Colored Cavalry of Cincinnati, Ohio, Read before the Ohio Commandery of the Loyal Legion, March 4, 1908*. MOLLUS-Ohio (Cincinnati: n.p., 1908): 1–14.

Buck, Irving A. "Negroes in Our Army: General Pat. Cleburne, the First to Advance Their Use." *SHSP* 31 (1903): 215–28.

Callender, Eliot. "What a Boy Saw on the Mississippi." In *Military Essays and Recollections*, vol. 1, MOLLUS-Ill. (Chicago: McClurg, 1891): 51–67.

Carter, Solon A. "Fourteen Months' Service with Colored Troops." In *CWP* 1, MOLLUS-Mass. (Boston: By the Commandery, 1900): 155–79.

Clark, George P., ed. "Remenecence of My Army Life." *IMH* 101, no. 1 (March 2005): 15–57.

Coleman, S. B. "A July Morning with the Rebel Ram 'Arkansas.'" In *War Papers*, vol. 1, MOLLUS-Mich. (Detroit: Winn & Hammond, 1890): 3–13.

Disbrow, Donald W., ed. "Lincoln's Policies as Seen by a Michigan Soldier." *Michigan History* 45 (December 1961): 360–64.

Duren, C. M. "The Occupation of Jacksonville, February 1864 and the Battle of Olustee." *Florida Historical Quarterly* 32, no. 4 (April 1954): 262–87.

Durham, Ken, ed. "'Dear Rebecca': The Civil War Letters of William Edwards Paxton, 1861–1863." *LH* 20 (1979): 169–96.

Early, Jubal A. "Early's March to Washington in 1864." *B&L* 4: 492–99.

Everson, Guy R., ed., "Service Afield and Afloat: A Reminiscence of the Civil War." *IMH* 89, no. 1 (March 1993): 35–56.

Fairfax, D. MacNeill. "Captain Wilkes's Seizure of Mason and Slidell." *B&L* 2: 135–42.

Gift, George W. "The Story of the Arkansas," *SHSP* 12 (1884): 48–54, 115–19, 163–70, 205–12.

Goulding, Joseph H. "The Colored Troops in the War of the Rebellion." *Proceedings of the Reunion Society of Vermont Officers* 2 (read Nov. 3, 1892; Burlington: n. p., 1906): 137–54.

Grant, Frederick D. "A Boy's Experiences at Vicksburg." In *Personal Recollections of the War of the Rebellion*, Ser. 3, MOLLUS-N.Y. (New York: Putnam, 1907): 86–100.

Gregory, Edward S. "Vicksburg during the Siege." In Philadelphia Weekly Times, *Annals of the War*. Reprint, Gettysburg, Pa., 1974. 111–33.

Harmon, George D., ed. "Letters of Luther Rice Mills—A Confederate Soldier." *CHR.* 4, no. 3 (July 1927): 285–310.

Heslin, James J., ed. "A Yankee Soldier in a New York Regiment." *NYHSQ* 50, no. 2 (April 1966): 109–49.

Heyman, Max L., Jr., ed. "The Gay Letters: A Civil War Correspondence." *Journal of the West* 9, no. 3 (July 1970): 377–412.

Huch, Ronald K., ed. "The Civil War Letters of Herbert Saunders." *Register of the Kentucky Historical Society* 69 (January 1971): 17–29.

Kautz, Albert. "Incidents of the Occupation of New Orleans." *B&L* 2: 91–94.

Kilmer, George L. "Gordon's Attack at Fort Stedman." *B&L* 4: 579–83.

Kroll, Kathleen, and Charles Moran, eds. "The White Papers: Letters (1861–1865) of Pvt. Herman Lorenzo White, 22nd Regiment Massachusetts Volunteers." *Massachusetts Review* 18 (Summer 1977): 248–70.

Landon, William. "The Fourteenth Indiana Regiment, Peninsular Campaign to Chancellorsville." *IMH* 33, no. 3 (September 1937): 325–48.

Lennard, George W. "Give Yourself No Trouble about Me: The Shiloh Letters of George W. Lennard." Ed. Paul Hubbard and Christine Lewis. *IMH* 76, no. 1 (March 1980): 21–53.

Levstik, Frank, ed. "The Civil War Diary of Colonel Albert Rogall." *Polish American Studies* 27 (spring-autumn 1970): 33–79.

Lockett, S. H. "The Defense of Vicksburg." *B&L* 3: 482–92.

Longacre, Edward G., ed. "The Task before Them." *CWTI* 21, no. 10 (February 1983): 36–43.

———. "'Would to God That War Was Rendered Impossible': Letters of Captain Rowland M. Hall, April-July 1864." *Virginia Magazine of History and Biography* 89 (October 1981): 448–66.

Meredith, William T. "Farragut's Capture of New Orleans." *B&L* 2: 70–73.

Michie, Peter S. "The Dutch Gap Canal," *B&L* 4: 575.

Milligan, John D. "Gunboat War at Vicksburg." *American Heritage* 29 (August-September 1978): 62–68.

Morgan, Thomas J. "Reminiscences of Service with Colored Troops in the Army of the Cumberland, 1863–1865." *PN*, Ser. 3, no. 13. Providence: RISSHS, 1885.

Nolin, Kelly, ed. "The Civil War Letters of J. O. Cross, 29th Connecticut Volunteer Infantry (Colored)."*ConnHS Bulletin* 60, nos. 3-4 (summer-fall 1995): 211–35.

Park, Robert E. "Diary of Robert E. Park, Macon, Georgia, late Captain Twelfth Alabama Regiment, Confederate States Army." *SHSP* 1 (1876): 370–386.

Porter, David D. "The Opening of the Lower Mississippi." *B&L* 2: 22–54.

Prescott, Royal S. "The Capture of Richmond." In *CWP* 1, MOLLUS-Mass. (Boston: Printed for the Commandery, 1900): 64–70.

Read, Charles W. "Reminiscences of the Confederate States Navy." *SHSP* 1, no. 5 (May 1876): 331–62.

Redkey, Edwin S., ed. "Rocked in the Cradle of Consternation." *American Heritage* 31 (October-November 1980): 70–79.

Robertson, James L., ed. "'The Boy Artillerist'": Letters of Colonel William Pegram, C.S.A." *VMH&B* 98 (April 1990): 221–60.

Robertson, Melville C. "Journal of Melville Cox Robertson." *IMH* 28, no. 2 (June 1932): 116–37.

Romeyn, Henry. "With Colored Troops in the Army of the Cumberland." In *War Papers* 51, MOLLUS–Washington, D.C. (Washington, D.C.: n.p., 1904): 3–26.

Shaw, James. "Our Last Campaign and Subsequent Service in Texas." *PN* 6, no. 9 (Providence: RISSHS, 1905): 10–52.

Shelly, Joseph F. "The Shelly Papers." Ed. Fanny Anderson; trans. from the German by Sophie Gemant. *IMH* 44, no. 2 (June 1948): 181–98.

Sherman, George R. "Assault on Fort Gilmer and Reminiscences of Prison Life." *PN* 5, no. 7 (Providence: RISSHS, 1894): 5–33.

———. "The Negro as a Soldier," *PN* 7, no. 7 (Providence: RISSHS, 1904-5): 5–33.

Silver, James W., ed. "Diary of Robert A. Moore, Private in Co. G, 17th Mississippi Regiment, Confederate Guards, Captain, C. W. Sears." *Louisiana Historical Quarterly* 39 (July 1956): 243–374.

Simonton, Edward. "The Campaign up the James River to Petersburg." In *Glimpses of the Nation's Struggle* 5 (1897–1902), MOLLUS-Minn. (St. Paul, 1903): 481–95.

Smith, Rebecca W., and Marion Mullins, eds., "Diary of H. C. Medford," *Southwestern Historical Quarterly* 34 (July 1930–April 1931): 106–40, 203–30.

Soley, James R. "Gulf Operations in 1862 and 1863." *B&L* 3: 571.

Swift, Lester L., ed. "Letters from a Sailor on a Tinclad." *CWH* 7, no. 1 (March 1961): 48–62.

Synnestvedt, Sig, ed. "The Earth Shook and Quivered," *CWTI* 11, no. 8 (December 1972): 30–37.

Throne, Mildred, ed. "An Iowa Doctor in Blue: The Letters of Seneca B. Thrall, 1862–1864." *Iowa Journal of History* 58, no. 2 (April 1960): 97–188.

Wagandt, Charles L., ed. "The Civil War Journal of Dr. Samuel Harrison." *CWH* 13 (1967): 131–46.

Walke, Henry. "The Gun-Boats at Belmont and Fort Henry." *B&L* 1: 358–67.

———. "The Western Flotilla at Fort Donelson . . . and Memphis," *B&L* 1: 430–52.
Warley, A. E. "The Ram *Manassas* at the Passage of the New Orleans Forts." *B&L* 2: 89–91.

PRIMARY SOURCES: PERIODICALS

Anglo-African; Baltimore *American*; Boston *Daily Evening Transcript*; Chicago *Tribune*; *Harper's Weekly*; New York *Herald*; *New York Times*; *Philadelphia Inquirer*; Willmantic (Conn.) *Chronicle*

SECONDARY SOURCES

Ambler, Charles H. *Francis H. Pierpont, Union War Governor of Virginia and Father of West Virginia*. Chapel Hill: UNC Press, 1937.
Anderson, Bern. *By Sea and by River: The Naval History of the Civil War*. New York: Knopf, 1962. Reprint. New York: Da Capo, 1989.
Andrews, J. Cutler. *The North Reports the Civil War*. Pittsburgh: University of Pittsburgh Press, 1955.
Baldwin, Thomas W. *Michael Bacon of Dedham, 1640 and His Descendants*. Cambridge, Mass.: Press of Murray and Emery, 1915.
Ballard, Michael B. *Vicksburg: The Campaign That Opened the Mississippi*. Chapel Hill: UNC Press, 2004.
Barnes, Lewis. "Pliny A. Jewett, A.M., M.D., New Haven." *PCMS* (1887): 189–72.
Bennett, Michael J. *Union Jacks: Yankee Sailors in the Civil War*. Chapel Hill: UNC Press, 2004.
Bernstein, Iver. *The New York City Draft Riots*. New York: Oxford University Press, 1990.
Binder, Frederick M. "Philadelphia's Free Military School." *Pennsylvania History* 17 (October 1950): 281–91.
Boatner, Mark Mayo, III. *The Civil War Dictionary*. New York: David McKay, 1959.
Brown, Elizabeth Mills. *New Haven: A Guide to Architecture and Urban Design*. New Haven: YU Press, 1976.
Burkhardt, George S. *Confederate Rage, Yankee Wrath: No Quarter during the Civil War*. Carbondale: Southern Illinois University Press, 2007.
Butler, John A. *Sailing on Friday: The Perilous Voyage of America's Merchant Marine*. Washington, D.C.: Brassey's, 1997. Paperback ed., 2000.
Calhoun, Charles C. *Longfellow: A Rediscovered Life*. Boston: Beacon Press, 2004.
Carrison, Daniel J. *The Navy from Wood to Steel, 1860–1890*. New York: Franklin Watts, 1965.
Chaffin, Tom. *Sea of Gray: The Around the World Odyssey of the Confederate Raider Shenandoah*. New York: Hill and Wang, 2006.
Cimprich, John. *Fort Pillow: A Civil War Massacre, and Public Memory*. Baton Rouge: LSU Press, 2005.
Cleaves, Freeman. *Rock of Chickamauga: The Life of General George H. Thomas*. Norman: University of Oklahoma Press, 1948.
Coggins, Jack. *Arms and Equipment of the Civil War*. New York: Doubleday, 1962.
Concise Dictionary of American Biography. New York: Scribner, 1964.
Cornish, Dudley. *The Sable Arm: Negro Troops in the Union Army, 1861–1865*. New York: Longmans, Green, 1956. Reprint. New York: Norton, 1966.

Current, Richard Nelson. *Lincoln's Loyalists: Union Soldiers from the Confederacy.* Boston: Northeastern University Press, 1992.

Dalzell, George W. *The Flight from the Flag: The Continuing Effect of the Civil War upon the American Carrying Trade.* Chapel Hill: UNC Press, 1940.

Davis, Hugh. *Leonard Bacon: New England Reformer and Antislavery Moderate.* Baton Rouge: LSU Press, 1998.

Davis, Peter. "Mid-Victorian RN Vessels, HMS *Cadmus.*" Access at www.pdavis.nl and search for Cadmus (Feb. 23, 2009).

Dictionnaire des bâtiments de la Flotte de guerre française de Colbert a nos jours—Extrait du tome 1 (1671–1870). Access at www.netmarine.net/dico;tome1-a.pdf.

Dorris, Jonathan T. *Pardon and Amnesty under Lincoln and Johnson.* Chapel Hill: UNC Press, 1953.

Dunkelman, Mark H. "George Bosley: Soldier, Medical Cadet, Assistant Surgeon," *Military Images,* 25, no. 4 (January-February 2004): 15–16.

Dyer, Frederick H. *A Compendium of the War of the Rebellion.* Des Moines, Ia.: Dyer, 1908. Reprint. Dayton, Ohio: Morningside, 1978.

Foner, Eric. *Forever Free: The Story of Emancipation and Reconstruction.* Picture ed. Joshua Brown. New York: Knopf, 2005.

Fox, William F. *Regimental Losses in the American Civil War.* Albany, N.Y.: Albany, 1889.

Glatthaar, Joseph T. *Forged in Battle: The Civil War Alliance of Black Soldiers and White Officers.* New York: Free Press, 1990.

Goldfinch, Charles W., and José T. Canales, *Juan N. Cortina: Two Interpretations.* New York: Arno Press, 1974.

Gosnell, H. Allen. *Guns on the Western Waters: The Story of River Gunboats in the Civil War.* Baton Rouge: LSU Press, 1949.

Greene, Francis V. *The Mississippi.* New York: Scribner, 1882.

Hamersly, Lewis R. *The Records of Living Officers of the U. S. Navy and Marine Corps.* Philadelphia: Lippincott, 1870.

Harrod, Frederick S. "Jim Crow in the Navy (1798–1941)." *Proceedings of the United States Naval Institute* 105 (September 1979): 46–53.

Headley, Joel T. *Farragut, and Our Naval Commanders.* New York: E. B. Trent, 1867.

Holice, Clayton, and Deb Hollice. "The History of Genesee, MI." Access at www.usgennet. org/usa/mi/county/lapeer/gen (Dec. 1, 2008).

Hollandsworth, James G., Jr. "The Execution of White Officers from Black Units by Confederate Forces during the Civil War." *LH* 35, no. 3 (fall 1994): 475–89.

Jones, Archer. *Civil War Command and Strategy: The Process of Victory and Defeat.* New York: Free Press, 1992.

Kelley, Brooks M. *Yale: A History.* New ed. New Haven: Yale University Press, 1999.

Levine, Bruce. *Confederate Emancipation: Southern Plans to Free and Arm Slaves during the Civil War.* New York: Oxford University Press, 2006.

Lewis, Charles Lee. *David Glasgow Farragut: Our First Admiral.* Annapolis: United States Naval Institute, 1943.

Livermore, Thomas L. *Numbers and Losses in the Civil War in America, 1861–1865.* Boston: Houghton Mifflin, 1901. Reprint. Dayton, Ohio: Morningside, 1986.

Lonn, Ella. *Desertion during the Civil War.* New York: Century, 1928. Reprint. Gloucester, Mass.: Peter Smith, 1966.

Lord, Francis A. *They Fought for the Union*. Harrisburg, Pa.: Stackpole, 1960. Reprint. New York: Bonanza, 1960.

Lowry, Thomas P., and Jack Welsh. *Tarnished Scalpels: The Court-Martials of Fifty Union Surgeons*. Mechanicsburg, Pa.: Stackpole, 2000.

Miller, Francis T., ed. *The Photographic History of the Civil War*. 10 vols. New York: Review of Reviews, 1911.

Moat, Louis S. *Frank Leslie's Illustrated Famous Leaders and Battle Scenes of the Civil War*. New York: Mrs. Frank Leslie, 1896.

Musicant, Ivan. *Divided Waters: The Naval History of the Civil War*. New York: Harper-Collins, 1995. Reprint. Edison, N.J.: Castle Books, 2000.

Nash, Howard P., Jr. *A Naval History of the Civil War*. South Brunswick, N.J.: Barnes, 1972.

Nicolay, Helen. *Lincoln's Secretary: A Biography of John G. Nicolay*. New York: Longmans, Green, 1949.

Noel, John V., Jr., and Edward L. Beach. *Naval Terms Dictionary*. 4th ed. Annapolis: Naval Institute Press, 1985.

Osborn, Norris G., ed. *Men of Mark in Connecticut: Ideals of American Life Told in Biographies and Autobiographies of Eminent Living Americans*. 5 vol. Hartford: W. R. Goodspeed, 1906–10.

Paludan, Phillip Shaw. *The Presidency of Abraham Lincoln*. Lawrence: University Press of Kansas, 1994.

Penn, William A. *Rattling Spurs and Broad-Brimmed Hats*. Midway, Ky.: Battle Grove Press, 1995.

Perry, Milton F. *Infernal Machines: The Story of Confederate Submarine and Mine Warfare*. Baton Rouge: LSU Press, 1965.

Phisterer, Frederick. *Statistical Record of the Armies of the United States*. New York: Scribner, 1883, Reprint. New York: Blue & Gray Press, n.d.

Quarles, Benjamin. *The Negro in the Civil War*. Boston: Little, Brown, 1953.

Ramold, Steven J. *Slaves, Sailors, Citizens: African Americans in the Union Navy*. DeKalb: Northern Illinois University Press, 2002.

Randall, J. G. *The Civil War and Reconstruction*. Boston: Heath, 1937. Reprint, 1953.

Ringle, Dennis J. *Life in Mr. Lincoln's Navy*. Annapolis: Naval Institute Press, 1998.

Rowell, John W. *Yankee Cavalrymen: Through the Civil War with the Ninth Pennsylvania Cavalry*. Knoxville: University of Tennessee Press, 1971.

Sargent, F. W. *England, the United States, the Southern Confederacy*. London: Hamilton, Adams, 1864. Reprint. New York: Negro Universities Press, 1969.

Semmes, S. Spencer. "Admiral Raphael Semmes." *SHSP* 38 (Richmond, Va., 1910): 28–40.

Shumway, Floyd, and Richard Hegel. *New Haven: An Illustrated History*. Woodland Hills, Calif.: Windsor, 1981. Rev. ed., 1987.

Smart, Jeffery K. "Chemical & Biological Warfare Research & Development during the Civil War," *Chemical and Biological Defense Information Analysis Center Newsletter* (Spring 2004): 3, 11–13, 15.

Sommers, Richard J. "The Dutch Gap Affair: Military Atrocities and Rights of Negro Soldiers." *CWH* 21 (1975): 51–64.

Steiner, Bernard C. *Life of Reverdy Johnson*. Baltimore: Norman, Remington, 1914. Reprint. New York: Russell & Russell, 1970.

Thomas, Benjamin P., and Harold M. Hyman. *Stanton: The Life and Times of Lincoln's Secretary of War*. New York: Alfred A. Knopf, 1962.

Thompson, Jerry, and Lawrence T. Jones III. *Civil War and Revolution on the Rio Grande Frontier: A Narrative and Photographic History*. Austin: Texas State Historical Association, 2004.

Tucker, Spencer C. *Blue & Gray Navies: The Civil War Afloat*. Annapolis: Naval Institute Press, 2006.

University of Medicine and Dentistry of New Jersey. "A History of Tuberculosis Treatment." Access at www.umdnj.edu/globaltb/tbhistory.htm (Dec. 2, 2008).

Urwin, Gregory J. W., ed. *Black Flag over Dixie: Racial Atrocities and Reprisals in the Civil War*. Carbondale: Southern Illinois University Press, 2004.

Ward, Andrew. *River Run Red: The Fort Pillow Massacre in the American Civil War*. New York: Viking, 2005.

Ward, Julius H. "Presentation Week at Yale." *Harper's New Monthly Magazine* (September 1864), 497–501.

Warner, Ezra J. *Generals in Blue: Lives of the Union Commanders*. Baton Rouge: LSU Press, 1964.

Weigley, Russell F. *Quartermaster General of the Union Army: A Biography of M. C. Meigs*. New York: Columbia University Press, 1959.

Weinberg, Adelaide. *John Elliott Cairnes and the American Civil War: A Study in Anglo-American Relations*. London: Kingswood Press, [1969].

Wert, Jeffry D. *Mosby's Rangers*. New York: Simon and Schuster, 1990.

West Virginia Humanities Council. "Reorganized Government of Virginia." Access at www.wvhumanities.org/Statehood/reorganized.htm (Dec. 2, 2008).

Wiley, Bell Irvin. *Southern Negroes, 1861–1865*. New Haven, Conn.: YU Press, 1938.

INDEX

George S. Burkhardt is an independent scholar and writer who lives in Long Beach, California. A former news reporter and writer, he was the editor, publisher, and owner of California's smallest daily newspaper, the *Corning Daily Observer*. He is the author of *Confederate Rage, Yankee Wrath: No Quarter in the Civil War*.